Computational Sanskrit & Digital Humanities

AA001587

Selected papers presented at the 18th World Sanskrit Conference

Canberra, Australia
9-13 January 2023

Editors:

Amba Kulkarni
Oliver Hellwig

ISBN: 978-1-7138-9031-7

Printed from e-media with permission by:

Curran Associates, Inc.
57 Morehouse Lane
Red Hook, NY 12571

Some format issues inherent in the e-media version may also appear in this print version.

Copyright© (2022) by the Association for Computational Linguistics
All rights reserved.

Printed with permission by Curran Associates, Inc. (2024)

For permission requests, please contact the Association for Computational Linguistics
at the address below.

Association for Computational Linguistics
209 N. Eighth Street
Stroudsburg, Pennsylvania 18360

Phone: 1-570-476-8006
Fax: 1-570-476-0860

acl@aclweb.org

Additional copies of this publication are available from:

Curran Associates, Inc.
57 Morehouse Lane
Red Hook, NY 12571 USA
Phone: 845-758-0400
Fax: 845-758-2633
Email: curran@proceedings.com
Web: www.proceedings.com

Proceedings of the
Computational Sanskrit & Digital Humanities

Selected papers presented
at the 18th World Sanskrit Conference

(in online mode)
Canberra, Australia
January 9 – 13, 2023

Edited by
AMBA KULKARNI & OLIVER HELLWIG

©2022 The Association for Computational Linguistics

Preface

This volume presents edited versions of shortlisted papers accepted for presentation in the session 'Computational Sanskrit and Digital Humanities' at the 18th World Sanskrit Conference during Jan 9-13, 2023 in online mode. The physical conference was delayed by two years due to the global pandemic situation. Thus there were two rounds of calls for submissions. In order to disseminate the research among the scholars, the convenors of the Computational Sanskrit and Digital Humanities decided to hold an online event after the first round of submission. We thank the organisers of the World Sanskrit Conference and in particular the International Association of Sanskrit Studies for giving us permission to hold this event online. The papers shortlisted in the first round were presented at the online event during Jan 11-12, 2022, as well.

We received a total of 29 submissions in the two rounds. Each submission was reviewed by at least three reviewers and 15 submissions were shortlisted for presentation.

A good number of papers focus on how machine learning approaches can be applied to Sanskrit texts, paying special attention to its status as a low resource language. The contribution of Krishna et al. is an in-depth study of data-driven parsing algorithms for Classical Sanskrit. It discusses various parsing architectures, the choice of input features and possible sources of parsing errors. Another aspect of data-driven NLP is covered in the contribution of Sandhan et al. who compare static and contextualized word embeddings on a range of semantic classification tasks and obtain remarkably good results given the small size of the digital Sanskrit corpus. As a foundation for data-driven methods, Krishnan et al. discuss endeavors towards merging existing annotated corpora of Classical Sanskrit in a common format. Building NLP resources is also the topic of the paper by Sarkar et al. who develop a simple, yet effective machine learning approach for pre-annotating an NER data set. While the papers mentioned so far use quantitative models for language analysis, Maity et al. discuss the problem of disambiguating the kāraka notion of oblique cases from a Pāṇinian perspective and evaluate their approach on a small sample of annotated sentences.

The remaining papers of this volume cover aspects of (Sanskrit) NLP that go beyond the identification and analysis of basic linguistic structures. Mahesh and Bhattacharya evaluate how well high-level textual features can be predicted with contextualized word embeddings. The contribution of Neill describes the open-source project Skrutable, a tool for identifying meters in Sanskrit texts, and sketches directions for future research in this field. Another paper focusing on meter identification is presented by Terdalkar and Bhattacharya whose system also includes a fuzzy search option. Ajotikar et al. propose an extension of the TEI standard for encoding various levels of information present in the Sanskrit commentarial literature and discuss which research questions can be addressed by applying XSLT templates to textual sources encoded in this way. Another contribution by Scharf et al. describes the TEI encoding of the Rāmopakhyāna and the Kramapha system used to interactively display its content in the web. Terdalkar et al. report about ongoing work on building knowledge graphs from Āyurvedic texts. Their paper elaborates on the annotation process and its prerequisites as well as on the design of an appropriate medical and botanical ontology. The problem of extracting and representing the knowledge structure of śāstra texts is also addressed in the paper by Susarla et al. who concentrate on sentence level features of scientific texts. Hellwig et al. describe an extension of Bloomfield's concordance of Vedic mantras and discuss its application to open issues in Vedic Studies.

Finally, two papers address aspects of Middle Indo-Aryan languages and the Buddhist literature composed in them. Harnsukworapanich et al. give an overview of D-Tipitaka, an online version of the Dhammachai Tipiṭaka Edition with linked manuscript images and contextual information. Zigmond discusses how Pāli commentaries can be distinguished from the commented canonical texts by applying standard clustering algorithms to frequent words in these texts.

We thank the Convenors, Programme Committee members and the numerous experts who helped us in the review process, and all our authors who responded positively to the reviewer's comments and improved their manuscripts accordingly. We thank the entire 18th WSC organising committee, led by Prof McComas Taylor, which provided us the necessary logistic support for the organisation of this section.

Amba Kulkarni & Oliver Hellwig

Programme Committee

- **Convenors:**
  - Gérard Huet (Inria, Paris, France) (Chair)
  - Amba Kulkarni (University of Hyderabad, India)
- **Chairs:**
  - Amba Kulkarni (University of Hyderabad, India)
  - Oliver Hellwig (University of Zurich, Germany)
- **Members:**
  - Ivan Andrijani (University of Zagreb,Croatia)
  - Stefan Baums (University of Munich, Germany)
  - Arnab Bhattacharya (IIT Kanpur, India)
  - Brendan Gillon (McGill University,Canada)
  - Pawan Goyal (IIT Kharagpur, India)
  - Malhar Kulkarni (IIT Bombay, India)
  - Dhaval Patel (Ahmedabad, India)
  - Wiebke Petersen (University of Düsseldorf, Germany)
  - Pavan Kumar Satuluri (Chinmaya Vishwavidyapeeth, Veliyanad, India)
  - Sai Susarla (MIT, Pune,India)
  - Peter Scharf (IIIT Hyderabad, India)
  - Srinivasa Varakhedi (KKSU, Ramtek,India)

Table of Contents

Neural Approaches for Data Driven Dependency Parsing in Sanskrit

Amrith Krishna, Ashim Gupta, Deepak Garasangi, Jivnesh Sandhan, Pavankumar Satuluri, Pawan Goyal
University of Cambridge, University of Utah, Manipal Institute of Technology, IIT Kanpur, Chinmaya Vishwavidyapeeth, IIT Kharagpur
ak2329@cam.ac.uk, pawang@cse.iitkgp.ac.in

Abstract

Data-driven approaches for dependency parsing have been of great interest in Natural Language Processing for the past couple of decades. However, Sanskrit still lacks a robust purely data-driven dependency parser, probably with an exception to Krishna (2019). This can primarily be attributed to the lack of availability of task-specific labelled data and the morphologically rich nature of the language. In this work, we evaluate four different data-driven machine learning models, originally proposed for different languages, and compare their performances on Sanskrit data. We experiment with 2 graph based and 2 transition based parsers. We compare the performance of each of the models in a low-resource setting, with 1,500 sentences for training. Further, since our focus is on the learning power of each of the models, we do not incorporate any Sanskrit specific features explicitly into the models, and rather use the default settings in each of the paper for obtaining the feature functions. In this work, we analyse the performance of the parsers using both an in-domain and an out-of-domain test dataset. We also investigate the impact of word ordering in which the sentences are provided as input to these systems, by parsing verses and their corresponding prose order (anvaya) sentences.

1 Introduction

Dependency parsing, specifically data-driven dependency parsing, has garnered considerable attention from the computational linguistics and the Natural Language Processing (NLP) communities in the past few decades. The ability of the parsing approach to capture syntactic and shallow semantic information over multiple languages and often in cross-lingual settings has led to widespread adoption of the syntactic parsing approach (Tiedemann, 2015; Li et al., 2019; McDonald et al., 2013). Transition based parsing and Graph based parsing are two of the dominant approaches in data-driven dependency parsing (McDonald and Nivre, 2007). Parsers proposed under either of these approaches vary widely in terms of the input representations, learning paradigms and inferences employed. The parsers range from linear machine learning models to neural network based nonlinear models for learning, whereas the input representations vary from discrete hand-crafted features to continuous word representations such as pre-trained word embeddings, contextualised word representations etc. (Kulmizev et al., 2019; Peters et al., 2018). In this work, we evaluate and present a comparative error analysis of the performance of several of these recently proposed data-driven approaches for parsing sentences in Sanskrit.

Our work closely follows the analysis framework proposed in several of the previous works on dependency parsing. McDonald and Nivre (2007), which was later extended in McDonald and Nivre (2011), performed an empirical analysis which contrasts the performance of graph-based and transition based parsers. They identified characteristics of these parsers and profiled the structural divergences in the predictions and the errors made by each of them. This was further extended by Kulmizev et al. (2019), where they performed a similar analysis on neural dependency parsers. Further, they investigated the impact of using contextualised word representations (Peters et al., 2018). Here, they observed that with neural architectures and contextualised word embeddings, both graph based and transition based approaches, tend to converge

Proceedings of the Computational Sanskrit and Digital Humanities, 18th World Sanskrit Conference 2023, pages 1–20

Parser	Parsing Approach	Learning Framework	Input Representation
YAP (More et al., 2019)	Transition	Neural	Hand-crafted features
Dozat and Manning (2017)	Graph	Neural	Word representations
Self-training (Rotman and Reichart, 2019)	Graph	Neural	Contextualised word representations
Learning to Search (Chang et al., 2016)	Transition	Neural	Hand-crafted features

Table 1: Overview of the data-driven models evaluated in this work.

on their performance characteristics more as compared to the corresponding linear models. The analysis framework essentially measures the empirical performance of various models based on the sentence length, relative distance between words connected by a dependency arc, distance of nodes to the root and on non-projective arcs. In this work, we replicate these analyses exclusively for Sanskrit. Further, we add an additional dimension crucial for Sanskrit, i.e., analysis of differences in parsing poetry and prose data.

Table 1 gives an overview of the various systems we use along with the parsing approach, model and input representation used in these models. Here, all the four models use neural learners. However, both the transition based models we evaluate use hand-crafted features while the graph based parsers automatically learn the word representations as features. Neural parsers, both graph-based and transition based, that use the learned word representations as features currently report the state of the art results for many languages including English (Mrini et al., 2019; Qi et al., 2018).[1] However this need not hold true for morphologically rich and relatively free word order languages. For instance, YAP (More et al., 2019) currently reports state of the art parsing results for the morphologically rich language, Hebrew and hence we include the model in our evaluation. YAP makes use of word n-grams and morphological information of the words from the input sentence as features. Similarly, we chose to include the Learning to Search model due to its training procedure that is designed to mitigate the effects of exposure bias and label bias. Since the prediction of individual arcs are dependent on the previous arc predictions for a sentence in dependency parsing, Learning to Search (Chang et al., 2016) exposes the system to incorrect parsing decisions during training. This enables the system to recover from early incorrect predictions made during inference and thereby resulting in lower exposure bias and label bias (Wiseman and Rush, 2016). The graph based parsers we employ learn neural word representations as features. This results in requirement for large amount of training data, or availability of large monolingual corpora to obtain pre-trained embeddings (Che et al., 2018). Rotman and Reichart (2019) addresses this issue by proposing a self-training approach that augments the biaffine parser from Dozat and Manning (2017). Here, first a base parser is trained with as low as 500 trained samples and then, dependency trees are predicted for unlabelled data. The predictions are used to train on auxiliary tasks which results in contextualised representations of the input sequence based on those auxiliary tasks. As Rotman and Reichart (2019) is promising as a parser for low-resource languages, we include the model in our experiments. Further, since Dozat and Manning (2017) is the base parser to Rotman and Reichart (2019), we include the model as well for a fair comparison between the models. Based on our experiments, our major observations are:

1. The self-training based dependency parser by Rotman and Reichart (2019) performs the best when tested on our in-domain test dataset (Kulkarni, 2013) and also on the out of domain Śiśupāla-vadha dataset, with word arrangements in prose as well as poetry.

[1] `https://nlpprogress.com/english/dependency_parsing.html`

2. All the models provide competitive results even on out-of-domain Śiśupāla-vadha test data, when the sentence follows prose ordering. However, the performance of all the models falls drastically, often halves, when the same sentences from Śiśupāla-vadha in its verse ordering are provided as input during inference.

3. We find that use of automated feature functions learned using LSTM based word-representation can be benefited in a low-resource morphologically rich language like Sanskrit. Both such graph based parsing models we use (Dozat and Manning, 2017; Rotman and Reichart, 2019) are the best 2 models in our experiments. Transition based parsers in general tend to perform poorly when it comes to predictions on longer sentences. However, the learning to search transition parser remains relatively stable often competitive to the graph based parsers we use.

2 Data-Driven Dependency Parsing

Early attempts at data-driven models for parsing dependency structures could be traced back to the later half of the 1990s. Collins (1996) and Eisner (1996), proposed multiple probabilistic-models for dependency parsing of English sentences. Similarly, Kudo and Matsumoto (2000) proposed an SVM based classifier for classifying dependencies in Japanese, and this was later extended to English (Yamada and Matsumoto, 2003). In the tenth CoNLL-X shard task on multi-lingual dependency parsing (Buchholz and Marsi, 2006), it was observed that graph-based and transition based parsing approaches have emerged to be the two dominant approaches for parsing dependency structures. Though the shared task identified these approaches as "all-pairs" and "stepwise", McDonald and Nivre (2007) later termed these approaches as graph based and transition based. Even though most of the proposed parsers fall under either of these categories, these parsers vary widely in terms of the input representations, learning algorithms and learning architectures. In this section, we provide a brief overview of the graph based and transition based parsers along with the developments that occurred in the past couple of decades. For a detailed understanding of these approaches, we recommend the readers to refer to McDonald and Nivre (2011) and Kulmizev et al. (2019).

2.1 Graph-Based Parsing

Given an input sentence, the sentence is converted into a dense graph (or a complete graph), where each word in the sentence is a node and every possible dependency relation between two words forms a labelled arc. In this 'all-pairs' approach (Buchholz and Marsi, 2006) every possible word pair is scored based on the likelihood of the pair to form a dependency relation. Then, using a search mechanism the parser identifies the best parse for the given sentence. We can generalise graph-based dependency parsing as an approach to score a dependency tree by the linear combination of scores of its local sub-graphs. The task here is to find an induced subgraph of the input graph, which structurally is a tree that spans all the nodes of the graph, i.e. a spanning tree. The inference then translates to finding the spanning tree with maximum (or minimum) score. The score for a tree is obtained by decomposing the structure into sub-graphs, and is scored using a global optimisation approach with a non-local greedy search. The decomposed sub-graphs can be as simple as an edge that connects a pair of nodes, and such models are called arc-factored models. The learning involves creating a gap between the score of the ground truth tree with that of other candidate tress. As per Kübler et al. (2009), any graph-based parsing system must define four things:

1. A set of sub-structures Ψ_G, to which the input graph G will be decomposed.

2. A defintion of the parameters λ for each substructure in Ψ_G.

3. A method for learning λ.

4. A parsing algorithm.

In an arc-factored model, Ψ_G will be the edge set in the input graph G and λ will be a function that maps edges into real values. Here an edge can be represented as a vector of fixed features and the function will be learnt to map this vector into a scalar real-value. The score of candidate structures (spanning trees in this case) will be calculated by summing the score of their edges. The parsing algorithm is then reduced to searching for a suitable structure, generally a spanning tree. The search procedure can be modified to enforce additional constraints on the specific structure to be searched. Additional constraints, such as the structure should only have one edge labelled with the subject relation, and relaxations, such as allowing cycles on the predicted structures, were incorporated in the inference in several works (Kübler et al., 2009). McDonald et al. (2005b) formalised the search procedure as a search for spanning tree with maximum score. Here the score of the tree is nothing but the sum of the scores of its edges. They employed the Chu-Liu-Edmond's algorithm (Edmonds, 1967).

Arc-factored models , such as McDonald et al. (2005b), perform exact search and hence they do not suffer from search errors. However, the features that can be incorporated are restricted to the local sub-graphs. McDonald et al. (2005a) used a feature function that contains 18 feature templates relevant to each of the edges. The features for an edge essentially are the word and POS information of the nodes connected by the edge, and the word and POS information of adjacent words to these nodes as per the linear order of the sentence. Although we learn a function to score the individual edges, the training still is global as the parameters of the model are set relative to the classification of the entire dependency tree, and not locally over single edges (McDonald and Nivre, 2011). The graph parsers are typically trained using margin based structured learning approaches which attempt to widen the gap between the score (need not always be a probabilistic score) of the correct dependency tree to that of other candidate dependency trees.

Graph-based parsers were extended to higher-order models and also in terms of the arity of a node. The arity of a node measures the likelihood of the node to have a fixed number of dependents. These extensions were primarily to improve the parsing performance for non-projective dependency structures. The arity information was trivially incorporated by modifying the scoring function of arc-factored models by adding the likelihood of arity as an additional parameter (Kübler et al., 2009). In the case of higher order-models, McDonald and Pereira (2006), score adjacent arcs with a common head. Similarly Carreras (2007) considered head-modifier chains of length two. Third order models by Koo and Collins (2010) consider set of various three arc subgraphs, such as adjacent siblings or grand-siblings. However, the inference and learning becomes NP-Hard (McDonald and Satta, 2007) when the score is factored over higher order structures than edges, especially for non-projective dependency parses. Martins et al. (2009) and Martins et al. (2010) proposed parsing approaches with exact inference, though with NP-hard complexity, to incorporate higher order features. To make the inference more efficient, an approximate inference using cube pruning was introduced in Zhang and McDonald (2014). However recent neural approaches reverted to using first order models and still achieve state of the art results (Kulmizev et al., 2019).

2.2 Transition based parsing

In transition based parsing approaches, instead of considering all the possible word pairs, the parsing decisions are taken incrementally. The approach is inspired from shift-reduce parsing approaches originally proposed for analysing programming languages (Aho and Ullman, 1972). Essentially this reduces the parsing task to that of iteratively predicting the next immediate parsing action as a greedy search. The system is trained on partial parser configurations, where the immediate next action needs to be predicted. Transition based parser parses a sentence sequentially from left to right.[2]

[2]The parsing can be done sequentially from right to left as well.

The parsing system is an abstract machine, consisting of a set of states and transitions between them. We start from an initial state and then follow a valid sequence of transitions, terminating at one of the terminal states. By the time a terminal state is reached, it would lead to the dependency tree for the given sentence. The parser essentially consists of a stack, a buffer and a set of dependency labels. At a given instance, the stack maintains the partial parses, the buffer maintains the words to be parsed and additionally the labels assigned so far is kept track of. The combination of the configuration of these three entities result in a parser configuration, i.e. a state. The parser is initialised with empty stack with a dummy root node in it, a buffer with all the words in the sentence and an empty set of actions. Words one after other are pushed into the stack and popped from it. A final configuration is a configuration when the buffer is empty and the stack is left only with the dummy root node. The given system is a non-deterministic system, i.e. there can be multiple possible transitions from a given state. However, the system can be amenable to a deterministic parsing approach, assuming the presence of an oracle that can guide the transition decisions at each state. The oracle can be approximated by training classifiers using labelled data (Kübler et al., 2009) and guide the parsing process.

Summarily, given a classifier, the parsing procedure is about finding a trajectory, i.e. an optimal sequence of transitions, that leads from the initial configuration to a terminal configuration. The behaviour of the parser is defined in terms of various transitions (McDonald and Nivre, 2011). Apart from initialisation and termination transitions, the basic version of the parser included four more transitions. The other transitions are Shift, reduce, left-arc, right-arc. The shift operation simply pushes the next input word into the stack, while reduce pops the word from the top of the stack. The left-arc assigns an arc from the next input word to word on the top of the stack and right-arc performs vice versa (McDonald and Nivre, 2007). Transition parsers enable to incorporate non-local features into the configurations of the parser. However, since the approach performs a local search, it is exposed to label bias resulting in compounding of errors. Though initially, transition based parsers employed greedy search approaches, models with global learning were later proposed. Further McDonald and Nivre (2011) proposed an enriched feature function with 72 different feature templates. The features vary from uni-gram to tri-gram word and POS information of words in the stack and the buffer, distance between the word at the top of the stack and front of the buffer queue, valency, third order features and set of dependency labels with the words at the top of the stack and the front of the buffer queue. More et al. (2019) adapted the feature function to meet the needs of free-word order languages, by replacing positional information with labelled grammatical functions.

In Goldberg and Nivre (2013), the static oracle was replaced with dynamic oracles. Dynamic oracles could guide the system to optimal trajectory, even from a configuration which is not present in the ground-truth. Introduction of dynamic oracles could reduce the error propagation, especially when an early mistake in prediction is made. While the transition based approaches initially were trained to handle projective dependency structures, these were later extended to handle non-projective dependency structures. Further, modifications to transition approaches were proposed, primarily for English. Apart from Arc-standard, which we already defined, arc-eager and arc-(Z)eager are two other systems of transition based parsing. The arc-eager system allows a right-dependent to eagerly attach to the head. Here, the dependent word will be pushed onto the stack so as to enable attaching to its dependents. Arc-(Z)eager is an augmentation to arc-eager approach, where it employs an additional stack to hold the head nodes and enabling certain constraints for the head words during transitions (More et al., 2019).

2.3 Neural Dependency Parsing

Though neural network based approaches for dependency parsing have been explored towards the end of the last decade (Titov and Henderson, 2007; Attardi et al., 2009), these parsers have come to prominence since the last five years (Kulmizev et al., 2019). Use of neural approaches for dependency parsing has brought in great advancements in the learning methods, architectures and improvements in performance. However, most of these parsers still belong to graph based or transition based approaches. Neural parsers have enabled to bring down the complexities in the parsing approaches and revert back to simpler inference approaches without any loss in performance. We can observe that neural transition parsers with local learning and greedy inference, and similarly neural graph based parsers making use of first order models now report competitive, often better, results as compared to complex parsing approaches previously employed. Yet another major advantage with neural architectures is that they have alleviated the need for hand-crafted feature engineering, and instead started to rely on dense features in the form of embeddings. Chen and Manning (2014) and Weiss et al. (2015) have shown how neural network based dense features can be employed instead of hand-crafted features for transition based and graph-based parsers respectively. Kiperwasser and Goldberg (2016) has employed BiLSTM based word features, coupled with POS tags, that could capture the contextual representation of the words within the sentence. However these models are constrained by the need for high amount of training data. Moreover, for morphologically rich languages like Hebrew or Turkish, state of the art models are the ones that still use hand-crafted features (More et al., 2019; Seeker and Çetinoğlu, 2015).

3 System Description of the Parsing Models

The Pāṇinian theory of kāraka, proposed for dependency analysis of sentences in Sanskrit, is well studied in the computational linguistics community. Bharati et al. (1991) proposed a computational framework for multiple Indian languages based on this framework. Further a dependency tagset and a dependency parser using the tagset was developed over the years for multiple Indian languages (Tandon and Sharma, 2017; Begum et al., 2008). Rule based systems for dependency parsing in Sanskrit was proposed by Kulkarni et al. (2010) and was later improved in Kulkarni (2013) using dynamic programming approaches. However both the systems require the input sequence to be in prose (anvaya) order, as the systems build constraints based on the (relative) positional information of the words in the sentence. A dependency parser for verses in Sanskrit was later proposed in Kulkarni et al. (2019). A statistical data-driven dependency parser was proposed by Krishna (2019), which uses an energy based model for the dependency parsing. All of these models use the tagset based on the relations described in Ramkrishnamacharyulu (2009). In this work, we do not consider any of the aforementioned works for comparison, as we focus on completely data-driven approaches with no explicit linguistic information incorporated into the models. Hence, we compare four different systems as shown in Table 1. While all of them use a neural network for training the models, 2 of them still use hand-crafted features and the other two rely on LSTM based encoders for capturing the feature information about the words and the sequence information of the words in context.

3.1 Yet Another Parser (YAP)

The parser proposed by More et al. (2019), is a transition based parser. It currently reports the state of the art results for Hebrew, a morphologically rich language. The model uses hand-crafted features, adapted from Zhang and Nivre (2011) for free word order languages. The model uses a variant of the generalised perceptron (Zhang and Clark, 2011) with early-update (Collins and Roark, 2004) for training. The focus of feature engineering is on selectional preferences, subcategorisation frames and their distributional characterisation. The transition based system has provisions for Arc-standard, Arc-eager and Arc-(Z)eager transition paradigms. We use the Arc-eager apparoach in our models. While the paper originally proposes a joint morpho-syntactic parser that can jointly perform morphological parsing and syntactic parsing for Hebrew, we make use of the system as a standalone dependency parser.

3.2 Learning to Search (L2S)

Learning to search is a framework that enables the formulation of a structured prediction problem as a search problem (Ross et al., 2011; Collins and Roark, 2004; Daumé et al., 2009). Here, an explicit search space is generally defined as a finite state machine over a set of states. The search problem essentially consists of a set of states, including an initial state, terminal states and actions that enable transition from one state to another. The learning problem here is to learn a function, referred to as a policy, that maps a trajectory (sequence of actions) from the initial state to a goal state with the lowest cost or dually the highest score. Here each state configuration is represented using a bag of features, which is used for learning. L2S integrates the learning and prediction in a unified framework. This framework is similar to a reinforcement learning setting, and indeed in many ways it is. However, L2S uses a reference policy obtained from labelled examples before the training starts (Chang et al., 2015). During training, the supervision in the form of labelled data is used to define the loss function and to construct a reference policy (Chang et al., 2016). Based on these signals, the classifier (or the current policy) gets iteratively trained.

Once a search space is obtained for a given problem, the training can be started. It needs to be noted that the loss during training is not calculated based on individual actions, but based on the trajectory of actions taken for a given data point. In our case, the data point is a sentence, For a sentence, the training happens in 3 phases called as roll-in, roll-out and one-step deviation. The roll-in and roll-out policies can be the reference policy, current policy or a mixture of both. Since, the prediction at a given step is dependent on the history of predictions made so far for the input sentence, each of those mistakes has a different cost to pay. This is called a credit assignment problem. To handle such cases and thereby alleviate the exposure bias of such systems, we do a one step deviation at several all time steps during different iterations. The action taken during the deviation would be an alternate action from the set of possible actions. All the actions prior to the deviation follow from the roll-in policy and the actions after the deviation follows the roll-out policy. The loss is calculated based on the trajectory obtained as a consequence of these 3 steps.

We employ a transition based parsing approach for the L2S framework. Here, the state space consists of all possible configurations of the parser. As with other standard transition based parsers (Kuhlmann et al., 2011), we use the word-level and POS-level (morphological tags) information of upto three words in the stack and the buffer to construct the feature representation for each state. We follow the arc-hybrid system proposed by Goldberg and Nivre (2013) and the corresponding L2S implementation from Chang et al. (2016). The optimal reference policy is computed using the dynamic oracle approach by Goldberg and Nivre (2013). The loss is computed by computing the differences in the number of parents in the predicted tree and that of the gold-standard tree. Here, when an action is predicted, the dependency relation is also predicted whenever the action is a reduce operation.

3.3 BiAFFINE Parser (BiAFF)

The BiAFFINE parser (Dozat and Manning, 2017) is a neural graph-based dependency parsing approach similar to Kiperwasser and Goldberg (2016). The neural approaches, in general, have been beneficial for dependency parsing as it considerably reduces the complexities involved in generating feature representations. The feature representations are learned as embeddings from the surface forms of the words and also from their POS. For learning contextual embeddings that can capture the sentence context, LSTM (or BiLSTM) layers are used. Here, the authors introduce bi-affine attention instead of bilinear or MLP based attention, which were used in previous works in dependency parsing. The representations learned from LSTMs are subjected to MLP based dimensionality reduction and a biaffine dependency label classifier is used. Here, a biaffine classifier differs from an affine classifier in the following way. For an input vector $\vec{x}$, while an affine classifier could be expressed as $W\vec{x} + b$, then a biaffine classifier could be expressed as $W'(W\vec{x} + b) + b'$.

The model inputs a sequence of tokens and their POS tags, which is then passed through multiple layers of a BiLSTM network. In order to obtain specialised representations, the hidden vector from the final layer of the LSTM network is passed to four separate ReLU activation layers. This produces four separate representations, each for a separate purpose. One for word as a dependant looking for its head and another for its label. Similarly, we have one each for a word as head looking for its dependents and the labels of those dependents (Dozat and Manning, 2017). Two biaffine classifiers are used, where these representations are passed. The classifiers are used to predict the head and the label, respectively for a given word pair.

3.4 Deep Contextualized Self-training (DCST)

Deep Contextualized Self-training (Rotman and Reichart, 2019) extends the graph-based parser of Dozat and Manning (2017) with a self-training approach (Clark et al., 2018; Rybak and Wróblewska, 2018) for low resource dependency parsing. The work primarily addresses the scarcity of task-specific labelled data for low resource languages (or scarcity of in-domain data) and suggests a self-training based solution. Here, a base-learner is trained on a limited set of labelled data and then applied on a larger set of unlabelled data. Then the predictions from unlabelled data and the gold-standard labelled data are combined to retrain the final model, which is often performed iteratively. Specifically, in this work, it first trains the BiAFFINE parser as a base learner, with as low as 500 labelled training sentences and then uses the same to generate predictions from unlabelled data. The predicted dependency trees from the unlabelled data are then used to train neural networks for several auxiliary tasks. The auxiliary tasks performed are sequence level tagging tasks, where the input is the predicted dependency tree adapted to a suitable sequence tagging scheme. LSTM based taggers are used for training these tasks. Once the training is completed, the BiLSTM encoder layers are used for generating representations for the input word. The encoder layers from the auxillary tasks are combined with the representations from the encoder layers of the BiAFFINE parser using a gating mechanism (Sato et al., 2017). Here, during training, the representation layers of the parser are randomly initialised, while the representation layers from the auxiliary task are initialised to what it learned for the auxiliary task. The auxiliary tasks that are employed are, predicting the number of children for each word, predicting the distance of the word from the root in the tree and predicting the head word of a given word using the relative POS tagging scheme (Rotman and Reichart, 2019). Here, the relative POS tagging scheme enables to mark ahead word by its relative position from the current dependent node and the corresponding POS tag of the head word.

The basic intuition behind the approach in this work is similar to pretraining and multi-task approaches used in deep learning networks previously. However, in pretraining settings, though unlabelled data are used, they are used to train the LSTM encoders on language model based objective. In this work, they are trained on sequence level tagging tasks based objectives. This is similar to multi-task learning approaches where several related tasks are trained together or are reused, but those approaches typically use labelled data, unlike in this case.

4 Experiments

4.1 Dataset

The dataset for the dependency parsing is obtained from the department of Sanskrit studies, UoHyd[3]. We use about 1,500 prose sentences from the Sanskrit Tree Bank Corpus, henceforth to be referred to as STBC (Kulkarni et al., 2010; Kulkarni, 2013). Further, we use 1,000 sentences from STBC as the test data. Additionally, we take 300 sentences from the Śiśupāla-vadha corpus[4] for testing. Here, we make use of the prose order (anvaya) and the corresponding verse order of the sentences to provide as input to the different models. For all the models, we provide the segmented surface-form of the words in the sentence and their corresponding morphological tags as input. However, the entries in STBC corpus did not contain morphological tags for the words. For these sentences, we used the Sanskrit Heritage reader (Goyal and Huet, 2016; Huet and Goyal, 2013), a shallow parser, for obtaining the exhaustive enumeration of all the possible morphological analyses of the input. We only selected those sentences where none of the words

[3]`http://sanskrit.uohyd.ac.in/scl/`

[4]`http://sanskrit.uohyd.ac.in/scl/e-readers/shishu/`

	System	STBC Prose		Śiśupāla-vadha Prose		Śiśupāla-vadha Poetry	
		UAS	LAS	UAS	LAS	UAS	LAS
1	L2S	77.29	68.53	75.42	68.48	38.80	31.76
2	YAP	72.14	63.15	65.27	55.88	26.79	21.10
3	BiAFF	78.97	70.83	76.77	70.24	38.45	34.32
4	DCST	**80.97**	**72.86**	**81.08**	**74.37**	**40.02**	**35.70**

Table 2: Performance evaluation of the four dependency parsers.

expressed syncretism or homonymy. While, the current morphological tag information is yet to be verified by a domain expert, we decided to include the morphological tag information in input. This decision was motivated by the empirical observation that the inclusion of morphological tags as input results in about 3 to 4 % of performance improvement for all the models, as compared to using only the surface-forms of the words as input. Moreover, the evaluation of the models is based only on the dependency arcs and the labels, and hence this decision does not interfere in our experimental settings.

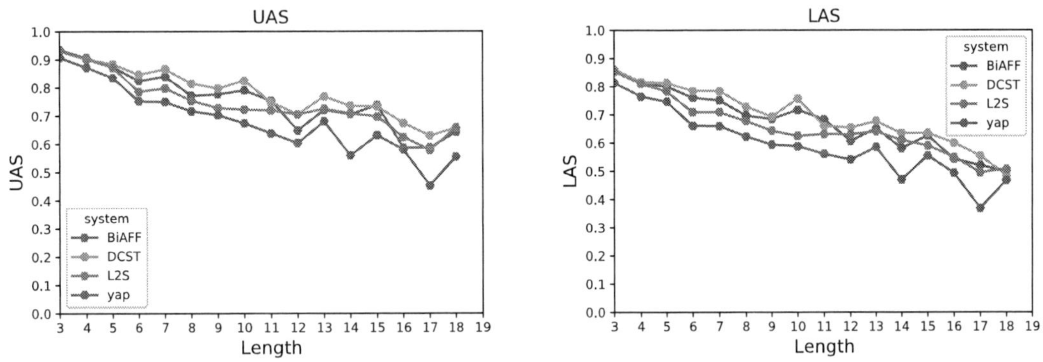

(a) Sentence length UAS - STBC

(b) Sentence length LAS - STBC

Figure 1: UAS/LAS of sentences grouped based on their sentence length on STBC corpus

4.2 Results

We report the performance of each system using the micro averaged Unlabelled Attachment Score (UAS) and the Labelled Attachment Score (LAS) as metrics (Nivre and Fang, 2017). UAS is the fraction of correct tokens with correct predicted heads and LAS is the fraction of tokens with the correct label (McDonald and Nivre, 2011). For micro averaged UAS and LAS, the denominator for normalising these fraction scores is the number of tokens in the corpus. Table 2 shows the results for all the four systems tested on the prose sentences from STBC, and prose and poetry data from Śiśupāla-vadha. It can be observed that DCST outperforms all the other models in all the three test data settings. The DCST model uses BiAFF as a base learner. However, it improves the performance of the model, by using better input representations obtained by self-training. We find that the performance differences between both the models are statistically significant.[5] Since, all the models are trained on the STBC train corpus, the STBC test data should ideally be most similar in terms of the data distribution with that of the training data. The data from Śiśupāla-vadha corpus can be seen as an out of domain dataset. Sentences from Śiśupāla-vadha, when arranged in their prose order, report comparable results with that of the

[5]We performed t-test for statistical significance with $p < 0.01$.

STBC prose test data for all the models, with YAP being a possible exception. However, the performance for all the models drops drastically when these systems are provided with poetry order data as input. In fact, for all the systems, the performance drops to half the UAS as compared to the corresponding prose order input. This is a strong indication that the order in which the data is input affects the performance of these systems.

Comparison to Linguistically involved Energy Based Model: We compare the performance of all the four models with the performance of the linguistically involved energy based model (EBM) proposed by Krishna (2019). We report two results based on the EBM model. Both the models use linguistic information in its input representation and in its feature engineering. However EBM* uses linguistic information to prune the search space and filter the candidates during the inference. Both the models use a graph-based input and are agnostic to the order in which a sequence is provided. Further, they report the Macro averaged UAS and LAS, i.e. average of sentence level UAS and LAS of sentences from both the STBC and Śiśupāla-vadha test data. Table 3 provides the macro averaged UAS and LAS for all the six systems. Here, we use the prose ordered data from Śiśupāla-vadha and STBC for the four models discussed in this paper. From the table, it can be observed that the EBM* model outperforms all the other models and reports a huge improvement in terms of LAS. However, DCST still outperforms the EBM, the model that does not incorporate explicit linguistic information during inference, in terms of UAS. This not only shows the relevance of incorporating linguistic information into the model, but also stresses on the significance of using contextualised word representations (like in the case of DCST).

	System	UAS	LAS
1	L2S	81.9	72.46
2	YAP	75.3	66
3	BIAFF	82.35	75.65
4	DCST	84.36	76.8
5	EBM	82.65	79.28
6	EBM*	**85.32**	**83.93**

Table 3: Macro averaged UAS and LAS for 1300 sentences from the STBC and Śiśupāla-vadha prose test datasets.

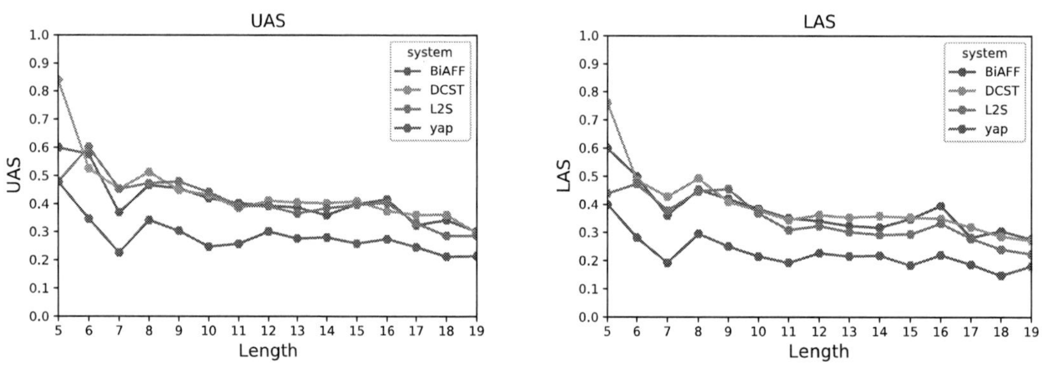

(a) Sentence length UAS - poetry

(b) Sentence length LAS - poetry

Figure 2: UAS/LAS of sentences in poetry order, grouped based on their sentence length on Śiśupāla-vadha corpus

Sentence Length Figure 1(a-b) and Figure 2(a-b) show the UAS and LAS for the sentences grouped based on the number of words in them, for each dataset. We show the lengthwise performance of only the poetry ordered sentences for the Śiśupāla-vadha dataset, as the prose ordered data's performance is similar to that of STBC prose test data. The figures show the performance for only those sentence lengths for which there exist at least 5 sentences in the corpus. All the systems perform the best on shorter sentences and generally the performance drops as the length of the sentence increases. However, the L2S system reports the lowest Mean

Absolute Deviation[6] (MAD) among the 4 models (0.07), followed by DCST (0.077) for the STBC corpus. YAP performs the worst and has the highest MAD (0.093). In the case of poetry data, the performance of the DCST dips drastically for sentences longer than 5 words as compared to its performance on sentences with 5 or less words. It shows the highest MAD (0.122) as well. The L2S system reports the lowest MAD among all the models (0.081). All the other systems have a MAD < 0.085. Sentences with 3 to 7 words form 68.7 % of sentences in the STBC corpus. In the case of Śiśupāla-vadha, 50 % of the sentences consist 11 to 15 words, and 85 % of the sentences consist of 7 to 17 words.

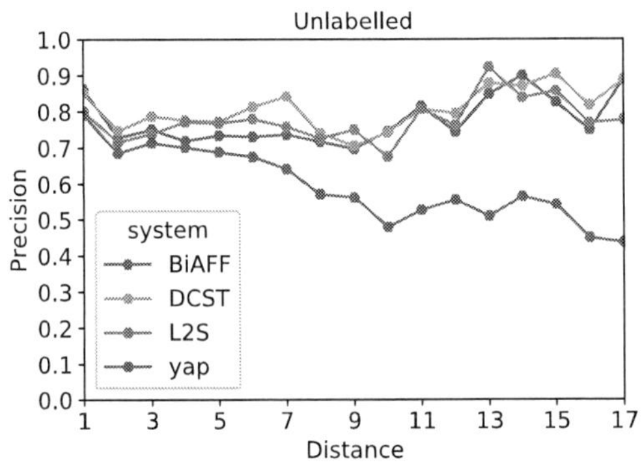

(a) Precision - unlabelled

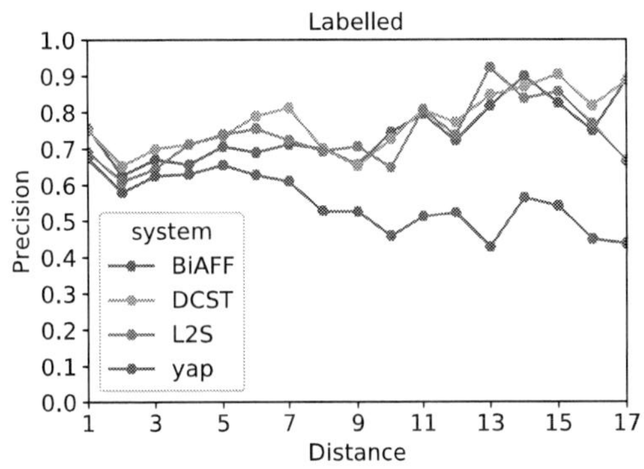

(b) Precision - labelled

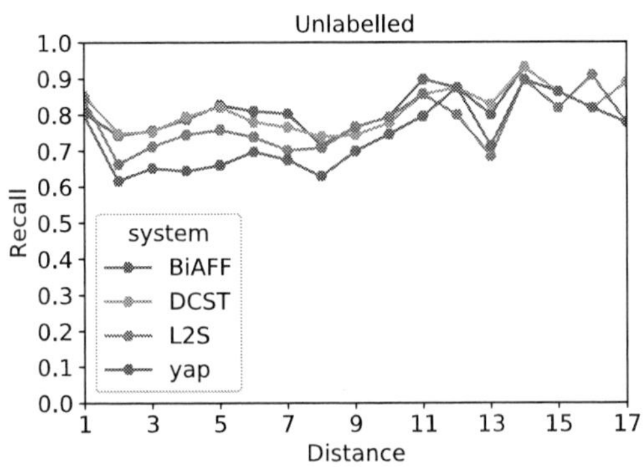

(c) Recall - unlabelled

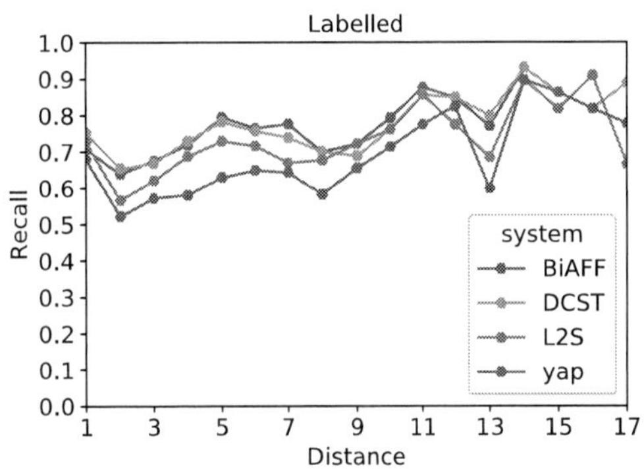

(d) Recall - labelled

Figure 3: Precision/Recall based on unlabelled/labelled edges for STBC prose w.r.t. dependency length

Dependency Length: Dependency length between two related words is the distance between those words based on their linear arrangement in the sentence (McDonald and Nivre, 2007). Figure 3(a-d), shows the precision/recall for dependency length on the STBC corpus based on unlabelled/labelled edges. Transition based parsers with greedy inference, in general, tend to perform worse on longer dependencies in terms of precision (McDonald and Nivre, 2007; McDonald and Nivre, 2011), though this becomes less evident in neural transition based parsing approaches (Kulmizev et al., 2019). Both the transition based systems in our experiments, YAP and L2S, use hand-crafted features. Aligning with observations made by McDonald and Nivre (2007), YAP's performance degrades considerably when predicting longer dependencies. However, L2S performs at par with the graph based parsing approaches we experimented with. We hypothesise, this is due to the training procedure followed in L2S, where the system is not just exposed to the ground truth trajectories but also to the one step deviations to the wrong

[6]The mean absolute deviation of a dataset is the average distance between each data point and the mean.(KhanAcademy, accessed 15 Apr 2020)

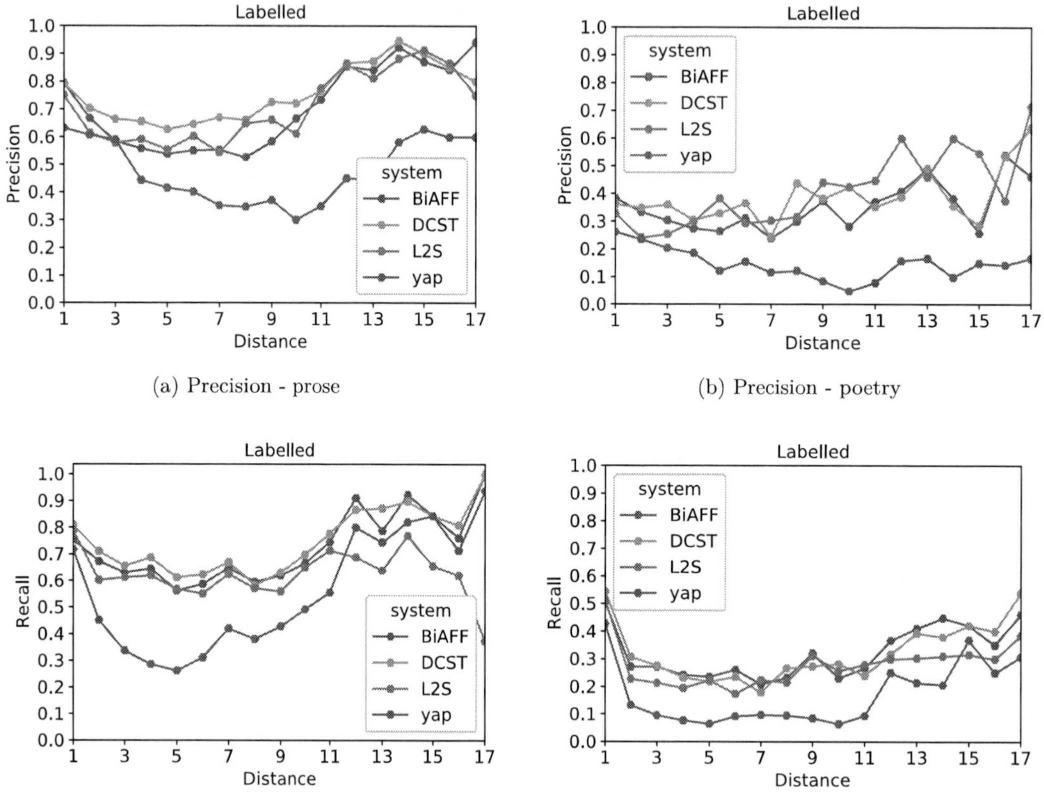

(a) Precision - prose

(b) Precision - poetry

(c) Recall - prose

(d) Recall - poetry

Figure 4: Precision/Recall based on labelled edges for Śiśupāla-vadha prose and poetry w.r.t. dependency length

states during training. This helps mitigating the exposure bias and label bias of these systems (Wiseman and Rush, 2016).

Figure 4(a-d) shows the precision/recall for dependency length on the prose and poetry data on the Śiśupāla-vadha based on labelled edges. In prose order sentences, the linear arrangement of words tends to follow the principle of Sannidhi (Kulkarni et al., 2015), i.e. dependency locality (Gibson et al., 2019). In terms of precision for prose data, similar to STBC prose data, YAP under-performs consistently as compared to all other systems. In the case of precision for poetry data, we can find that DCST and L2S systems, generally provide better performance as compared to other systems on longer dependency length word pairs. From Figure 5 we can observed that STBC corpus contains about 44.9 % of the word pairs with a dependency length of one. Similarly, word pairs with a dependency length greater than five is only about 13.5 % of the total word pair connections in the ground-truth. In contrast about 30.7 % of the word pairs have a distance more than 5 in the poetry data. More importantly, these systems have less than 0.6 % word pairs with a length of 1. Given that our

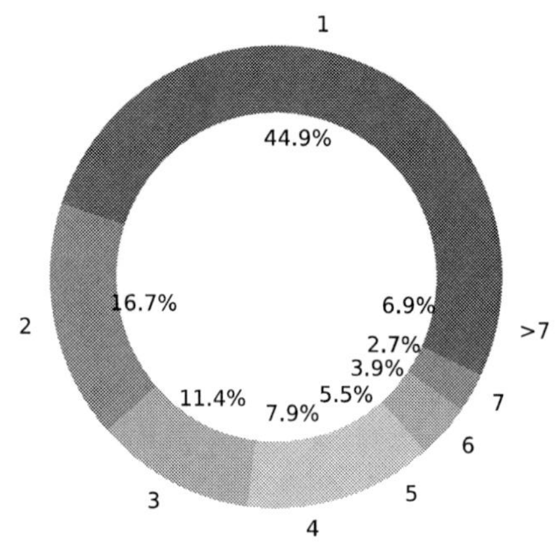

Figure 5: Dependency length percentage between word-pairs in STBC corpus ground truth

parsers are trained on prose data, these structural divergences with poetry ordered data might be a strong reason for poor performance of the parsing models on the poetry data.

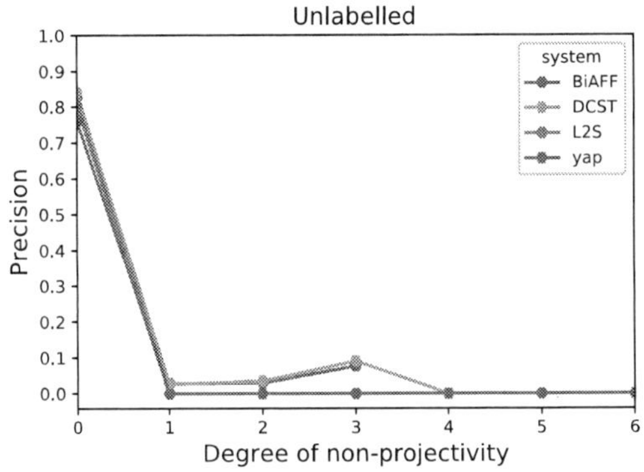

(a) Precision - Unlabelled

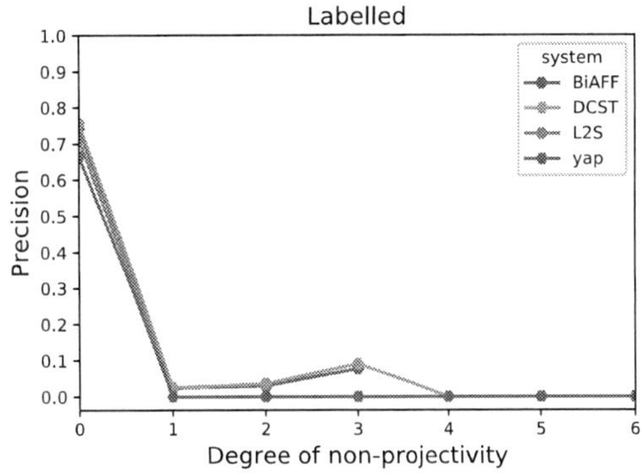

(b) Precision - Labelled

Figure 6: Precision based on the degree of non-projectivity of dependency arcs for STBC prose

Non Projective Dependencies: We further look into the performance of the systems on the non-projective dependencies. Here, we make use of degree of non-projectivity (McDonald and Nivre, 2007). The degree of non-projectivity of a dependency arc from a word w to word u is the number of words occurring between w and u which are not descendants of w and modify a word not occurring between w and u (Nivre, 2006). Figure 6(a-b) shows the precision for different models on the STBC corpus both in terms of labelled and unlabelled predictions. Similarly, Figure 7(a-b) shows the performance of the systems on the prose and poetry ordered data from Śiśupāla-vadha. Here we only show the performance for the labelled case, and the performance for the unlabelled case is similar to that of the labelled case. It can be observed that none of the models perform well for non-projective dependency arcs (those arcs with a non-zero degree of non-projectivity). Further, for the Śiśupāla-vadha poetry data, non-projective arcs constitute 19.24 % of the edges, as compared to just 7.12 % in the corresponding prose data. This is one of the factors for low-performance of the data in poetry ordering.

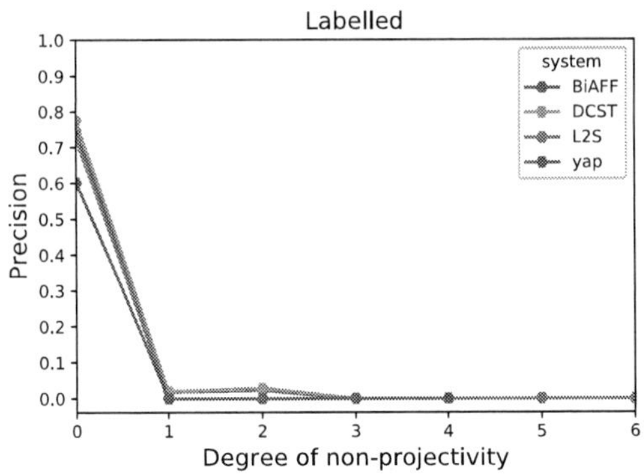

(a) Precision - prose

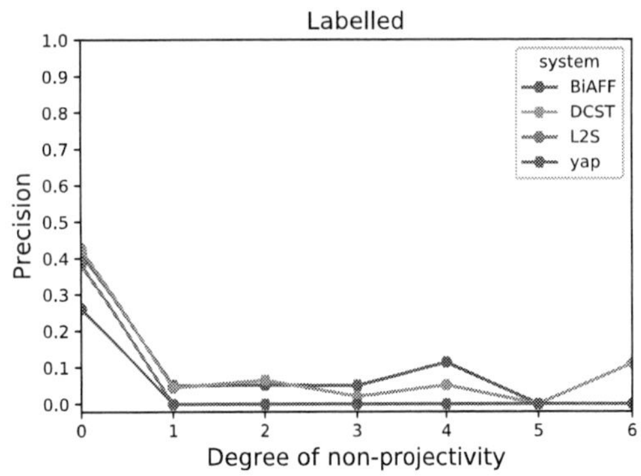

(b) Precision - poetry

Figure 7: Precision based on the degree of non-projectivity of dependency arcs for Śiśupāla-vadha prose and poetry

Distance to Root: We measure the performance of different systems based on the distance of a node from the root of the tree. Figure 8(a-d) shows the precision and recall for distance from the root on the STBC corpus based on unlabelled/labelled edges. The general trend for

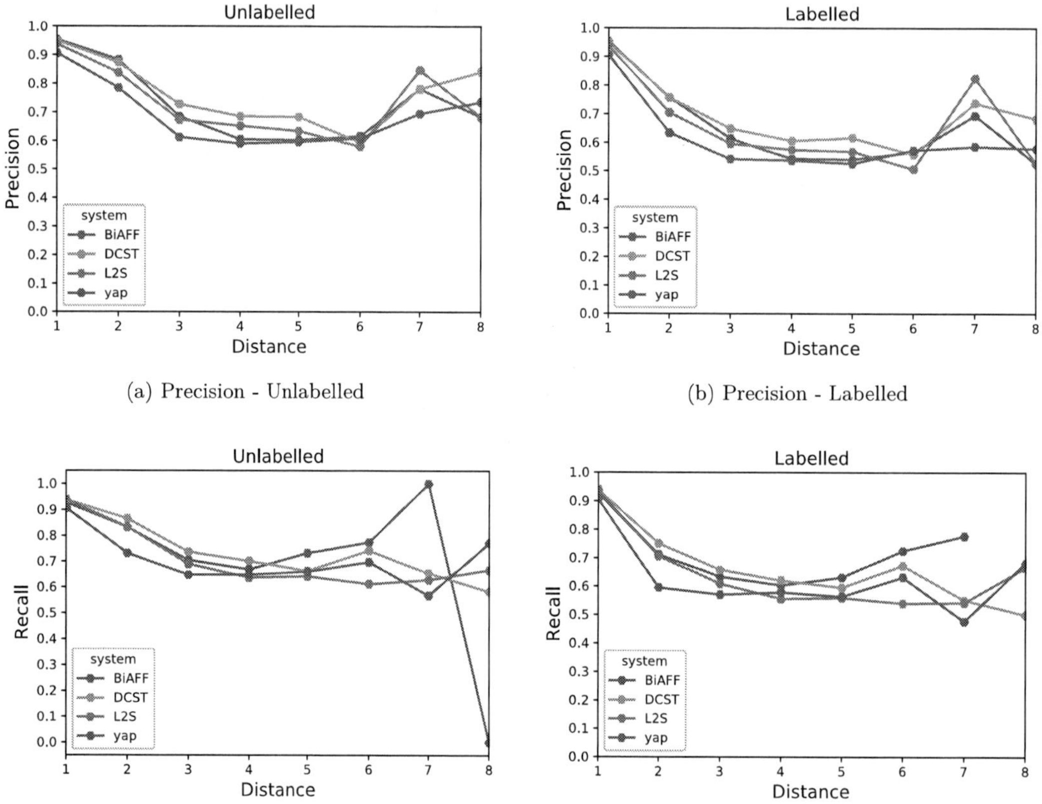

(a) Precision - Unlabelled

(b) Precision - Labelled

(c) Recall - Unlabelled

(d) Recall - Labelled

Figure 8: Precision/Recall based on unlabelled/labelled edges for STBC prose w.r.t. distance to the root

all the systems is that, the precision drops with nodes that have longer distances from the root. Similarly, Figure 9(a-d) shows Precision/Recall based on labelled edges for Śiśupāla-vadha prose and poetry. Transition based parsers generally tends to perform better than graph based approaches on arcs farther away from the root (McDonald and Nivre, 2011). However use of contextualised word representations tend to improve the results for graph based parsers (Kulmizev et al., 2019). Here, it needs to be observed that the graph based BiAFF parser, deteriorates in its performance with predictions that are far from the root. At the same time, DCST which uses BiAFF as its base parser reports better precision than L2S in most of the cases. We hypothesise that this is due to the improvement in the feature representations learned using the self-training approach in DCST. Further, it is interesting to note that both the graph parsers have the highest MAD on all the three dataset settings as compared to the transition based parsers. In fact, the transition based parser L2S outperforms BiAFF in most of the predictions with distance from root larger than 3, even though BiAFF reports a better overall performance than L2S.

5 Conclusion

In this work, we evaluated four standard neural dependency parsing models for parsing of Sanskrit sentences. We find that neural parsers that make use of neural word representations and contextualised word representations can be effectively used for parsing morphologically rich languages like Sanskrit. However, word ordering in these sentences affects the performance of these systems drastically. As of now, it would be difficult to conclude, whether this is a consequence of the linguistic characteristics of the language or because of the data distribution of the training

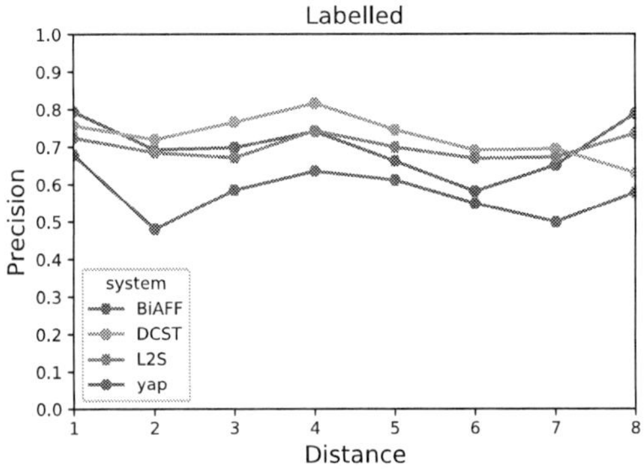

(a) Precision - prose

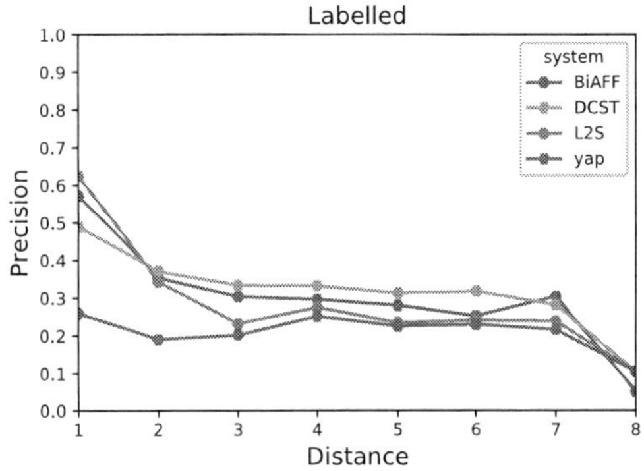

(b) Precision - poetry

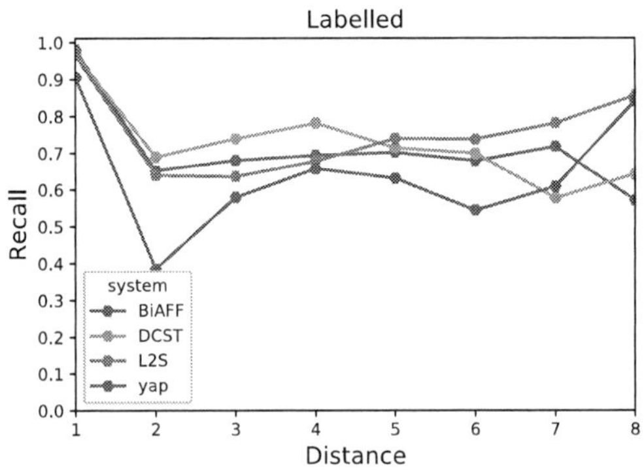

(c) Recall - prose

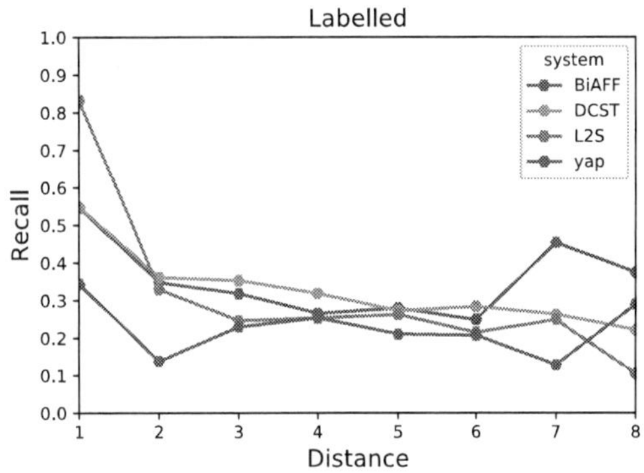

(d) Recall - poetry

Figure 9: Precision/Recall based on labelled edges for Śiśupāla-vadha prose and poetry w.r.t. distance to the root

data. To elaborate further, one possibility is that the current drop in result can be due to the distributional differences in the prose training data, with which the models were trained, and the poetry data. On the other hand, it further needs to be investigated whether the performance drop has to do with something which is more linguistically inherent, and not just confining to the distributional differences. For this, we would require to train the models using dependency tagged data in verse order. It would be worthwhile to pursue if there are schemes to shuffle the word ordering in verses that would benefit in parsing these sentences. The approaches can be to completely disregard the word order and convert the input as a graph as in the case of Krishna (2019), or to use syntactic linearisers such as Krishna et al. (2019) that convert a verse to its corresponding prose order or to perform word reordering/linearisation as an auxiliary task in the training for dependency parsing (Wang et al., 2018).

While in this work, we focused on evaluating the effect of standard parsers in their default settings, the next logical step would be to modify these models by incorporating design changes by keeping Sanskrit specific characteristics in mind. We plan to extend the work in two important directions. Currently, we provide the morphological tags of the words as input to the model. This often can be a bottleneck, as morphological disambiguation can be a challenge in itself for morphologically rich languages. We plan to augment the neural parsers, especially DCST, under a multi task setting where we would stack layers from a multi task morphological tagger so as to obtain enriched representations for the words. In this model, the user need not provide the morphological tags as input as the system would expect only the surface-forms of the words. Similarly, we find that the L2S model can be extended by incorporating linguistic knowledge as constraints into the inference, so as to effectively prune the search space. To elaborate, currently during one step deviation, transitions are made to incorrect states based on label predictions, including those states which can effectively be avoided by a rule based pre-processing step. The pre-processing step can bring down the search space transitions by allowing only those that are valid based on the given case information of the word pairs for which a decision needs to be taken.

Acknowledgements

We are grateful to Anupama Ryali for sharing the Śiśupāla-vadha dataset and Amba Kulkarni for the STBC corpus.

References

Alfred V. Aho and Jeffrey D. Ullman. 1972. *The Theory of Parsing, Translation, and Compiling.* Prentice-Hall, Inc., USA.

Giuseppe Attardi, Felice Dell'Orletta, Maria Simi, and Joseph Turian. 2009. Accurate dependency parsing with a stacked multilayer perceptron. In *Proceeding of Evalita 2009*, LNCS. Springer.

Rafiya Begum, Samar Husain, Arun Dhwaj, Dipti Misra Sharma, Lakshmi Bai, and Rajeev Sangal. 2008. Dependency annotation scheme for Indian languages. In *Proceedings of the Third International Joint Conference on Natural Language Processing: Volume-II.*

Akshar Bharati, Vineet Chaitanya, and Rajeev Sangal. 1991. A computational grammar for indian languages processing. *Indian Linguistics Journal*, 52:91–103.

Sabine Buchholz and Erwin Marsi. 2006. CoNLL-x shared task on multilingual dependency parsing. In *Proceedings of the Tenth Conference on Computational Natural Language Learning (CoNLL-X)*, pages 149–164, New York City, June. Association for Computational Linguistics.

Xavier Carreras. 2007. Experiments with a higher-order projective dependency parser. In *Proceedings of the 2007 Joint Conference on Empirical Methods in Natural Language Processing and Computational Natural Language Learning (EMNLP-CoNLL)*, pages 957–961, Prague, Czech Republic, June. Association for Computational Linguistics.

Kai-Wei Chang, Akshay Krishnamurthy, Alekh Agarwal, Hal Daume, and John Langford. 2015. Learning to search better than your teacher. In Francis Bach and David Blei, editors, *Proceedings of the 32nd International Conference on Machine Learning*, volume 37 of *Proceedings of Machine Learning Research*, pages 2058–2066, Lille, France, 07–09 Jul. PMLR.

Kai-Wei Chang, He He, Hal Daumé, John Langford, and Stephane Ross. 2016. A credit assignment compiler for joint prediction. In *Proceedings of the 30th International Conference on Neural Information Processing Systems*, NIPS'16, page 1713–1721, Red Hook, NY, USA. Curran Associates Inc.

Wanxiang Che, Yijia Liu, Yuxuan Wang, Bo Zheng, and Ting Liu. 2018. Towards better UD parsing: Deep contextualized word embeddings, ensemble, and treebank concatenation. In *Proceedings of the CoNLL 2018 Shared Task: Multilingual Parsing from Raw Text to Universal Dependencies*, pages 55–64, Brussels, Belgium, October. Association for Computational Linguistics.

Danqi Chen and Christopher Manning. 2014. A fast and accurate dependency parser using neural networks. In *Proceedings of the 2014 Conference on Empirical Methods in Natural Language Processing (EMNLP)*, pages 740–750, Doha, Qatar, October. Association for Computational Linguistics.

Kevin Clark, Minh-Thang Luong, Christopher D. Manning, and Quoc Le. 2018. Semi-supervised sequence modeling with cross-view training. In *Proceedings of the 2018 Conference on Empirical Methods in Natural Language Processing*, pages 1914–1925, Brussels, Belgium, October-November. Association for Computational Linguistics.

Michael Collins and Brian Roark. 2004. Incremental parsing with the perceptron algorithm. In *Proceedings of the 42nd Annual Meeting on Association for Computational Linguistics*, page 111. Association for Computational Linguistics.

Michael John Collins. 1996. A new statistical parser based on bigram lexical dependencies. In *34th Annual Meeting of the Association for Computational Linguistics*, pages 184–191, Santa Cruz, California, USA, June. Association for Computational Linguistics.

Hal Daumé, John Langford, and Daniel Marcu. 2009. Search-based structured prediction. *Machine learning*, 75(3):297–325.

Timothy Dozat and Christopher D. Manning. 2017. Deep biaffine attention for neural dependency parsing. In *5th International Conference on Learning Representations, ICLR 2017, Toulon, France, April 24-26, 2017, Conference Track Proceedings*. OpenReview.net.

Jack Edmonds. 1967. Optimum branchings. *Journal of Research of the national Bureau of Standards B*, 71(4):233–240.

Jason M. Eisner. 1996. Three new probabilistic models for dependency parsing: An exploration. In *COLING 1996 Volume 1: The 16th International Conference on Computational Linguistics*.

Edward Gibson, Richard Futrell, Steven P. Piantadosi, Isabelle Dautriche, Kyle Mahowald, Leon Bergen, and Roger Levy. 2019. How efficiency shapes human language. *Trends in Cognitive Sciences*, 23(5):389 – 407.

Yoav Goldberg and Joakim Nivre. 2013. Training deterministic parsers with non-deterministic oracles. *Transactions of the association for Computational Linguistics*, 1:403–414.

Pawan Goyal and Gerard Huet. 2016. Design and analysis of a lean interface for sanskrit corpus annotation. *Journal of Language Modelling*, 4(2):145–182.

Gérard Huet and Pawan Goyal. 2013. Design of a lean interface for Sanskrit corpus annotation. In *Proceedings of ICON 2013, the 10th International Conference on NLP*, pages 177–186.

Khan-Academy, accessed 15 Apr 2020. *Mean absolute deviation (MAD) review*.

Eliyahu Kiperwasser and Yoav Goldberg. 2016. Simple and accurate dependency parsing using bidirectional LSTM feature representations. *Transactions of the Association for Computational Linguistics*, 4:313–327.

Terry Koo and Michael Collins. 2010. Efficient third-order dependency parsers. In *Proceedings of the 48th Annual Meeting of the Association for Computational Linguistics*, pages 1–11, Uppsala, Sweden, July. Association for Computational Linguistics.

Amrith Krishna, Vishnu Sharma, Bishal Santra, Aishik Chakraborty, Pavankumar Satuluri, and Pawan Goyal. 2019. Poetry to prose conversion in Sanskrit as a linearisation task: A case for low-resource languages. In *Proceedings of the 57th Annual Meeting of the Association for Computational Linguistics*, pages 1160–1166, Florence, Italy, July. Association for Computational Linguistics.

Amrith Krishna. 2019. *Addressing Language Specific Characteristics for Data-Driven Modelling of Lexical, Syntactic and Prosodic Tasks in Sanskrit*. Ph.D. thesis, IIT Kharagpur, Kharagpur, West Bengal, India.

Sandra Kübler, Ryan McDonald, and Joakim Nivre. 2009. Dependency parsing. *Synthesis lectures on human language technologies*, 1(1):1–127.

Taku Kudo and Yuji Matsumoto. 2000. Japanese dependency structure analysis based on support vector machines. In *2000 Joint SIGDAT Conference on Empirical Methods in Natural Language Processing and Very Large Corpora*, pages 18–25, Hong Kong, China, October. Association for Computational Linguistics.

Marco Kuhlmann, Carlos Gómez-Rodríguez, and Giorgio Satta. 2011. Dynamic programming algorithms for transition-based dependency parsers. In *Proceedings of the 49th Annual Meeting of the Association for Computational Linguistics: Human Language Technologies*, pages 673–682, Portland, Oregon, USA, June. Association for Computational Linguistics.

Amba Kulkarni, Sheetal Pokar, and Devanand Shukl. 2010. Designing a constraint based parser for sanskrit. In Girish Nath Jha, editor, *Sanskrit Computational Linguistics*, pages 70–90, Berlin, Heidelberg. Springer Berlin Heidelberg.

Amba Kulkarni, Preethi Shukla, Pavankumar Satuluri, and Devanand Shukl. 2015. How Free is 'free' Word Order in Sanskrit. In *The Sanskrit Library, USA*, pages 269–304.

Amba Kulkarni, Sanal Vikram, and Sriram K. 2019. Dependency parser for Sanskrit verses. In *Proceedings of the 6th International Sanskrit Computational Linguistics Symposium*, pages 14–27, IIT Kharagpur, India, October. Association for Computational Linguistics.

Amba Kulkarni. 2013. A deterministic dependency parser with dynamic programming for Sanskrit. In *Proceedings of the Second International Conference on Dependency Linguistics (DepLing 2013)*, pages 157–166, Prague, Czech Republic, August. Charles University in Prague, Matfyzpress, Prague, Czech Republic.

Artur Kulmizev, Miryam de Lhoneux, Johannes Gontrum, Elena Fano, and Joakim Nivre. 2019. Deep contextualized word embeddings in transition-based and graph-based dependency parsing - a tale of two parsers revisited. In *Proceedings of the 2019 Conference on Empirical Methods in Natural Language Processing and the 9th International Joint Conference on Natural Language Processing (EMNLP-IJCNLP)*, pages 2755–2768, Hong Kong, China, November. Association for Computational Linguistics.

Zhenghua Li, Xue Peng, Min Zhang, Rui Wang, and Luo Si. 2019. Semi-supervised domain adaptation for dependency parsing. In *Proceedings of the 57th Annual Meeting of the Association for Computational Linguistics*, pages 2386–2395, Florence, Italy, July. Association for Computational Linguistics.

André Martins, Noah Smith, and Eric Xing. 2009. Concise integer linear programming formulations for dependency parsing. In *Proceedings of the Joint Conference of the 47th Annual Meeting of the ACL and the 4th International Joint Conference on Natural Language Processing of the AFNLP*, pages 342–350, Suntec, Singapore, August. Association for Computational Linguistics.

André Martins, Noah Smith, Eric Xing, Pedro Aguiar, and Mário Figueiredo. 2010. Turbo parsers: Dependency parsing by approximate variational inference. In *Proceedings of the 2010 Conference on Empirical Methods in Natural Language Processing*, pages 34–44, Cambridge, MA, October. Association for Computational Linguistics.

Ryan McDonald and Joakim Nivre. 2007. Characterizing the errors of data-driven dependency parsing models. In *Proceedings of the 2007 Joint Conference on Empirical Methods in Natural Language Processing and Computational Natural Language Learning (EMNLP-CoNLL)*, pages 122–131, Prague, Czech Republic, June. Association for Computational Linguistics.

Ryan McDonald and Joakim Nivre. 2011. Analyzing and integrating dependency parsers. *Computational Linguistics*, 37(1):197–230.

Ryan McDonald and Fernando Pereira. 2006. Online learning of approximate dependency parsing algorithms. In *11th Conference of the European Chapter of the Association for Computational Linguistics*, Trento, Italy, April. Association for Computational Linguistics.

Ryan McDonald and Giorgio Satta. 2007. On the complexity of non-projective data-driven dependency parsing. In *Proceedings of the Tenth International Conference on Parsing Technologies*, pages 121–132, Prague, Czech Republic, June. Association for Computational Linguistics.

Ryan McDonald, Koby Crammer, and Fernando Pereira. 2005a. Online large-margin training of dependency parsers. In *Proceedings of the 43rd Annual Meeting of the Association for Computational Linguistics (ACL'05)*, pages 91–98, Ann Arbor, Michigan, June. Association for Computational Linguistics.

Ryan McDonald, Fernando Pereira, Kiril Ribarov, and Jan Hajič. 2005b. Non-projective dependency parsing using spanning tree algorithms. In *Proceedings of Human Language Technology Conference and Conference on Empirical Methods in Natural Language Processing*, pages 523–530, Vancouver, British Columbia, Canada, October. Association for Computational Linguistics.

Ryan McDonald, Joakim Nivre, Yvonne Quirmbach-Brundage, Yoav Goldberg, Dipanjan Das, Kuzman Ganchev, Keith Hall, Slav Petrov, Hao Zhang, Oscar Täckström, Claudia Bedini, Núria Bertomeu Castelló, and Jungmee Lee. 2013. Universal dependency annotation for multilingual parsing. In *Proceedings of the 51st Annual Meeting of the Association for Computational Linguistics (Volume 2: Short Papers)*, pages 92–97, Sofia, Bulgaria, August. Association for Computational Linguistics.

Amir More, Amit Seker, Victoria Basmova, and Reut Tsarfaty. 2019. Joint transition-based models for morpho-syntactic parsing: Parsing strategies for MRLs and a case study from modern Hebrew. *Transactions of the Association for Computational Linguistics*, 7:33–48, March.

Khalil Mrini, Franck Dernoncourt, Trung Bui, Walter Chang, and Ndapa Nakashole. 2019. Rethinking self-attention: An interpretable self-attentive encoder-decoder parser. *arXiv preprint arXiv:1911.03875.*

Joakim Nivre and Chiao-Ting Fang. 2017. Universal dependency evaluation. In *Proceedings of the NoDaLiDa 2017 Workshop on Universal Dependencies (UDW 2017)*, pages 86–95, Gothenburg, Sweden, May. Association for Computational Linguistics.

Joakim Nivre. 2006. Constraints on non-projective dependency parsing. In *11th Conference of the European Chapter of the Association for Computational Linguistics*, Trento, Italy, April. Association for Computational Linguistics.

Matthew Peters, Mark Neumann, Mohit Iyyer, Matt Gardner, Christopher Clark, Kenton Lee, and Luke Zettlemoyer. 2018. Deep contextualized word representations. In *Proceedings of the 2018 Conference of the North American Chapter of the Association for Computational Linguistics: Human Language Technologies, Volume 1 (Long Papers)*, pages 2227–2237, New Orleans, Louisiana, June. Association for Computational Linguistics.

Peng Qi, Timothy Dozat, Yuhao Zhang, and Christopher D. Manning. 2018. Universal dependency parsing from scratch. In *Proceedings of the CoNLL 2018 Shared Task: Multilingual Parsing from Raw Text to Universal Dependencies*, pages 160–170, Brussels, Belgium, October. Association for Computational Linguistics.

K. V. Ramkrishnamacharyulu. 2009. Annotating sanskrit texts based on śābdabodha systems. In Amba Kulkarni and Gérard Huet, editors, *Sanskrit Computational Linguistics*, pages 26–39, Berlin, Heidelberg. Springer Berlin Heidelberg.

Stéphane Ross, Geoffrey Gordon, and Drew Bagnell. 2011. A reduction of imitation learning and structured prediction to no-regret online learning. In *Proceedings of the fourteenth international conference on artificial intelligence and statistics*, pages 627–635.

Guy Rotman and Roi Reichart. 2019. Deep contextualized self-training for low resource dependency parsing. *Transactions of the Association for Computational Linguistics*, 7:695–713.

Piotr Rybak and Alina Wróblewska. 2018. Semi-supervised neural system for tagging, parsing and lematization. In *Proceedings of the CoNLL 2018 Shared Task: Multilingual parsing from raw text to universal dependencies*, pages 45–54.

Motoki Sato, Hitoshi Manabe, Hiroshi Noji, and Yuji Matsumoto. 2017. Adversarial training for cross-domain universal dependency parsing. In *Proceedings of the CoNLL 2017 Shared Task: Multilingual Parsing from Raw Text to Universal Dependencies*, pages 71–79, Vancouver, Canada, August. Association for Computational Linguistics.

Wolfgang Seeker and Özlem Çetinoğlu. 2015. A graph-based lattice dependency parser for joint morphological segmentation and syntactic analysis. *Transactions of the Association for Computational Linguistics*, 3:359–373.

Juhi Tandon and Dipti Misra Sharma. 2017. Unity in diversity: A unified parsing strategy for major Indian languages. In *Proceedings of the Fourth International Conference on Dependency Linguistics (Depling 2017)*, pages 255–265, Pisa,Italy, September. Linköping University Electronic Press.

Jörg Tiedemann. 2015. Cross-lingual dependency parsing with universal dependencies and predicted PoS labels. In *Proceedings of the Third International Conference on Dependency Linguistics (Depling 2015)*, pages 340–349, Uppsala, Sweden, August. Uppsala University, Uppsala, Sweden.

Ivan Titov and James Henderson. 2007. A latent variable model for generative dependency parsing. In *Proceedings of the Tenth International Conference on Parsing Technologies*, pages 144–155, Prague, Czech Republic, June. Association for Computational Linguistics.

Wenhui Wang, Baobao Chang, and Mairgup Mansur. 2018. Improved dependency parsing using implicit word connections learned from unlabeled data. In *Proceedings of the 2018 Conference on Empirical Methods in Natural Language Processing*, pages 2857–2863, Brussels, Belgium, October-November. Association for Computational Linguistics.

David Weiss, Chris Alberti, Michael Collins, and Slav Petrov. 2015. Structured training for neural network transition-based parsing. In *Proceedings of the 53rd Annual Meeting of the Association for Computational Linguistics and the 7th International Joint Conference on Natural Language Processing (Volume 1: Long Papers)*, pages 323–333, Beijing, China, July. Association for Computational Linguistics.

Sam Wiseman and Alexander M. Rush. 2016. Sequence-to-sequence learning as beam-search optimization. In *Proceedings of the 2016 Conference on Empirical Methods in Natural Language Processing*, pages 1296–1306, Austin, Texas, November. Association for Computational Linguistics.

Hiroyasu Yamada and Yuji Matsumoto. 2003. Statistical dependency analysis with support vector machines. In *Proceedings of the Eighth International Conference on Parsing Technologies*, pages 195–206, Nancy, France, April.

Yue Zhang and Stephen Clark. 2011. Syntactic processing using the generalized perceptron and beam search. *Computational Linguistics*, 37(1):105–151.

Hao Zhang and Ryan McDonald. 2014. Enforcing structural diversity in cube-pruned dependency parsing. In *Proceedings of the 52nd Annual Meeting of the Association for Computational Linguistics (Volume 2: Short Papers)*, pages 656–661, Baltimore, Maryland, June. Association for Computational Linguistics.

Yue Zhang and Joakim Nivre. 2011. Transition-based dependency parsing with rich non-local features. In *Proceedings of the 49th Annual Meeting of the Association for Computational Linguistics: Human Language Technologies*, pages 188–193, Portland, Oregon, USA, June. Association for Computational Linguistics.

Evaluating Neural Word Embeddings for Sanskrit

Jivnesh Sandhan[1], Om Adideva Paranjay[3], Digumarthi Komal[1], Laxmidhar Behera,[1,2] and Pawan Goyal[4]

[1]Dept. of Electrical Engineering, IIT Kanpur,[2]Tata Consultancy Services,
[3]Dept. of Electrical and Systems Engineering, University of Pennsylvania,
[4]Dept. of Computer Science and Engineering, IIT Kharagpur
jivnesh@iitk.ac.in, pawang@cse.iitkgp.ac.in

Abstract

Recently, the supervised learning paradigm's surprisingly remarkable performance has garnered considerable attention from Sanskrit Computational Linguists. As a result, the Sanskrit community has put laudable efforts to build task-specific labeled data for various downstream Natural Language Processing (NLP) tasks. The primary component of these approaches comes from representations of word embeddings. Word embedding helps to transfer knowledge learned from readily available unlabelled data for improving task-specific performance in low-resource setting. Last decade, there has been much excitement in the field of digitization of Sanskrit. To effectively use such readily available resources, it is essential to perform a systematic study on word embedding approaches for the Sanskrit language. In this work, we investigate the effectiveness of word embeddings. We classify word embeddings in broad categories to facilitate systematic experimentation and evaluate them on four intrinsic tasks.

1 Introduction

The supervised learning paradigm has shown remarkable performance in many downstream Natural Language Processing (NLP) tasks. In this domain, the NLP community has witnessed the emergence of neural-based approaches with the state of the art performance. The dramatic popularity of such approaches has garnered considerable attention from Sanskrit Computational Linguistics (SCL) community. The primary prerequisite for the feasibility of such approaches is the availability of task-specific labeled data. Therefore, as a first step, there was a need for preparing such task-specific resources. As a result, laudable efforts have been put by the community for building task-specific labeled data for various NLP tasks (Krishna et al., 2017; Hellwig and Nehrdich, 2018; Hellwig et al., 2020). The availability of such resources triggered the emergence of the data-driven neural-based approaches into the SCL field. The wide success of neural-based data-driven approaches is greatly justified by the state of the art performance for many downstream tasks for Sanskrit, namely, segmentation (Hellwig and Nehrdich, 2018; Reddy et al., 2018; Krishna et al., 2018), dependency parsing (Krishna et al., 2020c; Krishna et al., 2020a; Sandhan et al., 2021; Krishna et al., 2020b), semantic type identification (Sandhan et al., 2019; Krishna et al., 2016), word order linearisation (Krishna et al., 2019; Krishna et al., 2020c) and morphological parsing (Gupta et al., 2020; Krishna et al., 2018).

The supervised approaches have shown remarkable performance in several downstream NLP tasks and many of these use word embeddings as a primary component. In 2013, Mikolov et al. (2013) proposed a new milestone in the field of word embedding, which completely revolutionized Natural Language Processing (NLP). From there, word embedding has been a buzzword in NLP and has become part and parcel of downstream applications. These word embedding approaches adopt a semi-supervised learning paradigm. They do not depend on any explicitly labeled data or human supervision. Availability of massive unlabelled corpora and ease of integration into downstream NLP tasks made them exciting for the researchers. Sanskrit, the cultural heritage of India, has 30 million extant manuscripts (Goyal et al., 2012). Last decade, there has been

Proceedings of the Computational Sanskrit and Digital Humanities, 18th World Sanskrit Conference 2023, pages 21–37

much excitement in digitization for Sanskrit, as a result, we have DCS[1], The Sanskrit Library[2] and GRETIL[3]. To reduce the labeled data dependency, it's crucial to take advantage of such cheaply available resources.

This motivates us to systematically investigate word embedding approaches that are originally proposed for resource-rich languages like English. Most of the research in NLP disproportionately focuses on resource-rich languages due to readily available language resources: digitized texts and gold standard labeled data (Joshi et al., 2020). Also, the recent word embedding approaches have been studied for resource-rich languages such as English. However, such analysis is lacking for Sanskrit. In addition to the morphological rich nature of language, the Sanskrit is a relatively free word order language, and most words are compound words (samāsa) that demand special attention for modeling the word embedding approach. To conduct a systematic study on the efficacy of these approaches, we categorize word embeddings into two categories, namely, *static* and *contextualized.* The *static* embeddings generate a single representation for all the senses possible for a word, irrespective of surrounding context words. In contrast to that *contextualized* embeddings generate a different representation for each sense of the meaning depending on the surrounding context words. This work provides fertile soil for investigating the following questions: (1) Which linguistic phenomenons are captured by word embeddings? (2) Out of existing word embedding approaches, which embeddings are most suitable for Sanskrit? (3) What are the shortcomings of existing approaches specific to Sanskrit? Based on our experiments, our major findings are as follows:

1. Our intrinsic evaluation results illustrate that word embedding models trained on Sanskrit corpus are able to capture exceptionally good amount of the syntactic information. However, they perform relatively poorly with the semantic notion of relatedness - similarity mainly due to Out of vocabulary problem.
2. The *contextualized* word embedding model by Peters et al. (2018) outperforms all the word embeddings in all the intrinsic tasks with a large margin except semantic categorization task (Section 5). We employ contextual models without a context to measure efficacy of these approaches compared to static approaches. Applying *contextualized* models without context is similar to just using their underlying static word representation.
3. The qualitative analysis shows that the *contextualized* representations generated by Peters et al. (2018) and Lan et al. (2020) for polysemous words indicating the same sense of meaning forms a cluster for each sense of meaning (Section 6.3). This is indeed a serendipitous outcome for such data-hungry models when trained on negligibly small amount of corpus available for Sanskrit.
4. We release our codebase, datasets and models publicly at: `https://github.com/jivnesh/EvalSan`. This might help the research community to do further analysis and apply these embeddings to downstream NLP applications of Sanskrit.

2 Neural Word Embedding

Neural word embedding methods construct vector space so that semantically related words are projected in closer vicinity compared to unrelated words. Word embedding is a dense representation of words in low-dimensional vector space. It mainly exploits the distributional hypothesis: neighboring words share similar meaning (Firth, 1957; Harris, 1954).

As shown in Table 1, we consider the two broader categories of embedding approaches, namely, *static* and *contextualized.* Further, we divide them based on an atomic unit of input fed to the model, i.e., token level, subword level and character level. First, we consider token level embeddings: `word2vec` (Mikolov et al., 2013) and `GloVe` (Pennington et al., 2014). We consider

[1] `http://www.sanskrit-linguistics.org/dcs/index.php`

[2] `https://sanskritlibrary.org/`

[3] `http://gretil.sub.uni-goettingen.de/gretil.html`

Category	Input level	Models
Static	Token	Word2vec, GloVe
	Subword	FastText
	Character	CharLM
Contextualized	Subword	ALBERT
	Character	ELMo

Table 1: Categorization of embedding models

word2vec as a strong baseline because it is the basic backbone of all the neural-based follow-up works in this domain. While word2vec focuses on the local context of a target word, GloVe is an alternative approach that considers the global context of a target word. Therefore, GloVe can be seen as representative of count-based models; hence we choose to include it in our study. However, these token-based approaches suffer from two serious issues: (1) Out of vocabulary (OOV) problem: they fail to obtain representation for words which are not seen during training (2) Polysemy problem: a single representation for multiple meanings of words. In order to handle the first drawback, sub-word (Wieting et al., 2016; Bojanowski et al., 2017; Heinzerling and Strube, 2018) and character level (Kim et al., 2016; Jozefowicz et al., 2016) compositional modeling is proposed. These models learn composition functions to obtain word-level representation of a word using character level or subword level modeling. In the next category, the advent of contextualized embeddings is attributed to the polysemy problem. The year 2018 is an inflection point in the field of NLP with the launching of contextualized embedding by Peters et al. (2018, ELMo). The specific meaning of the word can be understood by the context words surrounded by it. Hence, in contextualized embedding approach, the representation of each token word is a function of entire sentence as a input. The emergence of another contextual embedding by Devlin et al. (2019, BERT) can be seen as a clever recipe of a bunch of excellent ideas bubbled in the field of NLP in recent years. We consider a derivative of BERT known as ALBERT (Lan et al., 2020) which is light version of BERT with relatively less number of parameters.

3 System Description

Tokenizer: Token-based word embeddings such as word2vec and GloVe suffer from OOV problem, i.e., they are not capable of producing vector representation for words that are not seen during training. Here, word is defined as a continuous unsandhied string separated by delimiter. This problem is even more prominent for Sanskrit due to the following reasons: (1) morphological-rich nature (2) highly inflectional (3) most of the text is available in *sandhied* format. Hence, token-based approaches are highly ineffective for Sanskrit. We take inspiration from Heinzerling and Strube (2018) and leverage sentencepiece tokenizer (Kudo and Richardson, 2018) to overcome OOV problem. The sentencepiece is unsupervised tokenizer used for neural-based tasks such as machine translation and sequence generation task. This is a purely data-driven tokenizer and does not require any pretokenization. Also, this is language independent approach where words are considered as a sequence of unicode characters. The sentencepiece overcomes the challenge as mentioned earlier by creating a new vocabulary instead of relying on real word boundaries. This method uses a greedy approach to figure out subword units that maximize the likelihood of the language model (Kudo and Richardson, 2018). There exist other unsupervised tokenizers such as Wordpiece (Wu et al., 2016) and BPE (Sennrich et al., 2016). However, these approaches expect tokenized words as input and most of the available text for Sanskrit is in *sandhied* format. Hence, sentencepiece is the most befitting choice as a tokenizer. We demonstrate sentencepiece tokenization with an example as shown below.[4] Here, sentencepiece considers space character as a normal character and is replaced by "_" character. Note that *manā_bhava* is a word in our newly generated vocabulary, originally part of two words.

Sandhied sentence (original)

man-manā bhava mad-bhakto mad-yājī māṁ namaskuru
mām evaiṣyasi yuktvaivam ātmānaṁ mat-parāyaṇaḥ

Segmented by sentencepiece tokenizer

_man - manā_bhava _mad -bhakto _mad - yājī _māṁ _namas kuru
_mām _evai ṣyasi _yukt vaivam _ātmān aṁ _mat - parāyaṇ aḥ

3.1 Static Embeddings

Word2Vec: The work of Mikolov et al. (2013) is a new milestone in the field of word embeddings and popularly known as word2vec. This work was the basic backbone of the neural-based word embedding approach, which led to many of word embedding variants tackling various challenges. This model exploits the distributional semantics hypothesis: "semantically similar words are used in similar contexts" (Firth, 1957; Harris, 1954). Word2vec often considered as one of the seminal the deep learning models; however, technically, neither the architecture is deep, nor the model uses non-linearities. It adapts language modeling objectives to consider the additional context. Language modeling is the task where the next word is predicted given previous n words. However, word2vec also considers next n words as a context. The basic intuition behind this model is to project the words into n dimensional vector space such that semantically similar words are placed in closer vicinity than non-similar words. In other words, the dot product of similar (cosine similarity) words will be higher compare to that with non-similar words. In order to obtain geometric organization of words, authors propose two training methods: (1) Continuous Bag of Words (CBOW) (2) Skip-gram. While the CBOW uses context words to predict the target word, skip-gram predicts context words given the target word as an input. Note that context is considered as a window of n words surrounding target word from forward and backward direction. Unlike prior sparse representations, these learned vector representations are dense vectors of dimension ranging from 50-1000 and these dimensions do not have clear semantic interpretation.

GloVe: Prior to Mikolov et al. (2013), count-based models were prominent in the word embedding field. These count-based models (Bengio et al., 2003; Collobert and Weston, 2008; Collobert et al., 2011) are explicitly designed to model the global statistics of a entire corpus. Predictive models such as word2vec solely focus on the target word's local context. To gain the best of two worlds, Pennington et al. (2014) proposed an alternative word embedding technique that integrates global statistics via matrix factorization and local context via the sliding window method. This approach focuses on the co-occurrence of each word with all other words in the entire corpus, therefore called Global Vectors (GloVe). For the unsupervised models, the primary source of information to learn word representation is corpus statistics. However, how to exploit corpus statistics to generate word representations is an interesting problem. Pennington et al. (2014) show that the ratio of co-occurrence probabilities of words is more indicative of their relation than a direct co-occurrence probability . Although, GloVe does not use neural network, Levy et al. (2015) consider it as a predictive model due to following reason: Unlike other count-based models, GloVe use the Stochastic Gradient Descent (SGD) optimization for non-convex objective function. The GloVe outperforms it's peer models (including word2vec) in several intrinsic and extrinsic evaluation tasks. The model works well with a small-sized corpus but is highly scalable to a larger corpus. Although the model demands much memory to populate the co-occurrence matrix in large corpora, the authors term it as a "one-time, up-front cost".

[4]Originally, we apply tokenization on SLP1 transliterated data. Just to illustrate, we show an example in the romanized (IAST) transliteration scheme.

FastText: Token-level embeddings like `word2vec` and `GloVe` suffer from *Out of Vocabulary* (OOV) problem. That means these models cannot generate vector representation for words that are not present in vocabulary. For example, even if model learns embeddings for *pācikā* and *bhāryaḥ*, it will not be able to handle the word *pācikābhāryaḥ*, if it is not a part of vocabulary. Hence, such approaches could not serve the need of morphologically rich languages. Also, the model is not capable of handling different possible inflections of a word (for example, *rāmaḥ, rāmābhyām, rāmasya*) if such inflectional variants are not a part of the vocabulary. Hence, to overcome these shortcomings, Bojanowski et al. (2017, `FastText`) proposed a new word embedding technique, specifically, for learning reliable representations for OOV words. To accomplish this, the authors propose to incorporate subword level information into the model. While learning vector representation of target word, simultaneously, representations of all n-grams (n varies from 3 to 6) are also learned. For example, for n=4, the possible 4-grams of a word *ajñānam* are *<ajñ, jñāna, ñānam, ānam>*. The brackets are used for padding purposes to indicate the beginning and end of the word. With this modification, the training procedure similar to word2vec is applied. This subword level representation learning empowers the model to generate a representation for OOV words by simply summing representations of n-grams corresponding to the target word. `FastText` has been shown to improve performance on syntactic word analogy tasks, especially in the case of morphologically rich languages.

CharLM: Kim et al. (2016, `CharLM`) proposed a new variant of language model that learns subword information through a character-level convolutional neural network (CNN). In a standard neural language modeling setting, the model takes word-level vector representation as input and predicts word-level information. This modeling decision makes the model blind to subword information. For example, the inflected forms of a root word should have structurally similar word embeddings because they shared common sub-strings except for affixes. Therefore, to capture subword level information, `CharLM` takes a character-level input and learns composition function to generate word-level representation. This is achieved by extracting the features from CNN followed by a highway network. Finally, these extracted features are fed to a long short-term memory (LSTM) recurrent neural network language model to make word-level predictions. Kim et al. (2016) argues that without using word embeddings as input to the language model, their model gets the additional advantage of fewer parameters with competitive performance. Also, they show that the model is capable of encoding both semantic and orthographic information.

3.2 Contextualized Embedding

Each word has multiple meanings and their uses highly depend on the context they are used. However, irrespective of context, traditional approaches give a single vector representation for a word. Therefore, traditional word embeddings are called *static* embeddings. For example, there are two possible meanings of a word *cakrī*: (1) a potter (2) the holder of the disc and its uses highly depends on the context. In order to solve this polysemy problem, contextualized embeddings like `ELMo` (Peters et al., 2018) and `BERT` (Devlin et al., 2019) are proposed. In literature, there exists two domains for applying language representations to downstream tasks, namely, *feature-based* and *fine-tuned*. The feature-based approach simply augments the learned representation into the task-specific model architecture and well-known example in this category `ELMo`. A fine-tuned approach such as `BERT`, integrates pretrained model architecture into task-specific model and trains all the parameters, including the pretrained component. The emergence of these embeddings is described as a beginning of a new era in a word embedding. Their exceptional popularity in the field launched many of contextualized embedding variants. Hence, we include `ELMo` and `ALBERT` (A Light `BERT`: derivative of `BERT` model with significantly less number of parameters) (Lan et al., 2020) in our study. From an architectural point of view, `ELMo` belongs to LSTM based language model family and `ALBERT` belongs to the transformer-based language model family.

ELMo: Unlike traditional *static* word embeddings, ELMo computes a representation of each token word as a function of all the words in a sentence. Authors employ the language modeling objective; hence, these representations are also called as ELMo (Embeddings from Language Models). There are three salient features of ELMo: (1) *contextual:* the word representation depends on surrounding context words (2) *deep:* the word representation is weighted average of all the layers of model architecture (3) *character based:* character based modeling enables model to encode morphological clues to obtain robust representations for OOV words, especially, for languages with rich morphology. Prior state of the art neural language models (Kim et al., 2016; Jozefowicz et al., 2016) takes context-independent token-level representation as an input to forward language modeling objective where next word is predicted based on previous n words. Similarly, the backward language model predicts a word given n following words, i.e., precisely opposite to the forward model. ELMo coupled both forward and backward language model objective function together. Through ablations and intrinsic evaluation experiments, authors discover that higher-level layers in model architecture capture semantic properties and lower-level layers are syntactic. They show that a linear combination of internal representation helps obtain a rich representation, which is a better decision over just using top layer representation. Simultaneously providing enriched representation via a weighted linear combination of all layers, the model can choose the most relevant features for specific downstream tasks.

ALBERT: BERT is blend of several clever ideas that has been emerging in the field of NLP such as semi-supervised learning (Dai and Le, 2015), ELMO (Peters et al., 2018), ULMFIT (Howard and Ruder, 2018) and Transformer (Vaswani et al., 2017). The foundational concept used in BERT is a transformer architecture popularized by Vaswani et al. (2017). Inspired from Howard and Ruder (2018, ULMFIT), BERT adopts the fine-tuning approach to augment learned contextual representation in downstream applications. Authors argue that the previous language representations are unidirectional language modeling objective and this choice limits the model to learn effective representations. First, ELMo from the LSTM family demonstrated the effectiveness of a bidirectional language modeling for learning enriched representations. Suppose we introduce bidirectional language modeling into a transformer with a vanilla language modeling objective. In that case, the problem will become trivial and it will not be possible to learn robust representations. Therefore, to tackle this challenge, authors adapt a vanilla language modeling objective to a masked language objective. Here, instead of predicting the next word from previous n words, the model masks a few words from a sentence and learns to recover masked words from the remaining words. This is also called a denoising objective. In this way, BERT can take advantage of the surrounding context from both sides simultaneously.

This data hungry model reports the state of the art results in many downstream tasks on the leaderboard at the expense of huge parameters. Despite the great success of BERT, it is highly impractical to train such a monstrous model with limited available resources for Sanskrit. For example, BERT-base has 110 million trainable parameters, making it computationally very intensive and nearly impossible to train on consumer devices. Therefore, we choose a derivative of BERT called as ALBERT, a light BERT, which has significantly few parameters than traditional BERT model with significantly better performance. The authors achieved this by making three key changes to the original BERT's architecture. First, they factorize the large vocabulary embedding matrix used in BERT into two smaller ones such that dependency on the size of hidden layers is obliviated from the size of vocabulary embeddings. Second, they apply cross-layer parameter sharing. This way, the parameters are shared for similar sub-segments, thus ensuring that parameters are learned only once and are then reused for the subsequent blocks. This significantly reduces the number of trainable parameters in the model. Lastly, they propose a new inter-sentence coherence task called Sentence Order Prediction, instead of using original BERT's Next Sentence Prediction (NSP). NSP is a binary classification loss that was specifically created to improve performance on downstream NLP tasks. In summary, the ALBERT model is found to have 18x fewer parameters than BERT-large and trains 1.7x faster while achieving the state of the art results on many downstream tasks. This model is an important breakthrough as it brings the capabilities of BERT to a more practical and usable form that can be useful for real-world applications.

4 Intrinsic Evaluation

To evaluate the quality of the embedding model, two primary methods are proposed in literature: (1) Intrinsic evaluation (2) Extrinsic evaluation. Intrinsic evaluation refers to the class of methods to measure the quality of vector space without evaluating them on downstream tasks. For example, semantic similarity is the most traditional method to evaluate meaning representations intrinsically. On the other hand, extrinsic evaluation refers to the class of methods to assess the quality of vector representation when fed as an input to the machine learning-based model in the downstream NLP task. The wide range of NLP tasks that deals with lexical semantics such as chunking, part of speech tagging, semantic role labeling and named entity recognition can be used for the extrinsic evaluation. In this work, we restrict our study to intrinsic tasks. Intrinsic evaluation directly checks for syntactic and semantic properties of words (Mikolov et al., 2013; Baroni et al., 2014). These tasks rely on query inventory datasets consisting of a query word and semantically related target word. These query inventories are readily available for resource-rich languages but not for Sanskrit. We create such inventories for four different intrinsic tasks: relatedness, synonym detection, analogy prediction, and concept categorization. For creating such query inventory dataset for these intrinsic evaluation tasks, we use *Amarakoṣa*[5] (Nair and Kulkarni, 2010), Sanskrit WordNet[6] (Kulkarni, 2017) and Sanskrit Heritage Reader[7] (Goyal and Huet, 2016; Huet and Goyal, 2013). In extrinsic evaluation, feature extracted by word embeddings is fed as an input to downstream NLP task and corresponding performance metric is used as an indicator to compare across different embedding approaches. Although this family of evaluation methods gives signal on the relative strength of different word embedding approaches, it needs not be considered a general proxy for overall quality.

Relatedness: It is essential to distinguish between the notion of relatedness and synonyms (Agirre et al., 2009). Synonym words share many semantic properties and they can be substituted with each other without changing the meaning of the sentences. On the other hand, semantically related words can co-occur in the same context or document and share any one semantic relationship such as meronymy or antonymy. Unlike synonym words, we can not substitute related words in place of each other. The notion of semantic relatedness between word pairs is one of the fascinating concepts in lexical semantics with a variety of NLP applications (Pilehvar and Camacho-Collados, 2020). This task is considered as an in-vitro evaluation framework for judging the quality of word embeddings. The word pairs are annotated based on the degree of relatedness on a numerical scale by human annotators for evaluating semantic relatedness. For example, the distance between the *paricārikā* and *vaidya* in the numerical scale from 0 to 3 could be 2.5 because both words belong often found together. Similarly, the human judgment score for word pair *prādhyāpaka - karkaṭī* could be 0.5 because these two words do not share any semantic property. The word embedding performance is then evaluated by assessing the correlation between the average scores assigned by annotators and the cosine similarities between corresponding vector representations.

For the construction of such human-annotated test data for the new target language, a standard methodology is followed in the literature (Camacho-Collados et al., 2015). It is divided into two steps: (1) English word pairs of a standard English dataset are translated into the target language (2) language experts annotate these word pairs. For the English language, the dataset popularized by Hassan and Mihalcea (2011, WordSim353) has 353 word pairs with a human relatedness score. However, this dataset is criticized due to the human judgment criterion, which

[5]https://sanskrit.uohyd.ac.in/scl/amarakosha/index.html
[6]https://www.cfilt.iitb.ac.in/wordnet/webswn/index.php
[7]https://sanskrit.inria.fr/DICO/reader.fr.html

conflates similarity and relatedness. Another alternative is RG-65 (Rubenstein and Goodenough, 1965) dataset. In addition, we find that many words such as *automobile, cushion, autograph etc.* can not be naturally translated into Sanskrit. Therefore, we use *Amarakoṣa* to get word pairs due to its systematic organization of semantically related words. Here, synonymous words are categorized into synsets and semantically related words into *varga.* Therefore, we decide to select the word pairs from *Amarakoṣa.* This choice obliviates the need for translation and annotation of word pairs into Sanskrit. We exploit systematic categorization based on relatedness presents in the *Amarakoṣa.* We transform the relatedness task into a classification task where the task is to categorize word pairs into three classes based on cosine similarity scores between vector representations generated by corresponding embeddings. For selecting word pairs, we follow the following procedure. First, we sample 13,500 word pairs in such a way that an equal proportion of word pairs are selected from the following classes : (1) word pairs from the same synset (2) word pairs from same *varga* but not from the same synset (3) and the remaining word pairs such that each word from a word pair belongs to different *varga.* Out of 13,500, we use 4,500 word pairs as the development and remaining word pairs in the test set. We use a development set to find out cosine similarity thresholds to classify word pairs into respective classes. Here, we use the macro F-score as an evaluation metric to measure the performance.

Synonym Detection: Synonym detection (Baroni et al., 2014; Bakarov, 2018) is a task where the goal is to find the synonym of a given target word from the four synonym candidates. In this multiple-choice setting, a single answer is correct. For example, for target *sūryaḥ*, synonym candidates are *ādityaḥ* (correct), *cañcalā, candraḥ* and *ākāśa.* Here, we choose an option as a correct answer which shows the highest cosine similarity with the target word. We use accuracy as a metric to measure performance. We leverage *Amarakoṣa* (Nair and Kulkarni, 2010) synsets to build MCQs. It has 4,056 synsets categorized into 25 *vargas.* Out of 4,056, only 2,581 synsets have more than one element. We choose a word pair from each such synset, assign one word as the target word and another word as the correct answer. Then, for the remaining options, we use three words from the same *varga* but not from the synset where the target word belongs. The primary motivation of such a choice is that words belonging to the same *varga* are semantically related and picking such related words as synonym candidates make the task more interesting and challenging. Our test data has 3,034 MCQs. We consider accuracy as an evaluation metric for this task.

Analogy Prediction: The analogy prediction task popularized by Mikolov et al. (2013), a question is framed with word pairs exhibiting similar sense. For example, "If *kapi* is similar to *kapibhyām* then in the same sense *yati* is similar to ..." Authors propose that a simple algebraic operations suffice to answer these analogy questions. In above example, in order to find similar word for *yati*, we need to calculate $X = vector(\text{"kapibhyām"}) - vector(\text{"kapi"}) + vector(\text{"yati"})$. Then, we find the nearest neighbour to X as per cosine similarity metric and use it as answer to question.

To probe the information encoded in word embeddings, we build a comprehensive set of syntactic and semantic questions as illustrated in Table 2. We use the Sanskrit Heritage Reader (Goyal and Huet, 2016; Huet and Goyal, 2013) for generating syntactic questions. We consider the primary conjugation table for verbal root words and the declension table for nominal words for syntactic analogies. For conjugations, there are 10 families and popularly also called as *gaṇas.* Each *gaṇa* is further divided into *parasmaipadī* and *ātmanepadī.* Out of these 20 families, we choose 3 representative candidates to generate primary conjugations such that most of the inflectional variations are covered. Similarly, nominal words are broadly divided into *ajanta* and *halanta.* Further, they are divided based on gender and the end of root words (for example, *akārānta, ukārānta, nakārānta, jakāranta etc*). In this way, we consider 25 fine-grained families for nominals. From each family, we select 3 representative words. Words occurring in same family display similar inflections variations. Therefore, to make questions, we strictly choose

Relationship	Word Pair 1		Word Pair 2	
declension	kapi	kapayaḥ	yati	yatayaḥ
conjugation	ci	acīyethām	aś	āśyethām
absolutive	dṛ	dīrtvā	aś	aśitvā
infinitive	dṛ	daritum	aś	aśitum
husband - wife	viṣṇuḥ	lakṣmī	rāmaḥ	sītā
son - father	rāma	daśaratha	abhimanyu	arjuna
daughter - father	pārvatī	himavān	sītā	janaka
charioteer - warrior	dāruka	kṛṣṇa	śalya	karṇa
defeated - victorious	kicaka	bhīma	rāvaṇa	rāma
son - mother	kṛṣṇaḥ	yaśodā	rāmaḥ	kauśalyā

Table 2: Examples of syntactic (top) and semantic (bottom) questions in our test set

word pairs from the same family where the inflectional component belongs to the same position in the conjugation/declension table. For semantic questions, we extract semantic relation from *Amarakoṣa* (Nair and Kulkarni, 2010), *Rāmāyanam* and *Mahābhāratam.*[8] In semantic relationships, we consider six categories: husband - wife, son - father, daughter - father, charioteer - warrior, defeated - victorious, and son - mother. There are 6,415 semantic and 10,000 syntactic questions. We only consider single token words in our test set. We use accuracy as a metric to measure the performance. We evaluate accuracy separately for semantic and syntactic questions.

Categorization: As the name suggests, categorization is an evaluation task where the goal is to group nominal sets of concepts into natural categories (Baroni et al., 2014). For example, *narmadā, godāvarī, kāverī* and *gaṅgā* fall under the names of river category. This task is treated as an unsupervised clustering task where word representations are clustered into n clusters (n is the total number of gold standard categories). Here, performance is evaluated in terms of *purity*. This metric represents the degree to which elements from the single gold standard category belong to the same cluster. If unsupervised clustering exactly replicates the gold standard clusters, then the purity score reaches 100%. Otherwise, it decreases based on the inability to replicate gold standard partitions.

Following Baroni and Lenci (2010), we construct a test set of 15 common categories picked from *Amarakoṣa*. We exploit the ontological classification of *Amarakoṣa* based on *Vaiśeṣika* ontology. *Amarakoṣa* is also marked with semantic relations between words. These relations are mainly classified into hierarchical and associative. We use hierarchical relations such as hypernymy - hyponymy and holonymy - meronymy for this task. In each category, we select up to 10 concepts. Our categorization data contains the following categories: *vādyopakaraṇam, vṛttiḥ, grahaḥ, devatā, paśuḥ, pakṣī, nadī, vṛkṣaḥ, upakaraṇam, ābharaṇam, alaukikasthānam, vāhanam, parvataḥ, vṛkṣaphalam* and *puṣpam.* We also build a separate test set consisting of 45 syntactic categories where each category is made up of 25 concepts.[9] Each category represents a particular morphological class.

5 Experiments

Corpus: Our corpus contains texts from the Digital Corpus of Sanskrit (DCS), scraped data from Wikipedia and Vedabase corpus.[10] The number of words in each section is 3.8 M, 1.7 M, and 0.2 M, respectively. DCS and Vedabase are segmented, but the Wikipedia data is

[8]We extract word pairs holding specific relation from wikipedia.

[9]More details can be found at: `https://github.com/jivnesh/EvalSan`

[10]We use SLP1 transliteration scheme for training all the models.

unsegmented. We use this data for training all the embedding models. Most of the data in our corpus is in the form of poetry.

Hyper-parameters: For tackling OOV problem faced by token-based embedding models such as `word2vec` and `GloVe`, we leverage `sentencepiece` tokenizer with 32,000 vocabulary size. We train `word2vec` and `GloVe` on `sentencepiece` segmented corpus. We employ following hyper-parameter settings for `word2vec` and `GloVe` : the embedding dimension size of 300, window size as 11, minimum word count for vocabulary as 1 and the number of epochs equal to 80. We keep all the remaining parameters same as used by original authors of the respective works. Next, we use raw sentences (instead of using `sentencepiece` tokenized data) for training `FastText` and `CharLM`. We use following hyper-parameter setting for `FastText` : the embedding dimension of 300, window size of 11, the number of epochs 80, the minimum count for deciding vocabulary equals to 6, negative sampling loss with 5 negative samples, the learning rate as 0.025, minimum length of n-grams as 3 and maximum length of n-grams as 11. For `CharLM`, we use default parameters of small model architecture as Kim et al. (2016).[11] For `ELMo`, we use hyper-parameter settings of small model architecture.[12] For `ALBERT`, we use the same hyper-parameters as `albert-base-V2` model architecture except vocabulary size of 32,000 and the number of hidden layers equal to 6.

Results: Table 3 reports results on all the intrinsic tasks. We evaluate contextual models without context to assess how effective they are when compared with static models. Applying *contextualized* models without context is similar to just using their underlying static word representation. `ELMo` outperforms all the models in all the intrinsic tasks with a large margin except the semantic categorization task. Surprisingly, with limited training data, the contextualized `ELMo` model achieved impressive overall performance compared to static models across all intrinsic tasks. The subword level segmentation with the `sentencepiece` model empowered the `word2vec` and `GloVe` to such an extent that they outperform `FastText` in analogy prediction tasks and on par in the remaining tasks. For resource-rich languages, `ALBERT` have shown the state of the art performance on many evaluation tasks. However, despite a thorough hyper-parameter search, the performance of `ALBERT` could not compete with static models. This may be due to a lack of massive training data. Similarly, except relatedness and syntactic categorization, `CharLM` model shows low performance with a large margin.

	Relatedness	Categorization		Similarity	Analogy	
Model	f-score	syn	sem	acc	syn	sem
word2vec	30.90	0.22	0.41	37.34	30.65	11.01
GloVe	31.50	0.25	0.39	37.41	30.04	14.01
FastText	31.20	0.14	**0.47**	37.87	16.65	6.01
CharLM	35.21	0.33	0.28	35.94	2.11	0.03
ELMo	**37.17**	**0.86**	0.41	**42.15**	**56.80**	**32.70**
ALBERT	33.00	0.27	0.34	32.70	25.86	0.10

Table 3: Results on intrinsic evaluation tasks. For similarity and analogy prediction tasks, we use accuracy (acc) in terms of percentage as the evaluation metric, purity for categorization and f-score for the relatedness task. The syntactic and semantic tasks are denoted by *syn* and *sem* keywords, respectively.

[11] `https://s3.amazonaws.com/models.huggingface.co/bert/albert-base-v2-config.json`

[12] `https://s3-us-west-2.amazonaws.com/allennlp/models/elmo/2x1024_128_2048cnn_1xhighway/elmo_2x1024_128_2048cnn_1xhighway_options.json`

6 Analysis

6.1 Error Analysis

We conduct a detailed analysis of prominent mistakes done by the word embedding models. For the analogy prediction task, we find that all the models fail to correctly predict analogy questions where the root word gets modified while adding the affix to the root word. For example, in this analogy question (*lip : lepsyāmahe :: gur : gorişyāmahe*) while adding *syāmahe* the root gets modified. On the other hand, all the models perform surprisingly well for analogy questions where affix is added without modifying root word (*śak : śaknutam :: dagh : daghnutam*). In the incorrect answers of the subword enriched `FastText` model, at least the root word is predicted correctly. `CharLM` performs the worst among all models and the predictions made by the model seem almost random with no relation to the root word or the suffix. `CharLM` learns a character level composition function to generate word-level representation. Therefore, it often predicts the correct root with an incorrect suffix or no suffix. While in the case of syntactic analogy prediction task, the `GloVe` and `word2vec` perform comparably. However, the improved performance of `GloVe` at semantic analogy task can be attributed to consideration of the global statistics of word occurrences. We observe that all the embedding models majorly get those test cases correct for similarity and relatedness tasks, which have words already present in the model vocabulary. This indicates that these models are only capable of generating representation for OOV words based on orthographic similarity and fail to capture semantic meanings. Specifically, around 55% words present in the relatedness test set are OOV words.[13]

6.2 Qualitative inspection for rare word

We analyze the word representations captured by different models. We consider *contextualized* models also in this experiment. We use contextual models without a context to assess how effective are they when compared with static models. Applying *contextualized* models without context is very similar to just using their underlying static word representation. For systematic investigation, we choose three representative words from following categories: (1) In Vocabulary words (2) Out of Vocabulary words. Table 4 illustrates the top three nearest neighbors based on cosine similarity between embeddings learned by different models. For frequently occurring words present in vocabulary all the embeddings except `CharLM` and `ALBERT` are able to capture lexical meaning. The quality of nearest neighbour candidates of `CharLM` and `ALBERT` is relatively poor compared to other models. We suspect that the possible reason for this behaviour may be due to less amount of training data. The subword level modeling in `word2vec`, `GloVe` and `FastText` makes these models more inclined to find words which are orthographically similar. For these models, the representations seems to depend on surface string. For example, the nearest neighbours of *nityam* and *sukham* are very close in terms of edit distance. On the other hand, `ELMo` not only captures semantic level features but also orthographic features. This is very well evident from the following examples. The nearest neighbours produced by `ELMo` for *nityam* and *sukham* are lexically similar but orthographically different in terms of edit distance. However, the nearest neighbours of *tābhyām* exhibits suffix similarity. The last three words are OOV where *ahham, bahūhuni* are words with incorrect spelling and *sahasra-cakşo* is the compound word. For OOV words also similar trend holds. We generate representation for OOV for `word2vec` and `GloVe` using `sentencepiece` tokenizer. This tokenizer breaks OOV into subwords available in `sentencepiece` model vocabulary and representation of OOV word is sum of representations of these segmented subwords.

6.3 Qualitative inspection of contextualized embeddings

To investigate the contextualized nature of `ELMo` and `ALBERT`, we analyze the vector representation (using PCA to project the vectors into 2D space) of a two polysemous words in different

[13]Here, OOV referred as words which are not seen during training of embedding model.

	Vocabulary words			OOV words		
	nityam	*sukham*	*tābhyām*	*ahham*	*bahūhuni*	*sahasra-cakṣo*
word2vec	nityam-eva nityamiti sadā	sukhamayaṃ duḥkham sukha-duḥkham	āvābhyām dvābhyām tayā	allāh ahne ahrasat	mānini sani cūrṇitāni	pracakṣva suparṇāḥ-ca pracakṣmahe
GloVe	nityamiti nityam-eva sadā	sukhamayaṃ duḥkham duḥkhameva	adhikāribhyām pārṣṇibhyām jaṅghābhyām	allāh ahne ahnuvi	bahū behulā behulāyāḥ	tat-ca-eva tathā-ca yat-ca-eva
FastText	sadā satatam nitya-snāyī	su-sukham duḥkham sukha-duḥkham	tayoḥ tau cakṣuḍbhyām	siṃham tam yathā-aham	bahuni mandmatyoḥ bahavaḥ-tatra	sahasralaṃṇtra sahasra-kṛtvas sahasra-vedhī
CharLM	sṭeḍiyam saṃśayam yāpayan	somam saudham homam	sabhāyāḥ nyāyasabhāyāḥ hastābhyām	īḍyam bṛhantam gayam	vatsyati yotsyati setsyati	paryaṭanasthaleṣu naṣṭa-saṃjñaḥ cākṣuṣasya-antare
ELMO	martyam niṣṭham yugyam	sakham kulam sukhām	nābhyām yābhyām bhūbhyām	arham aṅkam andham	vilāsini mattakāśini jānuni	ajāta-śatro sahasra-śīrṣā ahu-rūpaḥ
ALBERT	dānam loke bhavitā	satām padam kṣayam	ardham mandam dhairyam	ahrasam allāh ahnuthāḥ	ityadīni hrasāni maṃdiram	ūrdhva-ge sahasra-śīrṣā sarva-mahīkṣitām

Table 4: Nearest neighbours (based on cosine similarity) for in vocabulary and OOV words for the models trained on Sanskrit corpus. Last three words are OOV words. We use contextual models without a context. Applying *contextualized* models without context is very similar to just using their underlying static word representation.

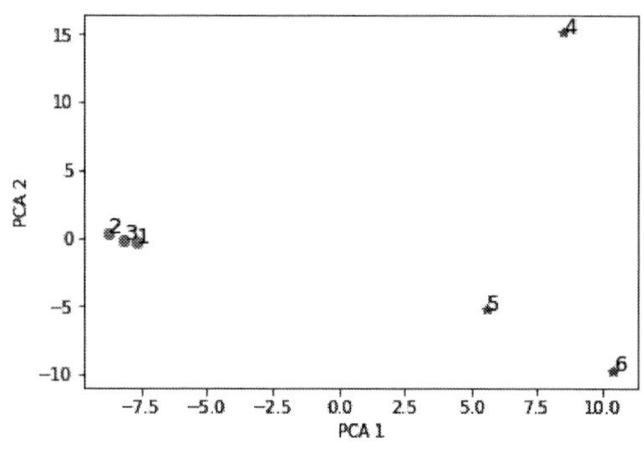

(a)

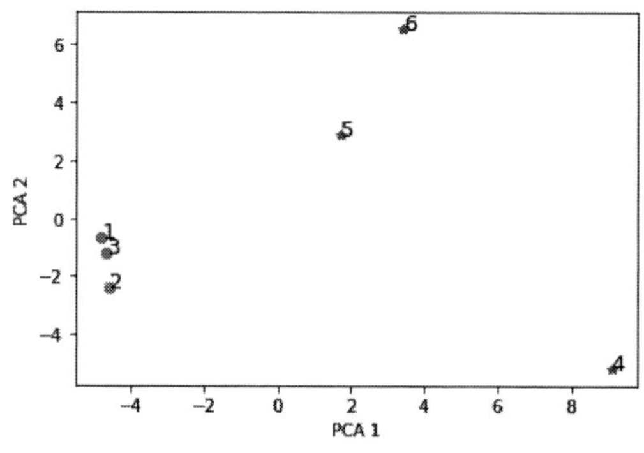

(b)

Figure 1: Projection of contextualized representation (the left side : `ELMo` and the right side `ALBERT`) for different sense of polysemous word *cakrī* denoted by following sentences: *(1) cakrī mṛdā jalena ca kumbhanirmāṇe viśāradaḥ (2) cakrī kevala jala mṛd cakra upajīvakaḥ (3) cakrī cakrasya upari mṛdaḥ kumbhaṃ nirmāti (4) svahaste bibharti sudarśanam sa cakrī (5) sudarśanena cakrī śiśupālam jaghāna (6) rakṣobhyaḥ svabhaktān trātum cakrī sudarśanam bibharti.*

context. In this experiment, each test case consists of 6 sentences in Sanskrit such that all sentences have one common polysemous word. Out of 6 sentences, 3 sentences represent one sense of meaning and the remaining represent another sense of meaning for that common polysemous

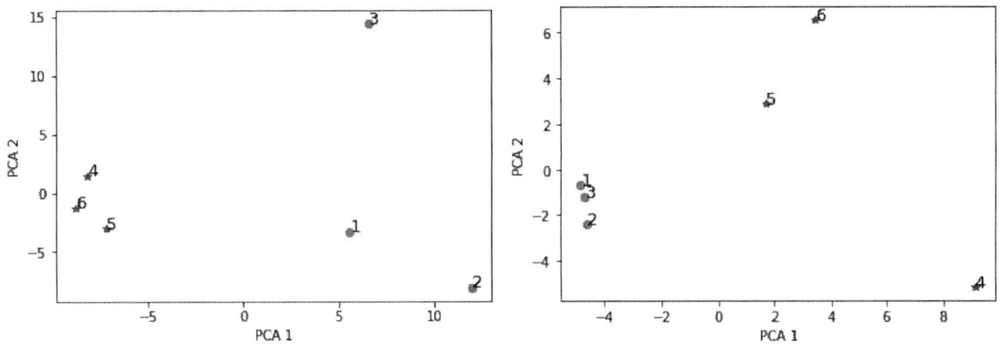

(a) (b)

Figure 2: Projection of contextualized representation (the left side : ELMo and the right side ALBERT) for different sense of polysemous word *hariḥ* denoted by following sentences: *(1) vāyusutaḥ hariḥ vānarāṇām toṣam vavardha (2) sugrīvaḥ nāma hariḥ vānarāṇām rājā āsīt (3) vānarāṇām vṛddhaḥ hariḥ jāmbavān (4) hariḥ baleḥ trailokyasampadam chalena jahāra (5) hariḥ hiraṇyākṣam nihatya devatānām khedam jahāra (6) hariḥ rukmiṇīm jahāra paśyatām*

word. Ideally, contextualized word vectors representing the same sense of meaning should form a cluster. For the polysemous word *cakrī*, we consider two senses of meaning, namely, potter and the Lord Viṣṇu. This test set consists of 6 sentences as follows: *(1) cakrī mṛdā jalena ca kumbhanirmāṇe viśāradaḥ (2) cakrī kevala-jala-mṛd-cakra-upajīvakaḥ (3) cakrī cakrasya upari mṛdaḥ kumbhaṃ nirmāti (4) svahaste bibharti sudarśanam sa cakrī (5) sudarśanena cakrī śiśupālam jaghāna (6) rakṣobhyaḥ svabhaktān trātum cakrī sudarśanam bibharti.* For the first three sentences, the sense of the meaning of the word *cakrī* is a potter and for the remaining sentences, the sense of meaning is the Lord Viṣṇu. Figure 1 illustrates visualization of polysemous word *cakrī*. Here, we observe that the contextualized representation indicating the same sense of meaning are clustered together. Similarly, we consider another polysemous word *hariḥ* consists of two senses of meaning, namely, monkey and the Lord Viṣṇu. *(1) vāyusutaḥ hariḥ vānarāṇām toṣam vavardha (2) sugrīvaḥ nāma hariḥ vānarāṇām rājā āsīt (3) vānarāṇām vṛddhaḥ hariḥ jāmbavān (4) hariḥ baleḥ trailokyasampadam chalena jahāra (5) hariḥ hiraṇyākṣam nihatya devatānām khedam jahāra (6) hariḥ rukmiṇīm jahāra paśyatām.* In Figure 2, we find the similar trend for this test case. The qualitative analysis suggests that the *contextualized* representations generated by Peters et al. (2018) and Lan et al. (2020) for polysemous words indicating the same sense of meaning forms a cluster for each sense of meaning (Section 6.3).

7 Conclusion and future work

In this work, we focused on evaluating word embedding approaches (initially proposed for resource-rich language English) for the Sanskrit language. Word embedding helps to transfer knowledge learned from readily available unlabelled data for improving the task-specific performance of data-driven approaches. We investigat the effectiveness of word embedding approaches for Sanskrit. To facilitate systematic experimentation, we classify word embeddings in the broad categories and evaluated on 4 intrinsic tasks, namely, relatedness, categorization, similarity identification and analogy prediction tasks. This work can be considered as the fertile soil for investigating the following questions: (1) Which linguistic phenomenons are captured by word embeddings? (2) Out of existing word embedding approaches, which embeddings are more suitable for Sanskrit? (3) What are the shortcomings of existing approaches specific to Sanskrit? Surprisingly, with limited training data, the Peters et al. (2018) achieved impressive overall performance compared to static models across all intrinsic tasks. The qualitative analysis suggests that the *contextualized* representations generated by Peters et al. (2018) and Lan et al. (2020) for polysemous words indicating the same sense of meaning forms a cluster for each sense of meaning (Section 6.3). This is indeed a serendipitous outcome for such data-hungry models when trained on negligibly small amount of corpus available for Sanskrit.

There are many limitations to this study. While in this work, we restrict our study to intrinsic evaluation tasks for the standard word embedding approaches with their default setting. We plan to extend this work on extrinsic evaluation tasks as well. Moreover, to get substantial empirical evidence on linguistics phenomenons captured by these models, we plan to evaluate them for context-sensitive tasks similar to Pilehvar and Camacho-Collados (2019). We find that all the models perform poorly on relatedness and similarity tasks since most of the words present in these evaluation test data are OOV words. However, these models perform relatively well for the words present in model vocabulary. This observation suggests investigating: What is the effect of the corpus size? We currently train our models with around 5 million tokens, which is negligible compared to the 840 billion tokens used by the resource-rich language models. We plan to investigate on applicability of the existing multi-lingual pretrained models for Sanskrit.

Acknowledgements

We are grateful to Amba Kulkarni for the discussion related to evaluation task decisions. We thank A V S D S Mahesh for helping us with the data preparation step. We thank the anonymous reviewers for their constructive feedback towards improving this work. The TCS Fellowship supports the work of the first author under the Project Number TCS/EE/2011191P.

References

Eneko Agirre, Enrique Alfonseca, Keith Hall, Jana Kravalova, Marius Paşca, and Aitor Soroa. 2009. A study on similarity and relatedness using distributional and WordNet-based approaches. In *Proceedings of Human Language Technologies: The 2009 Annual Conference of the North American Chapter of the Association for Computational Linguistics*, pages 19–27, Boulder, Colorado, June. Association for Computational Linguistics.

Amir Bakarov. 2018. A survey of word embeddings evaluation methods.

Marco Baroni and Alessandro Lenci. 2010. Distributional memory: A general framework for corpus-based semantics. *Computational Linguistics*, 36(4):673–721.

Marco Baroni, Georgiana Dinu, and Germán Kruszewski. 2014. Don't count, predict! a systematic comparison of context-counting vs. context-predicting semantic vectors. In *Proceedings of the 52nd Annual Meeting of the Association for Computational Linguistics (Volume 1: Long Papers)*, pages 238–247, Baltimore, Maryland, June. Association for Computational Linguistics.

Yoshua Bengio, Réjean Ducharme, Pascal Vincent, and Christian Janvin. 2003. A neural probabilistic language model. *The journal of machine learning research*, 3:1137–1155.

Piotr Bojanowski, Edouard Grave, Armand Joulin, and Tomas Mikolov. 2017. Enriching word vectors with subword information. *Transactions of the Association for Computational Linguistics*, 5:135–146.

José Camacho-Collados, Mohammad Taher Pilehvar, and Roberto Navigli. 2015. A framework for the construction of monolingual and cross-lingual word similarity datasets. In *Proceedings of the 53rd Annual Meeting of the Association for Computational Linguistics and the 7th International Joint Conference on Natural Language Processing (Volume 2: Short Papers)*, pages 1–7, Beijing, China, July. Association for Computational Linguistics.

Ronan Collobert and Jason Weston. 2008. A unified architecture for natural language processing: Deep neural networks with multitask learning. In *Proceedings of the 25th International Conference on Machine Learning*, ICML '08, page 160–167, New York, NY, USA. Association for Computing Machinery.

Ronan Collobert, Jason Weston, Léon Bottou, Michael Karlen, Koray Kavukcuoglu, and Pavel Kuksa. 2011. Natural language processing (almost) from scratch. *J. Mach. Learn. Res.*, 12(null):2493–2537, November.

Andrew M. Dai and Quoc V. Le. 2015. Semi-supervised sequence learning.

Jacob Devlin, Ming-Wei Chang, Kenton Lee, and Kristina Toutanova. 2019. BERT: Pre-training of deep bidirectional transformers for language understanding. In *Proceedings of the 2019 Conference of the North American Chapter of the Association for Computational Linguistics: Human Language Technologies, Volume 1 (Long and Short Papers)*, pages 4171–4186, Minneapolis, Minnesota, June. Association for Computational Linguistics.

John R Firth. 1957. A synopsis of linguistic theory, 1930-1955. *Studies in linguistic analysis*.

Pawan Goyal and Gérard Huet. 2016. Design and analysis of a lean interface for sanskrit corpus annotation. *Journal of Language Modelling*, 4:145, 10.

Pawan Goyal, Gérard Huet, Amba Kulkarni, Peter Scharf, and Ralph Bunker. 2012. A distributed platform for Sanskrit processing. In *Proceedings of COLING 2012*, pages 1011–1028, Mumbai, India, December. The COLING 2012 Organizing Committee.

Ashim Gupta, Amrith Krishna, Pawan Goyal, and Oliver Hellwig. 2020. Evaluating neural morphological taggers for Sanskrit. In *Proceedings of the 17th SIGMORPHON Workshop on Computational Research in Phonetics, Phonology, and Morphology*, pages 198–203, Online, July. Association for Computational Linguistics.

Zellig S Harris. 1954. Distributional structure. *Word*, 10(2-3):146–162.

Samer Hassan and Rada Mihalcea. 2011. Semantic relatedness using salient semantic analysis. In *Proceedings of the Twenty-Fifth AAAI Conference on Artificial Intelligence*, AAAI'11, page 884–889. AAAI Press.

Benjamin Heinzerling and Michael Strube. 2018. BPEmb: Tokenization-free pre-trained subword embeddings in 275 languages. In *Proceedings of the Eleventh International Conference on Language Resources and Evaluation (LREC 2018)*, Miyazaki, Japan, May. European Language Resources Association (ELRA).

Oliver Hellwig and Sebastian Nehrdich. 2018. Sanskrit word segmentation using character-level recurrent and convolutional neural networks. In *Proceedings of the 2018 Conference on Empirical Methods in Natural Language Processing*, pages 2754–2763, Brussels, Belgium, October-November. Association for Computational Linguistics.

Oliver Hellwig, Salvatore Scarlata, Elia Ackermann, and Paul Widmer. 2020. The treebank of vedic Sanskrit. In *Proceedings of the 12th Language Resources and Evaluation Conference*, pages 5137–5146, Marseille, France, May. European Language Resources Association.

Jeremy Howard and Sebastian Ruder. 2018. Universal language model fine-tuning for text classification. In *Proceedings of the 56th Annual Meeting of the Association for Computational Linguistics (Volume 1: Long Papers)*, pages 328–339, Melbourne, Australia, July. Association for Computational Linguistics.

Gérard Huet and Pawan Goyal. 2013. Design of a lean interface for sanskrit corpus annotation. 12.

Pratik Joshi, Sebastin Santy, Amar Budhiraja, Kalika Bali, and Monojit Choudhury. 2020. The state and fate of linguistic diversity and inclusion in the NLP world. In *Proceedings of the 58th Annual Meeting of the Association for Computational Linguistics*, pages 6282–6293, Online, July. Association for Computational Linguistics.

Rafal Jozefowicz, Oriol Vinyals, Mike Schuster, Noam Shazeer, and Yonghui Wu. 2016. Exploring the limits of language modeling.

Yoon Kim, Yacine Jernite, David Sontag, and Alexander M. Rush. 2016. Character-aware neural language models. In *Proceedings of the Thirtieth AAAI Conference on Artificial Intelligence*, AAAI'16, page 2741–2749. AAAI Press.

Amrith Krishna, Pavankumar Satuluri, Shubham Sharma, Apurv Kumar, and Pawan Goyal. 2016. Compound type identification in Sanskrit: What roles do the corpus and grammar play? In *Proceedings of the 6th Workshop on South and Southeast Asian Natural Language Processing (WSSANLP2016)*, pages 1–10, Osaka, Japan, December. The COLING 2016 Organizing Committee.

Amrith Krishna, Pavan Kumar Satuluri, and Pawan Goyal. 2017. A dataset for Sanskrit word segmentation. In *Proceedings of the Joint SIGHUM Workshop on Computational Linguistics for Cultural Heritage, Social Sciences, Humanities and Literature*, pages 105–114, Vancouver, Canada, August. Association for Computational Linguistics.

Amrith Krishna, Bishal Santra, Sasi Prasanth Bandaru, Gaurav Sahu, Vishnu Dutt Sharma, Pavankumar Satuluri, and Pawan Goyal. 2018. Free as in free word order: An energy based model for word segmentation and morphological tagging in Sanskrit. In *Proceedings of the 2018 Conference on Empirical Methods in Natural Language Processing*, pages 2550–2561, Brussels, Belgium, October-November. Association for Computational Linguistics.

Amrith Krishna, Vishnu Sharma, Bishal Santra, Aishik Chakraborty, Pavankumar Satuluri, and Pawan Goyal. 2019. Poetry to prose conversion in Sanskrit as a linearisation task: A case for low-resource languages. In *Proceedings of the 57th Annual Meeting of the Association for Computational Linguistics*, pages 1160–1166, Florence, Italy, July. Association for Computational Linguistics.

Amrith Krishna, Ashim Gupta, Deepak Garasangi, Jivnesh Sandhan, Pavankumar Satuluri, and Pawan Goyal. 2020a. Neural approaches for data driven dependency parsing in sanskrit.

Amrith Krishna, Ashim Gupta, Deepak Garasangi, Pavankumar Satuluri, and Pawan Goyal. 2020b. Keep it surprisingly simple: A simple first order graph based parsing model for joint morphosyntactic parsing in Sanskrit. In *Proceedings of the 2020 Conference on Empirical Methods in Natural Language Processing (EMNLP)*, pages 4791–4797, Online, November. Association for Computational Linguistics.

Amrith Krishna, Bishal Santra, Ashim Gupta, Pavankumar Satuluri, and Pawan Goyal. 2020c. A graph based framework for structured prediction tasks in sanskrit. *Computational Linguistics*, 46(4):1–63, December.

Taku Kudo and John Richardson. 2018. SentencePiece: A simple and language independent subword tokenizer and detokenizer for neural text processing. In *Proceedings of the 2018 Conference on Empirical Methods in Natural Language Processing: System Demonstrations*, pages 66–71, Brussels, Belgium, November. Association for Computational Linguistics.

Malhar Kulkarni, 2017. *Sanskrit WordNet at Indian Institute of Technology (IITB) Mumbai*, pages 231–241. Springer Singapore, Singapore.

Zhenzhong Lan, Mingda Chen, Sebastian Goodman, Kevin Gimpel, Piyush Sharma, and Radu Soricut. 2020. Albert: A lite bert for self-supervised learning of language representations. In *International Conference on Learning Representations*.

Omer Levy, Yoav Goldberg, and Ido Dagan. 2015. Improving distributional similarity with lessons learned from word embeddings. *Transactions of the Association for Computational Linguistics*, 3:211–225.

Tomas Mikolov, Ilya Sutskever, Kai Chen, Greg S Corrado, and Jeff Dean. 2013. Distributed representations of words and phrases and their compositionality. *Advances in neural information processing systems*, 26:3111–3119.

Sivaja Nair and Amba Kulkarni. 2010. The knowledge structure in amarakosa. pages 173–189, 01.

Jeffrey Pennington, Richard Socher, and Christopher Manning. 2014. GloVe: Global vectors for word representation. In *Proceedings of the 2014 Conference on Empirical Methods in Natural Language Processing (EMNLP)*, pages 1532–1543, Doha, Qatar, October. Association for Computational Linguistics.

Matthew Peters, Mark Neumann, Mohit Iyyer, Matt Gardner, Christopher Clark, Kenton Lee, and Luke Zettlemoyer. 2018. Deep contextualized word representations. In *Proceedings of the 2018 Conference of the North American Chapter of the Association for Computational Linguistics: Human Language Technologies, Volume 1 (Long Papers)*, pages 2227–2237, New Orleans, Louisiana, June. Association for Computational Linguistics.

Mohammad Taher Pilehvar and Jose Camacho-Collados. 2019. WiC: the word-in-context dataset for evaluating context-sensitive meaning representations. In *Proceedings of the 2019 Conference of the North American Chapter of the Association for Computational Linguistics: Human Language Technologies, Volume 1 (Long and Short Papers)*, pages 1267–1273, Minneapolis, Minnesota, June. Association for Computational Linguistics.

Mohammad Taher Pilehvar and Jose Camacho-Collados. 2020. Embeddings in natural language processing: Theory and advances in vector representations of meaning. *Synthesis Lectures on Human Language Technologies*, 13(4):1–175.

Vikas Reddy, Amrith Krishna, Vishnu Sharma, Prateek Gupta, Vineeth M R, and Pawan Goyal. 2018. Building a word segmenter for Sanskrit overnight. In *Proceedings of the Eleventh International Conference on Language Resources and Evaluation (LREC 2018)*, Miyazaki, Japan, May. European Language Resources Association (ELRA).

Herbert Rubenstein and John B. Goodenough. 1965. Contextual correlates of synonymy. *Commun. ACM*, 8(10):627–633, October.

Jivnesh Sandhan, Amrith Krishna, Pawan Goyal, and Laxmidhar Behera. 2019. Revisiting the role of feature engineering for compound type identification in Sanskrit. In *Proceedings of the 6th International Sanskrit Computational Linguistics Symposium*, pages 28–44, IIT Kharagpur, India, October. Association for Computational Linguistics.

Jivnesh Sandhan, Amrith Krishna, Ashim Gupta, Laxmidhar Behera, and Pawan Goyal. 2021. A little pretraining goes a long way: A case study on dependency parsing task for low-resource morphologically rich languages.

Rico Sennrich, Barry Haddow, and Alexandra Birch. 2016. Neural machine translation of rare words with subword units. In *Proceedings of the 54th Annual Meeting of the Association for Computational Linguistics (Volume 1: Long Papers)*, pages 1715–1725, Berlin, Germany, August. Association for Computational Linguistics.

Ashish Vaswani, Noam Shazeer, Niki Parmar, Jakob Uszkoreit, Llion Jones, Aidan N Gomez, Ł ukasz Kaiser, and Illia Polosukhin. 2017. Attention is all you need. In I. Guyon, U. V. Luxburg, S. Bengio, H. Wallach, R. Fergus, S. Vishwanathan, and R. Garnett, editors, *Advances in Neural Information Processing Systems*, volume 30. Curran Associates, Inc.

John Wieting, Mohit Bansal, Kevin Gimpel, and Karen Livescu. 2016. Charagram: Embedding words and sentences via character n-grams. In *Proceedings of the 2016 Conference on Empirical Methods in Natural Language Processing*, pages 1504–1515, Austin, Texas, November. Association for Computational Linguistics.

Yonghui Wu, Mike Schuster, Zhifeng Chen, Quoc V. Le, Mohammad Norouzi, Wolfgang Macherey, Maxim Krikun, Yuan Cao, Qin Gao, Klaus Macherey, Jeff Klingner, Apurva Shah, Melvin Johnson, Xiaobing Liu, Lukasz Kaiser, Stephan Gouws, Yoshikiyo Kato, Taku Kudo, Hideto Kazawa, Keith Stevens, George Kurian, Nishant Patil, Wei Wang, Cliff Young, Jason Smith, Jason Riesa, Alex Rudnick, Oriol Vinyals, Greg Corrado, Macduff Hughes, and Jeffrey Dean. 2016. Google's neural machine translation system: Bridging the gap between human and machine translation. *CoRR*, abs/1609.08144.

Validation and Normalization of DCS corpus and Development of the Sanskrit Heritage Engine's Segmenter

Sriram Krishnan[1], **Amba Kulkarni**[1], **and Gérard Huet**[2]
[1] Department of Sanskrit Studies, University of Hyderabad
[2] Inria Paris Center
sriramk8@gmail.com, apksh.uoh@nic.in, gerard.huet@inria.fr

Abstract

The Digital Corpus of Sanskrit records around 650,000 sentences along with their morphological and lexical tagging. But inconsistencies in morphological analysis, and in providing crucial information like the segmented word, urges the need for standardization and validation of this corpus. Automating the validation process requires efficient analyzers which also provide the missing information. The Sanskrit Heritage Engine's Reader produces all possible segmentations with morphological and lexical analyses. Aligning these systems would help us in recording the linguistic differences, which can be used to update these systems to produce standardized results and will also provide a Gold corpus tagged with complete morphological and lexical information along with the segmented words. Krishna et al. (2017) aligned 119,000 sentences, considering some of the linguistic differences. As both these systems have evolved significantly, the alignment is done again considering all the remaining linguistic differences between these systems. This paper describes the modified alignment process in detail and records the additional linguistic differences observed. It also proposes a modification to the existing Heritage segmenter where an additional ranking algorithm is introduced to rank solutions based on joint probabilities calculated from statistical data generated from the results of the alignment process. And finally, the datasets generated during this process are also released publicly.[1]

1 Introduction

Computational processing of Sanskrit is challenging due to sandhi, compounding and the free word order. Sandhi is mandatory between the components of a compound. While the sandhi between words in a sentence is left to the discretion of the speaker, due to the oral tradition, we find a greater tendency to use sandhi even in the written texts. The last decade has seen emergence of several computational tools for analysis of Sanskrit texts at various levels ranging from identification of sentence boundary (Hellwig, 2016), segmentation (Huet, 2005; Hellwig and Nehrdich, 2018), compound analysis (Gupta, 2012), morphological analysis (Kulkarni and Shukl, 2009; Huet, 2005) to sentential parsing (Kulkarni, 2019). The complexity of the sentential parser is reduced if it receives a morphologically analysed segmented text as an input. A collaborative effort between the developers of Sanskrit Heritage (SH) Platform and Saṃsādhanī team (Huet and Kulkarni, 2014) permitted to share efforts on these problematics. The Sanskrit Heritage Platform concentrated on the segmentation guided by the word forms validated through the lexicon. The Saṃsādhanī team focussed on the development of a parser (Kulkarni, 2019). The segmentation algorithm of SH Platform uses a novel approach to finite state technology, through Effective Eilenberg machines (Huet and Razet, 2015). The non-determinism involved in segmentation as well as during the morphological analysis results

[1]The Dataset can be accessed in the following github link: https://github.com/samsaadhanii/datasets under dcs_sh_alignment/

Proceedings of the Computational Sanskrit and Digital Humanities, 18th World Sanskrit Conference 2023, pages 38–58

in multiple possible segmentations of the given input string. The main reason behind the non-determinism is the absence of semantic compatibility check during the process of segmentation. The segmenter produces billions of possible segmentations with all relevant linguistic details such as morphological analysis, and links to the dictionary entry. In order to display these billions of solutions, an efficient compact shared representation of these solutions using tabulated display interface was developed (Goyal and Huet, 2016). Krishnan and Kulkarni (2019) enlisted these solutions by ignoring the linguistic details which are irrelevant from the segmentation point of view, merging the solutions that have same word level segmentation and prioritizing the solutions with the help of statistical information from the SHMT corpus.[2]

Some requirements of Sanskrit computational tools are very specific. Sanskrit has a vast literature spreading over several knowledge domains. Most of the important Sanskrit literature is already translated into several languages.[3] In spite of this, scholars want to have access to the original sources. Thus development of the computational tools with convenient user interfaces that allow seamless connectivity to and from the lexical resources, generation engines and analysis tools becomes meaningful. Though the user would like to have an access to all possible interpretations, it is desirable to rank the solutions and display a few of them. Only when none of the displayed solutions is correct, all other solutions should be made available to the user. In order to rank the solutions, one needs some annotated corpus which can be used to learn the priorities.

For this, Heritage segmenter is required to be facilitated with statistical analysis. Recently the digitization of Sanskrit manuscripts shot up. But the amount of annotated data available for Sanskrit is very small compared to the size of the texts available in it from ancient times. An effort towards having such an annotated data was initiated and resulted into the Digital Corpus of Sanskrit (DCS) (Hellwig, 2010 2019).[4] This data, being of reasonable size, can be used for both statistical analyses and machine learning algorithms.

This paper focuses on how DCS's data can be used along with the Heritage Engine's analysis so that we get a proper morphologically tagged and segmented corpus. It starts with describing the annotation schemes of the two systems, their advantages and limitations and the need for alignment. A similar effort towards aligning the DCS annotated data with the analysis of Heritage Engine's data was already reported by Krishna et al. (2017). This work is briefly described in section 3, along with some issues related to the alignment. Looking at the limitations of the previous work, an effort towards building a better dataset was started. A proper alignment between the representations of these systems was done. The alignment process is described in section 4. But there were some additional difficulties due to the differences in the design decisions of the two systems. These difficulties were recorded systematically and are discussed in section 5. The observations are put down in section 6. Statistical information was extracted from the segmented and morphologically tagged corpus. With the help of these statistical information, the Heritage Segmenter was updated with an additional ranking algorithm which is described in section 7. Testing the modified Heritage Segmenter using Bhagavad Gita verses and comparing the performance of the different statistical information, the different metrics, and with the model proposed in Hellwig and Nehrdich (2018) are under the same section.

---

[2]A corpus developed by the Sanskrit-Hindi Machine Translation (SHMT) Consortium under the funding from DeItY, Govt of India (2008-12). `http://sanskrit.uohyd.ac.in/scl/GOLD_DATA/tagged_data.html`

[3]Most of the literature is in poetry. In spite of having proper translations for these, the true essence of such poetry can be appreciated only in the original!

[4]`http://www.sanskrit-linguistics.org/dcs/`

2 Resources

Before going into the discussion, let us take a look at the morphological annotation and the segmentation annotation of The Digital Corpus of Sanskrit, and The Sanskrit Heritage Engine.

2.1 The Digital Corpus of Sanskrit

The DCS is a sandhi split corpus of Sanskrit texts with full morphological and lexical analysis. There are about 650,000 sentences with more than 4,500,000 word references and 175,000 unique words. All this data was collected from around 400 Sanskrit texts. For every word reference, the following list of attributes is present in DCS:

1. lemma
2. morphological class
3. case, number and gender for nouns along with a combined value termed CNG[5]
4. tense, person, and number values for verbs
5. prefix (optional)
6. finite verb form (optional)
7. infinite verb form (optional)
8. position in sentence, position inside chunk
9. meaning of the lemma

Krishna et al. (2017) represented this data as objects containing the sentence details like chunks, lemmas, and CNG values. A glimpse of what an object looks like is depicted in table 1. This object was used for alignment with the analysis done by Heritage Engine.

Sentence Id	83
Sentence	mauktike yadi saṃdehaḥ kṛtrime sahaje'pi vā
Chunks	['mauktika', 'yadi', 'saṃdeha', 'kṛtrima', 'sahaja', 'api', 'vā']
Lemmas	[['mauktika'], ['yadi'], ['saṃdeha'], ['kṛtrima'], ['sahaja'], ['api'], ['vā']]
Morphological Class (CNG)	[['171'], ['2'], ['29'], ['171'], ['171'], ['2'], ['2']]

Table 1: An example DCS Object data

DCS presents a lemma for each segment along with its morphological analysis. In some cases the derived stem is chosen as a lemma, and in some cases the underived one is chosen. The system is not uniform in deciding the lemmas. This might be a result of context-specific analysis, but in the absence of any tagging guidelines, we do not know the reason for such inconsistency. This corpus is curated single-handedly. Thus we can assume consistency in tagging. However, every human is prone to error. The quality of this data tested on a small sample (Hellwig and Nehrdich, 2018) revealed that around 5.5% of the compound splits are doubtful and around 2% errors are due to segmentation. The recently released data by Hellwig and Nehrdich (2018) contain the split points and sandhi rules proposed by the tagger, but these data are not easy to align with the DCS data.

2.2 The Sanskrit Heritage Engine

The Sanskrit Heritage Engine is a platform that hosts a lexicon (The Sanskrit Heritage Dictionary) and various tools like reader, lemmatizer, declension and conjugation engines. The Reader analyses any given text and segments it into all possible splits and displays them in a graphical interface where the user has the option to choose the required split. In addition to the graphical interface, it also enlists the solutions if the number of solutions is less than a threshold, say 100, also providing the sentential analysis. It closely follows Pāṇini's system i.e., all the rules governing the concept of *sandhi* that occur in *Aṣṭādhyāyī* are taken into consideration.

[5]A value denoting the case, number, and gender of the given word, for nouns. Or the tense, aspect, person, number, and gaṇa (present system class) for verbs.

This segmentation is lexicon directed, using forms systematically generated from its own lexicon.

Additionally, the morphological analyses (inflectional and if applicable derivational as well) are also provided for all the segments. This helps the user to disambiguate and correctly pick the intended split and prune the solutions that are not required. Such information also helps in the further stages of sentential analysis like parsing, disambiguation, and discourse analysis. Another advantage is that, this system combines a fast segmentation algorithm using finite-state transducers and dynamic programming with a first-pass of chunking that limits the inherently exponential complexity to small-length chunks, making the whole segmentation analysis fast enough in practice to be usable interactively.

One limitation of this system is that, it cannot arrive at a single solution mechanically. This owes to the fact that the current version does not take into account the meaning compatibility between various segments, which involves processing at sentential level. Another limitation is due to the Out of Vocabulary words. Though the dictionary contains high frequency words, as is the case with any NLP system, Heritage engine also suffers from automatic handling of Out of Vocabulary words. However the interactive interface allows the user to suggest the lemma for such words, which get stored in the local dictionary provided the lemmas are available in the Monier-Williams dictionary. And for some nominal words with certain prefixes like *su, vi, dur* and for words with *taddhita* suffixes, an explicit entry is required to be added in the dictionary.

This paper deals with the ways in which the DCS Gold data is aligned with one of the solutions of SH. This is an extension of the effort by Krishna et al. (2017) which is described in the next section. In addition to that, statistical information containing the frequencies for words, compound components, and sandhi rules are to be generated which are then used for:

1. updating the existing Segmenter in the Heritage Engine, and
2. testing the performance of the updated ranking algorithm and the frequencies

3 A Dataset for Sanskrit Word Segmentation

3.1 Description

Around 119,000 sentences from the originial DCS corpus were considered and an alignment between the DCS and the Heritage Engine was done by (Krishna et al., 2017). This lead to a huge dataset which had the input sequence, ground truth segmentation, and morphological and lexical information about all the phonetically possible segments. This was done primarily for the Word Segmentation task but is also useful for subsequent tasks. The main concern was to make this annotated corpus available for the use of statistical techniques and Machine learning algorithms.

Since there are differences in design decisions between DCS and Heritage Reader, the candidate segments provided by the Heritage Reader had to be adapted and a few additional segments were added so as to match the entries in DCS. The XML based GraphML format was used to represent the candidate space segments. The GraphML files consist of graph structures, $G(V, E)$ as the representation for the analyses of each of those sentences. The nodes, V, are the possible splits, and the values in the edges, E, denoting whether the participating nodes can co-exist in a solution or not i.e., whether or not they have an overlap in the position relative to the sentence, and that the overlapped portion does not follow any sandhi rule.

To match the two systems, the data from the Heritage Reader's analysis was scrapped and certain parameters such as word, lemma, position, morphological information, chunk number, word length, and pre-verbs were extracted. Corresponding to the morphological analysis the CNG was generated for the ease of alignment. With all these parameters as attributes of each of the nodes, graphs were built for each sentence. Standard graph processing libraries were used to extract the data from these graphs.

3.2 Issues already handled

The lemma provided by DCS and the CNG value are the attributes that help in mapping the two systems. Although direct mapping produced some results, there were multiple issues when the actual mapping was experimented with. Krishna et al. (2017) discusses these issues in detail and provides solutions for each of them. A short summary of the issues is presented below.

- One of the issues was with the compounds and Named entities. The DCS provided the lemma based on the context. If in a given context the compound has non-compositional meaning, then the compound was not split into its components. If the meaning in the given context is compositional, then the compound was split into components. The Heritage Reader's analysis is guided by the lexicon. If the lexicon contains a compound entry due to its non-compositional meaning or on account of being a Named entity, then the Reader in addition to producing all possible segmentations, also produced an entry without any segmentation. Deciding non-compositionality is a complex issue (Hellwig and Nehrdich, 2018).

- Another issue was with the derivative affixes, especially the secondary derivatives. These were treated separately in Heritage Reader, but DCS joins them.

- Third, there were inconsistencies while dealing with *anusvāras* which should have actually been the *anunāsikas* when followed by their respective class consonants.

- Fourth, in DCS, some of the non-final (iic) components of compounds have the same word-form as their stems. For example, *mahā*. But the Heritage Reader sticks to the Pāṇinian rules and produces the base stem (*mahat* in this case).

3.3 Issues yet to be handled

In addition to the above mentioned differences, we noticed following discrepancy at the level of analysis between the two systems.

- Use of homonymy index

  One important aspect of the Heritage Reader is that the dictionary has different entries for homonymous stems, and the morphological analyser provides the homonymy index of the stem. For example, the word *siddham* is analysed by Heritage Engine as shown below.

  ```
  [siddha_1 { pp. }[sidh_1]]{n. sg. acc.| n. sg. nom. | m. sg. acc}
  [siddha_2 { pp. }[sidh_2]]{n. sg. acc.| n. sg. nom. | m. sg. acc}
  ```

  If we look at the meanings of these two senses, we find that they are almost opposing each other.

  ```
  siddha_1  [pp. sidh_1] a. m. n. f. siddhā
  (French)  accompli, réalisé ; gagné, obtenu ; parfait
            qui a atteint son but, réalisé son objectif
  (English) accomplished, realized; won, obtained; perfect
            who achieved his goal, achieved his goal
  siddha_2  [pp. sidh_2] a. m. n. f. siddhā
  (French)  empêché, écarté, repoussé.
  (English) prevented, pushed aside, pushed back
  ```

  In DCS annotated data, homonymy of stems is available but mapping the sense of the stems found in the Heritage Reader with those in the DCS is not trivial. Hence Krishna et al. (2017) collapsed these two analyses into one ignoring the sense information. Although it is not used now, such distinctions would definitely be of greater use for sense disambiguation of such homonymous words.

- Level of analysis

  The engine provides both the inflectional as well as the derivational analysis for some *kṛdantas* (primary derivatives) i.e, participles, absolutives and infinitive forms. For example, the word *hitam* is an inflected form of the base root *hita* which can be derived in two different ways. This results in two different analyses for the word *hitam* as shown below.

  ```
  [hita_1 { pp. }[hi_2]]{n. sg. acc. | n. sg. nom. | m. sg. acc.}
  [hita_2 { pp. }[dhā_1]]{n. sg. acc. | n. sg. nom. | m. sg. acc.}
  ```

  The dictionary entries for these two stems show the meaning difference.

  ```
  hita_1     [pp. hi_2] a. m. n. f. hita
  (French)   envoyé, lancé, émis.
  (English)  sent, launched, issued
  hita_2     [pp. dhā_1] a. m. n. f. hita
  (French)   placé, mis, disposé | convenable, avantageux ;
             utile, propre à, bon pour <dat. g. loc.> ;
             salutaire | amical, bienveillant ; qui fait le bien
             avantage, profit, intérêt ; bien, chose utile ; bien-être.
  (English)  placed, put, disposed | suitable, advantageous;
             useful, suitable for, good for <dat. g. loc.>;
             beneficial | friendly, caring; who does good
             advantage, profit, interest; well, useful thing; well-being.
  ```

  The analyses of DCS data is dependent on the context or the meanings involved. So, DCS stores the analysis of the derived form sometimes and the analysis of the base form otherwise. As Heritage Reader proposes all possible analyses, it is thus challenging to map the Heritage Reader's analysis with the DCS' analysis due to the involvement of meaning. In the case of *hitam*, DCS chooses only the inflectional analysis according to the intended meaning in the sentence.

  In the case of causative forms of the verbs, DCS chooses the causative form of the verb *bhojay* as the stem for the word *bhojanīyāḥ*. But the Heritage Reader provides the following analysis for the same word.

  ```
  [bhojanīya {pfp. [2] }[bhuj_2]]{f.pl.acc. | f.pl.nom | m.pl.nom.} (1)
  [bhojanīya {ca. pfp. [2] }[bhuj_2]]{f.pl.acc. | f.pl.nom | m.pl.nom.} (2)
  [bhojanīya {pfp. [2] }[bhuj_1]]{f.pl.acc. | f.pl.nom | m.pl.nom.} (3)
  ```

  Of the three analyses provided by the engine, (2) has the causative form. Here one needs to construct the causative form *bhojay* from *bhuj+ca* in order to align the morphological analysis, which is not trivial and involves the rules from grammar. Additionally, the Heritage Engine analyses privative compounds like *anivṛttam* as *a-nivṛtta*, but is also updated regularly to lexicalize such compounds to have non-compositional meaning. Since DCS' analysis depends on the compositionality according to the context, the analysis might not map with Heritage Reader's analysis.

- Enhancement in the Heritage engine

  The Heritage Reader's Engine and the dictionaries have evolved in many ways in the past three years, and hence using the same GraphML files would neglect the improvements carried over during the last few years. One such change was with the way the Named Entities have been handled. In the earlier version, the compounds were always split into possible segments even if it represents a Named Entity. Another modification was regarding the pre-verbs. Earlier only the pre-verbs with derivational lemmas were joined, but in the current version the inflectional lemmas also have the pre-verbs attached alongwith.

In view of the above changes, and in order to resolve the problems with homonymy, we decided to align the Heritage Reader's analysis with the DCS afresh with modifications in the alignment process. This alignment of the manually tagged analyses of DCS with one of the analyses produced by the Heritage Engine would provide us with:

1. Identifying wrong annotations from DCS,
2. Consistent uniform analysis,
3. Probable compounds with non-compositional meaning,
4. Constituency analysis of compound words, and
5. Parallel corpus of segmented-unsegmented texts

4 Alignment Process

The DCS objects for the sentences are used in the same way they were used earlier. GraphML files are used for the representation of the mapped data. The same process of scrapping was used with a slight modification to scrap the derivational information, sense, and the correct representation of the morphological analysis.

The Mapping for every sentence was done in three stages:

1. Representing Heritage Reader's analysis as a graph,
2. Aligning the DCS annotation with Heritage Reader's analysis, and
3. Handling compounds with non-compositional meaning and words with derivational morphology

4.1 GraphML files creation

4.1.1 Scrapping

The first stage corresponds to scrapping data from the Heritage Reader's website and creation of GraphML files for each of the sentences from the DCS corpus. During this stage, CNG values corresponding to each morphological analysis are also obtained, and added as an additional attribute to help in connecting the Heritage Reader's analyses with the DCS entries (Krishna et al., 2017).

4.1.2 Graph Construction

The next part of this stage was creating graphs with nodes having the following form.

```
( id, { color_class, position, chunk_no, word, lemma, sense, cng, pre_verb,
morph, length_word, der_pre_verb, der_lemma, der_sense, der_morph, der_cng,
char_pos } )
```

All these values are extracted from the scrapped data. lemma, sense, pre-verb, morph and cng denote respectively the word's prātipadika/dhātu (stem/root), sense (based on different meanings), upasarga (pre-fix for verbs), morphological details, CNG - (case number and gender value) corresponding to the morphological information. der_lemma, der_sense, der_pre_verb, der_morph, der_cng correspond to the information pertaining to derivational morphology. color_class is an attribute for the interface and it denotes a particular color depending on the phase[6]. For example, iics have yellow, substantive/adjective forms have blue, indeclinable forms such as adverbs, conjunctions, prepositions have pink colors, etc.

Except for the derivational details, the sense information and the position based on character, all the others were created by Krishna et al. (2017). As in Krishna et al. (2017), the graph edge values are used to identify the co-existence of two nodes (segments) in a single solution. The edge value '1' indicates that the two nodes can be a part of a solution. The value '2' indicates that the two corresponding nodes cannot be in a single solution. For example, in the compound *pātālabhāsuram* (Figure 1), *pātāla* and *bhāsuram* are non-conflicting nodes and hence their edge is labeled '1'. But *bhā* and *bhāsuram* are separate nodes which are conflicting, and hence their

[6]Phases are the lexical categories like substantive, vocative, finite verbal forms, etc.

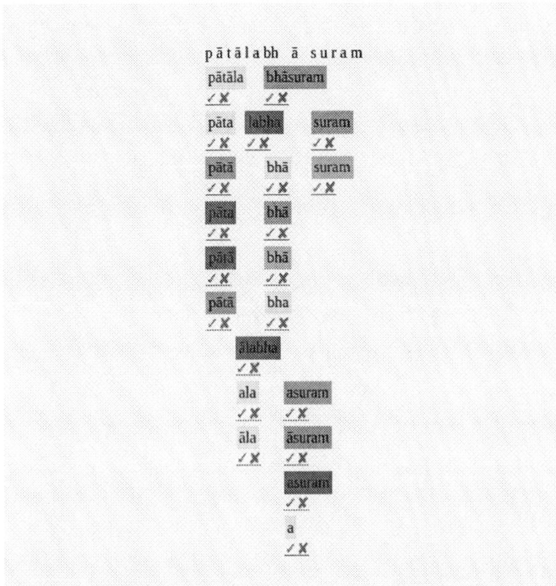

Figure 1: Heritage Reader's analysis of the compound *pātālabhāsuram*

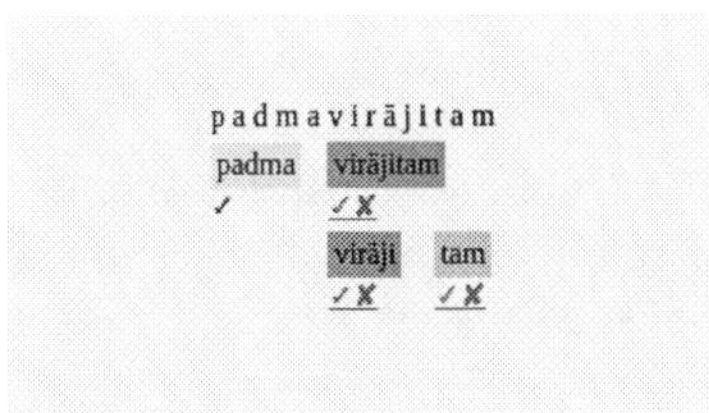

Figure 2: Heritage Reader's analysis of the compound *padmavirājitam*

edge is labeled '2'. Later, the value '3' will be stored for the edges in the correct segmentation solution.

As another example, let us consider the sentence *bindusthānaṃ madhyadeśe sadā padmavirājitam*. There are 2 possible ways in which the word *padmavirājitam* (Figure 2) can be analysed as depicted in table 2. So, the word *virājitam* is in conflict with the part *virāji* since they cannot co-occur together, and hence they will have an edge labeled as '2'. The nodes with *virāji* and *padma* will have an edge with label '1' since they can co-occur. Currently the edge information is not used but could be of use later.

Solution	Analyses
padma-virājitam	padma [padma]{iic.} virājitam [vi-rājita { pp. }[vi-rāj_1]]{n.sg.acc. | n.sg.nom. | m.sg.acc.}
padma-virāji-tam	padma [padma]{iic.} virāji [virāj_2]{m.sg.loc. | n.sg.loc. | f.sg.loc.} tam [tad]{m.sg.acc.}

Table 2: Analysis of the chunk *padmavirājitam*

4.1.3 Handling Homonymy

This involves merging the nodes with the same lemma and other parameters (like word, chunk, etc.) but different senses. Since it is not trivial to align DCS' sense analysis with Heritage

Engine's sense analysis, the individual nodes, having different senses, but the same lemma and same CNG value lead to multiple mappings with the DCS. Such nodes are collapsed into one, suppressing the information of senses. It was mentioned in section 3.3 that Krishna et al. (2017) collapsed all these nodes into one. As we have an additional attribute in 'sense', all the sense indices are temporarily stored in this attribute. New graphs were formed with the new nodes.

4.2 Comparison of DCS data and Heritage Reader's graph to analyze the parallels

The second stage of the alignment process deals with the actual analysis for creating the merged parallel database. First, both systems are normalized so that both of them have a uniform representation of the texts. Then the mapping process is initiated.

4.2.1 Normalization

Both the DCS data as well as the Heritage output are normalised to account for the variations in the use of *anunāsika* and doubling of consonants (*dvitva*). For example,

> *śrīśaṃkaraḥ* to *śrīśaṅkaraḥ*
> *satvena to sattvena*

4.2.2 DCS and Heritage Reader comparison

A comparison between the modified DCS data and modified Heritage Engine analyses was done in the following sequence in order to align them:

1. Mapping the base lemma, derived lemma (optional) and CNG.
2. Different conventions
   In the case of pronouns, both DCS and Heritage Engine follow different conventions while assigning the stem. For example, DCS analyses *tvam* as *tvad*, and the Heritage output following Pāṇini produces *yuṣmad* as the stem. These are treated as special cases with normal table lookup.
3. Mapping compound iics[7]
   In the case of iics (non-final components of compounds) of the DCS, the word-form and the stem for some segments are the same. But the Heritage Reader produces the original stem different from the word-form. For example, *mahādeva* is analysed as *mahā-deva* in DCS, but as *mahat-deva* in Heritage Reader. To handle this difference, the word-form (segment) is taken into consideration instead of the stem.

It was then observed that there were mappings with exactly one match, more than one match, at least one lemma not matched, and mappings with both multiple matches and unmatched lemmas.

So the results are categorized into 4 groups:

1. Single parallel mapping obtained for all lemmas in the sentence
2. Sentences that have at least one lemma with multiple parallels
3. Sentences that have at least one lemma without any parallel
4. Sentences that have at least one lemma with multiple parallels and at least one lemma without parallels

The unmapped sentences (3 and 4) are then sent for further modifications.

4.3 Modifications

Three kinds of modifications are done:

- Direct mapping of lemmas of verbs in the tenth gaṇa (class), having causative suffix *ṇic*.

  Eg, *pūjayati* is analysed in Heritage Engine as '*[pūj]pr. [10] ac. sg. 3*', but DCS has the lemma as *pūjay*. A separate list of such pairs like *pūjay-pūj*, *bhūśay-bhūś*, etc, was prepared. Additional nodes are created using such matching entries.

[7] *in initio compositi*

- The preverbs are sandhied with their corresponding lemmas, and derivational lemma is sandhied with its corresponding preverb labeled as der_pre_verb

  Eg, *praśaṃsanti* is analysed as '*[pra-śaṃs]pr. [1] ac. pl. 3*' in Heritage Reader, but DCS has the lemma *praśaṃs*. In this case, a new node with lemma *praśaṃs* is created by performing sandhi between the preverb *pra* and lemma *śaṃs*. Care should be taken when such sandhi is done, since there are certain required tranformations such as retroflexion of n (ṇ) and s (ṣ). For example, *pra* and *nam* become *praṇam*. Finally these new nodes are added to the graph.

- Merged possible components of compounds to form individual lemmas

  Eg, *śaṅkhaśuktyudbhavam* is analysed in Heritage Reader separately as *śaṅkha-śukti-udbhavam*, but *śaṅkha-śuktyudbhavam* is the expected solution according to DCS. So, for this chunk, all possible compounds are constructed and then each of it is compared to the DCS analysis. If the correct one is matched, a new node with the modified lemma, word and other information is created in the graph. The value for the attribute word, is kept as a hyphen-separated compound instead of the sandhied compound for future usage in constituency analysis. We should also make a note here that the total number of combinations is a Catalan number. So, generating all possible combinations for a given compound results in exponentially slow algorithm.

After these modifications, the second stage of analyzing the parallels is done for the modified graphs. Together with the previous results, the number of sentences with single parallels and multiple parallels is taken into consideration for observations.

5 Additional Problems

After the modifications, the mapping resulted in a reasonable amount of success. In the first phase, we were able to map 73,000 sentences and around 18,000 sentences had multiple possibilities. After the proposed modifications, 56,000 sentences were aligned and 66,000 sentences had multiple possibilities. Further results are available in Section 6. There were still issues regarding the lemmas that didn't match at all, and those which had multiple mappings. Let us first look into some of the issues that lead to the lemmas having multiple mappings.

Mapping for the CNG values is not one-to-one. For a given CNG value, there could be multiple morphological analyses. For example, the CNG value of -190 has morphological analyses as 'ca. pp.', 'des. pp.', and 'pp.'. We find multiple analyses being mapped for the same lemma. For the sentence *vasur ādyaṃ śivaṃ cādyaṃ māyābinduvibhūṣitam*, the lemma that had multiple parallels was *vibhūṣay*. On observing the morphological information, the difference between the multiple solutions was in the morphological analyses of the Heritage Engine. There were two entries with the same lemma - *vibhūṣay*. One had the morph as 'pp.' and the other had it as 'ca. pp.' (causative pp.). The DCS clubs both of them and assigns the CNG value as -190.

The DCS sticks with a single CNG value for primary and secondary derivatives but The Heritage Engine produces two levels of morphological analysis where the first level has the base stem and its analysis and the second level has the derived stem and its analysis. Considering the sentence *śrutaṃ vede purāṇe ca tava vaktre sureśvara*, the Heritage Engine's analysis for the word *śrutaṃ* is:

{[śruta { pp. }[śru]]{n. sg. acc. | n. sg. nom. | m. sg. acc.}}

The first level analysis is (*śru*, { pp. }), and the second level analysis is (*śruta*, n. sg. acc. | n. sg. nom. | m. sg. acc.). The CNG value for { pp. } is -190, and the CNG values for "n. sg. acc.", "n. sg. nom." and "m. sg. acc." are 31, 71, and 69, respectively. Although DCS refers to both the primary and secondary analyses, the CNG value assigned in DCS is -190. This lead to multiple mappings of DCS' analysis with the Heritage Reader's analysis.

The assignment of DCS' lemmas is also not uniform. Sometimes, even when the derivational lemma is available, it uses the inflectional lemma if the inflectional lemma is apt according to the context. For example, in the sentence *nīlaṃ nīlaṃ samākhyātaṃ marakataṃ haritaṃ hitam*, the analysis for *hitam* is provided as the inflectional form *hita*, and not it's derivational form *hi* or *dhā*. So, it is hard to map them because there is some amount of information missing.

Let us now look at an issue with compounds. For the sentence *ata eva hi tatrādau śāntiṃ kuryād dvijottamaḥ*, the compound *dvijottamaḥ* has its lemma as *dvijottama* in the DCS. But the compound modifications done to Heritage Reader's solutions leads to multiple entries with the same lemma. There are four possibilities: *dvija-uttamaḥ*, *dvi-ja-uttamaḥ*, *dvijā uttamaḥ*, and *dvi-jā uttamaḥ*. Of these, the last two are analysed as two words, and not a compound, and hence neglected but the first and the second are both possible compounds. In many such compounds, the differences are due to the combinations of the components.

In the Heritage Engine's analysis for the sentence *vada me parameśāna homakuṇḍaṃ tu kīdṛśam*, the word *parameśāna* is analysed as *parama-īśāna*. There are three analyses for the word *īśāna*. Two have participial forms generated from the root *īś*, and the other is generated from the lexicon entry *īśāna [agt. īś_1]* which states that it is an agent noun of the root *īś*. The participial forms and the agent noun belong to different phases (lexical categories) in the analysis - Krid and Noun, respectively. This distinction is present in the Heritage Reader because pre-verbs are not attached to general nominal entries but attached to participles. So, the nominal entry needs to be treated separately, and hence Noun is more preferred than being analysed as derived from the root *īś*. Since DCS has a single analysis which depends on context, and the Heritage Reader produces the possible distinctions, we arrive at multiple alignment. But, in this case, the agent noun, being derived from *īś*, is indeed a *kṛdanta* and should be present alongwith the other two.

In the sentence *kāraṇena mahāmokṣaṃ nirmālyena śivasya ca*, the word *mahāmokṣaṃ*'s analysis, according to DCS, has its lemma as *mahāmokṣa* with the CNG as 31. Such compounds' contexts need to be checked whether they are to be treated as compounds with non-compositional meaning, or whether they are to be split further.

Now, looking at the unmatched lemmas, we encounter the following difficulties. Some words are not analysed by the Engine at all either due to the absence of its *prātipadika* (stem) or *dhātu* (root) in the dictionary or, the engine fails to analyse the words. For example, the word *prameyatvam* is analysed by DCS as having the lemma *prameya* and *tvam*, but the Heritage Engine produces only parasite segmentations, in the absence of a lexical entry for *prameyatva*. Similarly certain *taddhitāntas* (secondary derivatives) like *nirguṇatvam* are not analysed in the Heritage Engine. Further modifications to the engine to analyse the secondary derivatives would help in aligning these words.

The secondary derivatives are treated like compounds in DCS. For example, in the sentence *prakuryāt tu dvijenaiva tadā brahmamayī surā*, the word *brahmamayī* is analysed as a compound of *brahman* and *maya*. The Heritage engine analyses it with the lemma as *brahmamaya*. Since DCS does not differentiate between compounds and words with secondary derivative suffixes, it is not possible to align such words with the Heritage Engine's analysis.

There is another issue with the way indeclinables like *api* are handled. The Heritage Reader analyses it as 'conj.' and 'prep.'. But DCS marks it as 'ind.' and assigns the CNG as 2. A normalization is required to classify properly such indeclinables under 'conj.', 'prep.' etc. The Heritage Reader has various classes for indeclinables like 'adv.'(adverb), 'abs.'(absolutive), 'part.'(particle), 'prep.'(preposition), 'conj.'(conjunction), etc. And *api* is stored both as 'prep.' and 'conj.' in the Heritage Reader. Either these are to be clubbed together or a mapping needs to be made from these two with the 'ind.' of DCS.

Sometimes the distinctions are present in the way certain *pūrva-padas* (non-final components) of compounds are analysed. For example, the component *rūpya* has the analysis as *rūpya* with the morphological analysis as 'iic'. But the Heritage Reader provides the lemma as *rūpya* with morphological analysis as 'pfp. iic.'.

These are just a handful of examples of the issues encountered. Further analysis of the missed alignments will bring out more such difficulties, but will also provide an opportunity to modify the corpus and the two systems.

6 Observations

Observations were recorded in three phases. In the first phase, the existing dataset from Krishna et al. (2017) (107,000 aligned sentences) was taken into consideration and the parallel corpus for unsegmented and segmented sentences was extracted. In the second phase, the alignment process was run by considering only the sentences from Krishna et al. (2017), and in the third phase, all the sentences from DCS which have proper analysis were considered for the alignment process. Similar to the first phase, the parallel corpora of unsegmented and segmented sentences were extracted.

Type	Phase II	Phase III
Overall Sentences	119,004	621,445
Aligned	65,699	130,439
Aligned (with multiple analyses)	36,755	84,469
Not aligned (with missed analyses)	4148	103,808
Not aligned (with both multiple analyses and missed lemma)	4265	110,760
Not aligned (modifications could not be done)	6925	165,456
Not aligned (due to other reasons)	1212	26,513

Table 3: DCS-SH Alignment Observations

The observations are noted in table 3. The problems discussed in section 5 were encountered in phase II, where the sentences from the existing dataset (Krishna et al., 2017) were passed to the alignment process, and 16,550 sentences have to be checked for issues either in the Heritage Segmenter or in the analyses present in DCS. In Phase III, where all the sentences from DCS had been considered for alignment, 406,537 sentences were not aligned and have to be analysed individually for such issues. If the issue is found to be in Heritage Engine's analyses, then those are solved systematically. In this way, the DCS acts as a tool to improve the Heritage Engine. Currently, only the aligned sentences are considered to form the parallel corpus of unsegmented-segmented sentences. From all the three phases of alignment, these parallel corpora are built and are used to extract the frequency lists which are described in the next section.

7 Modification to Heritage Segmenter

7.1 Statistics Generation

As seen previously, having obtained the aligned sentences, three different parallel corpora of unsegmented and segmented sentences were extracted as follows:

1. The parallel corpus from the alignment done by Krishna et al. (2017) (Phase I)
2. The parallel corpus obtained from the modified alignment done on the DCS sentences used by Krishna et al. (2017) (Phase II)
3. The parallel corpus obtained from the modified alignment done on all the DCS sentences (Phase III)

The following frequencies were obtained from these parallel corpora:

1. word
2. compound component
3. sandhi between words
4. sandhi between compound components

Additionally, frequencies from the SHMT corpus was used. The total list of frequencies is as follows:

1. Frequency list from SHMT corpus
2. Frequency list from DCS-SH aligned parallel corpus (130,000 aligned sentences - Phase III)
3. Frequency list obtained from modified alignment on sentences from Krishna et al. (2017) (70,000 aligned sentences - Phase II)
4. Frequency list obtained from Krishna et al. (2017) (107,000 aligned sentences - Phase I)

7.2 Updated Dovetailing Algorithm

The Sanskrit Heritage Engine's Reader enlists all solutions based on a dovetailing ranking algorithm. A threshold of 100 was used to enlist the best solutions based on the ranking algorithm. But it produces all possible solutions taking into consideration the phase (lexical category) and transition details of each of the segmented forms. Krishnan and Kulkarni (2019) proposed a modification to the Reader where the information about phase and lexical analyses is removed, and the segmented word forms alone are considered for the solutions. Also, an algorithm was introduced which ranks the solutions based on a joint probability calculated from word and transition frequencies of the SHMT corpus. The first metrics used to calculate the joint probability value was:

$$C_{total} = \prod_{i=1}^{n} P_{w_i} \times P_{t_i} \tag{1}$$

which is *word_probability* × *transition_probability* of every segment. The unigram probabilities of the segments (words) and the bigram probabilities of the transitions (sandhi) are taken into consideration and their cumulative product across all the segments is the the overall product presented above.

The second metrics considered the *word_probability* alone where the resultant value is the product of unigram probabilities of the segments/words:

$$C_{total} = \prod_{i=1}^{n} P_{w_i} \tag{2}$$

These metrics of joint probabilities of the segments and transitions are similar to First Order Markov Model except that the segments are not states and hence the probability of the segment does not depend on the previous segment. And the frequency list had unigram frequencies for the words and bigram frequencies for the transitions. The ranking of the solutions is based on the joint probability of the solution and also the number of segments in the solution. The solutions with higher joint probabilities combined with the least number of segments are ranked higher. These probability values were calculated from the statistical data mentioned in section 7.1. The frequency list that is chosen for the updated segmenter is mentioned in section 7.3. The performance comparison of these two metrics are shown in section 7.4.1.

Having obtained all the solutions, the sentences were ranked using the first metrics. Around 21,000 sentences (from SHMT corpus) with at most three split locations in each of them, were chosen for testing. Although it resulted into 98% recall, the algorithm increased the response time of the segmenter tremendously for long sentences and sentences with huge compounds. So, the algorithm was shifted to the graphical Segmenter that generates a graphical interface where the user can choose or reject specific segments. An example is shown in Figure 3. The sentence is initially divided into chunks based on sandhi rules. Each chunk is analysed further where segmentation and morphology recognition are done parallely and only if the segment obtained after the split is present in the lexicon of the Heritage Engine and is morphologically correct, it is registered into the graphical interface. This process developed by (Goyal and Huet, 2016) is now modified by adding a dovetailing algorithm to rank the solutions and maintain

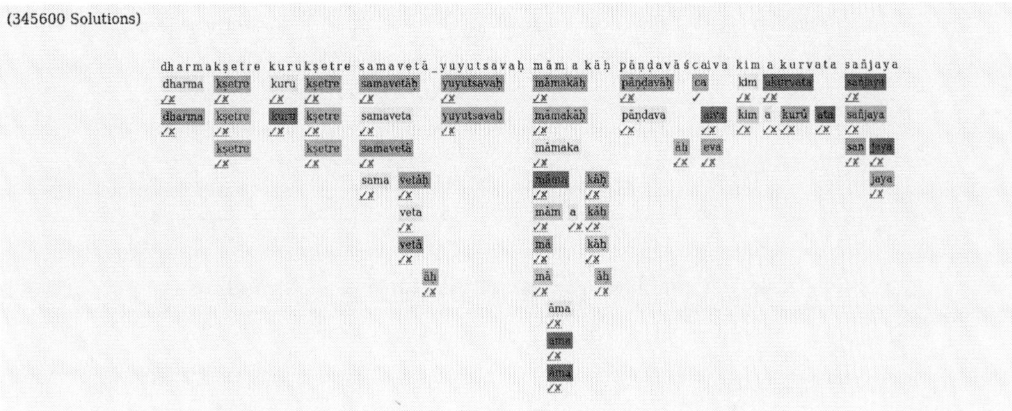

Figure 3: Heritage Segmenter Analysis for Bhagavad Gita 1.1

a bucket of best n solutions[8] based on the probabilities calculated from the frequencies. This value is calculated for every segment registered in the graph. For every chunk, a number of segments will be registered resulting into a number of segmentations each forming from non-overlapping segments in sequence. For each of the segmentations of the chunk, probabilities are also calculated cumulatively. After every chunk is segmented to form various segmentations, these are saved into a global list of chunk segmentations. And once the generation of the graphical interface is done, this list of chunk segmentations is run over the new dovetailing algorithm which traverses through this list and forms the entire list of solutions. And it keeps a bucket of the best n solutions based on the total joint probability of each solution. Finally, only these n solutions are displayed along with the graphical interface.

7.3 Choosing the correct frequency list

To compare the performance of the frequencies generated as shown in section 7.1, Bhagavad Gita Chapter Three's verses were run on the updated Segmenter with these four frequency lists. Of the four frequencies, SHMT performed the best by producing the correct solution (in the top 50 ranks) for 33 out of 43 verses. With the other frequencies, 29 out of 43 verses were analysed. Table 4 shows the distribution of solutions based on position for these four frequency lists.

Solution Rank	SHMT	Phase III (DCS-SH)	Phase II	Phase I
1	10	11	9	5
<= 2	15	13	11	5
<= 3	17	14	12	8
<= 4	19	15	12	9
<= 5	21	16	13	9
<= 10	23	20	17	13
	53.48%	46.5%	30.7%	39.53%

Table 4: Cumulative Position Distribution - Bhagavad Gita

Since there could be overlap of Bhagavad Gita in the lexical resources of SHMT, *Meghadhūta*[9] was chosen for the performance comparisons. 60 *pādas* from 15 verses were tested with all the four frequency sets and the results are shown in table 5.

It is clear from this observation that DCS-SH performs the best where the correct solution was found to be present in 55% of the sentences tested. Comparing both *Bhagavad Gīta's* and

[8] n is temporarily fixed as 100

[9] *Meghadūta* is a poetry text written by *Kālidāsa*.

Solution Rank	SHMT	Phase III (DCS-SH)	Phase II	Phase I
1	21	21	21	21
<= 2	27	28	27	27
<= 3	29	30	30	30
<= 4	30	31	30	30
<= 5	30	32	31	31
<= 10	31	33	32	32
	51.66%	55.0%	53.33%	53.33%

Table 5: Cumulative Position Distribution - Meghadūta

Meghadūta's observation would bring us to a conclusion that both the SHMT and DCS-SH have similar observations, but the scope of development of DCS-SH is high since more sentences might be added with annotations in the corpus. Around 400,000 sentences are to be checked for issues for not being aligned properly. If the issues in the missed sentences are solved, then the number of aligned sentences would increase. So, the statistical data obtained from DCS-SH aligned corpus was considered for calculating the probabilities of the segments.

7.4 Experiments with Bhagavad Gita corpus

7.4.1 On Heritage Segmenter

The unsegmented-segmented verses from Bhagavad Gita were used as development corpus on the updated Segmenter. For 278 verses, additional segmented solutions were added because of the differences in the way Heritage Segmenter deals with compounds. For example, named entities could be analysed as both standalone words as well as compounds with compositional meaning. For some of the compounds, the compositional analyses weren't present and had to be added. For the remaining verses, only one segmented solution was kept. The analysed sentences were put under three categories:

1. found the correct analysis and it is in the top 100 solutions (FOUND)
2. found the correct analysis and it is not in the top 100 solutions (MISSED)
3. could not find the correct analysis (WRONG)

Testing was done in two stages. The first stage was used for development of the Segmenter. Using the feedback from the first stage of testing, the segmenter was updated and the second stage was conducted. For the first stage only the first metrics described in section 7.2 was used. For the second stage, the performance of the ranking was checked with both the metrics separately and a comparison of the two stages was noted as given in table 6.

After the first stage of testing, the verses under MISSED and WRONG categories were analysed manually for possible issues in the Heritage Segmenter. Those under the WRONG category had the following reasons, predominantly:

- unrecognized words
- issue in sandhi
- improper compounding

Those under the MISSED category had solutions beyond the 100-mark. The joint probability had to be checked individually for each of the segments. Also, the issue was with the compositional analyses of compounds by the Heritage Engine. For some, the parallel corpus had to be modified. For the remaining verses, the issues were reported for updating the Segmenter.

The precision and recall values were calculated per sentence where the criteria for precision is to get the ratio of the number of sentences for which the correct solution was found to the total number of sentences. And recall was calculated as the ratio of the number of sentences for which solutions were obtained without leaving any word/chunk unrecognized to the total number of sentences. The precision increased from 74.28% to 98.28% (and 98.85%) from stage 1 to stage 2 while the recall remained the same. Also, there were 4 verses which couldn't be analysed in top

Category	Stage 1	Stage 2 (Metrics 1 - word * transition)	Stage 2 (Metrics 2 - word)
FOUND	520	688	692
MISSED	84	4	0
WRONG	94	6	6
TIMEOUT	2	2	2

Table 6: Bhagavad Gita on the updated Segmenter

100 solutions when the first metrics was used. The position difference between the two metrics is given in table 7.

Position	Metrics 1 - word * transition	Metrics 2 - word
1	308	364
2	89	118
3	51	48
4	32	40
5	39 (74.14%)	28 (85.42%)
6	20	18
7	12	9
8	11	9
9	13	5
10	10 (83.57%)	7 (92.28%)
11-20	58	28
21-30	16	8
31-40	12	4
41-50	8	5
51-100	9	1
> 100	4	0

Table 7: Bhagavad Gita on the updated Segmenter

With the first metrics, 74.14% of the verses had the correct solution in the top 5 ranks. With the second metrics, 85.42% of the verses had the correct solution in top 5 ranks. With both metrics, 6 verses could not be analysed at all. These are the reasons for such cases:

- periphrastic perfect forms: like *darśayāmāsa*, *āśvāsayāmāsa*, etc., are recognized as two segments instead of one. These aren't a combination of preverbs and verbs but are verbal compounds where the components are not strongly bound. Hence, it is difficult to glue them together to make them form a single segment.
- Since Bhagavad Gita is a part of the epic *Mahābhārata*, it is bound to contain certain words which were in use prior to Pāṇini's Aṣṭādhyāyī. Some of these are referred to as *ārṣaprayoga* (usage from *ṛṣis*. One such example is *priyāyārhasi*). It should actually be split into *priyāyāḥ* and *arhasi* according to the meaning, but the sandhi between these two words does not produce these splits.

7.4.2 Comparison with the model from Hellwig and Nehrdich (2018)

For comparing with similar models, the model from Hellwig and Nehrdich (2018) (rcNN) was chosen because it was also trained with DCS sentences. And the model used character level recurrent and convolutional neural networks for segmentation. Since DCS sentences were used for the alignment to generate the frequencies, a comparison was done between these two keeping in mind the following differences:

- The rcNN produces only one solution, whereas the updated Heritage segmenter produces the top n solutions, and

- rcNN is trained with DCS which has non-compositional analysis for the compounds, according to the context, while the Heritage Segmenter's compounds have compositional analysis predominantly.

So, the comparison was restricted to word level segmentations where the compound components were considered similar to the other words in the sentence. Thus, the parallel corpus generated earlier was modified to exhibit only the segmentations without differentiating the word splits with the compound component splits. And only the first solution was taken into account for comparison. 254/700 verses were analysed correctly by rcNN. In the case of the Heritage Segmenter, it was 308 with the first metrics and 364 with the second metrics.

Additionally, 1000 sentences from the test set of Hellwig and Nehrdich (2018) were tested on both the models (rcNN and the updated Segmenter). The Heritage Segmenter was unable to recognize at least one word in 385 of those sentences. So, the remaining 615 sentences were considered for a fair comparison. The rcNN was able to identify the ground truth segmentation for 371/615 sentences. The updated Heritage Segmenter was able to identify 295/615 sentences correctly. On observation, it was noted that the difference in the performance was predominantly due to the compositionality of the compounds in the Heritage Segmenter. While the ground truth segmentation in the test set has the non-compositional analysis, the Heritage Segmenter produces the components separately. A few such examples of the compounds are presented in table 8:

No.	Ground Truth Segment	Segment from Heritage Segmenter
1	kṣīramadhurā	kṣīra madhurā
2	tiktabījā	tikta bījā
3	mahārājaphalaḥ	mahārāja phalaḥ
4	pañcavidham	pañca vidham
5	ātmaka tvam	ātmakatvam
6	pañcarājiphalaḥ	pañca rāji phalaḥ
7	avakīrṇa vat	avakīrṇavat

Table 8: Comparison of Compositionality

As compositionality depends on context and cannot be finalised at the level of segmentation, and the Heritage Engine's lexicon has a limitation on many of the non-compositional lexicon entries of the compounds, the Segmenter specifies the compound components in the analysis. Hence, in the ground truth segmentations of the sentences that weren't segmented correctly, the compounds were split into their components for having compositional analysis in addition to the non-compositional analysis.

This increased the performance in both the systems. 401/615 sentences were analysed correctly by rcNN and the Heritage Segmenter was able to analyse 498/615 sentences of which 421 were analysed in the first position. The observations are presented in table 9.

615 test sentences	with ground truth compounds		with compositional analyses of compounds	
	rcNN	Updated Segmenter	rcNN	Updated Segmenter
FOUND	371	295	401	421
WRONG	244	320	214	117

Table 9: Comparison of rcNN vs Updated Segmenter

From the observations and the comparison of the compositionality, it is observed that the necessity of non-compositional analyses of certain compounds is questionable in the ground truth. In the same way, certain compounds which could have both compositional as well as non-compositional analyses (like named entities), are to be lexicalised in the Heritage engine's lexicon.

Thus, the differences in the way compounds are analysed in DCS and Heritage Segmenter is one of the main reasons for this performance difference. And that is the major obstacle to solve while trying to align these two systems to produce a proper dataset for segmentation tasks in Sanskrit.

8 Inferences and Conclusion

The alignment process and the experiments with the dataset obtained thereafter provided us three important cues to proceed forward towards the development of Heritage Segmenter. Several anomalies of the Segmenter were discovered and corrected with the help of the results from the experiments.

8.1 Improvement to the Heritage Engine

First, the lexicon was updated by the addition of words that went unrecognized by the engine. The Bhagavad Gita verses were used here as a development corpus to provide feedback for the Segmenter. As discussed in section 2.2, such entries were added to the lexicon to handle out of vocabulary words. Mostly, *taddhitas* with suffixes *tva, tā, vat*, compounds with prefixes *sa, su, vi, dus, etc.* and those agent nouns and action nouns which were encountered in the verses and which are not generated systematically by the engine were added.

Second, certain combinations of preverbs with root forms and kṛdantas were not permitted, which prevented the recognition of corresponding forms. The segmenter has a table, fixing for any root and gaṇa what voices are allowed for a given sequence of preverbs. Adding entries to the table allowed the recognition of the missing padas.

Third, to handle the words with suffixes *cit, cana* (refer section 7.4.1), the corresponding pronomial forms were glued with the suffixes and made to be generated by the engine.

Fourth, lexicalised compounds were treated as a whole even if they could be generated as a combination of component pieces (for the named entities whose meanings are non-compositional).

Having added these words, we were able to obtain better results (24% increase in precision). As discussed in 7.4.1, the engine couldn't produce solutions for 94 verses in stage 1 as each of the verse had at least one unrecognized word. In the second and third stages, solutions were found for 88 of these.

Also, the engine couldn't find the correct solution in the best 50 solutions for 84 verses because of the compounds which had their components split by the engine (not recognized as named entities). These were recognized after adding the lexical entries for these compounds.

Fifth, the dovetailing algorithm was also modified to make it consistent with the graphical interface. This was faster, produced more accurate results than the algorithm that was built for the Reader. Since the graphical interface does not narrow down to a single or a limited number of possible solutions, it requires additional effort from the user for providing the correct segmentation, although it is efficient and user-friendly. The updated ranking algorithm helps in truncating the entire list of possible solutions to a limited set (say, 5, 10, or 50), without any significant loss of recall. It is observed in table 7 that 85% of the verses have their solutions in top 5 ranks, and more than 90% of the solutions are found in the top 10 ranks owing to the improvement in the lexicon and the modified ranking algorithm.

Sixth, the frequencies were provided as a list in Krishnan and Kulkarni (2019) where accessing the frequencies delayed the process. To make it consistent with the data structures used in the engine and also to speed up the access rate, the frequencies were integrated into the newly formed decorated trie structure which holds both the words and frequencies by sharing the suffixes, similar to the trie structures built for the lexicon. Instead of populating the frequencies in the generated trie structure that holds the existing lexicon, a separate trie structure was built for these frequencies, making it a separate module.

Seventh, when only the word probability was used, correct solutions were produced in the top 10 ranks for 92% of the verses. The other metrics, where both the word probability and the sandhi probability of each of the segments was used, produces correct solutions in top 10 solutions for 83%. The metrics is similar to first order Markov model except that the current probability does not have any dependence on the previous state's probability because the segments are not considered as states as these segments are taken all at once. And the probabilities are calculated for each of the segments and cumulatively their product is obtained.

Finally, the alignment process provides for every word in the sentence, its base lemma, derived lemma, CNG value, preverb and morphological analysis. Currently, only the word and its frequency are being used by the algorithm. Experiments with other parameters should be tried for better results. Also, these could be used in further stages of sentential analyses.

8.2 Integrating the updates with *Saṃsādhanī* tools

The collaborative effort between the Sanskrit Heritage Engine and *Saṃsādhanī* team (Huet and Kulkarni, 2014) enables cross-platform analyses of sentences. Currently, it is left to the user to choose the correct or intended solution in the Heritage segmenter, and then send it to the *Anusāraka* in the *Saṃsādhanī* for parsing the sentence. With the help of the ranking incorporated in the engine, it is now possible to narrow down to the best n solutions, and choose from those. Again, looking at the performance comparison of the Bhagavad Gita corpus, 85% of the verses had their solutions in the top 5 ranks making it easy for the users to redirect to the *Saṃsādhanī*. So, the Heritage Segmenter acts as the front end to segment the sentence, and provide the best solution(s) where the user chooses one solution (instead of individual segments as in the original segmenter's interface), to parse with the help of the *Anusāraka* in the back-end.

With the development of the statistical data, the value of n should decrease gradually. As around 400,000 DCS sentences have to be dealt with further for analysing the issues in alignment, the number of aligned sentences is bound to increase. The frequencies of words and transitions also increases along with new words being added to the lists.

8.3 Improvement to the reference corpora

As discussed in section 2.1, there are a few limitations of DCS like the inconsistencies in the analysis, errors due to segmentation and compound splits. The alignment process helped in managing these issues and avoiding these in the resultant dataset. These are discussed here along with the state of the other corpora used - SHMT and Bhagavad Gita.

First, in some of the cases, the *anusvāras* were converted to corresponding *anunāsikas*.

Second, the inclusion of both the base and derived stems in the dataset with the help of the analyses from Heritage Engine, modifying the iics of certain compounds which were in the lemma format to the iic format, handling pre-verbs by gluing them to their corresponding word forms, etc were additionally done to modify the analyses of DCS.

Third, the analyses produced by the Heritage Segmenter has details like homonymy index which denotes the word sense. Mapping these with the senses of DCS words is a tedious task, as the mapping is one to many from DCS to Heritage's lexicon and hence, different senses of the same lemma were clubbed together in the analyses of the SH engine.

Fourth, many of the compounds which had non-compositional meaning were analysed as a whole entity. Sometimes, they have to be changed to components (iics and ifcs) depending on the context, which is out of the scope of current research.

Fifth, the main advantage of SH platform is the availability of morphological constructs which is obtained with the help of the generative tagset of the platform. And DCS provides abstract entities like CNG values which could have multiple analysis possibilities. The alignment process helped in mapping these CNG values with the morphological analyses, thus providing the resultant dataset both parameters.

SHMT corpus was used for comparisons of the performance of the Segmenter over different metrics, and different ranking algorithms. With the help of these comparisons, we can infer that the improvements to the alignment process would result into an improved dataset, which would then provide us better statistics. In section 7.3, the closeness of the three generated corpora with respect to the recall of the engine was discussed (29/43 verses producing results). SHMT stood out with 33/43 verses producing correct results. But in table 4 the closeness of the SHMT corpus with the dataset generated from overall alignment was shown (53% of the verses obtained the correct solution with SHMT corpus; 46% with the latest dataset from latest alignment). Two thirds of the DCS sentences are to be analysed for issues. Also, amongst the aligned sentences, 130,000 had single solution possibilities. The remaining 85,000 sentences had multiple mappings. Truncating these into a single solution is beyond the scope of the current research as the different possibilities arise mostly due to compound formations and contextual differences.

In section 7.4.1, it was mentioned that out of 700 verses of the Bhagavad Gita, 278 verses were provided with additional segmentation solutions because of the unmatched named entities or compounds which either require compositional analyses or non-compositional analyses. This is again beyond the scope of the current research as the differences are present in the meanings of the verses and also it depends on the design decisions of the systems under use.

Finally, the comparison with the model from Hellwig and Nehrdich (2018) (section 7.4.2) provided us clear distinctions on how this updated segmenter is better with respect to differentiating the segmentation within compounds and that between different words, providing limited multiple solutions owing to the different meaning possibilities, etc. The updated Segmenter did outperform the model with more number of verses analysed correctly for the Bhagavad Gita test verses. Although the neural network model performed better for the test sentences from Hellwig and Nehrdich (2018), when the compositionality of the compounds was included amongst the ground truth segmentations, the updated Segmenter did perform better. This showed the importance of compositionality at the segmentation level and how the Heritage Segmenter needs to handle the compositionality of the compound words. It also brought out the necessity of updating the lexicon with the unrecognized words. Other computational parameters like response time, training time and space, etc are also to be considered to propose a strong comparison of these two systems.

The intention behind this work was to provide a dataset which is rich in morphological and lexical analyses, and which provides as much details as possible regarding the sentences and words. The alignment process did pave the way to building such a dataset which was used on the existing Segmenter to improve it further. Thus, the resultant dataset could give rise to a homogeneous gold corpus which could in turn be used for various further tasks of sentential analysis.

References

Sushant Dave, Arun Kumar Singh, Prathosh A. P., and Brejesh Lall. 2021. Neural compound-word (sandhi) generation and splitting in sanskrit language. In *CODS-COMAD 2021: 8th ACM IKDD CODS and 26th COMAD, Virtual Event, Bangalore, India, January 2-4, 2021*, pages 171–177. ACM.

Pawan Goyal and Gérard Huet. 2016. Design and analysis of a lean interface for Sanskrit corpus annotation. *Journal of Linguistic Modeling*, 4(2):117–126.

Pawan Goyal, Gérard Huet, Amba Kulkarni, Peter Scharf, and Ralph Bunker. 2012. A distributed platform for Sanskrit processing. In *COLING*, pages 1011–1028.

Anilkumar Gupta. 2012. *Sanskrit Compound Processor.* Ph.D. thesis, University of Hyderabad, Hyderabad.

Oliver Hellwig and Sebastian Nehrdich. 2018. Sanskrit word segmentation using character-level recurrent and convolutional neural networks. In *Proceedings of the 2018 Conference on Empirical Methods in Natural Language Processing*, pages 2754–2763, Brussels, Belgium, October-November. Association for Computational Linguistics.

Oliver Hellwig. 2009. Sanskrittagger, a stochastic lexical and pos tagger for Sanskrit. In *Lecture Notes in Artificial Intelligence.*

Oliver Hellwig, 2010–2019. *The Digital Corpus of Sanskrit (DCS).*

Oliver Hellwig. 2016. Detecting sentence boundaries in Sanskrit texts. In *Proceedings of COLING 2016, the 26th International Conference on Computational Linguistics: Technical Papers*, pages 288–297, Osaka, Japan, December. The COLING 2016 Organizing Committee.

Gérard Huet and Amba Kulkarni. 2014. Sanskrit linguistics web services. In *Proceedings of COLING 2014, the 25th International Conference on Computational Linguistics: System Demonstrations*, pages 48–51.

Gérard Huet and Idir Lankri. 2018. Preliminary design of a Sanskrit corpus manager. In Gérard Huet and Amba Kulakrni, editors, *Proceedings of Computational Sanskrit and Digital Humanities, 18th WSC.*

Gérard Huet and Benoît Razet. 2015. Computing with relational machines. *Mathematical Structures in Computer Science*, pages 1–20, October.

Gérard Huet. 2003. Lexicon-directed segmentation and tagging of Sanskrit. In *XIIth World Sanskrit Conference, Helsinki, Finland. Final version in Themes and Tasks in Old and Middle Indo-Aryan Linguistics, Eds. Bertil Tikkanen and Heinrich Hettrich.*, pages 307–325, Delhi, August. Motilal Banarsidass.

Gérard Huet. 2005. A functional toolkit for morphological and phonological processing, application to a Sanskrit tagger. *J. Functional Programming*, 15,4:573–614.

Amrith Krishna, Pavankumar Satuluri, and Pawan Goyal. 2017. A dataset for sanskrit word segmentation. In *Proceedings of the Joint SIGHUM Workshop on Computational Linguistics for Cultural Heritage, Social Sciences, Humanities and Literature*, page 105–114. Association for Computational Linguistics, August.

Amrith Krishna, Bishal Santra, Sasi Prasanth Bandaru, Gaurav Sahu, Vishnu Dutt Sharma, Pavankumar Satuluri, and Pawan Goyal. 2018. Free as in free word order: An energy based model for word segmentation and morphological tagging in Sanskrit. In *Proceedings of the 2018 Conference on Empirical Methods in Natural Language Processing*, pages 2550–2561, Brussels, Belgium, October-November. Association for Computational Linguistics.

Amrith Krishna, Ashim Gupta, Deepak Garasangi, Pavankumar Satuluri, and Pawan Goyal. 2020a. Keep it surprisingly simple: A simple first order graph based parsing model for joint morphosyntactic parsing in Sanskrit. In *Proceedings of the 2020 Conference on Empirical Methods in Natural Language Processing (EMNLP)*, pages 4791–4797, Online, nov. Association for Computational Linguistics.

Amrith Krishna, Bishal Santra, Ashim Gupta, Pavankumar Satuluri, and Pawan Goyal. 2020b. A graph-based framework for structured prediction tasks in Sanskrit. *Computational Linguistics*, 46(4):785–845, December.

Sriram Krishnan and Amba Kulkarni. 2019. Sanskrit segmentation revisited. In *Proceedings of ICON 2019, the International Conference on Natural Language Processing*, Hyderabad, December.

Amba Kulkarni and Devanand Shukl. 2009. Sanskrit morphological analyser: Some issues. *Indian Linguistics*, 70(1-4):169–177.

Amba Kulkarni. 2019. *Sanskrit Parsing based on the theories of Śābdabodha.* IIAS, Shimla and D K Printworld.

Amba Kulkarni. 2021. Sanskrit parsing following indian theories of verbal cognition. *ACM Transactions on Asian and Low-Resource Language Information Processing*, 20(2):1–38, April.

Peter Scharf and Malcolm Hyman. 2009. *Linguistic Issues in Encoding Sanskrit.* Motilal Banarsidass, Delhi.

Pre-annotation Based Approach for Development of a Sanskrit Named Entity Recognition Dataset

Sujoy Sarkar
IIT Kharagpur
sujoys@iitkgp.ac.in

Amrith Krishna
IT University of Copenhagen
amrk@itu.dk

Pawan Goyal
IIT Kharagpur
pawang@cse.iitkgp.ac.in

Abstract

Recent NLP algorithms for Named Entity Recognition require a large amount of annotated resources. Low resourced languages such as Sanskrit lack adequate annotated data and manual annotation is costly as well as time-consuming. A sequence labeling tool that supports manual annotation with automatic suggestions to reduce time and increase annotators' productivity is appealing, especially for low-resourced languages. Most of the tools developed with such capabilities are for resource-rich western European languages and are not tuned to the need of morphologically rich language like Sanskrit. In our work, we deploy an annotation tool for crowd-sourcing a Sanskrit NER dataset annotation. The selected corpus is *Śrīmad-Bhāgavatam*. The annotation environment is augmented to help the annotators with automatic suggestions. The suggestions are pre-annotated using our proposed heuristic. The heuristic works based on string-matching algorithms. The key idea is to compare transliterated Sanskrit text with an English translation and identify words of similar forms as likely named entities (NE). A gazetteer is applied to further classify the NEs into semantic classes. On a small manually annotated dataset, the heuristic identified the NEs reasonably with an F-Score of 0.80.

1 Introduction

Named entity recognition (NER) is the task of finding spans of text that constitute proper names in unstructured documents, and classify them into predefined semantic categories such as person, location, etc. (Jurafsky and Martin, 2009). It has emerged from the field of Information Retrieval(IR) and has several downstream applications such as open domain question answering (Chen et al., 2017), co-reference resolution (Yang and Mitchell, 2016), improving semantic search (Caputo et al., 2009). One such motivating application is the use of NER to improve the searching and browsing capability of digital libraries (Borin et al., 2007; Caputo et al., 2009). A recent study on The Gallica digital library, a national heritage and encyclopedia library of France shows that 80% of the top 500 queries sent to the portal contained at least one named entity (NE) (Chiron et al., 2017). However, use of keyword-based search mechanisms often limit the effectiveness of search systems for such digital libraries. Words in natural languages tend to express polysemy and synonymy resulting in low precision and recall respectively of such keyword based search systems. An alternative approach is to search documents not only at the lexical level but also at the semantic level. "Named entities (NEs) mentioned in a document constitute an important part of its semantics" (Caputo et al., 2009). Indexing documents with named entities allow users to search the collection in novel ways (Bontcheva et al., 2002). Sanskrit has over 30 million manuscripts produced over a course of four millennia (Goyal et al., 2012). In the last few decades, a prodigious effort is put in to digitize these manuscripts and make them accessible through digital libraries (Krishna et al., 2017). These libraries can be enriched with NE metadata information to improve their functionalities. But to the best of our knowledge, there is no publicly available NE annotated data to facilitate research on Sanskrit NER.

Proceedings of the Computational Sanskrit and Digital Humanities, 18th World Sanskrit Conference 2023, pages 59–70

Recent advances in machine learning (ML) have achieved state-of-the-art performance on many sequence labeling tasks, including NER (Liu et al., 2018; Baevski et al., 2019). These ML algorithms rely on the availability of vast volumes of annotated data. However, creation of annotated text data is an expensive and a time-consuming process (Goyal et al., 2012; Yimam et al., 2014; Lin et al., 2019). Further, it puts a heavy demand on human annotators to maintain the quality annotations (Stenetorp et al., 2012). This makes direct application of such difficult for low-resource languages. Machine-assisted human validated semi-automatic annotation is already shown to be effective in reducing the annotation labor for preparing morphologically tagged corpus in Sanskrit (Goyal and Huet, 2016; Goyal et al., 2012). Generic tools are developed for text annotation including the NE annotation task. Most of these tools provide a good interface but does not provide machine-assisted support to human annotators (Bontcheva et al., 2013; Chen and Styler, 2013). More recently, tools are developed to combining automatic pre-annotation and manual annotation to improve the efficiency and quality of annotation (Teng et al., 2019; Yimam et al., 2014). In the pre-annotation approach, the annotation tool automatically suggests sequence labels to human annotators. The automatic suggestion of sequence labels can be static or dynamic. In static suggestion, data is pre-annotated using some rules before the annotation process begins (Lingren et al., 2013). Also, some tools give dynamic suggestions using ML algorithms that gradually learns from previously annotated data as annotation progresses (Teng et al., 2019; Lin et al., 2019). But these tools are developed for resource-rich western European languages and is not tuned to the need of morphologically rich language like Sanskrit. Automatic pre-annotation of NEs in Sanskrit is more challenging due to many challenges presented by the features of the language that varies significantly from typical Western European language features (Goyal et al., 2012). A large number of possible inflections of NEs, difficulty in identifying word boundaries due to phonemic changes and ambiguities between names and other parts-of-speech categories makes the task difficult.

In our work, we propose a heuristic based on string-matching algorithms to automatically pre-annotate Named Entities (NEs) in a Sanskrit corpus. The key idea is to compare transliterated text and English translation and identify words of similar forms as likely named entity. We use a name dictionary or gazetteer to further classify the NEs into three semantic classes: person, location and miscellaneous. The selected corpus is *Śrīmad-Bhāgavatam* in which words are already segmented and word by word English translation is available digitally. We present a web-based NE annotation platform for annotating *Śrīmad-Bhāgavatam*, based on an open-source text annotation framework. The annotation environment helps annotators by providing automatic NE suggestions based on the pre-annotated data. Currently, the scope is limited to static suggestions. Our platform is publicly available for crowd sourcing the task. Annotators can collaborate, modify the pre-annotations as well as add new annotations. An annotation-approver role also can be assigned to approve the annotations. We make the following specific contributions:

1. Our proposed string-matching based pre-annotation heuristic achieves 0.80 F1 in the task of identifying NEs on a set 60 manually annotated verses from *Śrīmad-Bhāgavatam.*

2. In our current experiment with variations of the heuristic we observe that the performances of string-matching algorithms do not significantly vary if inflected words are used instead of stems obtained by lemmatization. Among the string-matching algorithms that we selected, Jaro-Winkler similarity gives the best performance.

3. We deployed a web-based NE annotation platform for crowd-sourcing NE annotation in *Śrīmad-Bhāgavatam.*[0] The annotation environment is augmented to show annotation suggestions to annotators based on the pre-annotations by the heuristic.

https://sanskritner.herokuapp.com/

2 Named Entity Recognition Task

Named Entity Recognition is one of the fundamental tasks in NLP and Information Extraction. NER aims to find spans of text that constitute proper names in unstructured documents, and classify them into pre-defined semantic categories (Jurafsky and Martin, 2009). As natural language is polysemous, ambiguity exists among the name references. Resolving ambiguity involves recognizing the true referent entity of a name reference and then resolving the proper type. NER has achieved state of the art for western European languages using machine learning algorithms. NER task is more complex in Sanskrit compare to western European languages. Several challenges are posed by the rich morphological features of the language.

- Phonemic changes (*Sandhi*) obscure the word boundaries in a sentence by combining multiple words, resulting in long and complex word forms. A named entity may also get combined with other words. For example, *'śrībrahmovāca'* translates to *'Śrī Brahmā said'*. Here Brahmā is a named entity that is easily identifiable in English as it is present as a separate word. Also, the capitalization of the NE is a major feature used by NER systems for European languages. Even multiple NEs may be present in a single word. For example, the word *'sakarṇaduḥśāsanasaubalānā '* contains three NEs: *'karṇa, duḥśāsana, saubalānām'*. So to prepare a dataset one needs to segment the sandhied words in a corpus. However, word segmentation in Sanskrit is not a trivial task as the number of possible segments for a given sentence can be very large. Segmentation tools are available in popular computational Sanskrit platforms like Sanskrit Heritage Reader(SHR), but human intervention is required to decide the final solution (Goyal et al., 2012).

- NEs can also be a compound word, for example, *'kumbhakarṇa'*. Compounds are extensively used in Sanskrit literature but processing compound is a more complex task than *Sandhi* (Kumar et al., 2010). A word segmentation tool may consider the word *'kumbhakarṇa'* as two words making it difficult to identify it as a name.

- Another problem is there are up to 72 possible inflections of NEs due to gender, number and cases. Morphological analysis needs to be done to identify the stems (Krishna, 2019).

- In Indian languages names of persons, places, etc are more diverse and a lot of them can be found in the dictionary as common nouns. Also, ambiguities between names and adjectives, verbs and other parts-of-speech categories are prevalent. For example, *'vidūra'* is the name of a person which also means very far.

As our selected corpus is already in segmented form, we did not need to handle the problem of segmentation and compound word.

2.1 NER Tag-set

The task of NE expression identification in text was first defined in MUC-6 Named Entity task (Sundheim, 1995) where a total of seven NE tags were classified into three classes: ENAMEX (person, location and organization), TIMEX (date, time) and NUMEX (money, percentage). Only four categories of NEs are identified in the shared task 6 of CoNLL 2003 (Tjong Kim Sang and De Meulder, 2003): person, location, organization and miscellaneous. Text Encoding and Interchange guidelines (Burnard and Bauman, 2008) that maintain the XML standard for encoding and documenting have proposed hierarchical NEs. As our annotated data is meant for general-use linguistic resources, we have opted for CoNLL 2003 convention with three NE categories: person, location, and miscellaneous. *Bhāgavatam* is a spiritual text and lacks organizational entities, so we did not explicitly use the organization category.

3 Data

3.1 Corpus

Our approach of pre-annotation is based on a comparison of IAST (Williams et al., 1899) transliteration of Sanskrit text and the corresponding English translation. Many Sanskrit works of literature are translated into English over time. We have selected *Bhāgavatam* to demonstrate our approach and create an NER dataset. It can be extended to other Sanskrit texts with English translation as well. There are two reasons for selecting *Bhāgavatam*. The first reason is that word by word translation is done and made available online. The word by word translation makes it easier to apply our approach. We will discuss this further in Section 4. The second reason is that in the transliterated text words are already present in segmented form which makes it easier to identify the NEs. Also compared to other translated texts, it has a reasonable amount of text. *Bhāgavatam* contains a total of 18K verses with 0.23 million words. CoNLL 2003 English NER dataset (Tjong Kim Sang and De Meulder, 2003), which is one of the standard NER English data set, has 0.3 million words.

We have scrapped the total data of *Bhāgavatam* from online resources. In the online version sometimes, multiple verses are merged into a single verse. Total there are 12 cantos, 335 chapters, 13,004 occurrences of single or multiple verses, where each such instance is taken as one example to annotate at a time. The vocabulary contains a total of 41K unique words and inflections.

3.2 Gazetteer

Name dictionaries or gazetteer are very helpful NER resources. Modern names are collected from different sources like a telephone directory and named dictionaries. Identification of names using Gazetteer is difficult due to inflection, ambiguity etc., but it can be used to boost the performance of NER systems (Saha and Majumder, 2018). *Bhāgavatam* is a well discussed literary work. So, it is relatively easier to collect the list of names of characters or places. We have prepared a name dictionary by automatically scrapping names of characters from online resources. We have mainly collected person names, but the list can be extended further by adding names of other entity types. The gazetteer has 611 unique names.

4 System Description

In this work, we have attempted to develop a system that will provide a platform to crowdsource NER annotation. It will also assist the annotator to improve performance and speed by indicating which words are most likely a named entity and, in some cases, suggesting the possible class. As discussed earlier, suggestions can be static, i.e., prepared before the annotation process begins or these can be dynamically learned and improved as annotators annotate more and more data. The scope of our current work is restricted to static pre-annotation. In this section, we will present the details of the pre-annotation approach and also a description of the annotation framework.

4.1 Pre-annotation Approach

We want to compare Sanskrit transliteration and English translation to identify the named entities. The basic idea is that named entities do not change form in any language. So, the similar strings in transliteration and translation are most likely named entities.

For example, in Figure 1 we can see the English translation of the word *'kṛṣṇe'* has the word *'Lord Śrī Kṛṣṇa'*. Here the word *'kṛṣṇe'* and *'Kṛṣṇa'* have similar forms.

The second thing that we need to handle is the inflected forms of Sanskrit words. A word can appear in many different forms due to the morphological richness of the language. For example, one of the inflected forms of the word *'arjuna'* is *'arjunāya'* meaning *'to Arjuna'*.

https://vedabase.io/en/library/sb/
https://vaniquotes.org/wiki/Category:Personalities_from_Srimad_Bhagavatam
https://vedabase.io/en/library/sb/2/8/3/

kathayasva mahābhāga
yathāham akhilātmani
kṛṣṇe niveśya niḥsaṅgaṁ
manas tyakṣye kalevaram

kathayasva — please continue speaking; *mahābhāga* — O greatly fortunate one; *yathā* — as much as; *aham* — I; *akhila-ātmani* — unto the Supreme Soul; *kṛṣṇe* — unto Lord Śrī Kṛṣṇa; *niveśya* — having placed; *niḥsaṅgam* — being freed from material qualities; *manaḥ* — mind; *tyakṣye* — may relinquish; *kalevaram* — body.

Figure 1: Example of a verse (Śrīmad-Bhāgavatam 2.8.3) and word by word English translation.[0]

Here either we can apply approximate string matching directly using the inflected word or can apply morphological analysis to get the stem and then match. We have experimented with both the approaches. In second case, before applying string comparison the stems of the Sanskrit word is obtained using Sanskrit Heritage Reader (Goyal et al., 2012; Goyal and Huet, 2016). For string matching, we have opted for edit-distance based string similarity algorithms. String distance metrics are simple, fast and can be applied without prior knowledge of data. Cohen et al. (2003) have used string distance metrics for name-matching tasks. They have explored edit distance-based and token-based methods for matching named entities and found that Jaro and Jaro-Winkler metrics are better for short strings. In our data, we observed that most of the names are single word entities. So, we have tried only the edit distance-based methods such as Levenshtein distance, Monger-Elkan distance, Jaro similarity, and Jaro-Winkler similarity. Overall, the best-performing method is Jaro-Winkler similarity.

4.1.1 Jaro-Winkler Similarity

In record-linkage literature, good results have been obtained using Jaro-Winkler (Cohen et al., 2003). The similarity between two strings is measured in the range $[0, 1]$ based on the number and order of the common characters. Jaro-Winkler similarity uses Jaro similarity. Given two strings s_1 and s_2, Jaro similarity between these is defined as

$$Jaro(s_1, s_2) = \begin{cases} \frac{1}{3}\left(\frac{m}{|s_1|} + \frac{m}{|s_2|} + \frac{m-t}{m}\right) & : m > 0 \\ 0 & : otherwise \end{cases} \tag{1}$$

where $|s_1|, |s_2|$ are the lengths of the two strings, m is the number of matching characters, and t is the number of transpositions. Two characters from s_1, s_2 respectively, are considered matching if the maximum distance between the characters is, $w = \frac{max(|s_1|,|s_2|)}{2} - 1$. So a character from s_1 is matching to a character in s_2 if it is similar to any character from s_2 within the range of w charters before and after. The Jaro-Winkler similarity increases the Jaro similarity value if both the strings have common prefixes.

$$JaroWinkler(s_1, s_2) = \begin{cases} Jaro(s_1, s_2) + l \cdot p \cdot (1 - Jaro(s_1, s_2)) & : Jaro(s_1, s_2) \geq b_t \\ Jaro(s_1, s_2) & : otherwise \end{cases} \tag{2}$$

l is the length of the common prefix of both strings up to a maximum l_{bound}, b_t is the boost threshold with default value 0.7, p is the prefix scale with default value 0.1, and $l_{bound} \cdot p \leq 1$ must holds true (Keil, 2019). For example, if we compare the two words *'kṛṣṇe'* and *'kṛṣṇa'* the Jaro value is 0.86, and both have common prefix of length 4. So the Jaro-Winkler value is boosted to 0.92.

4.1.2 Word Selection for Comparison

The annotation heuristic is improved further taking advantage of the fact that in English, named entities always start with a capital letter. For example, the word *'abhimanyunā'* is translated in the context as *'by the hero Abhimanyu'*. So only those Sanskrit words are selected which have at least one word in translation starting with a capital letter. To reduce the number of comparisons, we compare *'abhimanyunā'* only with *'Abhimanyu'* as it starts with a capital, and avoid comparing to remaining words. An English dictionary is also used to avoid comparison to general English words. For example, *'om'* is translated as *'O my Lord'*. Clearly, *'om'* is not NE but, *'O'* and *'om'* have very high similarity. Here, although *'O'* and *'Lord'* start with a capital, both are present in the English dictionary. So, we do not calculate similarity and 'om' is marked as non-NE.

Finally, as transliterated verses and many words in the English translation also in the scrapped data are in IAST transliteration scheme, before applying string matching strings are converted to ASCII and case folded. The procedure of pre-annotation is presented in Algorithm 1.

4.1.3 Gazetteer Based Classification

Gazetteer based NE identification is not so simple for Indian languages as names can be ambiguous. Many common words are used as names in Indian languages. Ambiguity between nouns and NEs is observed in many languages. But in Indian languages ambiguity occurs between names and adjectives, verbs and other parts-of-speech categories also (Saha and Majumder, 2018). The problem is more prevalent in Sanskrit. For example, *'karṇa'* is name of a character and also translates as ear.

So, we do not use the gazetteer for the identification of NEs. Instead we use it to the classification of already identified NEs by the previous step. The advantage of the dataset is that it provides word by word meaning in the context which makes word sense disambiguation easier. For example, the word *'sakarṇaduḥśāsanasaubalānā '* is present in the dataset in split form as four words: *'saḥ — He (the Lord); karṇa — Karṇa; duḥśāsana — Duḥśāsana; saubalānām — Saubala'*. Another word *'hṛtkarṇarasāyanāḥ'* is present as three words: *'hṛt — to the heart; karṇa — to the ear; rasa-ayanāḥ — pleasing;'*. So, we can easily classify *'karṇa'* in the first example as the name of a person.

Algorithm 1: Preannotation algorithm

```
Result: List of annotated verses
begin
    θ ← Jaro Winkler Similarity Threshold
    for verse in list_of_verses do
        for sanskrit_word in verse do
            english_translation ← GetTranslation(sanskrit_word)
            for word in english_translation do
                if StartsWithCapital(word) = TRUE then
                    if EnglishDictionary(word) = FALSE then
                        d ← JaroWinklerSimilarity(sanskrit_word, word)
                        if d > θ then
                            NE [sanskrit_word] ← TRUE
                            if sanskrit_word in Gazetteer then
                                Label [sanskrit_word] ← GetLabel(sanskrit_word)
```

4.2 Annotation Framework

We have deployed a web-based crowd-sourcing annotation tool.[0] The UI design is based on an open-source Django framework named Doccano (Nakayama et al., 2018). The open-source framework provides annotation features for sequence labeling tasks. It can collect annotations from multiple (non-expert) contributors with lower cost and higher speed. It has Unicode support to display Sanskrit text in different encoding.

Figure 2 illustrates the annotation environment and how the tool presents the pre-annotated suggestions for the verse. The **NER→** tag suggests to annotators that the next word is most likely a named entity. In the figure, a total of seven suggestions are given. In that, the two words *'yudhiṣṭhiraḥ'* and *'madhu'* are further suggested as name of PERSON. If annotators want to remove the suggested tag or to correct the tag, they can simply click on the cross symbol. A new tag can be assigned by selecting the word and then clicking the right type appearing on the top. They can also press the shown shortcut key for quick tagging. For example, *'ānarta'* is the name of a place but it is not pre-annotated. So, an annotator can select that word and press 'l' on the keyboard or click on the LOCATION tag to assign the new tag. Additionally, there is a metadata button. Annotators can use it to read the verse in Devanagari or can use the URL to read about it in detail.

The tool is hosted on the public domain and anyone can register and contribute, once admin approves the registration. Admin can assign three types of roles for crowd-sourcing, annotator, annotation approver and project admin.

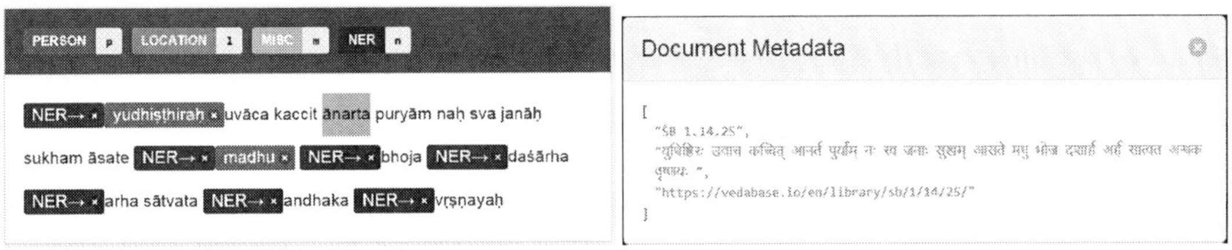

(a) A sample verse and tagging suggestions (b) Metadata

Figure 2: Annotation Environment

5 Experiment

To investigate the performance of the heuristics in the task of identification of NEs, we have experimented on a set of 60 manually annotated verses containing 997 words. 5 verses are selected randomly from each of the 12 cantos.To investigate the performance of the heuristics in the task of identification of NEs, we have experimented on a set of 60 manually annotated verses containing 997 words. 5 verses are selected randomly from each of the 12 cantos. We took the help of two annotators from Sanskrit background. The first annotator was given the raw verses and he adds 81 NE annotations. The second annotator was given the raw verses along with the annotations done by the previous annotator. The second annotator verified and accepted all those 81 NEs and added some additional NEs. However, as those additional NEs were not verified by a third person, we did not include it in our experiment. Both the annotators have used our deployed annotation platform for the task. So, it is a binary classification task where the classless are highly imbalanced, 81 NE and 916 non-NE words. We have reported Precision, Recall, and F-score only for NE class identification in Table 1. The F-score calculated is the harmonic mean between precision and recall.

$$P = \frac{True\ Positives}{(True\ Positives + False\ Positives)} \tag{3}$$

$$R = \frac{True\ Positives}{(True\ Positives + False\ Negatives)} \tag{4}$$

$$F1 = \frac{2 * P * R}{(P + R)} \tag{5}$$

As discussed earlier, the basic idea is to match the transliteration of a Sanskrit word with the words in English translation. The results in Table 1 shows the performance of two string matching algorithms, Levenstein distance, and Jaro-Winkler similarity. We also check the impact of

One annotator has Master and another has Doctorate degree

selecting only those words in English translation which starts with a capital and applying a dictionary to exclude general English words before performing string matching. Also, an experiment is done to check whether doing lemmatization of Sanskrit words before string matching improves the performance over using the actual word. The stems are obtained using SRH (Goyal et al., 2012).

If string similarity/distance between the Sanskrit transliteration and a word in the translation is above/below a certain threshold then the word in the translation is marked as NE. Changing the threshold value changes the performance of the heuristic. For Levenstein distance we tried thresholds in the range 0 to 8 and for Jaro-Winkler similarity in the range 0.5 to 1. Table 1 reports the maximum F1 value achieved using grid search over the range of thresholds.

	Using word			Using stem		
Heuristic	P	R	F1	P	R	F1
Levenstein	0.76	0.47	0.58	0.79	0.58	0.67
Capital + Levenstein	0.69	0.63	0.66	0.80	0.60	0.69
Capital + Dictionary + Levenstein	0.78	0.69	0.74	0.92	0.59	0.72
Jaro-Winkler	0.81	0.69	0.75	0.83	0.70	0.76
Capital + Jaro-Winkler	0.85	0.72	0.78	0.85	0.72	0.78
Capital + Dictionary + Jaro-Winkler	0.93	0.70	0.80	0.93	0.70	0.80

Table 1: Performance of different heuristics

Here we can observe, Jaro-Winkler is performing better than simple Levenstein distance. Also, checking whether the word starts with a capital and applying a dictionary to exclude general English words improves performance. It is observed that lemmatization improves performance if we use a tighter threshold value. For instance, if we apply direct string matching(Jaro-Winkler similarity threshold = 1), using stems 39 true positives(TPs) are identified while using the word 15 TPs are identified. But lemmatization is a costly operation and with tighter threshold though precision is high, recall drops reducing the overall F-score. Figure 3 plots the F-score of the best performing heuristic for different string matching threshold limits. The optimal threshold value for Jaro-Winkler similarity in both cases when matching is performed using the word and using the stems is 0.8. At this threshold, Jaro-Winkler similarity gives a similar performance without lemmatization also. So, the final pre-annotation of the data is done without performing lemmatization.

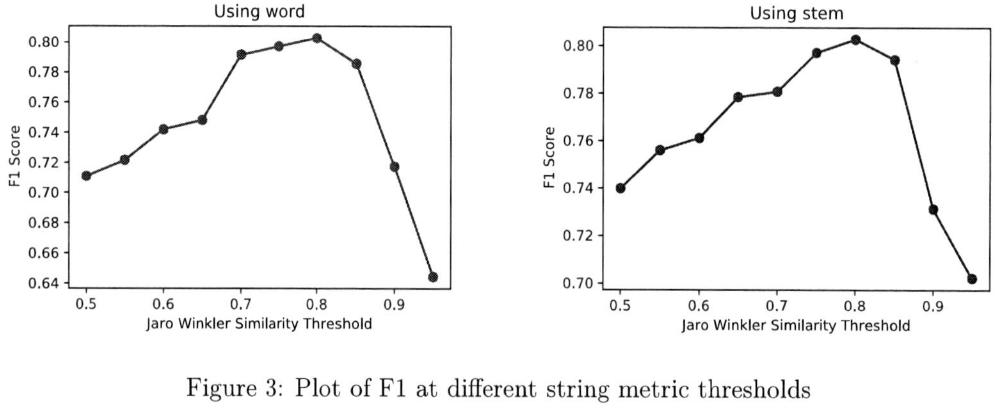

Figure 3: Plot of F1 at different string metric thresholds

6 Error Analysis

The heuristics work based on the assumption that NEs have a similar form in different languages. It is not always true. In *Bhāgavatam*, many times a single character has different names but in English translation uses only single name for all variation. For example, *'bhagavān rudraḥ'* is translated as *'Lord Śiva'*. So here the forms are not similar. Sometimes the translation instead of the name gives a description. For example, *'indra'* is translated as 'the King of heaven'. In another case, if the Sanskrit word is part of English vocabulary then also it is not marked. For example, *'buddhāya'* – *'to Lord Buddha'* , here *Budhha* is present in the dictionary as an English word, so the comparison is not done. The tool can be improved to handle these cases through dynamic suggestions. We have discussed it in Section 7.

7 Related Work

Our work aims to improve annotators' efficiency in preparing a Sanskrit NER dataset using pre-annotation. Pre-annotation has been wildly applied for the task of NER in different domains such as biomedical (Lingren et al., 2013), astrophysical (Hachey et al., 2005), etc. Lingren et al. (2013) studied the impact of pre-annotation on the speed of manual annotation of clinical trial announcements. They evaluated dictionary/gazetteer based approaches for pre-annotating entities related to symptoms and diseases. The study concluded that time savings were statistically significant and present in all of the experiments when the annotator used pre-annotated text. Savary et al. (2010) in their work of creating a largescale NE annotated dataset in Polish used a rule-based method to automatic pre-annotation of named entities, then the annotations are manually corrected and completed by linguistic experts. They customized a graphical tree editor TrEd to provide an annotation environment for manual correction of annotations. Similar works have been done for Indian regional languages also. Saha and Majumder (2018) developed a Hindi NER system without using any manually annotated training corpus. They prepared the initial training data using gazetteer and context patterns matching. They first extracted names from an English corpus using a pre-trained English NER system. Then the English gazetteer lists were used to transliterate into Hindi using a two-phase transliteration approach.

Annotation frameworks and tools are also developed which include some kind of pre-annotation module and use active learning to reduce the efforts of annotators. Yimam et al. (2014) applied their text annotation tool WebAnno that includes a machine learning component for automatic annotation suggestions of span annotations. They achieved an increase in annotation speed of about 21% with automatic suggestions in a German NE annotation project. Stenetorp et al. (2012) achieved 15% decrease in total annotation time using their rapid annotation tool BRAT on a multi-category entity mention annotation task by augmenting the annotation process with input from statistical and machine learning methods. Yang et al. (2018) from their experiment with open-source text span annotation tool YEDDA noted that annotation time can be compressed by 16.47% through intelligent recommendation. Experiments with more recent tools like EPAD showed that it shortened almost 60.0% of the total annotation time, and improved 12.7% of F-measure for annotation quality on a medical record named entity recognition task (Teng et al., 2019). Another tool, AlpacaTag which is implemented based on Doccano provides suggestions using active learning as well as a dictionary of frequent noun phrases and already annotated spans (Lin et al., 2019).

In computational Sanskrit, efforts are directed towards reducing annotation work by building software to allow semi-automated annotation. The SRH platform help linguists create a morphologically tagged corpus in a semi-automatic manner to reduce annotation labor (Goyal et al., 2012; Goyal and Huet, 2016). The interface allows a Sanskrit scholar to do segmentation (sandhi analysis), tagging, and parsing of a corpus by selecting from automatically presented words, stems, and morphological tags.

From these studies we hypothesize that one can take advantage of these approaches to easily build annotated resources for resource-poor languages like Sanskrit.

8 Conclusion and Future Direction

The approach to build Sanskrit NER dataset discussed in this paper is based on static pre-annotation. As there is no previous work in this direction, our work provides an overview and challenges of NER for Sanskrit. We explore the possibility of using external resources such as parallel corpora for the development of annotated datasets. An annotated dataset can help progress further research in this direction. Currently, in the annotation environment the annotators are given fixed suggestions based on the pre-annotation. The tool can be modified to improve the suggestions by taking into consideration the already annotated and verified annotation by annotators. To do so, we intend to integrate active learning strategy (Teng et al., 2019) in our system. Static suggestions also can be improved. The pre-annotation heuristic currently works based on language-independent string-matching algorithms by identifying strings of similar form in transliteration and translation of words. On a small manually annotated dataset it is able to perform reasonably with an F-measure of 0.80, precision 0.95 and recall 0.70. Language dependent analysis and rule-based approaches can be applied to handle difficult linguistic cases and to improve recall. Also, other approaches to compare the names, such as n-gram based approach (Jahangir et al., 2012), can be tested. Another way to improve the suggestions is by building a better gazetteer. One way the gazetteer can be improved is by identifying NEs from the translated text with the help of available NER systems of English (Saha and Majumder, 2018).

Acknowledgement

The authors are thankful to the anonymous reviewers for their valuable feedback. The authors would like to thank Malay Maity, University of Hyderabad, and Dr. Pavankumar Satuluri, Assitant Professor, Chinmaya Vishwavidyapeeth for their help in data annotation and helpful feedback.

References

Alexei Baevski, Sergey Edunov, Yinhan Liu, Luke Zettlemoyer, and Michael Auli. 2019. Cloze-driven pretraining of self-attention networks. In *Proceedings of the 2019 Conference on Empirical Methods in Natural Language Processing and the 9th International Joint Conference on Natural Language Processing (EMNLP-IJCNLP)*, pages 5360–5369, Hong Kong, China, November. Association for Computational Linguistics.

Kalina Bontcheva, Diana Maynard, Hamish Cunningham, and Horacio Saggion. 2002. Using human language technology for automatic annotation and indexing of digital library content. In Maristella Agosti and Costantino Thanos, editors, *Research and Advanced Technology for Digital Libraries*, pages 613–625, Berlin, Heidelberg. Springer Berlin Heidelberg.

Kalina Bontcheva, Hamish Cunningham, Ian Roberts, Angus Roberts, Valentin Tablan, Niraj Aswani, and Genevieve Gorrell. 2013. Gate teamware: a web-based, collaborative text annotation framework. *Language Resources and Evaluation*, 47(4):1007–1029.

Lars Borin, Dimitrios Kokkinakis, and Leif-Jöran Olsson. 2007. Naming the past: Named entity and Animacy recognition in 19th century Swedish literature. In *Proceedings of the Workshop on Language Technology for Cultural Heritage Data (LaTeCH 2007).*, pages 1–8, Prague, Czech Republic, June. Association for Computational Linguistics.

Lou Burnard and Syd Bauman. 2008. Tei p5: Guidelines for electronic text encoding and interchange.

Annalina Caputo, Pierpaolo Basile, and Giovanni Semeraro. 2009. Boosting a semantic search engine by named entities. In Jan Rauch, Zbigniew W. Raś, Petr Berka, and Tapio Elomaa, editors, *Foundations of Intelligent Systems*, pages 241–250, Berlin, Heidelberg. Springer Berlin Heidelberg.

Wei-Te Chen and Will Styler. 2013. Anafora: A web-based general purpose annotation tool. In *Proceedings of the 2013 NAACL HLT Demonstration Session*, pages 14–19, Atlanta, Georgia, June. Association for Computational Linguistics.

Danqi Chen, Adam Fisch, Jason Weston, and Antoine Bordes. 2017. Reading Wikipedia to answer open-domain questions. In *Proceedings of the 55th Annual Meeting of the Association for Computational Linguistics (Volume 1: Long Papers)*, pages 1870–1879, Vancouver, Canada, July. Association for Computational Linguistics.

Guillaume Chiron, Antoine Doucet, Mickaël Coustaty, Muriel Visani, and Jean-Philippe Moreux. 2017. Impact of ocr errors on the use of digital libraries: Towards a better access to information. In *Proceedings of the 17th ACM/IEEE Joint Conference on Digital Libraries*, JCDL '17, page 249–252. IEEE Press.

William W. Cohen, Pradeep Ravikumar, and Stephen E. Fienberg. 2003. A comparison of string distance metrics for name-matching tasks. In *Proceedings of the 2003 International Conference on Information Integration on the Web*, IIWEB'03, page 73–78. AAAI Press.

Pawan Goyal and Gérard Huet. 2016. Design and analysis of a lean interface for sanskrit corpus annotation. *Journal of Language Modelling*, 4:145, 10.

Pawan Goyal, Gérard Huet, Amba Kulkarni, Peter Scharf, and Ralph Bunker. 2012. A distributed platform for Sanskrit processing. In *Proceedings of COLING 2012*, pages 1011–1028, Mumbai, India, December. The COLING 2012 Organizing Committee.

Ben Hachey, Beatrice Alex, and Markus Becker. 2005. Investigating the effects of selective sampling on the annotation task. In *Proceedings of the Ninth Conference on Computational Natural Language Learning (CoNLL-2005)*, pages 144–151, Ann Arbor, Michigan, June. Association for Computational Linguistics.

Faryal Jahangir, Waqas Anwar, Usama Ijaz Bajwa, and Xuan Wang. 2012. N-gram and gazetteer list based named entity recognition for Urdu: A scarce resourced language. In *Proceedings of the 10th Workshop on Asian Language Resources*, pages 95–104, Mumbai, India, December. The COLING 2012 Organizing Committee.

Daniel Jurafsky and James H. Martin. 2009. *Speech and Language Processing (2nd Edition)*. Prentice-Hall, Inc., USA.

Jan Martin Keil. 2019. Efficient bounded jaro-winkler similarity based search. *BTW 2019*.

Amrith Krishna, Pavan Kumar Satuluri, and Pawan Goyal. 2017. A dataset for Sanskrit word segmentation. In *Proceedings of the Joint SIGHUM Workshop on Computational Linguistics for Cultural Heritage, Social Sciences, Humanities and Literature*, pages 105–114, Vancouver, Canada, August. Association for Computational Linguistics.

Amrith Krishna. 2019. *Addressing Language Specific Characteristics for Data-Driven Modelling of Lexical, Syntactic and Prosodic Tasks in Sanskrit*. Ph.D. thesis, IIT, Kharagpur.

Anil Kumar, Vipul Mittal, and Amba Kulkarni. 2010. Sanskrit compound processor. In Girish Nath Jha, editor, *Sanskrit Computational Linguistics*, pages 57–69, Berlin, Heidelberg. Springer Berlin Heidelberg.

Bill Yuchen Lin, Dong-Ho Lee, Frank F. Xu, Ouyu Lan, and Xiang Ren. 2019. AlpacaTag: An active learning-based crowd annotation framework for sequence tagging. In *Proceedings of the 57th Annual Meeting of the Association for Computational Linguistics: System Demonstrations*, pages 58–63, Florence, Italy, July. Association for Computational Linguistics.

Todd Lingren, Louise Deleger, Katalin Molnar, Haijun Zhai, Jareen Meinzen-Derr, Megan Kaiser, Laura Stoutenborough, Qi Li, and Imre Solti. 2013. Evaluating the impact of pre-annotation on annotation speed and potential bias: natural language processing gold standard development for clinical named entity recognition in clinical trial announcements. *Journal of the American Medical Informatics Association*, 21(3):406–413, 09.

Liyuan Liu, Jingbo Shang, Xiang Ren, Frank Fangzheng Xu, Huan Gui, Jian Peng, and Jiawei Han. 2018. Empower sequence labeling with task-aware neural language model. In *Thirty-Second AAAI Conference on Artificial Intelligence*.

Hiroki Nakayama, Takahiro Kubo, Junya Kamura, Yasufumi Taniguchi, and Xu Liang. 2018. doccano: Text annotation tool for human. Software available from https://github.com/doccano/doccano.

Sujan Kumar Saha and Mukta Majumder. 2018. Development of a hindi named entity recognition system without using manually annotated training corpus. *International Arab Journal of Information Technology*, 15:1088–1098, 11.

Agata Savary, Jakub Waszczuk, and Adam Przepiórkowski. 2010. Towards the annotation of named entities in the national corpus of polish. In *Proceedings of the Seventh International Conference on Language Resources and Evaluation (LREC'10)*, Valletta, Malta, May. European Language Resources Association (ELRA).

Pontus Stenetorp, Sampo Pyysalo, Goran Topić, Tomoko Ohta, Sophia Ananiadou, and Jun'ichi Tsujii. 2012. brat: a web-based tool for NLP-assisted text annotation. In *Proceedings of the Demonstrations at the 13th Conference of the European Chapter of the Association for Computational Linguistics*, pages 102–107, Avignon, France, April. Association for Computational Linguistics.

Beth M. Sundheim. 1995. Overview of results of the MUC-6 evaluation. In *Sixth Message Understanding Conference (MUC-6): Proceedings of a Conference Held in Columbia, Maryland, November 6-8, 1995.*

Fei Teng, Minbo Ma, Zheng Ma, Lufei Huang, Ming Xiao, and Xuan Li. 2019. A text annotation tool with pre-annotation based on deep learning. In Christos Douligeris, Dimitris Karagiannis, and Dimitris Apostolou, editors, *Knowledge Science, Engineering and Management*, pages 440–451, Cham. Springer International Publishing.

Erik F. Tjong Kim Sang and Fien De Meulder. 2003. Introduction to the CoNLL-2003 shared task: Language-independent named entity recognition. In *Proceedings of the Seventh Conference on Natural Language Learning at HLT-NAACL 2003*, pages 142–147.

Monier Monier Williams, Ernst Leumann, and Carl Cappeller. 1899. *A Sanskrit-English dictionary: Etymologically and philologically arranged with special reference to Cognate Indo-European languages.* At the Clarendon Press.

Bishan Yang and Tom M. Mitchell. 2016. Joint extraction of events and entities within a document context. In *Proceedings of the 2016 Conference of the North American Chapter of the Association for Computational Linguistics: Human Language Technologies*, pages 289–299, San Diego, California, June. Association for Computational Linguistics.

Jie Yang, Yue Zhang, Linwei Li, and Xingxuan Li. 2018. YEDDA: A lightweight collaborative text span annotation tool. In *Proceedings of ACL 2018, System Demonstrations*, pages 31–36, Melbourne, Australia, July. Association for Computational Linguistics.

Seid Muhie Yimam, Chris Biemann, Richard Eckart de Castilho, and Iryna Gurevych. 2014. Automatic annotation suggestions and custom annotation layers in WebAnno. In *Proceedings of 52nd Annual Meeting of the Association for Computational Linguistics: System Demonstrations*, pages 91–96, Baltimore, Maryland, June. Association for Computational Linguistics.

Disambiguation of Instrumental, Dative and Ablative Case suffixes in Sanskrit

Malay Maity, Sanjeev Panchal and Amba Kulkarni
{malayoham,snjvpnchl}@gmail.com, ambapradeep@gmail.com
Department of Sanskrit Studies,
University of Hyderabad

Abstract

Ambiguity is an integral part of any natural language. There are only seven different case markers in Sanskrit that encode both *kāraka* as well non-*kāraka* relations. This introduces an ambiguity at the level of case markers leading to a structural level ambiguity. Two most frequent relations expressed by the ablative case suffix are *apādāna* and *hetu*, by the dative case suffix are *sampradāna* and *prayojana*, and by the instrumental case suffix are *karaṇa* and *hetu*. The first among these pairs is a *kāraka* relation and the second one a non-*kāraka* relation. It is the *yogyatā* between the word meanings that plays an important role in the deciphering of these relations. In this paper we illustrate how by using minimum ontological information such as *dravya* and *guṇavacana*, we can get the correct solution in almost 80% of the cases.

1 Introduction

Ambiguity is an integral part of any natural language. A speaker while expressing his thoughts through language always encounters a tension between precision and brevity. The precision in linguistic expressions brings in clarity. But the natural tendency of a human being is to go for brevity. For example, look at the sentence

Skt: Rāmaḥ Śyāmāya pustakaṃ krīṇāti. (1)
Gloss: Rāma{m, sg, nom} Śyāma{m, sg, dat} book{n, sg, acc} purchase{pr, sg, 3p}
Eng: Rāma purchases a book for Syāma.

On the face of it, we will not find any difficulty in understanding it. But if we try to analyse it deciding the relations between various words, we notice that the word *Śyāmāya* is not directly related to the verb *kṛ* by any *kāraka* relation, nor it is related to any other word in the sentence by any direct relation. A grammarian would relate *Śyāma* to the action of *kṛ* by the relation of *prayojana* (purpose). But to be precise, it is not *Śyāma* but 'giving a book to Śyāma' is the purpose. Sentence (2) provides the precise expression providing this meaning literally.

Skt: Rāmaḥ Śyāmāya dātuṃ pustakaṃ krīṇāti. (2)
Gloss: Rāma{m, sg, nom} Śyāma{m, sg, dat} give{infinitive} book{n, sg, acc} purchase{pr, sg, 3p}
Eng: Rāma purchased a book for giving it to Śyāma.

In this sentence *Śyāma* is the *sampradāna* (beneficiary) for the action of giving (*dā*). Though the relations are different in both the sentences, they are expressed by the same dative case marker, making the dative case marker ambiguous.

The second reason for ambiguity is the lexical overloading. The conceptual space is a continuum while the words are the discrete representation of these concepts. This leads to the overloading

Proceedings of the Computational Sanskrit and Digital Humanities, 18th World Sanskrit Conference 2023, pages 71–88

sentence

Skt: Devadattaḥ odanaṃ pacati. (3)
Gloss: Devadatta{m, sg, nom} rice{n, sg, acc} cook{pr, sg, 3p}
Eng: Devadatta cooks rice.

the *vyāpāra* (activity) referred to by *pacati* is described as

adhiśrayaṇodakāsecanataṇḍulāvapanaidho'pakarṣaṇakriyāḥ (ma. bhā. 1.4.23. vā 8)
[an activity of putting a vessel on the stove, pouring water in it, adding rice, supplying fuel etc. and this activity refers to the activity of the *pradhāna kartṛ* (the chief doer of the activity).]

In the sentence
Skt: *sthālī pacati.* (4)
Gloss: vessel {f, sg, nom} cook{pr, sg, 3p}
Eng: A vessel cooks.

the activity is that of *dhāraṇa* (holding) (ma. bhā. 1.4.23.vā 9).

Finally, in the case of
Skt: edhāḥ pakṣyanti. (5)
Gloss: Wood{n, pl, nom} cook{fut, pl, 3p}
Eng: Wood will cook.

the activity is that of *jvalanakriyā* (to provide fire). (ma. bhā. 1.4.23.vā 10).

We observe that the same word *pacati* is being used to refer to different activities. Similarly the *prātipadikas* are also overloaded. These ambiguities in the meanings of the verbal roots and the nominal stems may be due to either homonymy or polysemy.

The third source of ambiguity is the linear representation of the underlying dependency or the constituency tree structure. When a two dimensional tree structure is flattened to a linear structure, loss of information is natural. The stock example of structural level ambiguity in a positional language like English is

He saw a man on the hill with a telescope. (6)

The ambiguity in this sentence is due to multiple possibilities of the attachment of the prepositional phrase 'with a telescope' to

- 'saw', where a telescope is an instrument,
- 'the hill', where a telescope is installed on the hill, and
- 'a man', where he is carrying a telescope.

Here we see that the ambiguity is essentially due to the overloading of the preposition to mark a relation of a noun phrase 'a telescope' with the verb ('saw') as well as another noun phrase ('a man' or 'the hill') and the flexibility of placement of the prepositional phrase not necessarily adjacent to the noun with which it is connected to.

Here is an example from Sanskrit which has a structural ambiguity.

Skt: Rāmaḥ kadaliphalaṃ chittvā khādantaṃ vānaraṃ paśyati. (7)
Gloss: Rāma{m, sg, nom} banana{n, sg, acc} after_peeling eating{m, sg, acc} monkey{m, sg,

acc} see{pr, sg, 3p}.
Eng: Rāma sees a monkey peeling a banana and eating it / Rāma, while peeling a banana, sees a monkey who is eating.

The ambiguity is related to the doer of the activity of peeling a banana. The *sūtra samānakartṛkayoḥ pūrvakāle* (3.4.21) says that if the two activities have the same *kartṛ* and one activity precedes another activity then the *kṛt* suffix *ktvā* is used with the verb that denotes the preceding activity. Now in this sentence, there are three activities viz. peeling, eating and seeing. And the verb *chittvā* 'peeling' is the preceding activity. If this peeling activity precedes the eating activity, then the monkey, who is the *kartṛ* of the eating activity, would also be the *kartṛ* of activity of peeling. If the eating activity precedes the activity of seeing, then the *kartṛ* of the peeling would be Rāma, the *kartṛ* of the activity of seeing.

Thus brevity and linear representation lead to an overloading at the lexical as well as structural level. In the process of interpretation, a reader or a listener uses various clues both linguistic as well as extra-linguistic to decipher such ambiguities. The mutual meaning compatibility between the words/components involved often helps resolve such ambiguities. In this paper we focus on the ambiguities due to the case markers, and suggest a method for automatic disambiguation of such cases.

In the next section, we look at the overloading of case markers in Sanskrit. This is followed by a discussion on the clues from the theories of *śābdabodha* for disambiguation. In the fourth section we look at the Pāṇinian *sūtras* which provide various semantic and/or syntactic conditions for the assignment of instrumental, dative and ablative case suffixes to the nouns. In the fifth section we show how the minimum ontological property of *dravya* and *guṇavacana* help in pruning out the wrong solutions. Finally we provide the results of evaluation and conclude with the observations.

2 Overloading of case markers

There are only seven different case markers that encode both *kāraka* as well non-*kāraka* relations. A list of various semantic relations between the words in a sentence was compiled by Ramakrishnamacaryulu (2009). This list contains a little over hundred relations. This list was further shortened by Kulkarni and Ramakrishnamacharyulu (2013) from the computational point of view by removing certain fine-grain distinctions of some *kāraka* relations such as *anubhavakartṛ*, *karmakartṛ*, *karaṇakartṛ* and so on. The main reason for removing these fine-grained relations is that in order to mark these relations, one needs an extra linguistic information. For example, in the sentence *kāṣṭhāni pacanti* 'the wood cook', to mark *kāṣṭha* as a *karaṇakartṛ*, one needs to know that it can be used as an instrument. This list of relations was later extended by adding semantic relations encoded by the *upapadas* (Madhusoodan, 2020; Panchal, 2020; Kulkarni, 2019 20), in the course of developing a parser and generator for Sanskrit. The list currently being in use is given in Appendix A, and has 56 relations.

Table 1 lists all the relations from this list, between a noun and a verb, and between two nouns extracted from the Appendix A, which take either the instrumental, dative or an ablative case marker.

From this table we note that all the three case markers viz. instrumental, dative and ablative are ambiguous between more than one relation. The instrumental case suffix is ambiguous between the four[1] relations viz *kartṛ, prayojakakartṛ, karaṇa*, and *hetu* (cause/reason). Sentences (9) and (10) illustrate the ambiguity due to the instrumental case.

[1]The cases of kriyāviśeṣaṇa, apavargasambandhaḥ and aṅgavikāraḥ involve words which more-or-less forms a closed list, and hence are not discussed here.

Relation	Case-marker
kartā	3 (Passive voice)
prayojakakartā	3 (Passive voice)
kriyāviśeṣaṇam	2,3
karaṇam	3
apavargasambandhaḥ	3
aṅgavikāraḥ	3
hetuḥ	3,5
sampradānam	4
prayojanam	4
apādānam	5
vibhaktam	5

Table 1: Ambiguities with case markers

Skt : *pituḥ ājñayā Rāmeṇa hastena phalaṃ khādyate.* (9)
Gloss: Father{m, sg, gen} permission{f, sg, inst} Rāma{m, sg, inst} hand{m, sg, inst} fruit{n, sg, nom} eat{pr, sg, 3p, passive}
Eng: With father's permission a fruit is eaten by Rāma with a hand.

In this sentence, *ājñā* is a *hetuḥ*, *Rāma* is the *kartṛ* and *hasta* is the *karaṇa*. In the case of a sentence in an active voice, the *kartṛ* being in nominative, the ambiguity is only between *karaṇa* and *hetu* as in (10).

Skt : *Daśarathasya ājñayā Rāmaḥ rathena vanaṃ gacchati.* (10)
Gloss: Daśaratha{m, sg, gen} permission{f, sg, inst} Rāma{m, sg, nom} chariot{m, sg, inst} forest{n, sg, acc} go{pr, sg, 3p}
Eng: With Daśaratha's permission Rāma goes to the forest by a chariot.

In the case of dative case, the ambiguity is between *sampradāna*, *prayojana* and *tādarthya.*[2]

Skt : *rājā brāhmaṇāya yāgāya dāru dadāti.* (11)
Gloss: The king{m, sg, nom} brāhmaṇa{m, sg, dat} sacrifice{m, sg, dat} wood{n, sg, acc} give{pr, sg, 3p}
Eng: The king gives a wood to a brāhmaṇa for sacrifice.

Skt : *rājā brāhmaṇāya yūpāya dāru dadāti.* (12)
Gloss: The king{m, sg, nom} brāhmaṇa{m, sg, dat} sacrificial_post{m, sg, dat} wood{n, sg, acc} give{pr, sg, 3p}
Eng: The king gives a wood to brāhmaṇa for (making) a sacrificial post.

In both sentences (11) and (12), *brāhmaṇa* is the *sampradāna*. In sentence (11) *yāgāya* is the *prayojana* for the action expressed by *dadāti* while in sentence (12) *yūpāya* is the *tādarthya* for *dāru*.

In the case of ablative case, the ambiguity is between an *apādāna, hetu* and *vibhakta* as shown in sentences (13) to (15).

[2]Tādarthya is not included in Table 1 or in Appendix A. The reason for its non-inclusion is discussed in section 4.1.3

Skt : vṛkṣāt parṇaṃ patati.(13)
Gloss: Tree{m, sg, abl} leaf{n, sg, nom} fall{pr, sg, 3p}
Eng: A leaf falls from a tree.

Skt : Rāmāt Śyāmaḥ nipuṇaḥ asti. (14)
Gloss: Rāma{m, sg, abl} Śyāma{m, sg, nom} smarter{m, sg, nom} be{pr, sg, 3p}
Eng: Śyāma is smarter than Rāma.

Skt : dhūmāt vahniḥ bhavati iti tarkaḥ kriyate. (15)
Gloss: smoke{m, sg, abl} fire{m, sg, nom} be{pr, sg, 3p} argue{m, sg, nom} do{pr, sg, 3p}
Eng: It is argued that the smoke causes fire.

In addition, in each of the cases, the adjective of these *kārakās* show concord with their head, and hence will have the same vibhakti. For example

Skt : vīreṇa Rāmeṇa tīkṣṇena bāṇena Vāliḥ hanyate. (16)
Gloss: Brave{m, sg, inst} Rāma{m, sg, inst} sharp{m, sg, ins} arrow{m, sg, ins} Vāli{m, sg, nom} kill{pr, sg, 3p, passive}
Eng: Vāli was killed by the brave Rāma by a sharp arrow.

Here the words *vīreṇa* and *tīkṣṇena* are the adjectives of *Rāmeṇa* and *bāṇena* respectively.

3 Handling ambiguity

The multiple choices exist both at the stage of generation as well as at the stage of analysis. During the generation process, the speaker based on his intention chooses an appropriate alternative among the multiple choices available. At the time of analysis, since the speaker's intention is not known to the listener, and due to the reasons mentioned earlier that result in ambiguous linguistic expressions, listener has an extra task of choosing the correct analysis among all possible analyses. The Indian theories of *śābdabodha* discuss three different factors viz. *ākāṁkṣā*, *yogyatā* and *sannidhi* to understand any text.[3] These factors help in resolving the ambiguity. *Ākāṁkṣā* helps in correctly identifying the relations between words following the Pāṇinian grammar and the usage (*loka-vyavahāra*). *Sannidhi* puts restrictions on the sentential structure. *Yogyatā* provides the semantic constraints on the establishment of relations between the words. While *ākāṅkṣā* provides a necessary condition for establishing a relation, *yogyatā* and *sannidhi* provide the sufficient conditions.

4 *Ākāṅkṣā*: necessary condition

In what follows now we look at the clues from the *Aṣṭādhyāyī* as the necessary condition for establishing the possible relations with ablative, dative and instrumental case markers.

4.1 Ablative Case Marker

In *Aṣṭādhyāyī*, *Pāṇini* has given nine different rules for designating *apādāna*. He starts with the rule

> *Dhruvamapāye apādānam* (1.4.24)
> [the fixed point in relation to moving away is called *apādānam*.][4]

[3]Earlier these were discussed by Kumarilabhatta in `Tantravārtikam`. Later on, these were also discussed by Grammarian and Logician.

[4]The English translations are borrowed from (Joshi and Roodbergen, 1975)

For example:

Skt: saḥ grāmāt āgacchati.(17)
Gloss: He{m, sg, nom} village{m, sg, abl} come{pr, sg, 3p}
Eng: He comes from village.

Here the *grāma*(village) is the fixed point with respect to moving away. So, it gets *apādāna* designation. This rule tells us the verbs which have an activity related to movement have an expectancy of *apādāna kāraka*. Pāṇini further lists several cases along with some specific verbs to define *apādāna*. These *sūtras* are provided in the *Aṣṭādhyāyī* from 1.4.25 to 1.4.31. They are as follow:

> *Bhītrārthānāṃ bhayahetuḥ* - 1.4.25
> [With having the meaning of *bhī* "fearing" or *trā* "protecting" the term which causes fear is called *apādānam*.]
>
> *Parājerasoḍhaḥ* - 1.4.26
> [With the verbal base *parā- ji* "to be overcome" the item which one cannot endure is called *apādānam*]
>
> *Vāraṇārthānām īpsitaḥ* - 1.4.27
> [With the verbal bases having the meaning of *vāraṇa* "warding off" the item desired to be reached is called *apādāna*, when it becomes instrumental in bringing about the action.]
>
> *Antarddhau yenādarśanamicchati* - 1.4.28
> [The person by whom one wishes not to be seen through the use of something which comes in between in called *apādāna*, when it becomes instrumental in bringing about the action.]
>
> *Ākhyātopayoge* - 1.4.29
> [The person who relates is called *apādāna*, when it becomes instrumental in bringing about the action provided that what he relates is useful.]
>
> *Janikartuḥ prakṛtiḥ* - 1.4.30
> [The material origin of the agent of the action denoted by the verbal base *jñā* - "to originate from" is called *apādāna*, when it becomes instrumental in bringing about the action.]
>
> *Bhuvaḥ prabhavaḥ* - 1.4.31
> [The source of the agent of the action denoted by the verbal base *bhū* - "to become" is called *apādāna*, when it becomes instrumental in bringing about the action.]

In this way, Pāṇini provides either a list of verbs or specifies the meaning of verbs which have the expectancy of *apādāna kāraka*.

4.1.1 Vibhakta (Isolated)

The second use of ablative case suffix is in the sense of *vibhakta*. This is a non-*kāraka* relation and is defined by the Pāṇini's *sūtra*

Pañcamī vibhakte - 2.3.42
[The fifth case endings are added after a *prātipadika* provided the referent is singled out or separated from another referent or a group on the basis of some property.]

For example:

Skt: Māthurāḥ Pāṭaliputrakebhyaḥ āḍhyatarāḥ santi. (18)
Gloss: the_inhabitantas_of_Mathurā{m, pl, nom} the_inhabitantas_of_Pāṭaliputra{m, pl, abl} richer{m, pl, nom} be{p, sg, 3p}
Eng: The inhabitants of Mathurā are more richer than the inhabitants of Pāṭaliputra.

Two other examples of this category are given below.

Skt: tayoḥ karmasannyāsāt karmayogaḥ viśiṣyate. (19)
Gloss: Among{n, pl, loc} karmasannyāsa{m, sg, abl} karmayoga{m, sg, nom} specify{p, sg, 3p, passive}
Eng: Among the two karamayoga(yoga of action) is better than karmasannyāsa(renunciation of action).

Skt: Rāmaḥ Śyāmāt nipuṇaḥ asti. (20)
Gloss: Rāma{n, sg, nom} Śyāma{m, sg, abl} smarter{n, sg, nom} be{p, sg, 3p}
Eng: Rāma is smarter than Śyāma.

4.1.2 *Hetu* (cause / reason)

The third major use of ablative case suffix is to mark the *hetu* (cause/reason). This time the word which is preffered to be a cause should be a guṇavācaka but not a feminine. The Pāṇini's *sūtra* definines these conditions as

vibhāṣā guṇe'striyām 2.3.25
[The fifth case endings are better not added after a *prātipadika* in the sense of *hetu* "ground, reason", when reference is to a *guṇa* "quality", provided that the *prātipadika* concerned is non-feminine.]

Here is an example.

Skt: jāḍyāt saḥ baddhaḥ. (21)
Gloss: Stupidity{n, sg, abl} he{m, sg, nom} imprisoned{m, sg, nom}
Eng: He was imprisoned on account of his stupidity.

4.2 Dative Case Marker

The dative case in Sanskrit is used to mark the *Sampradāna* (beneficiary) kāraka relation predominantly. In addition it is also used to mark two non-*kāraka* relations of *prayojana* (purpose) and *tādarthya* (being a thing for the sake of that).

4.2.1 *Sampradāna* (beneficiary)

Pāṇini in the *Aṣṭādhyāyī* has stated ten *sūtras* that provide the semantics of *sampradāna* followed by some exceptional cases that are extensions of the semantic definition of the *sampradāna kāraka*. The first *sūtra* which defines the *sampradāna* is:

> *Karmaṇā yamabhipraiti sa sampradānam* 1.4.32
> [The item which one has in view through the *karman* is called *sampradāna* when it becomes instrumental in bringing about an action.]

Here is an example:

Skt: Rāmaḥ brāhmaṇāya dhanaṃ dadāti. (22)
Gloss: Rāma{m, sg, nom} Brahmin{m, sg, dat} money{n, sg, acc} give{pr, sg, 3p}
Eng: Rāma gives money to a brahmin.

In the activity of giving, the *kartṛ* viz. Rāma aims at Brāhmin by offering him the money. Hence Brahmin is termed as a *sampradāna*.
Pāṇini further lists several exceptional cases where a verb assigns a dative case suffix to a noun it governs, however it is not obvious that the relation is that of beneficiary. For example, consider the Pāṇini's *sūtra*

> *Rucyarthānāṃ prīyamāṇaḥ* 1.4.33
> [With (verbal base) having the meaning of ruc - "to please" the one who is being pleased is called *sampradāna*, when he becomes instrumental in bringing about the action.]

The example sentence is:

Skt: Devadattāya modakaḥ rocate. (23)
Gloss: Devadatta{m, sg, dat} modaka{m, sg, nom} please{p, sg, 3p}.
Eng: Modaka pleases Devadatta.

In *sūtras* from 1.4.34 till 1.4.39, Pāṇini covers a few more special case of verbs that assign dative case to the nouns with a specific semantic condition, and he terms all such relations as *Sampradāna*. These *sūtras* are:

1. *ślāgha-hnuṅ-sthā-śapāṃ jñīpsyamānaḥ* - 1.4.34
   [With (the verbal base) *ślāgha* "to praise", *hnuṅ* "to hide oneself", *sthā* "to position", *śapāṃ* "to curse" the one who is desired to be informed is called *sampradāna* when he becomes instrumental in bringing about an action.]

2. *Dhāreḥ uttamarṇaḥ* - 1.4.35
   [With the causative verbal base *dhāri* "to owe" the creditor is called *sampradāna* when he becomes instrumental in bringing about an action.]

3. *Spṛheḥ īpsitaḥ* - 1.4.36
   [With the verbal base *spṛha* "to long for" the item desired to be reached is called *sampradāna* when he becomes instrumental in bringing about an action.]

4. *Krudha-druh-erṣyā-asūyā-arthānāṃ yaṃ prati kopaḥ* - 1.4.37
   [With the verbal base having the meaning of *Krudha* "to be angry", *druha* "to harm", *īrṣyā* "to be jealous" and *asūyā* "to find fault" the person towards whom anger (etc.) is directed is called *sampradāna* when he becomes instrumental in bringing about an action.]

5. *Rādhi-īkṣyoḥ yasya vipraśnaḥ* - 1.4.39
   [With the verbal base *rādhi* "to propitiate" and *īkṣi* "to look" the person about whom different questions are asked is called *sampradāna* when he becomes instrumental in bringing about an action.]

6. *Prati-āṅbhyāṃ śruvaḥ pūrvasya kartā* - 1.4.40
   [In connection with *śru* "to hear" preceded by prati and āṅ the agent(*kartā*) of the prior action of requesting is called *sampradāna* when he becomes instrumental in bringing about an action.]

7. *Anu-prati-gṛṇaḥ ca* - 1.4.41
   [Also with the verbal base *gṛ* "to call out" preceded by *anu* and *prati* the agent(*kartā*) of the earlier action is called *sampradāna* when he becomes instrumental in bringing about an action.]

8. *Parikrayaṇe sampradānam anyatarasyām* - 1.4.44
   [With regard to the action of hiring the most effective means is indifferently called *sampradāna* when he becomes instrumental in bringing about an action.]

Thus, Pāṇini provides either a list of all the verbs which assign dative case to its noun in the sense of beneficiary or specifies the meaning of the verbs (leaving the discretion of inclusion of a verb into this list to the speaker) that assign dative case to the noun in the given semantic sense.

There is one more exceptional case where dative case is used with the motion verbs to denote a *karman*, as in the sūtra:-

> *Gatyarthakarmaṇi dvitīyacaturthyau ceṣṭāyām anadhvani* -2.3.12
> [The second or the fourth case endings are added after a *prātipadika* in the sense of *karman* "(direct) object" of verbs of going, provided that movement actually occurs, except the object is the word *adhvan* "road".]

For example:

Skt: saḥ grāmāya vrajati. (26)
Gloss: He{m, sg, nom} village{m, sg, dat} go_out{pr, sg, 3p}
Eng: He proceeds to village.

In this case there is a condition that the action should be physical and not mental. Thus the following sentence is ungrammatical.

Skt: manasā saḥ Pāṭaliputrāya gacchati. (27)
Gloss: Mind{n, sg, inst} He{m, sg, nom} Pāṭaliputra{m, sg, dat} go{pr, sg, 3p}
Eng: He goes to Pāṭaliputra in his thoughts.

4.2.2 *Prayojana* (purpose)

Barring these verbs, in all other cases when a noun in dative case is related to a verb, the relation is that of *prayojana* (purpose). For example;

Skt: pākāya vrajati. (24)
Gloss: cooking{m, sg, abl} go_out{pr, sg, 3p}
Eng: (He) goes out in order to cook.

Here is another example.

Skt: randhanāya sthālī asti (25)
Gloss: cooking{n, sg, dat} pot{f, sg, nom} be{p, sg, 3p}
Eng: The pot is for cooking.

4.2.3 *Tādarthya* (Thing for the sake of that)

The third use of dative case suffix is to mark a relation of a noun with another noun when the first one is for the sake of the second one. The stock example of this relation is

Skt: yūpāya dāru asti. (28)
Gloss: Sacrificial post{m, sg, dat} wood{n, sg, nom} be{pr, sg, 3p}
Eng: The wood is for the sacrificial post.

Here the relation of *yūpa* is with *dāru*. But in this case also, there is an underlying verb *nirmāṇa* 'for the construction' (of a sacrificial post), and then with this verb, *yūpāya* becomes a purpose.[5] Therefore, in such cases also we mark the relation of *yūpāya* with the finite verb(*asti*) as a *prayojana*, and do not mark it as a relation between *yūpa* and *dāru*, as the tradition does. We have taken this decision for the following reasons.

1. As shown above, with every relation of *tādarthya*, there is an underlying action associated with it, which acts as a purpose (*prayojana*) for the main action.
2. Secondly, from the computational point of view, this brings in coarsity in the analysis resulting in a better performance.

4.3 Instrumental Case

In Sanskrit the instrumental case is used to mark three *kāraka* relations viz. *kartṛ*, *karaṇa* (an instrument) and *prayojaka kartṛ* (a causer), if they are not expressed by any other means such as verbal suffix etc.[6] In active voice, since the *kartṛ* is expressed by the verbal suffix, it is in nominative case. Only in the passive voice (*karmaṇi*) and the impersonal (*bhāve*) voice, the *kartṛ* is in the instrumental case. In the causative constructions, in passive voice, the *prayojaka kartṛ* is in instrumental case. Here are some examples.

Skt: Rāmaḥ bāṇena Vālim̥ hanti. (29)
Gloss: Rāma{m, sg, nom} arrow{m, sg, inst} Vāli{m, sg, acc} kill{pr, sg, 3p}
Eng: Rāma kills Vāli with an arrow.

In this sentence *bāṇa* in instrumental case and is the *karaṇa* (instrumental).

Skt: Rāmeṇa bāṇena Vāliḥ hanyate. (30)
Gloss: Rāma{m, sg, inst} arrow{m, sg, inst} Vāli{m, sg, nom} kill{pr, sg, 3p, passive}
Eng: Vāli is killed by Rāma with an arrow.

In this sentence two nouns viz. *Rāmeṇa* and *bāṇena* are in instrumental case, of which the first one is a *kartṛ* and the second one is a *karaṇa*.

Skt: mātrā śiśuḥ dugdham̥ pāyayate (31)
Gloss: Mother{f, sg, inst} child{m, sg, nom} milk{n, sg, acc} feed{pr, sg, 3p, passive}
Eng: The milk is fed to child by his mother.

In this sentence mother is a causer and the causative verb is in passive voice. Therefore it is in instrumental case.

In addition, the instrumental suffix also marks the relation of *hetu* (cause/reason). Here is an example:

Skt: saḥ adhyayanena atra vasati. (32)
Gloss: He{n, sg, nom} study{n, sg, inst} here{ind} stay{pr, sg, 3p}
Eng: He stays here because of study.

In this sentence the noun *ahyayanena* which is in the instrumental case is the *hetu* (cause/reason) for the stay.

The vārttika *prakṛtyābhya upasamkhyānam*[7] assigns instrumental case to the words belonging

[5] vā. tādarthye caturthī vācyā - siddhāntakaumudī, vol-I
[6] kartṛkaraṇayoḥ tṛtīyā (2.3.18)
[7] Under kartṛkaraṇayostṛtīyā(2.3.18) in the Mahābhāṣya

to this *gaṇa*. This is an open list. Here is an example.

Skt: saḥ prakṛtyā cāruḥ asti. (33)
Gloss: He{m, sg, nom} nature{f, sg, inst} good{m, sg, nom} be{pr, sg, 3p}
Eng: He is good by nature.

Pāṇini's *sūtra yenāṅgavikāraḥ* (2.3.20) assigns an instrumental case to the words denoting a cause for deformity, as in the following.

Skt: akṣṇā kāṇaḥ. (34)
Gloss: Eye{n, sg, inst} blind{n, sg, nom}
Eng: Blind with eye.

5 *Yogyatā*: sufficient condition

Now let us come to the problem of analysis. In order to choose among the possible relations proposed by the condition of expectancy, we need to decide the meaning compatibility among the meanings of the words involved. In Indian Tradition, the relation between a word and its meaning is considered to be of three types viz. *abhidhā* (the primary meaning), *lakṣaṇā* (the extended or the secondary or metaphoric meaning) and *vyañjanā* (the suggestive meaning) [8]. It has been pointed out that the suggestive meaning exists in parallel with the other two meanings (Kulkarni, 2015). In order to get the suggestive meaning one needs to look at the coherence between the texts at sentential and paragraph level. Thus, only on the basis of sentential analysis, it is not possible to decide the suggestive meaning even if it exists. In order to look at the meaning compatibility at sentential level, we need to look at the meaning compatibility with both *abhidhā* as well as *lakṣaṇā*. To devise rules for testing the meaning compatibility for each of the cases of various *kāraka* and non-*kāraka* relations covering both the primary and secondary meanings is a huge task. We have not decided in this momment what kind of information is needed, how to organize it and so on.

Yogyatā is defined as an absence of incompatibility and also as the presence of compatibility. Modeling it as an absence of incompatibility ensures less chance of type-2 error viz. the possibility of missing any correct solution. This helps in increasing the recall (Kulkarni, 2015; Panchal and Kulkarni, 2018). We get a clue to distinguish between the nouns which are related by a *kāraka* relation and those which are related by a non-*kāraka* ones in the *Aruṇādhikaraṇa* of the *Śābara bhāṣya*. Under the commentary of Mīmāṃsā sūtra 3.1.6, it is mentioned that

> *na ca amūrta-arthaḥ kriyātaḥ sādhanaṃ bhavatīti* (Jha, 1933, p 654)
> No unsubstantial object can ever be the means of accomplishing an act.

Thus anything other than *dravya* can not be a *kāraka*. There are some words which designate a quality and also a substance in which this quality resides. For example the word *śukla* (white). It designates a color. In addition, it also designates a thing which is white in color. Such words have a technical name in Sanskrit grammar. They are called the *guṇavacanas*. Since the *guṇavacanas* also can designate a *dravya*, all the *dravyas* as well as the *guṇavacanas* are qualified to be a *kāraka*. The rest, i.e. nouns which denote either a *guṇa* which is not a *guṇavacana* (for example *gandha*) or a *kriyā* (verbal nouns), would have a non-*kāraka* relation with a verb.

With this background now we discuss the disambiguation of the ablative, dative and the instrumental case markers in this order.

[8]These aspects are discussed by all the three school of śābdabodha tradition i.e - Vaiyākaraṇa, Naiyāyika and Mīmāṃsaka, and Ālaṅkārika also. Prominent discussions among them are accumulated by K. Kunjanni Raja in `Indian Theories of Meaning`.

5.1 *Deciding the meaning of ablative case marker*

The ablative case marker is used to mark three relations viz. *apādāna*, *hetu* and *vibhakta*. Among these, *apādāna* is a *kāraka* relation, and Pāṇini, in addition to the semantic definition of *apādāna*, has provided a list of exceptional cases[9] where he provides either a list or a semantics of the verbs involved. Thus only in case of these verbs, there is a possibility of *apādāna* relation.

Pāṇini's *sūtra*
vibhāṣā guṇe'striyām 2.3.25
[(The fifth case endings are) better not (added after a *prātipadika* in the sense of *hetu* "ground, reason"), when reference is to a *guṇa* "quality" provided that (the *prātipadika* concerned is) non-feminine.][10]
This *sūtra* provides two syntactic clues to infer the relation of *hetu*. They are

1. The word which is in the ablative case should be a *guṇa* (whose reference is a quality), and
2. it should not be in feminine gender.

In the case of *vibhakta*, the seperateness is indicated by a comparison. Pāṇini mentions four suffixes for expressing comparison. The relevant sūtras are *atiśāyane tamabiṣṭhanau*(5.3.55) and *dvivacanavibhajyopapade tarabīyasunau*(5.3.57). And the suffixes are - *tamap, iṣṭhan, tarap* and *īyasun.*

With these clues now the rules for disambiguating the ablative case suffix may be stated as

1. In the presence of words with the suffixes *tarap*, *tamap*, *iṣṭhan* and *iyasun*, the word in ablative case has a relation of *vibhakta* with another noun.
2. If the verb does not have any expectancy of *apādāna* and the noun in ablative case refers to a quality *guṇa* which is not a *guṇavacana*, then the relation of the noun in ablative case with the verb is that of *hetu.*
3. If the verb has an expectancy of *apādāna* and the noun in ablative case refers to a *dravya* or a *guṇavacana*, then the relation between the noun in ablative case and the verb is that of *apādāna* and otherwise it is a *hetu.* In the case of verbs in the sense of fear, this condition is further relaxed, and even a *guṇa* which is not a *guṇavacana* would be a possible *apādāna kāraka*, on the basis of the *sūtra* '*bhītrārthānām bhayahetuḥ* (1.4.24)'.

In addition to these, we also came across some special cases in Bhagvadgītā, where the verbs themselves indicate the seperateness such as *viśiṣyate* and *atiricyate.* Moreover words like *adhika*, *para*, *kuśala*, *pravīṇa* etc. also indicate a seperateness. In such cases the relation is marked as *vibhaktam.*

5.2 *Sampradāna* versus *Prayojana*

With the availability of Pāṇini's *sūtras* which provide a list of verbs or the meanings of the verbs that have an expectancy of *sampradāna*, we get an almost complete list of all the verbs that have a *sampradāna* expectancy. If a verb does not belong to this list, then it does not have any expectancy for a *sampradāna*, and safely we can say that any word in the dative case represents the *prayojana.* So the only challenge is with the verbs having an expectancy for *sampradāna.* In such cases we will have to decide whether the word in dative case is a *prayojana* or a *sampradāna* with respect to the given verb. With the above condition that a *kāraka* should necessarily be a *dravya*, in sentences such as (35), one can correctly assign a relation of *prayojana* to the dative word *paṭhanāya.*

Skt: Rāmaḥ paṭhanāya pustakaṃ dadāti. (35)
Gloss: Rāma{m, sg, nom} study{n, sg, dat} book{n, sg, acc} give{pr, sg, 3p}

[9]Patañjali explains how these are not exceptions but can be justified with the original definition of apādāna.
[10]By 'better not added' is indicated a less-preferred optionality.

Eng: Rāma gives a book for study.

Of course this condition is just a necessary and not a sufficient one. For example, consider a sentence

Skt: Rāmaḥ pustakāya dhanaṃ dadāti. (36)
Gloss: Rāma{m, sg, nom} Book{n, sg, dat} money{n, sg, acc} give{pr, sg, 3p}
Eng: Rāma gives money for a book.

Here *pustaka* is a matter(*dravya*) and hence it will be marked as a *sampradāna*. But we know that in this sentence *pustaka* is not a beneficiary. A beneficiary should be an object that has an ability of receive. The living beings have an ability to receive. But imposing this restriction can handle only sentences with *abhidhārtha* (primary meaning). It is possible that a word is used in a metaphoric sense as in

Skt: Rāmaḥ pāṭhaśālāyai dhanaṃ dadāti. (37)
Gloss: Rāma{m, sg, nom} school{n, sg, dat} money{n, sg, acc} give{ pr, sg, 3p}
Eng: Rāma gives money to a school.

In this sentence, the noun in dative *pāṭhaśālā* is used in the sense of an institution and not in the sense of a building. Though an institution is not a living body, but still it shares some properties of a living body such as an institution grows just like a living being. Untill a good model for *lakṣaṇā* is developed, we decided to keep the condition of mutual congruity as wide as possible so that the recall is closer to 100%. Thus, instead of allowing only living beings to be candidates for *sampradāna* we allow any *dravya* or a *guṇavacana* to be a possible *sampradāna*. This increases the type-1 error, allowing the cases of *pustaka* to be a *sampradāna* in the sentence (35), but reduces the type-2 error by allowing *pāṭhaśālā* to be a *sampradāna* as in (37).

Sentence (35) was an example of ellipsis. The complete sentence without ellipsis would be something like

Skt: Rāmaḥ Mohanāya pustakāya dhanaṃ dadāti. (38)
Gloss: Rāma{m, sg, nom} Mohana{m, sg, dat} book{n, sg, dat} money{n, sg, acc} give{ pr, sg, 3p}
Eng: Rāma gives money to Mohana for a book.

Now the parser with an extra condition that if there are two *dravyas* with dative case then the one which refers to a living being is preferred to be a *sampradāna*, would yield a correct result.

5.3 *Karaṇa* versus *Hetu*

There is similarity between the ambiguity of instrumental case suffix with that of dative and ablative case suffix. All the three are used for both *kāraka* as well as non-*kāraka* relations. But there is a major difference and that is: *Pāṇini* has provided a clues as to which verbs have an expectancy for *sampradāna kāraka* and *apādāna kāraka*. But no such list has been provided for the verbs with an expectancy for the *karaṇa*. In the case of *karaṇa*, there was no such major extension except two cases viz. the verb *div* and the verbs denoting *parikrayaṇa*.[11] The list of verbs having an expectancy of *sampradāna* or an *apādāna* is small in comparison with the verbs having an expectancy of an instrument.

Another difference is, it was easy to formulate a criterion to rule out the candidates for

[11] *divḥ karma ca*(1.4.43), *parikrayaṇe sampradānam anyatarasyām*(1.4.44)

sampradāna and *apādāna* simply using the criterion of being a substantial object. Thus a simple ontological information such as whether the word designates an object or not helped in the formulation of rules. However in the case of a *karaṇa*, the things are not that simple, for the following reasons.

First the number of the verbs having an expectancy for a *karaṇa* is much more than the number of verbs having an expectancy for *sampradāna* or *apādāna*. Therefore formulating a general semantic criterion that will cover all the verbs is difficult. Secondly in the case of passive voice, even the *kartṛ* takes the instrument case suffix along with an instrument and a cause or a reason. Finally the *karaṇa* has its own activity which is a part of the complex activity denoted by a verb. Thus in order to decide whether the denotation of a word can be an instrument or not completely depends on the nature of the activity denoted by the verb. Hence in order to decide whether something is an instrument or not, one needs to know the associated semantics of the verb. In view of these difficulties, we decided to look at the problem afresh and search for clues that will rule out the non-players than the clues that will shortlist the possible candidates.

Pāṇini defines *karaṇa* as *Sādhakatamaṃ karaṇam*(1.4.42). The most effective means is termed as a *karaṇa*. The *karaṇa* has an action associated with it and this action is a part of the activity indicated by the main verb, and is the last sub-activity among the group of activities associated with the activity of main verb. For example, consider the sentence (29). Here the action is denoted by a verb *han*. *Rāma*, the agent picks up an arrow, and then shoots his bow towards *Vāli*. Now this arrow, after leaving the hands of *Rāma* travels through the air and pierces *Vāli*. At this point *Vāli* gets killed. So, the activity of the arrow of piercing is the last activity in the complex activity of *han*, and is the activity of an instrument. Thus we observe that in order to qualify to be an instrument, the object under consideration should have an activity of its own. This is true only of the matter(*dravya*). Hence only (*dravya*) or a *guṇavacana*(those which refer to a quality as well as the one which possesses the quality) are qualified to be a *karaṇa*.

This criterion thus helps us in ruling out the possibility of *adhyayana* to be a *karaṇa*, in the sentence (32), since it does not refer to a *dravya*. Further, the condition that the instrument cannot be an animate object would further help disambiguate in the following example:

Skt: Rāmeṇa bāṇena Vāliḥ ahanyata. (39)
Gloss: Rāma{m, sg, inst} arrow{m, sg, inst} Vāli{m, sg, nom} kill{pr, sg, 3p passive}
Eng: Vāli is killed by Rāma with arrow.

In this sentence, both *Rāmeṇa bāṇena* are in instrumental case. But *Rāma* is the name of a person and thus denotes an animate object while *bāṇa* refers to an inanimate object and hence *bāṇa* is a *karaṇa* (instrument) and *Rāma* is a *kartṛ*.

We came across some examples where the *karaṇa* is not a *dravya*. Here is an example.

skt: ghoṣeṇa āpūrayan diśaḥ. (40)
Gloss: sound{m, sg, inst} fill_out{m, sg, nom} directions{f, pl, acc}
Eng: Fill out the directions with sound.

In this sentence, the word *ghoṣa* refers to a *guṇa* and yet it is an instrument for the activiy denoted by *āpūrayan*. We noticed that in the case of verbs that denote activities associated with mind, brain etc. such as *bhartsa, abhi-jñā* etc. words denoting *śabda* act as a *karaṇa*.

With these criteria, now the rules for ruling out non-candidates for *karaṇa* may be summarized as:

- If the verb denotes a mental activity, words denoting *śabda* can act as a *karaṇa*.
- In all other cases of verbs having an expectancy for a *karaṇa*, a word denoting a *dravya* (including the *guṇavacana*), is a potential candidate.
- If there are two words in instrumental case, and the verb is in passive voice, then the word denoting an animate object is preferred to be a *kartṛ*.

6 Evaluation

For evaluating the disambiguation rules thus framed, we chose `Srīmadbhagvadgītā`. This text is manually analysed at various levels such as morphological analysis and *kāraka* analysis. The current parser can not handle sentences with co-ordinate conjunction properly. Hence we selected only those verses which do not have the use of conjunctive particles. A verse with more than one finite verbs[12] were split. Each input sentence had only one finite verb, and the order of the words was the same as in the original verse. Since the implementation focuses on reduction of Type-2 error, we wanted to make sure that the recall is high. The recall for all the relations was found to be 100%. That is, each of the sentences produced one or more solutions and one of them was found to be correct. Table 2 shows the performance of the parser on sentences with ablative, dative and instrumental case. We note that in almost 80% of the times, the first solution is correct. And the parser could parse 93% of the sentences correctly. The failures were due to un-availability of morphological analysis for at least one word in the sentence.

relation	Sentences	Parsed	Failed	rank of correct solution		
				1	2-9	>9
apādāna	18	18 (100%)	0	13 (72.2%)	1	4
hetu(5)	20	18 (90%)	2 (10%)	10 (55%)	6	2
vibhakta	19	17 (90%)	2 (10%)	10 (60%)	4	3
sampradāna	26	23 (88.5%)	3 (11.5%)	16 (69.6%)	4	3
prayojana	25	23 (92%)	2 (8%)	22 (95.6%)	0	1
karaṇa	91	84 (92.3%)	7 (7.7%)	71 (84.5%)	11	2
hetu(3)	22	22 (100%)	0	13 (59%)	5	4
All	221	205 (92.8%)	16 (7.2%)	155 (78.9%)	31	19

Table 2: Performance of the parser

Analysis of the sentences where the correct solution was not at the top revealed that the sentence contains words with more than one possible morphological analysis. And the top solution displayed makes sense, if it is situated in an appropriate context. For example, consider the following feet of a verse
{m, sg, dat} Skt: tat te padaṃ saṅgraheṇa pravakṣye ahaṃ (41) (BhG 8.11)
Gloss: that{n, sg, acc} you{m, sg, dat} goal{n, sg, acc} briefly{m, sg, inst} tell{f, sg, 1p} I{m, sg, nom}
Eng: I will tell you that goal briefly.

Here the word *te* is ambiguous between a dative and a genitive case suffix of the second person pronoun *yuṣmad*. So it can be interpreted as either related to *padaṃ* by a possessive relation or related to the verb as a beneficiary. In this particular context, the second reading is more appropriate. A simple rule which checks if all the desired expectancies of the verb are fullfilled or not would push the correct solution to the top. But this rule can be used only if we always deal with complete sentences. If elliptical sentences are allowed, then this rule breaks down.

[12] *ekatiṅ vākyam*

Another observation is, if the word order is changed to

Skt: ahaṃ tat padaṃ te saṅgraheṇa pravakṣye (42) (BhG 8.11)
Gloss: I{m, sg, nom} that{n, sg, acc} goal{n, sg, acc} you{m, sg, dat} briefly{m, sg, inst} tell{f, sg, 1p}
Eng: I will tell you that goal briefly.

then the parser produces the intended solution as the first solution. Most of the cases of *sampradāna kāraka* where the solutions were pushed down were due to such ambiguities.

In the case of instrumental case, the cases where the solution was pushed down were due to the ambiguity between a *kartṛ* and *karaṇa* having the same instrumental case marker in passive voice. When there is an ellipsis of one of them, then the sentence can be parsed in more than one ways. Only the context helps you in deciding which one is the correct. For example,

Skt: indriyaiḥ sṛjyate yat. (43)
Gloss: organs{m, pl, inst} produce{pr, sg, 3p, passive} which{n, sg, nom}
Eng: which is produced by organs

This phrase can be interpreted in two different ways: with *indriya* as either a *kartṛ* or a *karaṇa*. And it is only the context that helps in selecting the correct one.

7 Conclusion

In this paper we have discussed the problems in disambiguation of three case suffixes ablative, dative and instrumental. There is always a trade-off between precision and recall. Since our aim is to provide complete access to the original text and not merely a translation system, recall is more important for us. This implies, we need to consider both the primary and the secondary meanings of the words for checking the meaning congruity for establishing the relations. The mīmāṁsā texts very clearly advocate the use of primary meaning first, and only in the absence of any appropriate primary meaning, they advocate the use of secondary meaning. However, since the task of framing rules for meaning congruity is a gigantic task, and our aim is to increase the recall, we decided to use *yogyatā* as an absence of non-congruity. This reduces the precision, but helps in using some simple ontological properties to rule out the non-players. With the help of only two classes viz *dravya* and *guṇa*, and occasionally words denoting *śabda*, and animacy, we could get satisfactory results.

We are aware of the fact that the sample on which the parser was tested is very small, and belongs to a specific domain. In order to test it on better corpus, we still do not have annotated corpus of large size.

Improving the performance of this parser would help in its use for building a tree bank for Sanskrit semi-automatically, at the same time making it useful for those who would like to access the original text with the help of these tools.

References

Vaman Sivaram Apte. 2012. *Sanskrit-Hindi Kosha.* Motilal Banarasidas Varanasi.

Nagesh Bhatta. 1987. *Laghuśabdenduśekharaḥ.* Chowkhamba Sanskrit Sanshthan, Varanasi.

Nagesh Bhatta. 2006. *Paramalaghumañjūṣā.* Chowkhamba Surabharati prakashan, Varanasi.

K A Subramania Iyer. 1969. *Bhartṛhari: A Study of Vākyapadīya in the light of Ancient commentaries.* Deccan College, Poona.

K A Subramania Iyer. 1971. *The Vākyapadīya of Bhartṛhari.* Deccan College, Poona.

Ganganatha Jha. 1933. *Śābara Bhāṣya Vol 1.; Translated into English.* Oriental Institute Baroda.

Jinendrabuddhi. 1981. *Nyāsa.* Sanskrit Parishat, Osmania University, Hyderabad.

S D Joshi and J.A.F. Roodbergen. 1975. *Patañjali's Vyākaraṇa Mahābhāṣya Kārakāhnikam (P 1.4.23–1.4.55).* Center of Advanced Study in Sanskrit, Pune.

S D Joshi and J.A.F. Roodbergen. 1998. *The Aṣṭādhyāyī of Pāṇini with Translation and Explanatory Notes,*, volume 7. Sahitya Akadamy, Rabindra Bavan, Ferozshah Road, New Delhi 01.

András Kornai. 2020. *Semantics.* Springer.

Amba Kulkarni and K. V. Ramakrishnamacharyulu. 2013. Parsing Sanskrit texts: Some relation specific issues. In Malhar Kulkarni, editor, *Proceedings of the 5th International Sanskrit Computational Linguistics Symposium.* D K Printworld.

Amba Kulkarni, Sheetal Pokar, and Devanand Shukl. 2010. Designing a Constraint Based Parser for Sanskrit. In G N Jha, editor, *Fourth International Sanskrit Computational Linguistics Symposium,* pages 70–90. Springer-Verlag, LNAI 6465.

Amba Kulkarni. 2013. A deterministic dependency parser with dynamic programming for Sanskrit. In *Proceedings of the Second International Conference on Dependency Linguistics (DepLing 2013),* pages 157–166, Prague, Czech Republic, August. Charles University in Prague Matfyzpress Prague Czech Republic.

Amba Kulkarni. 2015. *Sanskrit Parsing based on the theories of Śābdabodha.* IIAS, Shimla and D K Printworld.

Amba Kulkarni. 2019-20. Appropriate dependency tagset for Sanskrit analysis and generation. *Acta Orientalia,* 80:401–425.

Amba Kulkarni. 2021. Sanskrit parsing following indian theories of verbal cognition. *Transactions on Asian and Low-Resource Language Information Processing,* 20(2):1–38.

J Pai Madhusoodan. 2020. *Sanskrit Sentence Generator: A prototype.* Ph.D. thesis, University of Hyderabad, Hyderabad.

Daniel Jurafsky & James H. Martin. 2008. *Speech and Language Processing: An introduction to natural language processing,computational linguistics, and speech recognition.* Prentice Hall.

Harekanta Mishra, editor. 2016. *Bṛhaddhātukusumākaraḥ.* Chowkhamba Sanskrit Pratishthan, New Delhi.

M. Monier-Willaiams. 2008. *Sanskrit-English Dictionary.* Indica Books, Godowlia, Varanasi.

Sanjeev Panchal and Amba Kulkarni. 2018. Yogyatā as an absence of non-congruity. In Gérard Huet and Amba Kulkarni, editors, *Computational Sanskrit and Digital Humanities.* D K Publishers.

Sanjeev Panchal. 2020. *Modeling Ākāṅkṣā following Pāṇinian grammar for Sanskrit.* Ph.D. thesis, University of Hyderabad, Hyderabad.

Gopal Dutt Pande. 2012, Reprint Edition. *Vaiyākaraṇa-Siddhāntakaumudī of Bhattojidikshita.* Chowkhamba Surabharati Prakashan, Varanasi.

Patanjali. 1987. *Pāṇinīyavyākaraṇamahābhaṣyam.* Chowkhamba Sanskrit Pratishthan, New Delhi.

K Kunjunni Raja. 1963. *Indian Theories of Meaning.* Adayar Library and Research Center, Madras.

K V Ramakrishnamacaryulu. 2009. Annotating Sanskrit texts based on Śābdabodha systems. In Amba Kulkarni and Gérard Huet, editors, *Proceedings Third International Sanskrit Computational Linguistics Symposium,* pages 26–39, Hyderabad India. Springer-Verlag LNAI 5406.

Preeti Shukla, Amba Kulkarni, and Devanand Shukl. 2013. Geeta: Gold standard annotated data, analysis and its applicationa. In *Proceedings of ICON 2013, the 10th International Conference on NLP,* Noida, India, December.

Vijaypal Vidhyavaridhi. 1969. *Kāśikā.* Ramlal Kapur Trast, Sonipat, Hariyana.

A Tagset of Dependency Relations

- **Kāraka-sambandhāḥ**
  - kartā
    - prayojaka-kartā
    - prayojya-kartā
  - karma
    - mukhya-karma
    - gauṇa-karma
    - vākya-karma
  - karaṇam
  - sampradānam
  - apādānam
  - adhikaraṇam
    - kāla-adhikaraṇam
    - deśa-adhikaraṇam
    - viṣaya-adhikaraṇam
- **Kāraketara-sambandhāḥ**
  - **Kriyā-kriyā-sambandhāḥ**
    - pūrva-kālaḥ
    - vartamāna-samāna-kālaḥ
    - bhaviṣyat-samāna-kālaḥ
    - bhāvalakṣaṇa-pūrva-kālaḥ
    - bhāvalakṣaṇa-vartamāna-samāna-kālaḥ
    - bhāvalakṣaṇa-anantara-kālaḥ
    - sahāyaka-kriyā
  - **Kriyā-nāma-sambandhāḥ**
    - sambodhyaḥ
    - hetuḥ
    - prayojanam
    - kartṛ-samānādhikaraṇam
    - karma-samānādhikaraṇam
    - kriyāviśeṣaṇam
    - pratiṣedhaḥ
  - **Nāma-nāma-sambandhāḥ**
    - ṣaṣṭhī-sambandhaḥ
    - aṅgavikāraḥ
    - vīpsā
    - viśeṣaṇam
    - sambodhana-sūcakam
    - vibhaktam
    - abhedaḥ
    - nirdhāraṇam
    - atyanta-saṃyogaḥ
    - apavarga-sambandhaḥ
    - vakyakarmadyotakaḥ
- **Upapada-sambandhāḥ**
  - sandarbhabinduḥ
  - tulanābinduḥ
  - viśayādhikaraṇam
  - nirdhāraṇam
  - prayojanam
  - udgāravācakaḥ
  - saha-arthaḥ
  - vinā-arthaḥ
  - svāmī
  - srotaḥ
- **Vākyetarasambandhāḥ**
  - anuyogī
  - pratiyogī
  - nitya-sambandhaḥ
- **Samuccayādisambandhāḥ**
  - samuccitaḥ
  - samuccaya-dyotakaḥ
  - anyataraḥ
  - anyatara-dyotakaḥ

Note: The bold entries are the headings and do not indicate relation labels

Creation of a Digital Rig Vedic Index (Anukramani) for Computational Linguistic Tasks

A V S D S Mahesh and **Arnab Bhattacharya**
Dept. of Computer Science and Engineering
Indian Institute of Technology Kanpur
maheshak@cse.iitk.ac.in, arnabb@cse.iitk.ac.in

Abstract

Rig Veda, the oldest text in Vedic Sanskrit, is a collection of hymns addressed to various *devatā*s. We present an index of Rig Vedic verses along with the respective *devatā*, *ṛṣi* and *chandas* which is, in short, a digitized form of the well known Rig Vedic *Anukramaṇī*. We then build several deep learning based language models from the corpus. The models are tested on a downstream classification task that predicts the *devatā* associated with a given verse. The six classifiers we test are based on FastText, ELMo, ALBERT, Word2Vec, GloVe and RoBERTa language models pretrained on the GRETIL data. We find that RoBERTa outperforms the other models on this task and achieves an accuracy of 77.3%.

Keywords— Vedic Sanskrit, Rig Vedic Anukramani, Text Classification

1 Introduction

The *Anukramaṇī* is an index of the Rig Vedic hymns; it contains the details about the *author* (**ṛṣi**), the *divinity* that a hymn is dedicated to (**devatā**), and the *meter* (**chandas**) for each hymn. The widely found *Anukramaṇī* is that of *Kātyāyana* and is known as the *Sarvānukramaṇī* (Macdonell, 1885). The details present are considered to be accurate to a good extent (Jamison and Brereton, 2014). In particular, the *devatā* addressed can easily be cross-checked from the content of the hymns. To the nest of our knowledge, we are the first to present this data in a machine-readable format. One may find in the text form of Griffith's Rig Veda (Griffith, 1889) an index of hymns each labeled with the *devatā*. However, these labels are not verse-wise and the *devatā* addressed is often not the same for the entire hymn. Hence, to our consensus, the data we provide is not available before. We also referred the Maharishi International University's Vedic Reserve's[1] materials in the process of annotation. We use this information about the *devatā*s as a *text classification* dataset with the verses as input texts and their respective *devatā*s as labels.

1.1 Motivation

To be able to benchmark the performance of computational natural language models, it is necessary to judge their realiability in downstream tasks. The same applies to Vedic Sanskrit of Rig Veda, which is an ancient form of Sanskrit. We present one such benchmark dataset, the Rig Vedic *Anukramaṇī*. Although it has been available from historical times, it was not in any machine-readable form.

Thus, upon this dataset, we run six classifiers that respectively use the embeddings from FastText (Joulin et al., 2016; Bojanowski et al., 2016), ELMo (Peters et al., 2018), ALBERT (Lan et al., 2019), Word2Vec (Mikolov et al., 2013), GloVe (Pennington et al., 2014), and RoBERTa (Liu et al., 2019) pretrained language models. We carried out the pretraining of FastText, ELMo, ALBERT and RoBERTa based models on the GRETIL data[2] and whereas pretraining of Word2Vec and GloVe are carried out on lemmatized text from Digital Corpus of Sanskrit (DCS) (Hellwig, 2010–2021). The results thus obtained show that the transformer (Vaswani et al., 2017) based RoBERTa model outperforms the other ones in this classification task.

1.2 Contributions

Our contributions in this work are two-fold:

[1] https://vedicreserve.miu.edu/
[2] http://gretil.sub.uni-goettingen.de/gretil.html

Proceedings of the Computational Sanskrit and Digital Humanities, 18th World Sanskrit Conference 2023, pages 89–96

1. We present a digital Rig Vedic index (*Anukramaṇī*) dataset consisting of *devatā*, *ṛṣi* and *chandas* information, labeled for each verse. This acts as a benchmark dataset in Vedic Sanskrit.
2. We apply six classifiers based on pretrained ALBERT, FastText, ELMo, Word2Vec, GloVe and RoBERTa embeddings on the above dataset.

The dataset and the models are available from `https://github.com/mahesh-ak/WSC2023`.

1.3 Organization

The rest of the paper is organized as follows. The details about the classification data are given in Section 2, while the information about the pre-training and training of the various classifiers applied are described in Section 3. The results obtained on the classifiers are discussed in Section 4 and, finally, the paper is concluded in Section 6.

2 Dataset

2.1 Rig Vedic *Anukramaṇī*

There are a total of 10,552 verses in the Rig Veda. Each verse is assigned with a *devatā* label. Although most hymns are associated with a single *devatā*, for example, *Agni*, there are many hymns where a verse has more than one *devatā* labels. Some have two *devatā*s addressed in dual tense, for example, *Indrāgnī*, i.e., *Indra* and *Agni*. Some have a special designated group of *devatā*s, for example, *Viśvedevā*s or the *āditya*s. Some again may just be a case where multiple *devatā*s are addressed together, for example, *Iḻā-Sarasvatī-Bhāratī*. In these cases, we make no attempt to present these labels as a mixture of the compositional *devatā*s. Rather, we present them as they are. For example, a dual like *Mitrāvaruṇau* is not decomposed into *Mitra* and *Varuṇa*, but is treated as a single label only. In future, it will be worthwhile to present them in a decomposed format. Similary, a verse generally has only a single *ṛṣi*, but can have multiple *ṛṣi*s rarely. There is always a unique *chandas* of a hymn by definition of a meter. An example line from *Anukramaṇī* from first *Maṇḍala* and its annotation is demonstrated as follows:

(27) saptaviṃśaṃ sūktam
(1-13) trayodaśarcasyāsya sūktasyājīgartiḥ śunaḥśepa ṛṣiḥ ।
(1-12) prathamādidvādaśarcām agniḥ (13) trayodaśyāśca devā devatāḥ ।
(1-12) prathamādidvādaśarcāṃ gāyatrī (13) trayodaśyāśca triṣṭup chandasī

The annotation for the above is:

27.13.ājīgartiḥ śunaḥśepaḥ.(1-12)agniḥ,(13)devāḥ.(1-12)gāyatrī,(13)triṣṭup

The fields of hymn, verse, *ṛṣi*, *devatā* and *chandas* are separated by a period, whereas muliple entries within a field are seperated by a comma. This yields a format that can be easily processed in an automated fashion.

It can be seen that the original *anukramaṇī*, even if made available in a machine-readable format, requires manual annotation since the sentences are in a natural language, whose processing would, in turn, require a gold standard.

2.2 Classification Task

For the classification task, the focus is on a single label classification, that is, a single *devatā* prediction for a verse. We attempt to group *devatā*s that are fundamentally the same under one single label. For example, *Rakṣoghna Agni* is labeled as only *Agni*. However, although the classes labeled *Soma* and *Pavamāna Soma* may look like one one, we leave them unmerged since there is a subtle difference between the two classes. The hymns of *Pavamāna Soma* almost always invoke the purifying nature of *Soma* like *Somaḥ pavate* which is not the case with the class labeled just *Soma*. Additionally, the several *Dānastuti*s or the praises of patrons are labeled as just *Dānastuti* without the names of the patrons like *Paijavana Sudās*. This produces an overall list of 216 labels.

From this data, we consider the labels with at least 30 instances or verses for the classification task. This brings the label count down to 28. The number of instances corresponding to these 28 labels is

9,496, which is still a fairly large size. We keep aside 15% of the data consisting of 1,424 hymns as the *test* set. The rest of the data is split using a 90:10 ratio into *training* (7,265 hymns) and *validation* (807 hymns) sets. The splits are done in a *stratified* manner.

3 Training the Classifiers

As mentioned earlier, we evaluate on this task six classification models based on FastText, ELMo, ALBERT, Word2Vec, GloVe and RoBERTa. Training these models involve pre-training as a first step and then fine-tuning for the classification task at hand. These two steps are next discussed separately.

3.1 Pre-training

The models, except for Word2Vec and GloVe, are pre-trained on the GRETIL data[3] that consists of over 2000 Sanskrit texts. These are cleaned to remove pieces of text that are not in Sanskrit as much as possible to produce over 450 MB of textual data with about 45 million words. Note that a word here can refer to a compound word (*sandhi* or *samāsa* or *both*) as well. In case of Word2Vec and GloVe, the pretraining was done on lemmatized text available from the Digital Corpus of Sanskrit (DCS)(Hellwig, 2010–2021) corpus, consisting about 34 MB of text data and 5 million words. The pre-training is carried on an RTX 2080 GPU machine with 11 GB memory for ELMo, ALBERT and RoBERTa and on a 12-core CPU with 32 GB RAM for FastText, Word2Vec and GloVe. The details are discussed next.

1. **FastText** (Bojanowski et al., 2016) is a skip-gram based model that learns continuous word representations from character n-grams. It can be trained fast on a CPU unlike the deep neural network models that require GPU. In our case, it was trained in less than an hour on a 12-core CPU. The FastText software provided on the official website[4] is used.

2. **ELMo** (Peters et al., 2018) is a deep learning model consisting of CNN embedders of input characters and bidirectional LSTM encoders that train on the bidirectional language modeling task. ELMo demonstrated significantly the power of transfer learning in the realm of NLP. We use the small model with about 13 million parameters. It still took about 3 days to pre-train on the GPU. We used the official TensorFlow implementation of ELMo[5].

3. **ALBERT** (Lan et al., 2019) is a variant of the transformer (Vaswani et al., 2017) based BERT model (Devlin et al., 2018) with smaller number of parameters. It trains on a masked language modeling task. We use unigram language model tokenization (Kudo, 2018) with a vocabulary size of 5,000. Our model has about 8 million parameters (albert-base with vocabulary size 5,000) and the training converged in about 3 days on the GPU. We used the Huggingface (Wolf et al., 2019) library here.

4. **Word2Vec** (Mikolov et al., 2013) is a skip-gram based model that learns distributed word representations. In implementation, this is special case of FastText with window size parameter set to 0. So, the same FastText software is used. The training details are same as that of FastText.

5. **GloVe** (Pennington et al., 2014) is an unsupervised algorithm for learing word vector representations based on word-word co-occurrence statistics. Training details including hardware and time taken is similar to that of FastText. The GloVe software provided on the official website[6] is used.

6. **RoBERTa** (Lan et al., 2019) is a variant of the transformer (Vaswani et al., 2017) based BERT model (Devlin et al., 2018) with robust training method. It trains on a masked language modeling task like ALBERT. We use byte-pair encoding (BPE) tokenization (Sennrich et al., 2016) with variable vocabulary sizes of 2,500, 5,000, 10,000 and 20,000. The best-performing model has about 90 million parameters (roberta-base with vocabulary size 20,000) and the training converged in about 3 days on the GPU. We used the Huggingface (Wolf et al., 2019) library here.

[3]http://gretil.sub.uni-goettingen.de/gretil.html
[4]https://fasttext.cc
[5]https://github.com/allenai/bilm-tf
[6]https://nlp.stanford.edu/projects/glove/

3.2 Fine-tuning

We use the training classification data mentioned in Section 2 to fine-tune the pretrained models for the classification task. As previously mentioned, we consider only 28 labels for this task. The details for each the models including the architecture and algorithms are next discussed. The fine-tuning time for this task is always less than 15 minutes on respective hardwares.

- **FastText** classifier involves averaging the input word representations to form the hidden layer which is fed foward into a linear classifier (Joulin et al., 2016). Again the software provided in the official website is used here.
- **ELMo** embeddings of the input words learned previously, similar to above, are summed up to form the hidden layer which is fed forward into a linear classifier. This simple architecture is known to often outperform the complex ones (Perone et al., 2018). Here, we use the AllenNLP library (Gardner et al., 1803).
- **ALBERT** classifier takes as input the ALBERT final hidden representation layer of the CLS token and feeds it to a linear classifier. We use the implementation provided in the Huggingface library (Wolf et al., 2019).
- **Word2Vec, GloVe**: FastText classifier is used by loading pretrained vectors from Word2Vec and GloVe respectively. GloVe vectors are converted into Word2Vec format using the Gensim (Řehůřek and Sojka, 2010) library.
- **RoBERTa**: The details are similar to those of ALBERT.

4 Results

The F1 scores for each of the 28 classes is reported in Table 1. From overall macro-averaged F1 scores, it can be seen that RoBERTa performs the best. The RoBERTa here refers to the one with vocabulary size of 20K, which is the one that performs the best. The comparison of results of RoBERTa for different vocabulary sizes is given in Table 2.

We also report in Table 1, the performance of only the *under-represented* classes or in other words, the classes which see very few instances relative to the other classes. Here, we consider the under-represented classes as those which have less than overall 70 instances. That gives about 20-50 instances for training. The macro and weighted average F1 scores for only these under-represented classes are reported in the last two rows of Table 1. RoBERTa performs the best in the classification of under-represented classes as well except in case of the classes *Dānastuti*, *Aśva* and *Āpas*. Word2Vec outperforms RoBERTa in these classes. These results are discussed further in the following section.

It should be noted from Table 1 and Table 2 that RoBERTa outperforms ALBERT while having same vocabulary size of 5,000 as well. This is expected since ALBERT shares parameters across the layers and hence has small number of parameters to train.

From the confusion matrix of RoBERTa predictions provided in Figure 1, which is normalized across rows (i.e., true labels), one can see the patterns in wrong predictions. For instance, one can observe that various other labels are being predicted instead of the *Viśvedevā*s (index 3 on y-axis); this happens since *Viśvedevā*s is like an umbrella term for 'many' or rather 'all *devatā*s'. For instance, the following verse (RV 6.055.03) labeled as *Viśvedevā*s invokes *Aditi* and *Uṣāsānaktā*. The predicted label is *Uṣas* which is indeed close.

prá pastyā̀(3)m áditiṃ síndhum arkaíḥ svastím ī̱le sakhyā́ya devī́m |
ubhé yáthā no áhanī nipā́ta uṣā́sānáktā karatām ádabdhe ||

Note that the accents are provided only for the purpose of reading. They are not considered while training and testing.

Also, one can observe that the class *Soma* (index 13 on y-axis) is often wrongly being predicted as *Pavamāna Soma* (index 2 on x-axis) which can be understandable in the sense that both are almost the

Class	Label	Count	ALBERT	FastText	ELMo	Word2Vec	GloVe	RoBERTa
1	Indra	2887	0.855	0.844	0.836	0.778	0.810	**0.858**
2	Agni	2000	0.789	0.804	0.785	0.667	0.756	**0.825**
3	Pavamāna Soma	1087	0.799	0.834	**0.890**	0.750	0.793	0.824
4	Viśvedevās	815	0.435	0.426	0.404	0.364	0.414	**0.519**
5	Aśvinau	631	0.840	0.807	0.819	0.783	0.791	**0.864**
6	Marutas	425	0.656	0.641	0.656	**0.823**	0.589	0.651
7	Mitrāvaruṇau	183	0.638	0.429	0.378	0.403	0.439	**0.653**
8	Uṣas	182	0.576	**0.739**	0.585	0.222	0.622	0.655
9	Indrāgnī	117	0.737	0.684	0.789	0.606	0.718	**0.829**
10	Ādityās	100	0.609	0.400	0.286	**0.762**	0.333	0.538
11	Varuṇa	99	**0.600**	0.545	0.222	0.222	0.471	0.522
12	Ṛbhavas	96	0.690	**0.833**	0.545	0.759	0.500	0.733
13	Savitṛ	83	0.714	0.545	0.250	**0.727**	0.222	0.667
14	Soma	80	0.308	0.417	0.444	0.300	0.316	**0.588**
15	Pūṣan	77	0.552	0.385	0.167	0.286	0.385	**0.625**
16	Bṛhaspati	74	**0.923**	0.600	0.800	0.667	0.857	0.833
17	Indrāvaruṇau	70	**0.923**	0.667	0.870	0.593	0.667	**0.923**
18	Dānastuti	65	0.286	0.250	0	**0.667**	0.154	0.167
19	Sūrya	62	0.500	0.316	0.471	0.417	0.353	**0.600**
20	Vāyu	53	0.667	0.588	0.182	0.556	0.667	**0.778**
21	Dyāvāpṛthivyau	48	0.444	0.400	0.286	0.524	0.500	**0.545**
22	Brahmaṇaspati	48	0.545	0.444	0.500	0.560	**0.667**	**0.667**
23	Āpas	45	0.286	0.364	0.333	**0.500**	0.286	0.286
24	Rudra	38	**0.667**	0.333	0	0.261	0.250	**0.667**
25	Aśva	35	0	0	0	**0.333**	0	0.200
26	Indravāyū	33	**1**	0.667	0.500	0.727	0.750	**1**
27	Sarasvatī	32	0.714	0.364	0	0.333	0.400	**0.750**
28	Viṣṇu	31	0.444	0.545	0	0.800	0.286	**1**
	Overall (Weighted)		*0.745*	*0.730*	*0.710*	*0.668*	*0.693*	***0.773***
	Overall (Macro)		*0.614*	*0.531*	*0.429*	*0.550*	*0.500*	***0.670***
	Few-instance classes (Weighted)		*0.490*	*0.382*	*0.221*	*0.519*	*0.392*	***0.573***
	Few-instance classes (Macro)		*0.505*	*0.388*	*0.207*	*0.516*	*0.392*	***0.605***

Table 1: F1 scores for the classification task

Vocabulary Size	2.5K	5K	10K	20K
Overall (Weighted)	0.774	0.766	**0.775**	0.773
Overall (Macro)	0.639	0.638	0.634	**0.670**
Few-instances (Weighted)	0.458	0.485	0.483	**0.573**
Few-instances (Macro)	0.488	0.513	0.515	**0.605**

Table 2: Performance of RoBERTa for different vocabulary sizes

same. Note that, by our assumptions, in this case, *Soma* and *Pavamāna Soma* should have been clubbed into a single class in the first place. However, this is not done in order to observe how the model would get confused of either label. Their difference is better captured by ELMo (see in Table 1).

Another interesting case is the class that is labeled as *Aśva*. This occurs in a single hymn (RV 1.162) which talks about a sacrifice of a horse. Except for Word2Vec and RoBERTa, none of the other models appear to have learned anything of this class. From the confusion matrix (Figure 1), the label *Aśva* (index 24 on y-axis) is wrongly predicted as *Agni* often. The following is one such instance (RV 1.162.15):

mā́ tvāgnír dhvanayīd dhūmágandhir mókhā bhrā́janty abhí vikta jághriḥ |
iṣṭáṃ vītám abhígūrtaṃ váṣaṭkṛtaṃ táṃ devā́saḥ práti gṛbhṇanty áśvam ||

This is not surprising since the verse not only talks about *Agni*, which is the Sacred Fire, but also invokes many concepts and terms related to the Fire such as the word *vaṣaṭkṛta*, an exclamation made while making an offering to the Fire.

The class *Āpas* or the Waters is also poorly predicted by RoBERTa. A possible factor attributing to this

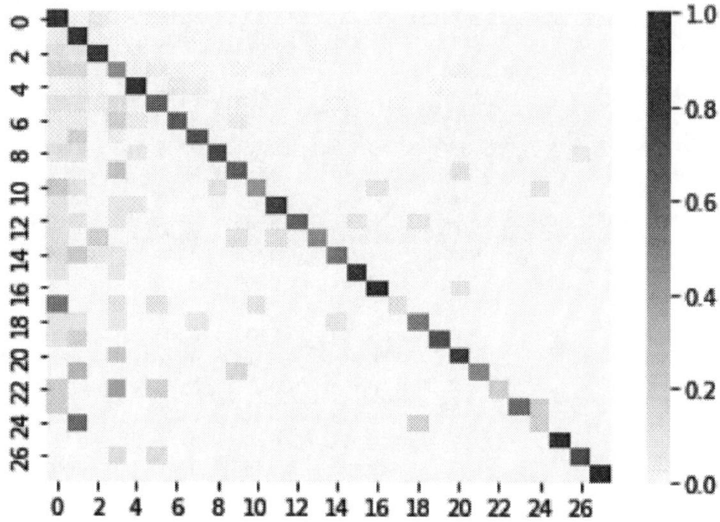

Figure 1: Confusion matrix with label indices for the best model, i.e., RoBERTa (see Table 1)

result could be that compared to other few-instance classes like *Rudra*, *Viṣṇu* etc., the word *āpaḥ* which means water appear quite regulary throughout the Rig Veda and this is not the case with aforementioned classes. Apart from these classes, the class of *Dānastuti* hymns, which are dedicated to some patron describing their generous donations, are also poorly predicted by RoBERTa. This is not surprising since this class denotes an abstract meaning that is not limited to a single word. Word2Vec surprising learns these classes to a good extent.

It should also be noted that Word2Vec outperforms RoBERTa with vocabulary sizes other than 20K in the case of under-estimated classes. This is likely due to the fact that Word2Vec has an advantage of being trained and tested on a lemmatized dataset. The behaviour of Word2Vec on *Dānastuti*, a semantically difficult class is noteworthy and a potential topic of future exploration. ELMo, probably owing to that fact that it starts from the character level, is outperformed by all others in case of few-instance classes. On the other hand, this does not happen with FastText since it considers a higher window of size 2-5 in our case.

5 Related Work

A transformer based architecture was tested for Sentence segmentation in (Hellwig and Nehrdich, 2018) probably for the first time for Sanskrit. Classification task related to compounds were seen in (Krishna et al., 2016; Sandhan et al., 2019) where use of neural network based models like Word2Vec, GloVe and LSTM are found. Various neural embeddings are explored for Classical Sanskrit in (Sandhan et al., 2021).

6 Conclusions

In this paper, we have produced a machine readable form of Rig Vedic *Anukramaṇī* that can be used as a benchmark dataset in Vedic Sanskrit Compuational Linguistics. Also, we have benchmarked six neural network based models namely, FastText, ELMo, ALBERT, Word2Vec, GloVe and RoBERTa on this dataset and found that the transformer-based RoBERTa outperforms the other models, especially in case of classification of under-represented classes. It is desirable to benchmark the BERT based models on more such tasks. Improving the classification scores can be taken up as a future task. As it was pointed out earlier, study of semantically difficult classes like *Dānastuti* can also be a potential future task.

References

Piotr Bojanowski, Edouard Grave, Armand Joulin, and Tomas Mikolov. 2016. Enriching word vectors with subword information. *arXiv preprint arXiv:1607.04606.*

Jacob Devlin, Ming-Wei Chang, Kenton Lee, and Kristina Toutanova. 2018. Bert: Pre-training of deep bidirectional transformers for language understanding. *arXiv preprint arXiv:1810.04805.*

Matt Gardner, Joel Grus, Mark Neumann, Oyvind Tafjord, Pradeep Dasigi, Nelson Liu, Matthew Peters, Michael Schmitz, and Luke Zettlemoyer. 1803. Allennlp: a deep semantic natural language processing platform (2018). *arXiv preprint arXiv:1803.07640.*

Ralph Thomas Hotchkin Griffith. 1889. *The Hymns of the Rig Veda*, volume 1-4. Benares : E.J. Lazarus.

Oliver Hellwig. 2010–2021. *The Digital Corpus of Sanskrit (DCS).*

Oliver Hellwig and Sebastian Nehrdich. 2018. Sanskrit word segmentation using character-level recurrent and convolutional neural networks. In *Proceedings of the 2018 Conference on Empirical Methods in Natural Language Processing*, pages 2754–2763, Brussels, Belgium. Association for Computational Linguistics.

Stephanie W Jamison and Joel P Brereton. 2014. *The Rigveda: the earliest religious poetry of India*, volume 1. South Asia Research.

Armand Joulin, Edouard Grave, Piotr Bojanowski, and Tomas Mikolov. 2016. Bag of tricks for efficient text classification. *arXiv preprint arXiv:1607.01759.*

Amrith Krishna, Pavankumar Satuluri, Shubham Sharma, Apurv Kumar, and Pawan Goyal. 2016. Compound type identification in Sanskrit: What roles do the corpus and grammar play? In *Proceedings of the 6th Workshop on South and Southeast Asian Natural Language Processing (WSSANLP2016)*, pages 1–10, Osaka, Japan. The COLING 2016 Organizing Committee.

Taku Kudo. 2018. Subword regularization: Improving neural network translation models with multiple subword candidates. In *Proceedings of the 56th Annual Meeting of the Association for Computational Linguistics (Volume 1: Long Papers)*, pages 66–75, Melbourne, Australia. Association for Computational Linguistics.

Zhenzhong Lan, Mingda Chen, Sebastian Goodman, Kevin Gimpel, Piyush Sharma, and Radu Soricut. 2019. Albert: A lite bert for self-supervised learning of language representations. *arXiv preprint arXiv:1909.11942.*

Yinhan Liu, Myle Ott, Naman Goyal, Jingfei Du, Mandar Joshi, Danqi Chen, Omer Levy, Mike Lewis, Luke Zettlemoyer, and Veselin Stoyanov. 2019. Roberta: A robustly optimized BERT pretraining approach. *CoRR*, abs/1907.11692.

Arthur Anthony Macdonell. 1885. *Die Sarvanukramani des Katyayana zum Rigveda, zum ersten mal mit kritischen anmerkungen hrsg. von Arthur Macdonell.* Ph.D. thesis, Leipzig.

Tomas Mikolov, Ilya Sutskever, Kai Chen, Greg Corrado, and Jeffrey Dean. 2013. Distributed representations of words and phrases and their compositionality. In *Neural and Information Processing System (NIPS).*

Jeffrey Pennington, Richard Socher, and Christopher Manning. 2014. GloVe: Global vectors for word representation. In *Proceedings of the 2014 Conference on Empirical Methods in Natural Language Processing (EMNLP)*, pages 1532–1543, Doha, Qatar. Association for Computational Linguistics.

Christian S. Perone, Roberto Silveira, and Thomas S. Paula. 2018. Evaluation of sentence embeddings in downstream and linguistic probing tasks.

Matthew E. Peters, Mark Neumann, Mohit Iyyer, Matt Gardner, Christopher Clark, Kenton Lee, and Luke Zettlemoyer. 2018. Deep contextualized word representations. In *Proceedings of the 2018 Conference of the North American Chapter of the Association for Computational Linguistics: Human Language Technologies, Volume 1 (Long Papers)*, pages 2227–2237, New Orleans, Louisiana. Association for Computational Linguistics.

Radim Řehůřek and Petr Sojka. 2010. Software Framework for Topic Modelling with Large Corpora. In *Proceedings of the LREC 2010 Workshop on New Challenges for NLP Frameworks*, pages 45–50, Valletta, Malta. ELRA. `http://is.muni.cz/publication/884893/en`.

Jivnesh Sandhan, Om Adideva, Digumarthi Komal, Laxmidhar Behera, and Pawan Goyal. 2021. Evaluating neural word embeddings for sanskrit. *arXiv preprint arXiv:2104.00270.*

Jivnesh Sandhan, Amrith Krishna, Pawan Goyal, and Laxmidhar Behera. 2019. Revisiting the role of feature engineering for compound type identification in Sanskrit. In *Proceedings of the 6th International Sanskrit Computational Linguistics Symposium*, pages 28–44, IIT Kharagpur, India. Association for Computational Linguistics.

Rico Sennrich, Barry Haddow, and Alexandra Birch. 2016. Neural machine translation of rare words with subword units. In *Proceedings of the 54th Annual Meeting of the Association for Computational Linguistics (Volume 1: Long Papers)*, pages 1715–1725, Berlin, Germany. Association for Computational Linguistics.

Ashish Vaswani, Noam Shazeer, Niki Parmar, Jakob Uszkoreit, Llion Jones, Aidan N Gomez, Łukasz Kaiser, and Illia Polosukhin. 2017. Attention is all you need. *Advances in neural information processing systems*, 30.

Thomas Wolf, Lysandre Debut, Victor Sanh, Julien Chaumond, Clement Delangue, Anthony Moi, Pierric Cistac, Tim Rault, Rémi Louf, Morgan Funtowicz, et al. 2019. Huggingface's transformers: State-of-the-art natural language processing. *arXiv preprint arXiv:1910.03771*.

Skrutable: Another Step Toward Effective Sanskrit Meter Identification

Tyler Neill
Leipzig University
Institute for Indology and Central Asian Studies
Schillerstraße 6, 04109
Leipzig, Germany
tyler.g.neill@gmail.com

Abstract

There has been good progress toward making computational identification of Sanskrit meter accurate and easy to use. The present project continues this work with a new online tool offering whole-file analysis and detailed scansion output. It also presents a preliminary meter analysis data set of 150,000 verses from a range of genres as a resource to be collaboratively developed to help power future, machine learning-based iterations of the identification task.

1 Introduction

It is already very clear that verse is an important part of Sanskrit literature, and also that having a computer tool to help identify the meter of a given verse is useful. Previous work has laid out the numerous motivations for computational work in Sanskrit meter in particular (Ingalls, 1985; Smith, 1999; Murthy, 2003; Sellmer, 2013), explained the theoretical background (Deo, 2007; Rama N. and Lakshmanan, 2010; Hahn, 2014; Melnad et al., 2015; Rajagopalan, 2018; Scharf, 2018), and presented several usable tools already (especially those of Melnad et al. 2015 and Rajagopalan 2018).

Taken together, this represents good progress toward making computational identification of Sanskrit meter accurate and easy to use. The present project continues this work with a new online tool offering whole-file analysis, detailed scansion output, and a number of other features. It also presents a preliminary meter analysis data set of 150,000 verses from a range of genres as a resource to be collaboratively developed to help power future, machine learning-based iterations of the identification task.

1.1 Basic Task

The basic meter identification task is as follows:

> Given a Sanskrit verse as textual input, output information useful for assessing how it compares to known metrical patterns, including first and foremost a traditional label when possible (e.g., "anuṣṭubh", "śārdūlavikrīḍitā", "āryā", etc.) but also further scansion details for inspection especially in the case of greater variation from conventional patterns.

1.2 Standard Approach

The standard approach to this task reproduces the mechanical method of the student, especially one not immersed in an oral tradition:

1. Understand the textual input as Sanskrit (the data cleaning and "transliteration" step).
2. Break the text into syllables using one simple set of rules, and evaluate each syllable as either light or heavy using another set of rules (the "scansion" step).

Proceedings of the Computational Sanskrit and Digital Humanities, 18th *World Sanskrit Conference 2023*, pages 97–112

3. Compare this pattern of syllable weights against a set of known patterns, looking for a best match (the "identification proper" step).

Depending on particular interests and goals, more detail is also possible, including other analytic units (e.g., pādas, gaṇas, yatis, etc.), specific treatment of partial matches, additional output features (e.g., traditional definitions, sound files), and so on.

1.3 Specific Motivation

Because most users of Sanskrit are not (yet) also computer programmers, a tool that can perform this task must also be user-friendly enough that, for example, a philologist can easily analyze one or more entire texts in this way without needing to know what a "for-loop" is. If students and scholars can be empowered to interact with large amounts of textual data in this way, then not only does their individual research stand to gain, but also, if they aggregate their results, everyone can benefit. Namely, not only do these results immediately serve for scholarly reference, but also, if designed to be machine-readable, they can additionally serve as training data for machine learning-based upgrades of the identification task. One possible such upgrade could consist in the detection of metrical material from among non-metrical material using sequence-to-sequence labeling.

2 Skrutable

The current project, called Skrutable (as in "let's make Sanskrit less inscrutable"), provides just such a forward-looking resource. It may not outperform its peers in every last technical respect (see §4), but it does certainly contribute by empowering its users with access to whole-file analysis and a number of other engaging features. Furthermore, its modular design will allow it to be improved through user feedback and open-source cross-pollination in due time.

2.1 Relation to Previous Work

The present project began in 2015 with direct inspiration from the "Meter Identifying Tool" (at `http://www.sanskritlibrary.org:8080/MeterIdentification`, hereafter "MIT-2015") of Keshav Melnad, Pawan Goyal, and Peter Scharf (Melnad et al., 2015). Two years earlier, in 2013, I had also met and spoken with Anand Mishra in Heidelberg, whose similar 2007 "Sanskrit metre recognizer" tool (formerly at `http://www.sanskrit.sai.uni-heidelberg.de/Chanda/HTML`) is today unfortunately no longer found online. Further motivation to continue developing a Python-based toolkit for Sanskrit came from speaking with two creators of the Classical Language Toolkit (Kyle Johnson and Patrick Burns) at a conference in Leipzig in 2017. Then, while late in the project, I found out about Shreevatsa Rajagopalan's "Metre Identifier" (at `http://www.sanskritmetres.appspot.com`, hereafter "MI-2018"), begun in 2013 and presented in 2018. Finally, while revising this paper, I became aware that work on MIT-2015 had continued (Scharf, 2018).[1] In accordance with my interest in what is easily accessible to

[1]This 2018 paper by Scharf introduced TEITagger, a system for preparing digital editions of texts in accordance with the Text-Encoding Initiative Guidelines. Sections §4–5 of this paper ("TEITagger software" and "Philological use of the TEITagger software", respectively) discuss the further development of MIT-2015, its incorporation into TEITagger, and its application to the Mahābhārata. The paper also does a good job of discussing the following additional previous scholarship, the citations for which are worth mentioning in full:

Edgerton, Franklin. 1939. "The epic triṣṭubh and its hypermetric varieties." Journal of the American Oriental Society 59.2: 159–74. doi: www.jstor. org/stable/594060.

Fitzgerald, James L. 2004. "A meter-guided analysis and discussion of the dicing match of the Sabhāparvan of the Mahābhārata."

—. 2006. "Toward a database of the non-anuṣṭubh verses of the Mahābhārata." In: Epics, Khilas, and Purāṇas: continuities and ruptures. Proceedings of the Third Dubrovnik International Conference on the Sanskrit Epics and Purāṇas. Ed. by Petteri Koskikallio. Zagreb: Croatian Academy of Sciences and Arts, pp. 137–48.

—. 2009. "A preliminary study of the 681 triṣṭubh passages of of the Mahābhārata." In: Epic undertakings: proceedings of the 12th World Sanskrit Conference. Ed. by Robert Goldman and Muneo Tokunaga. Delhi: Motilal Banarsidass, pp. 95–117.

all, I will focus my comparative discussion here only on the two tools that are freely available online: MIT-2015 and MI-2018.

For step 1 (data cleaning and transliteration, see §1.2 above), each of the Sanskrit meter projects named above appears to use its own code for transliteration, drawing on neither the "Sanscript" package (`https://www.github.com/sanskrit/sanscript`) — (I surmise) originally written collaboratively in Javascript and also PHP by the online "Sanskrit Coders" / "Sanskrit Programmers" group but adapted for easy importation in Python in 2013 by Arun K. Prasad — nor the "Aksharamukha" (`https://www.github.com/virtualvinodh/aksharamukha`) by Vinodh Rajan, going back to 2010 and also importable in Python. As a result, there is varying support for transliteration schemes among the different meter projects, and additional use of other tools is sometimes required. For its part, Skrutable, written in Python 3, currently supports the following: Unicode-based International Alphabet for Sanskrit Transliteration (IAST); ASCII-based "Sanskrit Library Phonetic Basic" (SLP1),[2] Harvard-Kyoto (HK), Velthuis (VH), Indian languages Transliteration (ITRANS), "WX" (scheme developed at IIT Kanpur); and Unicode-based Devanagari, Gujarati, and Bengali.[3]

For step 2 (scansion), each of the three online meter tools (MIT-2015, MI-2018, and Skrutable) also solves the relatively simple problems in syllabification and weight calculation on their own, to no major effect on subsequent processing, as far as I can tell. Instead, their main differences lie in the precise handling of step 3, the "identification proper" step (see §1.2 above) and in what other features they offer (e.g., display of scansion information).

2.2 Algorithm

Skrutable's basic algorithm for meter identification does not differ much from other rule-based programming solutions. At its most basic, once relevant characters have been filtered and transformed (via internal processing in SLP1) into the corresponding sequence of light and heavy syllable weight values, this sequence is run through what I will call a "cascade" of checks against regular expressions for known and named patterns. The order of this cascade is fixed, as follows:

- Anuṣṭubh śloka
  - two perfect halves
  - two halves, one perfect, one imperfect
  - a single perfect half
- Varṇavṛttas
  - perfect samavṛtta
  - perfect ardhasamavṛtta
  - perfect viṣamavṛtta
  - perfect upajāti (triṣṭubh etc.)
  - imperfect samavṛtta (two or three out of four pādas)
  - imperfect upajāti (two or three out of four pādas)
- Mātrāvṛttas a.k.a. jātis (perfect only)

If ever an overall perfect match (four out of four perfect pādas) is found, the cascade breaks and the match is reported. All verses are treated as consisting of four parts, and identification of overall imperfect verses currently relies on the internal support of a certain number of perfect individual components within the same verse. As a consequence of this design, not currently supported are: 1) verse types with numbers of pādas other than four (e.g. the three-pāda

[2] More accurately, this project uses only a subset of SLP1, e.g. being less strict about punctuation.

[3] Character frequency-based automatic detection of schemes is also soon to be supported but is still under repair at the time of this publication.

gāyatrī and five-pāda paṅkti of Vedic literature); 2) imperfect ardhasamavṛtta, viṣamavṛtta, or jāti verses; and 3) all cases of partial verses (e.g., single pādas and half verses) or overfull verses (i.e., anything over four pādas) except half-anuṣṭubh. Also, relatively few samavṛttas (less than 100) have been programmed for recognition.

This cascade is then assisted by pāda-resplitting, which happens outside of it. That is, Skrutable always first uses its cascade to try to identify the verse with pāda breaks as given by the user. Having this no-resplit, "WYSIWYG" behavior at the core of the identification algorithm was seen as desirable for both practical and pedagogical purposes. As soon as this fails, however, Skrutable can in turn also produce a series of alternative pāda-break configurations (hereafter: "resplits") for similar cascade testing. This resplitting is initialized by accepting user input as provided (supported string sequences are set as a config variable) and otherwise by dividing the overall length in syllables into four. Resplit points are then moved progressively further out from their starting points, which privileges more likely configurations earlier and helps the identification process successfully complete sooner. Experience found use for two additional parameters here: 1) an option to further privilege the frequently informative user-input midpoint of the verse, i.e., the "bc" pāda break (hereafter: the "keep mid" option); and 2) a distance option determining the total maximum number of resplits to be attempted, with one setting ("resplit max") looking further and one option ("resplit lite") quitting sooner. Skrutable's approach to pāda breaks is thus similar to that of MI-2018 in its concern to reduce the number of resplits tested,[4] but different in its implementation.

The third major component of Skrutable's identification algorithm is result scoring. For as long as no perfect match is found, resplitting and testing against the cascade continues. All results, including partial matches defined by two or three correct pādas out of four (for supported verse types), are collected and scored according to an empirically calibrated look-up table (values being again set as config variables). The highest scoring result is reported as the best match, and other results (as well as statistics on total resplits i.e. identification attempts) are stored as an internal object attribute. In the rare case of a tie as determined by the scoring system, both results are reported with the phrase "atha vā" ("or").

In this way, although resplitting greatly increases the number of checks performed, it allows for comprehensive handling of even difficult cases, even as input in a natural way, and it leads to better performance in cases with pādas of uneven length, either inherently (e.g., jāti, ardhasamavṛtta) or because of data errors. Also, on a modern machine, such as the server currently running the public-facing deployment of the tool, total computation time per verse generally remains in the millisecond range (cp. §4.3 below).

2.3 Implementation

Code

Skrutable is written as an importable Python 3 library with modules for transliteration, scansion, and meter identification.[5] In combination with an associated front-end user interface (hereafter: "the UI") written primarily in Flask, and secondarily with HTML, CSS, and Javascript, Skrutable also functions as a web app, which is currently deployed online at `https://www.skrutable.info` and which can also be installed and run locally if desired.[6] All code and content is on GitHub,[7] and documentation is provided throughout, for both developer and student consultation.

---

[4]Cp. Rajagopalan 2018, pp. 125ff.

[5]A simple wrapper module also provides access to a pretrained version of the Hellwig-Nehrdich Sanskrit Sandhi and Compound Splitter (Hellwig and Nehrdich, 2018).

[6]The web interface was initially found at the address `http://www.skrutable.pythonanywhere.com`.

[7]Library at `https://www.github.com/tylergneill/skrutable`, and front-end at `https://www.github.com/tylergneill/skrutable_front_end`.

User Interface

The Skrutable UI (Fig. 1) is designed to provide convenient access to the library's three major functions and to help tailor output to user needs.

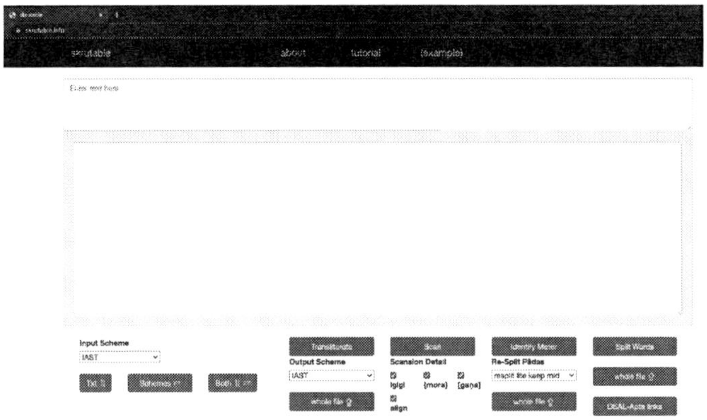

(a) On desktop device

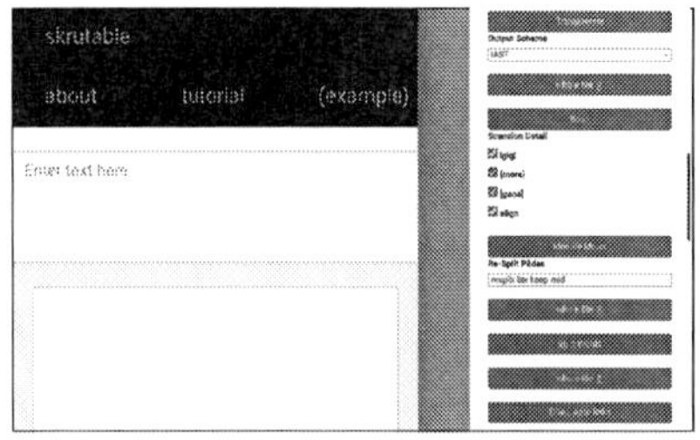

(b) On mobile device

Figure 1: Screenshots of blank UI

These three major functions and their interrelations are represented in the UI by its centermost top blue buttons, read left to right (see Fig. 2). That is, after first controlling for the input text's transliteration scheme, Skrutable can next "scan" the input text for its straightforward and essential metrical properties. Then, if desired, it can also, in a third and final separate step, attempt to "identify" the verse as being of a particular meter. Showing the user two separate buttons for the latter two functions is meant to help clarify this important difference.

Figure 2: *Major function buttons*

As explained above (§2.2), when the "Scan" button is clicked, Skrutable's "scansion" module does not remove pāda breaks, such that this basic stage of the output exactly reflects the breaks in the input.[8] Scansion output detail (hereafter just "scansion detail") is broken down into four optional components, each of which can be toggled with its own checkbox below the "Scan" button: 1) raw syllable weights, 2) mora count, 3) syllable count and grouping into gaṇa abbreviations, and 4) syllable-to-weight alignment (using a simple monospace font with fixed per-character width plus spaces for filler). In general, any Romanization scheme would work well for this scansion output, but since Indic scripts do not yet also display well in this context, I opt to output only IAST for now.

Then, if "none" is chosen as the meter identification "Re-Split Pādas" option using that drop-down box and if the "Identify Meter" button is clicked, Skrutable's "meter_identification" module first internally invokes the separate "scansion" module to fetch the appropriate scansion information, and then it runs the identification cascade a single time with the pāda breaks as given and outputs the result. If the verse was, for example, not input as four separate lines, then this no-split identification will certainly fail, regardless of the textual content (see Fig. 3). In fact, I see this possibility for very literal behavior as desirable from a pedagogical standpoint. That is, a user may, if he or she wishes, use the scansion output to iteratively work toward a proper pāda break solution him- or herself, visually scrutinizing patterns, manually changing

[8]Surrounding or multiple pāda-break sequences are currently treated as extraneous and simplified.

the input pāda breaks, adding or subtracting "scansion detail" features, and again clicking the "Scan" and/or "Identify Meter" buttons, until a positive result is found.

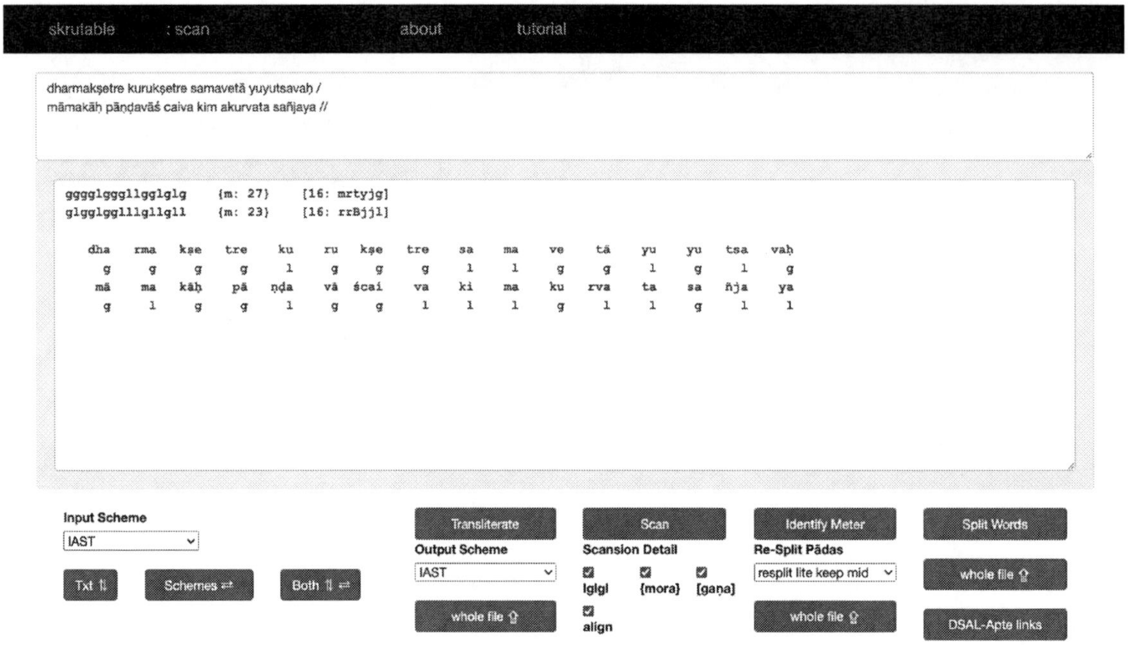

Figure 3: *Meter id., resplit "none", on two lines, with failure id. label "na kiṃcid adhyavasitam"*

A few more things to note here: 1) Both input and output are in plain-text, making them easy to play with and/or copy-paste as needed. 2) Swap buttons are also provided for text buffers and input schemes. 3) The "scansion detail" options apply equally for both the "Scan" and "Identify Meter" buttons. 4) Text-buffer contents and all selected options will persist between visits to the site.[9]

Frequently, however, a user will not be interested in splitting the verse manually in this way, and so the meter identification module also includes functionality for resplitting, described above (§2.2). Internally, scansion and the identification cascade are simply repeated for each resplit, in a simple loop. In the UI, however, when "Identify Meter" is clicked with a resplit option active, all that appears as output is the highest-ranking pāda break configuration, its scansion details, and a label describing the result (Fig. 4).

For users also interested in multi-verse, i.e., whole-file metrical analysis, it is then as easy as looking past the "Identify Meter" button and instead clicking the "whole file" upload button located below it. One then can follow the instructions to upload a file,[10] and once processing and downloading are finished, output can be retrieved from one's normal browser download location. This output consists of a plain-text file (Fig. 5), containing for each verse its full text, its scansion detail according to chosen settings, and its meter identification label. Additionally, if desired, the system can also be made to output a summary of detected verse types in tab-separated value (TSV) format (Fig. 6).[11] In this table, perfect meter types and their associated frequencies appear to the left, while imperfect outcomes and their frequencies appear to the right.

[9]This out-of-the-box, client-side "*session*" feature of the Flask web-development framework works essentially like a cookie.

[10]The file currently must be in plain-text, properly encoded in UTF-8 and in the chosen transliteration scheme, with one verse per line, and with an ASCII-only filename.

[11]This recently developed feature is demonstrated in the "Jupyter Notebook" folder of the GitHub repo and should be incorporated into the UI before long.

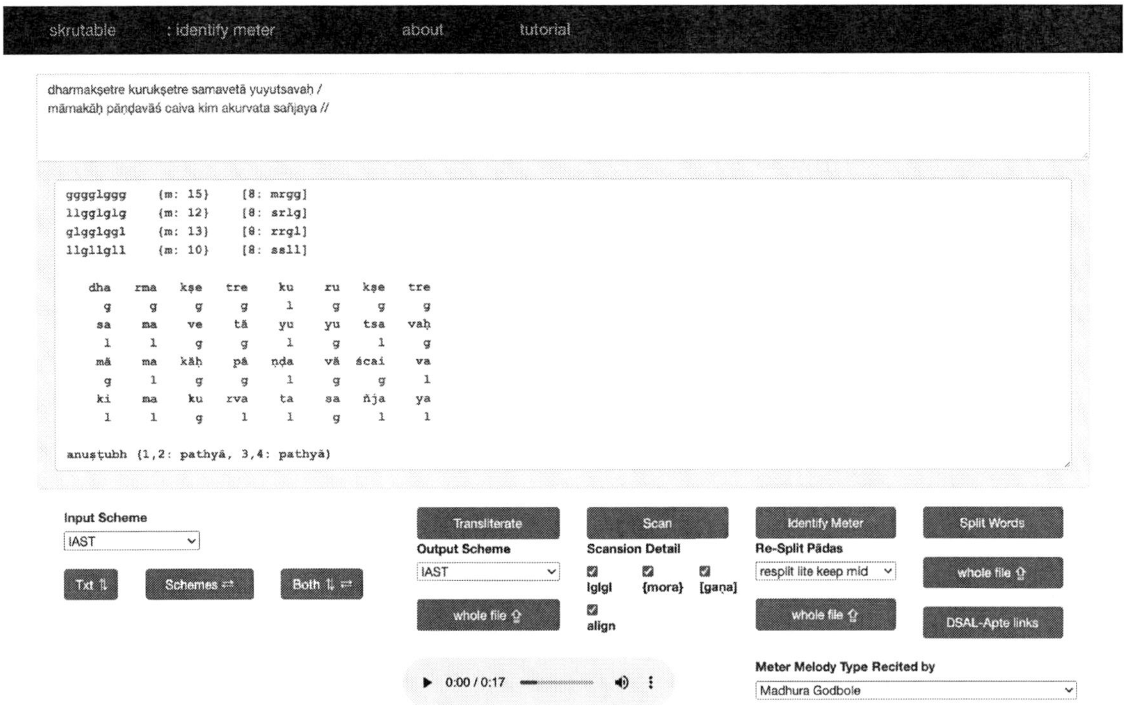

Figure 4: *Meter id., "resplit lite keep mid", with correct four-pāda solution (pathyā anuṣṭubh)*

Whole-file processing takes just a few seconds in most cases (see §4.3 below), so trial-and-error adjustment of input content and settings is not costly.

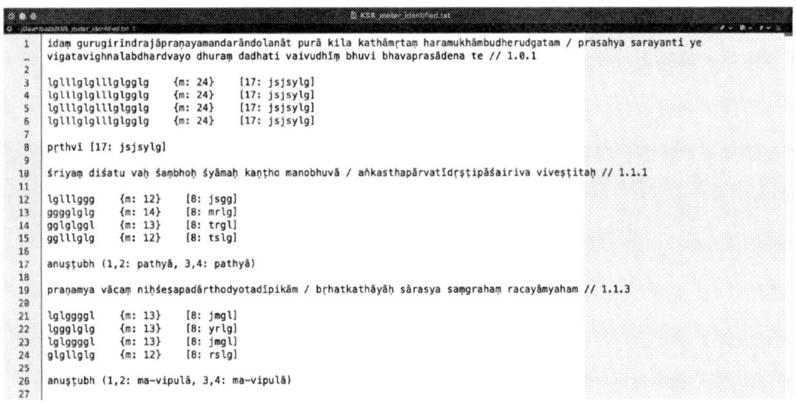

Figure 5: *Text-file output (in BBEdit), KSS examples (pṛthvī, anuṣṭubh pathyā, ma-vipulā)*

Finally, in addition to the meter identification functionality already described, the UI also offers a few more power features, both regarding meter and otherwise:[12]

- Whole-file transliteration
- Transliteration scheme encoding standardization (e.g., to ensure precomposed IAST "ṝ")
- A melody player for successful single-verse meter id. (multiple voice/melody options, details available at `https://www.skrutable.info/reciters`)

[12] Additional features still undergoing development in late 2021 include: Indic-style (i.e. "varṇamālā"/"akṣaramālā"-order) list alphabetization; virāma options for Indic output (both more and less); and options for punctuation preservation in word splitting.

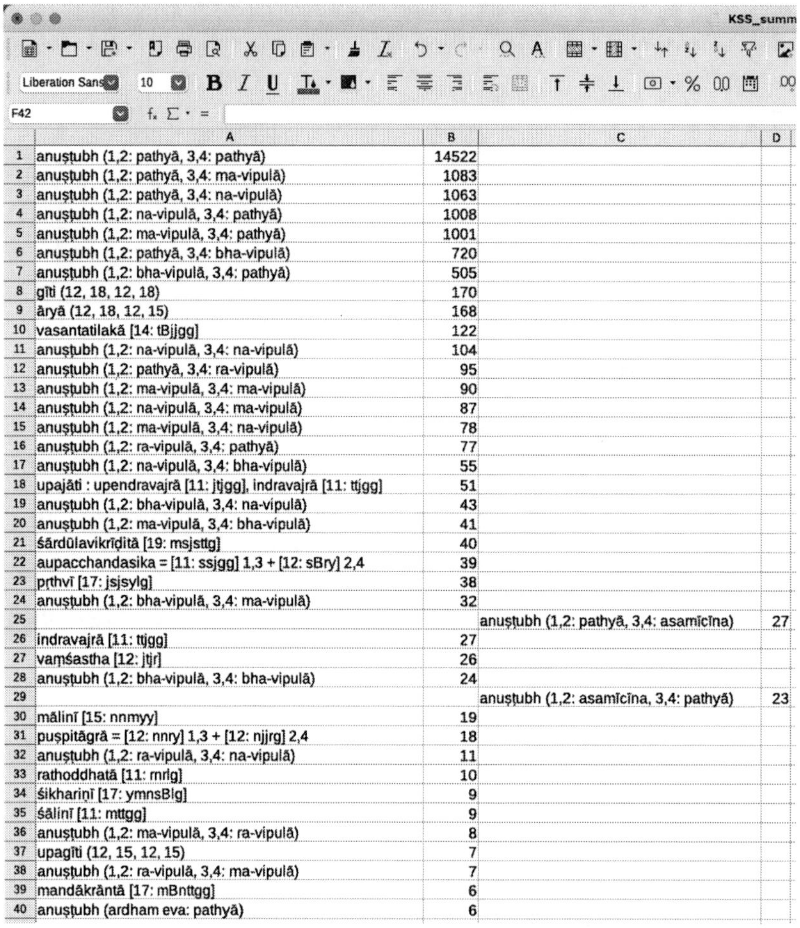

	A	B	C	D
1	anuṣṭubh (1,2: pathyā, 3,4: pathyā)	14522		
2	anuṣṭubh (1,2: pathyā, 3,4: ma-vipulā)	1083		
3	anuṣṭubh (1,2: pathyā, 3,4: na-vipulā)	1063		
4	anuṣṭubh (1,2: na-vipulā, 3,4: pathyā)	1008		
5	anuṣṭubh (1,2: ma-vipulā, 3,4: pathyā)	1001		
6	anuṣṭubh (1,2: pathyā, 3,4: bha-vipulā)	720		
7	anuṣṭubh (1,2: bha-vipulā, 3,4: pathyā)	505		
8	gīti (12, 18, 12, 18)	170		
9	āryā (12, 18, 12, 15)	168		
10	vasantatilakā [14: tBjjgg]	122		
11	anuṣṭubh (1,2: na-vipulā, 3,4: na-vipulā)	104		
12	anuṣṭubh (1,2: pathyā, 3,4: ra-vipulā)	95		
13	anuṣṭubh (1,2: ma-vipulā, 3,4: ma-vipulā)	90		
14	anuṣṭubh (1,2: na-vipulā, 3,4: ma-vipulā)	87		
15	anuṣṭubh (1,2: ma-vipulā, 3,4: na-vipulā)	78		
16	anuṣṭubh (1,2: ra-vipulā, 3,4: pathyā)	77		
17	anuṣṭubh (1,2: na-vipulā, 3,4: bha-vipulā)	55		
18	upajāti : upendravajrā [11: jtjgg], indravajrā [11: ttjgg]	51		
19	anuṣṭubh (1,2: bha-vipulā, 3,4: na-vipulā)	43		
20	anuṣṭubh (1,2: ma-vipulā, 3,4: bha-vipulā)	41		
21	śārdūlavikrīḍitā [19: msjsttg]	40		
22	aupacchandasika = [11: ssjgg] 1,3 + [12: sBry] 2,4	39		
23	pṛthvī [17: jsjsylg]	38		
24	anuṣṭubh (1,2: bha-vipulā, 3,4: ma-vipulā)	32		
25			anuṣṭubh (1,2: pathyā, 3,4: asamīcīna)	27
26	indravajrā [11: ttjgg]	27		
27	vaṃśastha [12: jtjr]	26		
28	anuṣṭubh (1,2: bha-vipulā, 3,4: bha-vipulā)	24		
29			anuṣṭubh (1,2: asamīcīna, 3,4: pathyā)	23
30	mālinī [15: nnmyy]	19		
31	puṣpitāgrā = [12: nnry] 1,3 + [12: njjrg] 2,4	18		
32	anuṣṭubh (1,2: ra-vipulā, 3,4: na-vipulā)	11		
33	rathoddhatā [11: rnrlg]	10		
34	śikhariṇī [17: ymnsBlg]	9		
35	śālinī [11: mttgg]	9		
36	anuṣṭubh (1,2: ma-vipulā, 3,4: ra-vipulā)	8		
37	upagīti (12, 15, 12, 15)	7		
38	anuṣṭubh (1,2: ra-vipulā, 3,4: ma-vipulā)	7		
39	mandākrāntā [17: mBnttgg]	6		
40	anuṣṭubh (ardham eva: pathyā)	6		

Figure 6: *TSV-file output (in LibreOffice), KSS, top 40 meters, with frequencies*

- Point-and-click access to the powerful plain-text Sanskrit Sandhi and Compound Splitter[13]
- Conversion of split words into hyperlinks for V.S. Apte's Practical Sanskrit-English Dictionary (1957-59 ed.) as provided by Digital Dictionaries of South Asia (allied with Digital South Asia Library or DSAL)

3 Data

Here I will describe the textual data, in total about 150,000 Sanskrit (and Prakrit) verses, pertaining to the assessment of Skrutable's meter identification system.

3.1 Input

Data was sourced largely from GRETIL. Other sources used include 1) the author's own repository of NLP-ready philosophical texts,[14] and 2) the repository of Vishvas Vasuki.[15]

[13] Using the pretrained model at `https://www.github.com/OliverHellwig/sanskrit/tree/master/papers/2018emnlp` (Hellwig and Nehrdich, 2018). The Skrutable wrapper also supports unlimited input length and punctuation preservation.

[14] At `https://www.github.com/tylergneill/pramana-nlp`, used here specifically for Ślokavārtika, Pramāṇavārtika, Pramāṇavārtikālaṃkāra, and Tattvasaṃgraha. In addition to GRETIL, this repository uses data from 1) SARIT, 2) the unofficially circulating work of Jongcheol Lee and Helmut Krasser, and 3) original digitization.

[15] At `https://www.github.com/sanskrit/raw_etexts`, used here specifically only for Mālatīmādhava. This repository draws on `http://www.sanskrit.nic.in/ebooks.php`, a number of other scraped text repositories, and also some unknown sources.

The following nineteen texts from various genres (Epic, Story, Kāvya, Philosophy) and generally of large size were chosen for analysis: Mahābhārata (MBh), Kathāsaritsāgara (KSS), Rāmāyaṇa (Ram), Pañcatantra (PT_vv), Mahāsubhāṣitasaṃgraha (MSS), Śiśupālavadha (SpV), Raghuvaṃśa (RVams), Kirātārjunīya (Kir), Sattasaī/Saptaśatī (SS, in Prakrit), Kumārasaṃbhava (KuS), Meghadūta (MgD), Śatakatraya (ST), Mālatīmādhava (MM_vv), Tattvasaṃgraha (TS), Ślokavārtika (SV), Pramāṇavārtikālaṃkāra (PVA_kk), Pramāṇavārtika (PV_kk), Bodhicāryāvatāra (BCA), and Mūlamadhyamakakārikā (MMK). Metrical details for the individual texts, including their respective lengths in verses, are given below in Figs. 7–10.

Original files are provided in the Skrutable_front_end GitHub repo, along with cleaned versions actually used for input. Cleaning interventions included 1) extracting verse from "mixed"-style (i.e., miśraka) texts (PV1_kk from PV-Svavṛtti, TS from TS-Pañjikā, PVA_kk, and MM_vv); 2) re-applying sandhi in certain of these cases (PV_kk); and 3) adjusting numbering, for example, breaking verses that obviously consist of three or more verse halves (pādadvayas) into multiple verses, or simply removing non-canonical material (e.g., from the digitized critical MBh). Digitization quality (not to mention edition quality) is known to be mixed, but as has been observed (Rajagopalan 2018: 128–130), partly erroneous data is actually a virtue in the present context, as the ability to gracefully handle and illuminate data problems on a large scale is one of most useful potential applications of such tools.

3.2 Output

For the present study, the meter identification settings "resplit max" and "keep mid" were used. The exact output text-files produced by Skrutable, both with all available scansion details and in a more abbreviated form (verse number and meter label only), are available on the GitHub repo. Also provided are TSV summary files generated during the analysis, both for individual texts and overall. It is also easy enough to repeat the analysis for oneself by uploading the same input data to the Skrutable website, for example to see how quickly the script runs on a given text or to try out other settings. Since exact output will also vary depending on ongoing project upgrades, the exact code used for generating this particular data is archived as a package release on Zenodo.[16]

4 Evaluation

For a meter-identification tool like Skrutable, it would be desirable to evaluate four things: 1) identification accuracy, 2) usefulness of output information, 3) speed, and 4) ease of use.

4.1 Accuracy

I'll begin my discussion of system accuracy by providing some background on how the two similar projects up for comparison here have been assessed. MIT-2015 was tested on "a database of 1031 verses in the Pañcākhyānaka, including 291 verses in 23 different types of meters besides Anuṣṭubh" (Melnad et al. 2015: 325). The tool was iteratively calibrated during testing, and overall performance was evaluated as follows: "MIT correctly recognized 1018 out of the 1031 verses (98.7%) and 287 out of the 291 non-Anuṣṭubh verses (98.6%). There were no cases in which a meter was recognized incorrectly" (ibid.: 342). The MIT-2015 software is not easily available online, but I was able to obtain from Peter Scharf updated software for the 2018 TEITagger project (JAR file, v28) into which MIT-2015 was incorporated. I also received the relevant Pañcākhyānaka database file (XML), and with some help, I was able to get TEITagger working on this file to identify the meters. Since these results sometimes differ from those of MIT-2015 online, I cannot yet speak to the above accuracy claims. Time permitting, I will continue to work on this verification process.

In turn, Rajagopalan 2018, while noting that "the lack of a reliable (and nontrivial) 'gold standard' hinders attaching a numeric value to the accuracy" describes how for its tool "a large

[16] Available for download at `https://zenodo.org/badge/latestdoi/103173253` (Skrutable) and `https://zenodo.org/badge/latestdoi/328881004` (Skrutable_front_end).

number of texts such as from GRETIL were examined", again enabling tool calibration and resulting in a "recall of 100% in the examples tested" and a precision that is "lower and harder to measure because of errors in the input" (2018: 128–129). Although the underlying GRETIL texts are themselves relatively accessible, the exact "example" input used is not easily available for inspection, nor is exact output. However, a useful table of summary statistics, not featured in Rajagopalan 2018 but mostly coinciding with the texts mentioned therein, is found on the project website.[17] The data from this table is incorporated into Figs. 7 and 8 below. As for the software itself, I found the Python code relatively easy to download and apply to numerous verses.

In the absence of a gold-standard, Skrutable is not yet evaluated with a percentage accuracy. Instead, in order to enable more direct comparison with other projects and thereby begin to approach such a standard, Skrutable was tested on texts similar to those used to test the other two projects discussed here, and all results are being made publicly available: one text for comparison with MIT-2015, the Pañcākhyānaka a.k.a. Pañcatantra (only the GRETIL version so far), and six texts for comparison with MI-2018, namely, MSS, SpV, RVams, Kir, KuS, and ST (again all GRETIL). In addition to these (seven texts in about 17,000 verses), Skrutable was also tested on considerably more and diverse material (eleven additional texts in about 133,000 verses) in the hopes of attracting the interest of more scholars who can help produce the needed gold-standard annotations. The overall summary statistics are presented here in two pairs of tables, the first pair (Figs. 7 and 8) for material overlapping with previous projects, and the second pair (Figs. 9 and 10) for original analysis of novel data.[18]

Visual inspection of the first pair of tables (Figs. 7 and 8) reveals a great deal of numerical agreement between MI-2018 and Skrutable, but many individual discrepancies as well. The latter are strongly suspected to be due mostly to differences in how imperfect verses are handled (see §4.2 below). For Skrutable, in line with the detailed data it was designed to produce, three additional types of information are given: 1) a few important meter subtypes (for anuṣṭubh and upajāti); 2) two numbers instead of one in those cases (anuṣṭubh, upajāti, and samavṛtta) where Skrutable is made to explicitly distinguish imperfect verses (e.g., for indravajrā in Kirātārjunīya, 18 perfect and 2 imperfect); and 3) explicit labels for specific kinds of categorical failures ("ajñātasamavṛtta", "ajñātārdhasamavṛtta", "no id", and in fact most cases of "non-triṣṭubh upajāti"). In short, Skrutable, like the other tools, seems generally capable of correct identification in the case of good data.

4.2 Usefulness of Output Information

On the other hand, especially in the case of worse data, Skrutable's basic scansion output (cp. Fig. 4) is designed especially for iterative exploration after identification fails. Whereas the user interfaces of both MIT-2015 and MI-2018 use HTML text formatting (color and bold weighting, respectively) to highlight syllable weight patterns, Skrutable's strictly plain-text output — with

[17]`http://www.sanskritmetres.appspot.com/statistics`, sourced from GitHub repo "templates" folder.

[18]Note that Scharf 2018 also presents similar analysis for over 73,000 verses of the Mahābhārata and compares results with Fitzgerald 2009 (see footnote 1 above). I quote here a summary of Scharf's MBh results (p. 242) in full:

> TEITagger version 2 tagged 73,436 verses and 1,057 prose sentences in 386 paragraphs. The verses include 68,860 Anuṣṭubhs, 2,970 Triṣṭubhs, 431 Jagatī, 322 Indravajrā, 0 Upendravajrā, 496 of the standard Upajāti variety alternating the two preceding, 88 Śālā, 78 Vāṇī (other Upajātis), 31 Aparavaktra (an ardhasamavrtta meter), 22 Praharṣiṇī, 16 Rucirā, 9 Mālinī, 4 Vasantatilakā, 4 Puṣpitāgrā, 1 Śārdūlavikrīḍita, 1 Halamukhī, 1 Āryāgīti (a type of Āryā), 1 mixture of half Kāmakrīḍā and half Kāmukī, and a hundred unidentified. The unidentified metrical patterns include for instance, 1 mixture of half Kāmukī and half unidentified, 1 mixture of a deviant pāda with subsequent Anuṣṭubh, jagatī, and Triṣṭubh pādas, as well as 98 other uninvestigated unidentified patterns.

Comparison of this paragraph (or Table 1 in Scharf 2018, p. 244 — or Table 3, pp. 245–6 presenting the results of "TEITagger version 17") with Figs. 9–10 here reveals only a rough correspondence between the two attempts. Clearly a more careful comparison is a desideratum for future study.

(Skr vs. MI and MIT)	Kir		KuS		MSS		RVams		SpV		ST		PT_vv	
	1,040		613		9,979		1,637		1,645		324		1,105	
anuṣṭubh śloka	(MI)	(Skr)	(etc.)										(MIT)	(Skr)
pathyā (MI: all)	125	103, 2	157	120, 1	4457	3309, 185	565	433, 55	231	104, 36	35	29, 1	740	639, 154
vipulā		20		36		629, 14		71, 5		76, 13		5		57, 5
upajāti														
comm.triṣṭ. (MI: all)	132	129	187	180	490	436	463	425	62	37	14	7		21
other triṣṭubh		6		4		63		58		34		2		6
non-triṣṭubh						18, 51		0, 1		18, 2		2		3, 2
samavṛtta														
pramāṇikā					16									
indravajrā	20	18, 2	30	30, 3	149	104, 8	104	66, 24	21	6, 22	1	1		6, 5
upendravajrā	24	22, 1	9	9, 1	41	27, 5	28	9, 16	25	5, 18		0, 1		2
rathoddhatā	38	37, 1	90	88	99	86, 3	151	120, 18	87	80, 3	3	2, 1		1
śālinī	3	3			45	27, 1	1	1	81	63, 5	3	3		1, 1
svāgatā	77	71			102	79, 1	1		91	44, 14				
toṭaka					19	18	1	1	2	1				
drutavilambita	33	32, 1			106	101, 5	64	48, 16	69	37, 28	5	3, 1		2
pramitākṣarā	51	49, 2			35	33, 1			82	52, 23				1
vaṃśastha	214	203, 11	84	83, 1	197	167, 16	74	63, 10	145	40, 34	3	2, 1		7, 5
praharṣiṇī	50	46, 4			42	36, 2	8	6, 2	76	35, 35				
mañjubhāṣiṇī					15	15	1	1	69	59, 10				
rucirā					9	7, 2	1	0, 1	68	62, 6				
vasantatilakā	24	23, 1	4	4	728	595, 57	46	40, 6	88	41, 38	34	22, 11		28, 2
mālinī	13	13	6	5, 1	209	193, 16	13	6, 7	72	52, 18	11	7, 4		2
pṛthvī					72	67, 4			1	1	5	1, 4		
mandākrāntā					163	136, 8	7	4, 3	3	2	8	6		4
śikhariṇī	3	3			327	309, 18			1		50	31, 15		2, 1
hariṇī					105	99, 6	1	0, 1	1		8	5, 3		3
śārdūlavikrīḍitā					1221	979, 91			5	4	104	73, 27		29, 7
sragdharā					237	181, 24			1	1	21	12, 8		1, 1

Figure 7: *Summary statistics, Overlap (anuṣṭubh, upajāti, samavṛtta), other tools in grey*

(Skr vs. MI and MIT)	Kir		KuS		MSS		RVams		SpV		ST		PT_vv	
	1,040		613		9,979		1,637		1,645		324		1,105	
ardhasamavṛtta	(MI)	(Skr)	(etc.)											
aparavaktra		1			1	4								
puṣpitāgrā	69	67	2	2	106	99	4	3	78	45	1	1		
viyoginī	62	60	44	44	91	79	97	72	79	71	2	1		1
aupacchandasika	36	33			68	64	2	2	83	68				
viṣamavṛtta														
udgatā	52	38			2	1			91	51				
jāti														
āryā					696	668		1			12	6		67
(MI: āryā "loose")	1				10		1		4		1			
gīti		1			140	144		9		4	1			
upagīti					53	61				1				4
udgīti					35	33								
āryāgīti		4				14		1	1	36				
not identified														
ajñātasamavṛtta		0, 19		0, 1		6, 40		0, 21		0, 128		0, 4		0, 9
ajñātārdhasamavṛtta		1				10		4		51		2		1
no id		1			43	34		5	7	9		19		28

Figure 8: *Summary statistics, Overlap (ardhasamavṛtta, viṣamavṛtta, jāti, errors), other tools in grey*

(Skrutable only)	MBh	Ram	KSS	SS	MM_vv	MMK	BCA	SV	PV_kk	PVA_kk	TS
	77,810	19,354	21,545	999	226	448	913	3,351	1,452	2,674	3,646
anuṣṭubh śloka	(Skr)	(etc.)									
pathyā	54811, 591	14576, 235	14528, 50		14	298, 21	638, 13	2985, 152	889, 139	1919, 254	3345, 92
vipulā	17463, 109	3636, 35	6151, 12		1	127, 2	181, 3	149, 5	335, 24	379, 35	201, 2
upajāti											
comm.triṣṭ.	1075	344	51		2		33	9		11	
other triṣṭubh	2162	15		1			3	3		3	
non-triṣṭubh	17, 6	2, 7	2, 4	0, 1	1			0, 1	0, 3	1, 2	0, 2
samavṛtta											
pramāṇikā	38, 1										
indravajrā	174, 87	36, 8	27		8		6	3		2	
upendravajrā	94, 81	80, 15	4		1		2			4, 1	
rathoddhatā	5		10		3					2	
śālinī	38, 62		9		2		0, 1			2	
svāgatā			1							2	
toṭaka											
drutavilambita			1		4			0, 1		2	
pramitākṣarā	0, 3										
vaṃśastha	360, 108	268, 40	26, 3		2			1		3, 1	
praharṣiṇī	8, 1	4	2		7						
mañjubhāṣiṇī					7						
rucirā	28, 13	5, 1									
vasantatilakā	3		122		49		3			2	
mālinī	9		19		21		2	3, 1		1	
pṛthvī			38		4				1		
mandākrāntā			6		14						
śikhariṇī			9		22						
hariṇī					12						
śārdūlavikrīḍitā	1		40		32		1				
sragdharā			1		6		3				

Figure 9: *Summary statistics, Original (anuṣṭubh, upajāti, samavṛtta)*

(Skrutable only)	MBh	Ram	KSS	SS	MM_vv	MMK	BCA	SV	PV_kk	PVA_kk	TS
	77,810	19,354	21,545	999	226	448	913	3,351	1,452	2,674	3,646
ardhasamavṛtta											
aparavaktra	27	9			1		2			1	
puṣpitāgrā	33	26	18		5		2				
viyoginī			3		1		3				
aupacchandasika			39		1		9				
viṣamavṛtta											
udgatā											
jāti											
āryā	1	1	168	956	11		1		3	4	
gīti			170	18							
upagīti	46		7	9				5	11	12	
udgīti			1	2			1	1			
āryāgīti										1	
not identified											
ajñātasam.	5, 166	0, 3	0, 16	0, 5	0, 2		0, 1	0, 18	0, 23	0, 8	0, 2
ajñātārdhasam.	51	2			1		2	1		10	
no id	60	1	3	7				16	23	12	2

Figure 10: *Summary statistics, Original (ardhasamavṛtta, viṣamavṛtta, jāti, errors)*

its tightly printing block of "l" and "g" characters, line-by-line syllable and mora counts, and syllable-weight alignment — relies primarily on the visible geometry of the line-separated raw syllable weights, and secondarily on the other scansion information calculated therefrom (morae, syllable counts, and gaṇas), also presented as line-separated. Since each way has advantages, there is no reason not to eventually offer both as options, at least in a UI.

In the case of anuṣṭubh and upajāti, Skrutable's identification behavior and output labels are uniquely specific. For anuṣṭubh, Skrutable recognizes and names the various vipulās with sensitivity to their usual conditioning (Murthy 2003, Hahn 2014), and it outputs the caveat "not right" (asamīcīna) whenever any conditioning rule is violated, whether it be one of a vipulā or either of the two more fundamental anuṣṭubh rules, "Piṅgala 1" (akṣaras 2 and 3 in odd pāda cannot both be short) and "Piṅgala 2" (akṣaras 2 through 4 in an even pāda cannot be a ra-gaṇa) (Murthy 2003: 103). By contrast, while MI-2015 does recognize the basic vipulā, it uses obscure numerical labels (e.g., "anuṣṭubh3" for a na-vipulā), and it does not explicitly note the role of conditioning. That is, when either of Piṅgala's rules is violated, MIT-2015 fails silently. Meanwhile, MI-2018 seems to be sensitive to none of these details, issuing the label "anuṣṭubh (Śloka)" regardless. Similarly, Skrutable's particular handling of upajātis allows it to distinguish them into subtypes of standard triṣṭubh (indravajrā and upendravajrā), other triṣṭubh (e.g., including vātormī, vāṇī, or also unnamed 11-syllable patterns, e.g. as found in abundance in the Bhagavadgītā), and non-triṣṭubh (the widest meaning of the term "upajāti", as used also for combinations of e.g. 12-syllable i.e. jagatī pādas). Currently, Skrutable takes no further details like āryā syncopation structure (Ollett, 2012) or yatis into consideration.

For the case of imperfect or failed identification, Skrutable's output is again designed to be practical and to avoid both false positives and false negatives. Where some structural pattern is still discernible on the basis of internal support within the verse itself (see §2.2), the suspected type is suggested in the identification label along with a caveat of "unrecognized" ("ajñāta") or "only # pādas correct" ("# eva pādāḥ yuktāḥ") or "not right" ("asamīcīna"), depending on the case. On the other hand, apart from whatever help the basic scansion output may provide for real-time iterative problem-solving, the null identification label ("na kiṃcid adhyavasitam") itself currently provides no specifically helpful information in the following cases: 1) imperfect anuṣṭubhs with zero perfect halves (whether out of one or two), 2) samavṛttas with three or more imperfect pādas, 3) imperfect ardhavṛttas, 4) imperfect viṣamavṛttas, and 5) imperfect jātis.

Here it is useful to consider the alternative strategy of MI-2018, most clearly visible in the case of samavṛttas, to find the nearest identification match using string-alignments of the calculated syllable weight pattern against known patterns (Rajagopalan 2018, pp. 127–128). This allows for extremely clear output in certain cases (see e.g. the red-colored "[-]" in Fig. 11 below, and also the example in Rajagopalan 2018, p. 115).

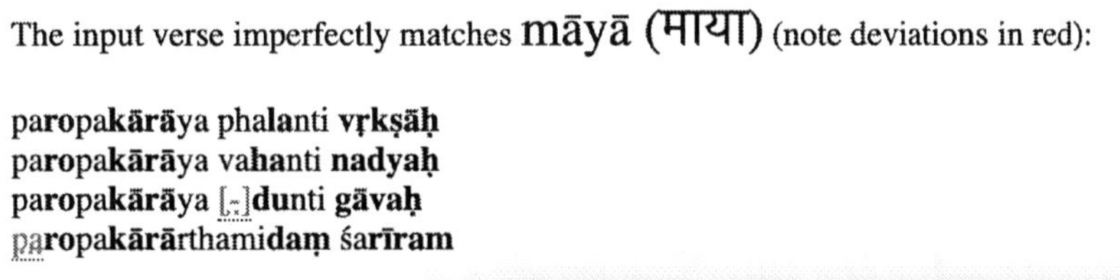

Figure 11: *Screenshot from MI-2018 of samavṛtta alignment output ("dunti" for "duhanti")*

However, this strategy does not appear to work equally well in all cases, and its usefulness is occasionally mitigated by the tendency of MI-2018 (anticipated at Rajagopalan 2018: 132–33) to produce misleading false positives. An example of this is seen in Fig. 11 with the label of "māyā" for an upendravajrā that is missing a syllable in pāda c.[19] Most likely, some combination of these two strategies (reliance on internal structure plus string-alignment), perhaps combined

[19]According to Piṅgala's Chandaḥśāstra (Kedāranātha, 1938), the name "māyā" refers to an upajāti with the specific sequence upendravajrā, upendravajrā, upendravajrā, indravajrā. It is for this reason that the first syllable "pa" of pāda d in Fig. 11 is also mootly colored red as deviating from this "māyā" pattern.

with Skrutable's supplementary scoring strategy — and the latter perhaps also augmented by frequency-based score penalties for very rare meters — may be the best way forward for improving the deterministic approach. Since MI-2018 does also in fact have an unpublished "fulltext" (i.e., whole-file) upload feature in its UI,[20] and since the tool is open source, more systematic comparison of these different output strategies is only a matter of time.

4.3 Speed

I adopt the Tokunaga-Smith digitization of Valmīki's Rāmāyaṇa (19,354 verses) and Ollet's digitization of Weber's Sattasaī/Saptaśatī (999 verses) as speed-run test cases. Comparable speeds can probably also be expected for other tools once they are adapted as necessary,[21] but the main point here is simply to illustrate that text size need no longer pose a significant barrier to such analysis whatsoever.

Rāmāyaṇa

Run on the PythonAnywhere server with the "Re-Split Pādās" option "resplit lite keep mid", the task of analyzing meter for the entire Rāmāyaṇa completes in about 14.5 seconds, i.e., an average of about 1,330 verses per second. With "resplit max keep mid", the time is 23.5 seconds, or about 820 verses/sec, but performance remains nearly identical, with different outcomes only for a dozen cases of triṣṭubh and/or jagatī verse types with data problems. On the other hand, if run on a local machine,[22] "resplit lite keep mid" finishes in about 9.0 seconds, or 2,150 verses/sec, and "resplit max keep mid" again in about 14.5 seconds. If additional explicit pāda break information[23] is used, namely by automatically choosing the relatively confident no-resplit option for such cases and "resplit lite keep mid" for other cases, the time is again reduced to 7.5 seconds, or about 2,580 verses/sec. Again, identification results remain basically constant.

Sattasaī/Saptaśatī

This text, consisting entirely of āryā verses (or because Prakrit, actually gāhā i.e. gāthā), demonstrates the usefulness of Skrutable's "resplit max" option. Because success in identifying āryā is so much better with this option, I do not discuss the "resplit lite" option here. With "resplit max", the successful analysis completes in about 14.5 seconds when run on the PythonAnywhere server (68.9 verses/sec) and in about 10.5 seconds (95.1 verses/sec) when run locally. The slower speed (still less than 1/100th of a second for an individual verse) is due to jāti verses requiring many more resplits before a best match is found.

4.4 Ease of Use

Ease of use is necessarily quite subjective, but some comments are still warranted. With Skrutable, great care has been taken with the UI to reduce effort and possible confusion on the user's part. User focus is maintained on a single display window, which is formatted simply and cleanly with basic Bootstrap CSS and which thus also displays relatively comfortably on mobile devices (see Fig. 1b). Settings allow for users to choose from among numerous transliteration schemes, as well as a range of scansion-detail and other options, all of which are conveniently preserved between sessions. Above all, whole-file processing is available with just a few clicks. In short, user convenience is highly valued, and further feedback is most welcome.

[20] See `http://www.sanskritmetres.appspot.com/fulltext`.

[21] MI-2018 would most accurately be compared by directly utilizing its code. Submission of moderately large texts to its unpublished "fulltext" website endpoint so far suggests speeds slower by one order of magnitude, whereas processing seems to hang in the case of very large texts of 10,000 verses or more (likely a file-size constraint of the server). Inspection of output is also complicated by this mode's emphasis on complex HTML formatting, which makes output rendering prohibitively slow.

[22] Here, on a MacBook Pro 2020 with 2 GHz Quad-Core Intel Core i5. The Jupyter Notebook used for local runs is also available for inspection at `https://www.github.com/tylergneill/skrutable/tree/master/jupyter_notebooks`.

[23] E.g., such as was formerly available on GRETIL at least as late as December 2018 in the form of semicolons between ab and cd pādas.

5 Conclusion

With digitized texts and capable computing resources becoming ever more available, it is high time that students and scholars of Sanskrit be able to use a tool to analyze the metrical properties of a given text without themselves needing to know how to code. Skrutable empowers users to do just that, for any number of verses at a time, accurately, with detailed output, at speed, and (in good cases) with only minimal data prep. As a bonus, those who do code and who want to include such scansion or meter-identification functionality in their own computational projects can also take advantage of Skrutable's being written modularly and in a popular language with robust community support. What's more, Skrutable provides a number of additional practical features, which e.g. may help users better understand certain kinds of imperfect metrical Sanskrit text.

Going forward, Skrutable has room to grow. As an open-source project, others can take it and develop versions as they wish. As for the master branch of its development, as more thorough comparison with similar tools more clearly reveals relative strengths and weaknesses, advantageous features, whether pertaining to core algorithm or to final display, can be either incorporated centrally or included as additional options. For example, MI-2018 makes numerous practical advances yet to be emulated in Skrutable, including the illustrative highlighting of erroneous syllables, and it seems clear to me that even the online version of MIT-2015 (not to mention the further developments thereof in TEITagger) is much more accurate and detailed with regard to certain kinds of good data. That said, even as-is, Skrutable can already make a useful contribution. Alongside its pedagogical value, it can help specialists to not only augment their own research but also contribute annotated material toward a collaborative meter dataset, begun here with 150,000 verses. Such aggregated data can serve both as an interesting reference tool in its own right and as a model-training resource for very exciting technological applications to come.

Acknowledgements

The author's thanks are due to Peter Scharf and The Sanskrit Library, for a formative period of part-time employment cataloging Sanskrit manuscripts at Houghton Library in 2015 and for sharing software and data; to Shreevatsa Rajagopalan, who in a personal communication permitted reference to his unpublished table of summary statistics and to the "fulltext" endpoint of his MI-2018 website; and to Oliver Hellwig and Sebastian Nehrdich, for allowing me to feature their Splitter.

References

Ashwini S. Deo. 2007. The Metrical Organization of Classical Sanskrit Verse. *Journal of Linguistics*, 43(1):63–114.

Michael Hahn. 2014. A brief introduction into the Indian metrical system (for the use of students). Handout. Accessed at `academia.edu/6353023` on Mar. 31, 2021.

Oliver Hellwig and Sebastian Nehrdich. 2018. Sanskrit Word Segmentation Using Character-level Recurrent and Convolutional Neural Networks. In *Proceedings of the 2018 Conference on Empirical Methods in Natural Language Processing*, pages 2754–2763, Brussels, Belgium. Association for Computational Linguistics.

Daniel H. H. Ingalls. 1985. The "Mahābhārata": Stylistic Study, Computer Analysis, and Concordance. *Journal of South Asian Literature*, 20(1):17–46.

Pt. Kedāranātha. 1938. *Śrī-Piṅgalanāga-viracitaṃ Chandaḥ-śāstram: Śrī-Hālāyudha-bhaṭta-viracitayā Mṛtasaṃjīvanyākhyayā vṛttyā sametam. Samīkṣācakravarti-rāja-paṇḍita-śrī-Madhusūdanavidyāvācaspati-racita-Chandonirukti-sanāthī-kṛtaṃ ca = The Chhandas-śāstra of Piṅgalanāga.* Nirnaya Sāgar Press, Bombay, 3rd edition.

Keshav Melnad, Peter Scharf, and Pawan Goyal. 2015. Meter Identification of Sanskrit Verse. In *Sanskrit Syntax: Selected Papers Presented at the Seminar on Sanskrit Syntax and Discourse Structures, 13-15 June 2013, Université Paris Diderot, with an Updated and Revised Bibliography by Hans Henrich Hock*, pages 325–346. Sanskrit Library, Providence.

G. S. Srinivasa Murthy. 2003. Characterizing Classical Anuṣṭup: A Study in Sanskrit Prosody. *Annals of the Bhandarkar Oriental Research Institute*, 84:101–115.

Andrew Ollett. 2012. Moraic Feet in Prakrit Metrics: A Constraint-Based Approach. *Transactions of the Philological Society*, 110(2):241–282.

S. Rajagopalan. 2018. A user-friendly tool for metrical analysis of Sanskrit verse. In *Computational Sanskrit & Digital Humanities, Selected papers presented at the 17th World Sanskrit Conference, July 9-13, 2018*, pages 113–142, University of British Columbia, Vancouver, Canada. Department of Asian Studies, University of British Columbia.

Rama N. and Meenakshi Lakshmanan. 2010. A Computational Algorithm for Metrical Classification of Verse. *International Journal of Computer Science*, 7(2):46–53, March.

Peter Scharf. 2018. TEITagger: Raising the standard for digital texts to facilitate interchange with linguistic software. In *Computational Sanskrit & Digital Humanities, Selected papers presented at the 17th World Sanskrit Conference, July 9-13, 2018*, pages 229–257, University of British Columbia, Vancouver, Canada. Department of Asian Studies, University of British Columbia.

Sven Sellmer. 2013. Computer-aided detection of unusual passages in the Mahābhārata. In *CEENIS Current Research Series*, volume 1, pages 44–54. Dom Wydawniczy Elipsa, Warsaw.

John D. Smith. 1999. Winged Words Revisited: Diction and Meaning in Indian Epic. *Bulletin of the School of Oriental and African Studies, University of London*, 62(2):267–305.

Chandojnanam: A Sanskrit Meter Identification and Utilization System

Hrishikesh Terdalkar **Arnab Bhattacharya**
hrishirt@cse.iitk.ac.in arnabb@cse.iitk.ac.in
Department of Computer Science and Engineering,
Indian Institute of Technology Kanpur,
India

Abstract

We present Chandojñānam, a web-based Sanskrit meter (chanda) identification and utilization system. In addition to the core functionality of identifying meters, it sports a friendly user interface to display the scansion, which is a graphical representation of the metrical pattern. The system supports identification of meters from uploaded images by using optical character recognition (OCR) engines in the backend. It is also able to process entire text files at a time. The text can be processed in two modes, either by treating it as a list of individual lines, or as a collection of verses. When a line or a verse does not correspond exactly to a known meter, Chandojñānam is capable of finding fuzzy (i.e., approximate and close) matches based on sequence matching. This opens up the scope of a meter based correction of erroneous digital corpora. The system is available for use at `https://sanskrit.iitk.ac.in/jnanasangraha/chanda/`, and the source code in the form of a Python library is made available at `https://github.com/hrishikeshrt/chanda/`.

1 Introduction

Majority of the Sanskrit literature is in the form of poetry that adheres to the rules of Sanskrit prosody or Chandaḥśāstra, which is the study of Sanskrit *meters*, known as chandas. The purpose of chanda is primarily to add rhythm to the text so that it is easier to memorize. Additionally, it also helps in preserving the correctness to some extent.

In this paper, we introduce a web-based system, Chandojñānam, to detect the chanda in Sanskrit text. The text can be either a single line or a verse or even an image. With increasing efforts towards digitization of Sanskrit literature, our system serves as the go-to portal to detect, study and analyze vṛttas in Sanskrit text.

The digitization of Sanskrit text is achieved primarily through two methods: (1) manual data entry and (2) scanning of documents followed by optical character recognition (OCR). The former suffers from human error while the latter is prone to inaccuracies due to automated processing. Further, with the rise of social media, blog sites and Unicode, there is a large replication of Sanskrit text on the Internet with little quality control, thereby further increasing errors in the text.

We argue that a non-trivial portion of the errors introduced in texts through various sources can be detected by the process of meter identification. The Chandojñānam system exhibits tolerance towards erroneous texts and is able to locate the errors as well as make suggestions for fixing them.

1.1 Motivation

The motivation behind Chandojñānam can be better understood with the following scenarios.

- A Sanskrit enthusiast wants to identify the meter of a verse from a PDF file with Sanskrit text. She however, lacks the capability to effectively type the Sanskrit text, and prefers to

Proceedings of the Computational Sanskrit and Digital Humanities, 18th *World Sanskrit Conference 2023*, pages 113–127

upload a screenshot of the specified verse to identify the meter. With Chandojñānam, she is able to perform meter identification directly from the image.

- A teacher of Chandaḥśāstra wants to explain the rules of Sanskrit prosody to her students using several examples. She does not want to spend precious time on writing down all the intermediate steps in the identification of a meter. Instead, she wants a system that will do this job for her. Chandojñānam fits the bill nicely.

- A budding poet is trying to compose Sanskrit poetry adhering to a specific meter. However, she is not an expert, and may have made some errors. She wants to locate these errors so that she can correct it. Chandojñānam lets her locate these errors, and also provides suggestions for correction.

- A Sanskrit researcher wants to analyse a large Sanskrit text file and obtain metrical statistics of the entire corpus. Chandojñānam allows her to upload the text file and quickly obtain the required statistics to aid her in her research.

These examples highlight the utility of Chandojñānam, in addition to just satisfying one's curiosity about Sanskrit meters.

1.2 Background

The classification of syllables into laghu (*short*) and guru (*long*) forms the core concept of Chandaḥśāstra Deo (2007). The classification is related to the amount of time it takes to pronounce a specific syllable; in particular, the short syllables are termed laghu and the long syllables guru. Specific sequences or combinations of laghu and guru letters result in a particular rhythm or chanda.

A verse (śloka) is composed of four parts, each known as a pāda. Every meter has a constraint on the sequence of syllables that should be followed in a pāda. For example, the meter Pañcacāmara is defined by each pāda having 16 syllables with the following laghu-guru sequence of syllables: `LGLGLGLGLGLGLGLG`[1]. The perfect alternation of laghu and guru syllables is a reason for its energetic tempo, as can be experienced in the hymns such as Śivatāṇḍavastotram[2] or Narmadāṣṭakam[3]. In a similar manner, numerous Sanskrit meters have been defined in the texts on Sanskrit prosody such as Vṛttaratnākara.

The unique sequence of laghu-guru markers used to identify a meter is hereon referred to as *lg-signature* of that meter. The term, in reference to an arbitrary Sanskrit line, is used to refer to its decomposition in the laghu-guru sequence. Chandaḥśāstra, for brevity and ease of remembering, identifies all laghu-guru sequences of length 3 with a unique letter. This unique 3-length sequence is known as a Gaṇa. The possible number of gaṇas is $2^3 = 8$. More details about the terminology and rules of Chandaḥśāstra can be found at `https://sanskrit.iitk.ac.in/jnanasangraha/chanda/help`. Several previous works (Deo, 2007; Mishra, 2007; Melnad et al., 2013) also discuss the theory of Chandaḥśāstra in detail.

1.3 Related Work

There have been several efforts in the area of automatically identifying meter from Sanskrit text. Some of these tools (Mishra, 2007; Melnad et al., 2013) were only presented as web interfaces, which are no longer functional.

More recent works (Rajagopalan, 2020; Neill, 2022) provide both a web interface and a software library. However, the web interfaces provided by Rajagopalan (2020) and Neill (2022) both assume that a single verse will be provided as an input, limiting its usability to quickly check meters for a set of verses. Thus, even for a text consisting of a small number of verses, the

[1] We use letters `L` and `G` to denote laghu and guru syllables respectively.

[2] `https://shlokam.org/shivatandavastotram/`

[3] `https://shlokam.org/narmadashtakam/`

Features		Mishra (2007)	Melnad et al. (2013)	Rajagopalan (2020)	Neill (2022)	Chandojñānam
Availability	Web Interface	✓[4]	✓[5]	✓	✓	✓
	Software Library			✓	✓	✓
Input	Text	✓	✓	✓	✓	✓
	Arbitrary Lines					✓
	Multiple Verses					✓
	Textfile Upload				✓	✓
	Image Upload					✓
Functionality	Meter Identification	✓	✓	✓	✓	✓
	Error Tolerance			✓	✓	✓
	Fuzzy Matching			✓		✓

Table 1: Feature comparison of extant meter identification systems

input has to be provided as many times as there are number of verses. Neill (2022) attempts to address this issue by allowing upload of text files. However, it still lacks a display in case one wants to visualize meters for multiple verses. More significantly, identifying the meter of a single pāda or a partial verse is not possible at all, as any text entered is assumed to consist of exactly four pādas.

Error tolerance, i.e., the capacity to identify the meter of a verse in the presence of errors, is an important requirement for a meter identification system. To be useful for error correction, a system should be further able to detect exact locations of error and suggest corrections. Neill (2022) uses a scoring system resembling majority rule on the pādas of a verse to identify its meter. However, it assumes pāda matching to be exact. In other words, even if there is a single error in a pāda, the system reports that pāda as a mismatch. As a result, when there are errors in three pādas, due to the majority of pādas being mismatched, the overall meter for the verse is reported as '*unknown*'. Further, it lacks any suggestion mechanism. Barring the admirable work by Rajagopalan (2020), none of the other tools attempts to perform *fuzzy matching* (i.e., *approximate matching*) to handle erroneous text. The chanda suggested by Rajagopalan (2020) is, however, the one that is perceived as the best by its fuzzy matching algorithm, which may not always be the actual chanda of the verse. Therefore, providing a top-k ranked list of matches is more useful.

Further, none of the existing tools has a functionality to upload images for meter identification.

Chandojñānam attempts to overcome the shortcomings of the previous tools by providing a comprehensive set of user-friendly features. There is a special focus on *fuzzy matching* (explained in §2.4.2) and the utility of Chandaḥśāstra for correction of digital corpora.

Table 1 presents a feature matrix comparing the other works with Chandojñānam.

1.4 Contributions

We present, Chandojñānam, a Sanskrit meter identification and utilization system, which in addition to identifying a meter, also aims to catch errors in the text and suggest corrections. The aim of the tool is to make this process easy for a non-programmer. The salient features of Chandojñānam can be summarized as follows:

- The tool is available as a web-application that can be used from any standard browser and requires no other installation from the user. The library is also made available for the benefit of programmers.
- There are three prominent input options: (1) plain text, (2) images (screenshots) and (3) text files.
- The input can be in any of the standard transliteration scheme that can be detected by the

[4]`http://sanskrit.sai.uni-heidelberg.de/Chanda/HTML/` is no longer functional.

[5]`https://sanskritlibrary.org:8080/MeterIdentification/` is no longer functional.

indic-transliteration (Sanskrit-programmers (2021)) library. This applies to all three input methods.

- The image files can be processed using one of the two OCR engines, namely, Google OCR and Tesseract OCR, and the detected text can be further edited.
- The lines from input are detected based on several standard line-end markers, such as '\n', '।', '॥' and '.'
- Meter identification can be performed on the line (pāda) level. The input is treated as a set of lines. Therefore, the input can be any arbitrary set of pādas.
- Meter identification can also be performed on a verse (śloka) level. In this case, the system treats the lines as being parts of a verse. Cumulative cost of each line is minimized to identify the meter of the verse. Multiple verses can be provided.
- For erroneous inputs, the tool provides a robust fuzzy matching support using edit distance comparison, which helps in identifying and highlighting the places where an error might be present. Additionally, there is a suggestion module to help the user understand what changes can be made to the input.
- Informative display shows the steps involved in the meter identification, which is aimed to help learners of Chandaḥśāstra.
- Results can be downloaded in the JSON format.

The Chandojñānam system is a available online at https://sanskrit.iitk.ac.in/jnanasangraha/chanda/. The source code can be found at https://github.com/hrishikeshrt/chanda/.

2 The Chandojñānam System

In this section, we discuss the inner workings of the Chandojñānam system. Figure 1 illustrates the overall workflow of the system. Initially, definitions of Sanskrit meters are read into the system and stored in the form of a dictionary, referred to hereon as the *metrical database*. A user may specify the input in any of the three specified formats, namely, plain text, image containing text, and text file. For image, the text is extracted using OCR systems. After the text is extracted, the transliteration scheme is detected, and converted to the internal transliteration scheme, which is 'Devanagari'. From the text, lines are detected which, in turn, are split into syllables to obtain the *lg-signature* of the lines. The metrical database is then queried using the meter detection algorithm and the matches are presented to the user along with useful information. In case of erroneous inputs, $k = 10$ closest matches are also shown, along with the suggestions for corrections.

2.1 Chanda Definitions

There are two main types of meters, Varṇavṛtta and Mātrāvṛtta (Melnad et al., 2013). Currently, the system only deals with Varṇavṛtta. In future, we will enable the system to handle Mātrāvṛtta as well. Varṇavṛtta can be further divided into three categories, namely, Samavṛtta, Ardhasamavṛtta and Viṣamavṛtta. This categorization is performed based on the symmetry or lack thereof of the metrical pattern exhibited by the four pādas of a śloka adhering to the meter. All four pādas following the same pattern is termed as Samavṛtta, odd and even pādas following a different pattern is termed as Ardhasamavṛtta, and all four pādas following a different pattern corresponds to Viṣamavṛtta.

Chanda definitions are specified in the tabular format as illustrated in Figure 2. The legend is described in Table 2. It can be noted that the value corresponding to the column pāda denotes

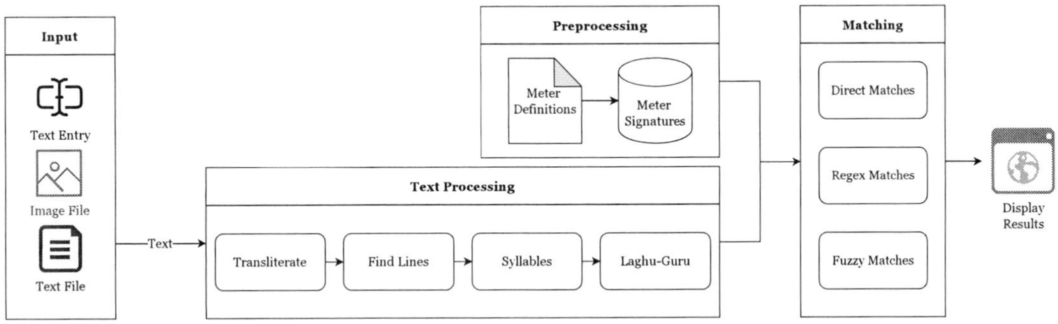

Figure 1: Workflow of the Chandojñānam system

वृत्त	पाद	गण	लक्षण	अक्षरसङ्ख्या	मात्रा	यति
शार्दूलविक्रीडित		मसजसततग	गगगललगलगललगगगलगगलग	19	30	12,7
शालिनी		मततगग	गगगगगलगगलगग	11	20	4,7
अपरवक्त्र	1	ननरलग	ललललललगलगलग	11	14	
अपरवक्त्र	2	नजजर	ललललगललगलगलग	12	16	
सौरभ	1	सजसल	ललगलगलललगल	10	13	
सौरभ	2	नसजग	लललललगलगलग	10	13	
सौरभ	3	रनभग	गलगलललगललग	10	14	
सौरभ	4	सजसजग	ललगलगलललगलगलग	13	18	
अनुष्टुभ्	1	----लग--	----लग--	8		
अनुष्टुभ्	2	----लगल-	----लगल-	8		

Figure 2: Generic Chanda definition format

the index of pāda in the meter described in that row. This way of specifying definitions results in a uniform treatment of samavṛtta, ardhasamavṛtta and viṣamavṛtta. Additionally, a regex pattern (*regular expression*) definition can also be specified, where the metrical restriction only applies to a part of the pāda. The most commonly used meter in Sanskrit, namely, anuṣṭubh, is a prime example of such regex patterns. Specifically, the requirements for anuṣṭubh chanda are:

- Every pāda must contain exactly 8 syllables.
- The 5th syllable of every pāda must be a laghu syllable.
- The 6th syllable of every pāda must be a guru syllable.
- The 7th syllable of the even pādas must be a laghu syllable.
- There is no other restriction on the other syllables, i.e., they can be either laghu or guru.

Therefore, the regex patterns `[LG][LG][LG][LG]LG[LG][LG]` and `[LG][LG][LG][LG]LGL[LG]` correspond to the *lg-signatures* for the odd numbered and even numbered pādas of Anuṣṭubh respectively.

Internally, the meter database is stored in the form of dictionaries in two ways: signature of individual pādas is stored as `CHANDA_SINGLE`, while signature of consecutive pādas is stored as `CHANDA_MULTIPLE`. It may often happen that two pādas of the input verse are given as a single

Column	Requirement	Description
Vṛtta	required	Name of the meter described in the row
Pāda	required	Index of pāda in the corresponding vṛtta; the possible values are <blank>, 1, 2, 3 and 4.
Lakṣaṇa	required	*lg-signature* of the meter
Gaṇa	optional	Signature of the meter in the compressed (trika) notation
Akṣarasaṃkhyā	optional	Number of letters in the pāda
Mātrā	optional	Number of mātrās in the pāda
Yati	optional	Indices corresponding to yati

Table 2: Chanda Definitions specification format

line without any kind of line marker. The second dictionary acts as a fail-safe when the lines couldn't be split in a proper manner due to lack of punctuation or line-breaks.

For example, for the meter Bhujaṅgaprayāta, which has a signature यययय[6], corresponding to the *lg-signature* of LGGLGGLGGLGG, two independent entries are maintained.

```
CHANDA_SINGLE = {
    'LGGLGGLGGLGG': ['Bhujaṅgaprayāta'],
    '[LG][LG][LG][LG]LG[LG][LG]': ['Anuṣṭubh (Pāda 1)'],
    '[LG][LG][LG][LG]LGL[LG]': ['Anuṣṭubh (Pāda 2)']
}
CHANDA_MULTIPLE = {
    'LGGLGGLGGLGGLGGLGGLGGLGG': ['Bhujaṅgaprayāta (Pāda 1-2)'],
    '[LG][LG][LG][LG]LG[LG][LG][LG][LG][LG][LG]LGL[LG]': ['Anuṣṭubh (Pāda 1-2)']
}
```

Currently, the system has data for more than 200 meters. This number is less as compared to the database used by Rajagopalan (2020); however, the detailed discussion of why more data need not always mean better is also provided by Rajagopalan (2020). The primary reason for not importing a large number of meters is that the lower number results in less false positives when dealing with erroneous input. More meters may be included in the system in future based on user feedback.

2.2 Input

The input for meter identification is Sanskrit text, and it can be provided to our system in three ways. The simplest form of input is a direct text entry, wherein, a user may type or copy-paste Sanskrit text in any valid transliteration scheme into a text input box.

Perhaps a more useful option, which is a novelty of our tool, is the ability to process images containing text. Two well-known OCR engines, Google Drive OCR[7] and Tesseract OCR[8] (Kay, 2007) are supported. Google Drive OCR functions by making use of Google's Drive API v3[9] to upload files to Google Drive, while Tesseract OCR v5 is a neural network (LSTM) based OCR engine. Python libraries `google-drive-ocr`[10] (Terdalkar, 2022) and `pytesseract`[11] (Lee, 2022) are utilized respectively to access the OCR systems. Google Drive OCR is generally more accurate than Tesseract OCR but slower due to the network latency imposed by upload of files. The output of either of the OCR systems, i.e., the recognized text, is treated as if directly

[6] Gaṇa य corresponds to the *lg-sequence* LGG.

[7] https://support.google.com/drive/answer/176692?hl=en

[8] https://github.com/tesseract-ocr/

[9] https://developers.google.com/drive/api/v3/reference

[10] https://github.com/hrishikeshrt/google_drive_ocr

[11] https://github.com/madmaze/pytesseract

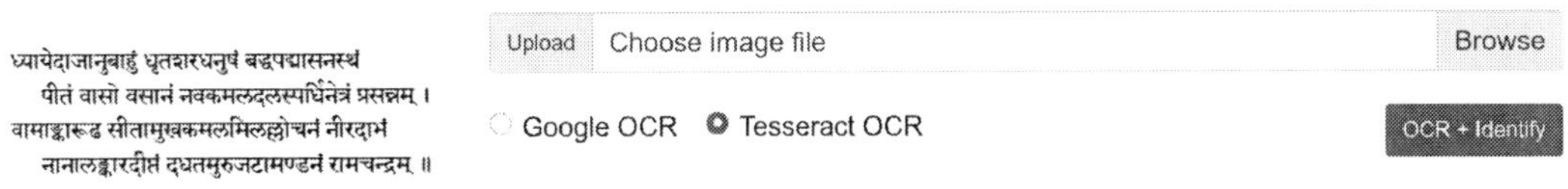

Figure 3: Upload a screenshot of a verse to Chandojñānam for meter identification

entered by the user. The output is not always accurate, especially if the image contains noisy text. Therefore, the system also lets user edit the optically recognized text and re-submit it to the system. Figure 3 shows the interface to upload images for meter identification.

For bulk processing, the option to upload a text file is also available. After reading the uploaded file, the text is again treated as if directly entered by the user.

The identical treatment of all input allows the same meter identification pipeline to follow. For example, as the transliteration module is triggered after the processing of input text, all three input methods have full support for input in any valid transliteration scheme.

2.3 Text Processing

Once the text input is obtained and cleaned, it passes through four primary processing steps.

1. **Transliteration:** The problem of transliteration of Devanagari text can be considered to be a solved one due the presence of robust tools such as `indic-transliteration`[12] (Sanskrit-programmers, 2021) and `Aksharamukha`[13] (Rajan, 2018). We rely on `indic-transliteration` for detection of input scheme; thus, any transliteration scheme detectable by `indic-transliteration` is also supported by our system. The internal transliteration scheme is set to 'Devanagari', which is a convenience choice as we believe that it makes the code easier to follow.

2. Pāda **Split:** The contiguous text is now split into lines (pādas) based on several standard line-end markers, such as '\n', '।', '॥' and '.'. Chandojñānam uses pāda as a unit for meter identification.

3. **Syllabification**: The process of splitting text into syllables is fairly straightforward for majority of Indian languages due to phonetic consistency of the alphabet. The Devanagari Unicode has special vowel markers for all vowels except 'अ' (a). The presence of vowels with consonants, therefore, can be easily identified with these markers, and syllables can be separated. The absence of vowel marker for the vowel 'अ' (a) can be treated by noting that for a joint consonant, Unicode always uses the halanta marker '◌्'. So, two consecutive consonant characters indicate the presence of a vowel 'अ' with the first consonant. For example, the Unicode string "भारत" consists of 4 Unicode characters: 'भ', '◌ा', 'र' and 'त'. However, it corresponds to 6 Devanagari letters (varṇa), namely, 'भ्', 'आ', 'र्', 'अ', 'त्' and 'अ'. Every vowel signifies an end of a syllable, resulting in three syllables, namely, 'भा', 'र' and 'त'. Thus, in a single scan of the string, syllabification can be performed. We use the `sanskrit-text`[14] Python library to perform this task.

4. Laghu-Guru **Marks**: The syllabification process is a prerequisite for obtaining the *lg-signature* of a Sanskrit line. Standard rules of Sanskrit prosody described in numerous articles (Deo, 2007; Melnad et al., 2013; Rajagopalan, 2020) are followed to mark each syllable as laghu or guru. A general rule of Piṅgala's Chandaḥśāstra states that the last syllable of a pāda should be treated as a guru. However, there exist meters in the Chandaḥśāstra whose signatures contain the last syllable as laghu (Pādānta Laghu). Therefore, we compute the *lg-signature* without forcing the last letter to be guru.

[12] `https://pypi.org/project/indic-transliteration/`
[13] `https://aksharamukha.appspot.com/`
[14] `https://pypi.org/project/sanskrit-text/`

Algorithm 1: Meter Identification

```
Data: Metrical Database (MD)
Input: lg-signatures corresponding to each 'line' in the input (T = {lg1, lg2, ..., lgn})
Output: Result set containing exact or fuzzy matches
forall lg ∈ T do
    SM1 = FindDirectMatch(lg, 'CHANDA_SINGLE')
    SM2 = FindDirectMatch(lg, 'CHANDA_MULTIPLE')
    RM = FindRegexMatch(lg, 'CHANDA_SINGLE' + 'CHANDA_MULTIPLE')
    DM = SM1 + SM2 + RM
    FM = ϕ
    if DM = ϕ then
        FM = FindFuzzyMatch(lg)
    end
    return DM + FM
end
```

Algorithm 2: Direct Matching

```
Input: lg-signature
Output: Result set containing exact matches
Function FindDirectMatch(lg, 'MD')
    M1 = Query(lg, 'MD')          // dictionary lookup
    M2 = ϕ
    if M1 = ϕ then                // if no match found
        if the last letter of lg is laghu then
            lg1 = replace last letter of lg with guru
            M2 = Query(lg1, 'MD')
        end
    end
    return M1 + M2
```

This completes the text processing which makes the text ready for the next stage, which is meter identification.

2.4 Meter Identification Algorithm

The *meter identification* problem, in its simplest form, is a dictionary lookup on *lg-signatures* of meters. In practice, however, there can be several additional considerations. The algorithm used by our system is described in Algorithm 1. The algorithm consists of a direct dictionary lookup, regular-expression based lookup and fuzzy matching. These are explained in the subsequent sections.

2.4.1 Direct Matching

Finding a direct match involves trying to find the match in the both the dictionaries in the metrical database that store the meter signatures. Further, for meters with regex specification, regular-expression-based matching is performed.

As mentioned in §2.3, we compute the *lg-signature* without enforcing the last syllable to be guru. If the last syllable was laghu and no direct match was found, we attempt to find a direct match by treating the last syllable as guru. Algorithm 2 describes this process. The function `Query` corresponds to a simple dictionary lookup and returns a set of matches.

In theory, this should be sufficient. However, in practice, one often encounters erroneous text. This is expected since a large amount of Sanskrit text available digitally is a result of either

Figure 4: Meter identification with fuzzy matching and suggestions

manual entry or post-scanning OCR followed by manual correction. As a result, due to human errors or OCR inaccuracies, the following errors may be found in the texts available online.

- Characters may be misspelt, e.g., रु (ru) as रू (rū)
- Characters may be missing, e.g., वर्गैं (vargai) as वगैं (vagai)
- Characters may be misidentified, e.g., ऋ (ṛ) as क्र (kra)
- Characters may get split, e.g., ख (kha) as रव (rava)

Most of these errors may also affect the metrical pattern of a line and, therefore, meter identification is a useful tool to identify them. It should be mentioned here that not all errors lead to metrical mismatch. For example, an error such as the confusion between letter pairs such as व, ब or म, स would not affect the meter pattern and, thus, cannot be captured by only meter identification.

2.4.2 Fuzzy Matching

For non-exact matches, we model the problem as that of finding the *nearest matching string* for the *lg-signature* of the text. In particular, we compute the Levenshtein edit distance of the observed pattern with all the known patterns. We then find the similarity by first normalizing the edit distance using the length of the target match, and then subtracting it from 1.

$$\text{Similarity} = 1 - \frac{\text{Levenshtein distance}}{\text{length of target match}}$$

We present the topmost k matches as the possible fuzzy matches (currently, $k = 10$). Algorithm 3 and Algorithm 4 describes the core functions pertaining to fuzzy matching. The *Similarity* column in the interface (Figure 4) shows the similarity instead of the edit distance.

For finding the edit-distance and edit-operations, we use the `python-Levenshtein`[15] library (Haapala, 2014). The `AddEditOpsMarkers` function (line 5) formats the original list of syllables by adding suggestions based on the edit operations. The suggestions shown contain the characters from the original string, along with the suggested places where a change might be required. Suggested changes for each meter correspond to the changes needed to transform the given line into that meter.

The suggestions are identified by three letters `i`, `d` and `r`, indicating *insert*, *delete* and *replace* operations respectively. They are used in the following manner.

[15] `https://pypi.org/project/python-Levenshtein/`

Algorithm 3: Fuzzy Matching

```
Input: lg-signature and k
Output: Result set containing top-k fuzzy matches
Function FindFuzzyMatch(lg, 'MD', k)
    results = ϕ
    forall chanda in 'MD' do
        cost, suggestion = Transform(lg, lg-signature of chanda)
        if suggestion then
            results += (chanda, cost, suggestion)
        end
    end
    return top-k results with lowest cost
```

Algorithm 4: Transform String Sequences

```
Input: String sequences seq1, seq2
Output: Suggested edit operations required to transform seq1 into seq2 and the cost of
        transformation
Function Transform(seq1, seq2)
    edit_ops = GetLevenshteinEditOps(seq1, seq2) // using python-Levenshtein
    weights = {'replace': 1, 'delete': 1, 'insert': 1}
    cost = Σ_{op ∈ edit_ops} weights[op]
    suggestion = AddEditOpsMarkers(seq1, edit_ops) // add suggestions
    return cost, suggestion
```

- `i(L/G)`:
  This notation indicates the insertion of a new syllable. `i(L)` (respectively, `i(G)`) indicates that a **laghu** (respectively, **guru**) syllable needs to be inserted.

- `r(letter)[L/G]{suggestion}`:
  This notation indicates that the syllable needs to be replaced by a **laghu** or a **guru** syllable (depending upon the marker). In some of the cases, a suggested change of syllable may be included. A simple heuristic that is followed replaces the **laghu** syllables corresponding to the **laghu** vowels 'इ', 'उ' and 'ऋ' by their **guru** vowel counterparts, namely, 'ई', 'ऊ' and 'ॠ', respectively, and vice versa.

- `d(letter)`:
  This notation indicates that the syllable needs to be deleted.

The process of fuzzy matching can be better understood with the help of an example. Consider the first line of the example depicted in Figure 4.

- Line: नमस्ते सदा वत्सले मातृभुमे
- LG-Signature: `LGGLGGLGGLLG`
- Nearest Match: `LGGLGGLGGLGG` (cost 1) (Bhujaṅgaprayāta)
- Suggestion: [['न', 'म', 'स्ते'], ['स', 'दा'], ['व', 'त्स', 'ले'], ['मा', 'तृ', 'r(भु)[G]{भू}', 'मे']]

The exact match for the line is not found in the system and, therefore, we find the edit-distance of this *lg-signature* with every *lg-signature* from the database. It is found that the *lg-signature* `LGGLGGLGGLGG` of Bhujaṅgaprayāta meter is the closest and is only 1 edit-distance away. The required change is to replace the 11th letter from `L` (laghu) to `G` (guru). It is also suggested to replace the **laghu** letter भु into a **guru** letter भू.

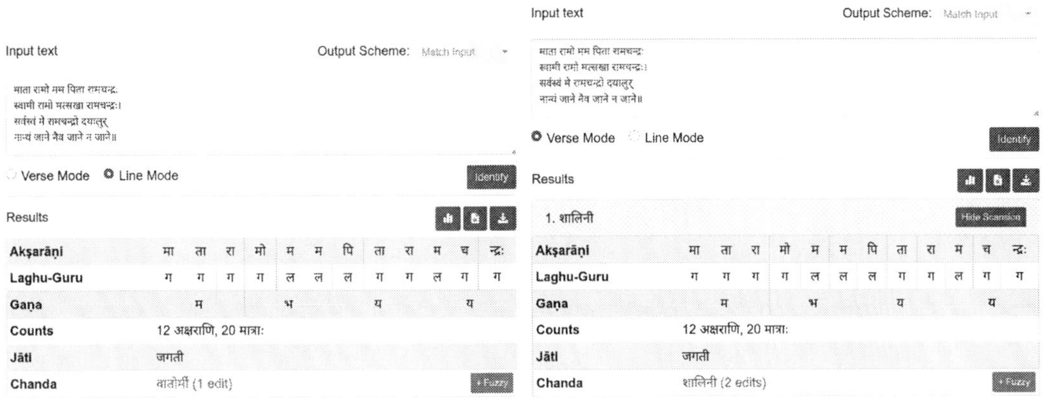

Figure 5: Meter identification from a verse in (a) *Line mode* and (b) *Verse mode*

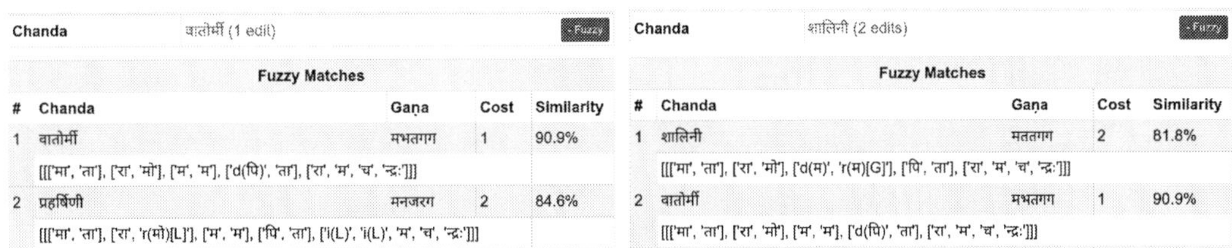

Figure 6: Fuzzy matches in (a) *Line mode* and (b) *Verse mode*

2.4.3 Verse Processing

Meter identification can be performed by treating the input either as a set of arbitrary lines (*Line mode*) or as a collection of verses (*Verse mode*). The *Line mode* is useful for checking meter of a single line or a set of lines. The treatment of the text as a verse differs insofar as it attempts to minimize the cumulative cost of the meter matches over each line.

Consider a sample verse adhering to the meter Śālinī, albeit with a deliberate small error in the first pāda. Figure 5 highlights the difference between the two modes of meter identification. The correct word मत्पिता has been replaced by two words मम पिता. As a result, the first pāda does not find an exact match. Further, the closest match based on edit distance is found to be the meter Vātormī with an edit distance of 1. Therefore, when in the *Line mode*, the suggestion is made as Vātormī. However, rest of the three pādas are exact matches for Śālinī. Therefore, the cumulative cost of Śālinī over the entire śloka is the lowest (here, it is 2). Thus, in the *Verse mode*, the identified meter for the verse is Śālinī. This highlights the utility of the *Verse mode*.

In the list of fuzzy matches shown, the meter identified for the verse is shown first. Figure 6 shows that the meter Śālinī is shown for the first pāda despite having a higher edit cost.

2.5 Output

A blackbox that only identifies meter would not be as interesting as a system that also explains ('teaches') the steps. Therefore, in addition to the meter name, scansion details such as *lg-signature*, gaṇa-signature, count of letters and count of mātrās are also displayed. Additional information displayed in the case of fuzzy matches is already discussed in §2.4.2. Entire result is displayed in a neat tabular format (as displayed in Figure 4) which makes the system useful for learners of Chandaḥśāstra.

Cumulative statistics such as number of lines identified, number of lines not identified, frequency distribution of exact and fuzzy matches etc. can also be viewed. Additionally, the data can also be downloaded. The data download supports two formats, a compact format for quick visual inspection, and a detailed JSON format for further computational processing.

Figure 7: Meter identification from other Indian languages, e.g., (a) Marathi (b) Telugu

2.6 Utility

We can identify several use-cases for Chandojñānam, some of which have already been discussed in §1.1:

- The primary use-case, naturally, is the ability to identify meters from Sanskrit text.
- Ability to upload of images and identification of meters from it is another important scenario.
- Identification of errors from the Sanskrit text which has been created through the process of OCR, but not manually corrected yet, serves as another prominent use-case.
- Additionally, the system can be used to obtain metrical statistics from large texts automatically. These statistics may also help a user identify errors, if any, at a quick glance. For example, in the case of texts such as Meghadūta, which follows a single meter, namely, Mandākrāntā, any anomaly will be quickly spotted by appearance of a different meter in the statistics.
- A user may be interested in creating poetry in Sanskrit, and may require assistance in quickly checking the metrical consistency of her creation.
- Learners of Chandaḥśāstra may want to try out several examples to understand the process of meter identification in-depth.
- Several Indian languages, e.g., Marathi, Telugu, etc., exhibit rules of prosody similar to Sanskrit. Due to comprehensive transliteration support provided by the `indic-transliteration` library, text written in scripts other than Devanagari can be also used in the same manner. Figure 7 illustrates the usage of Chandojñānam for meter identification from Marathi and Telugu. Here, we are assuming that the same metrical database is used. However, there may be language-specific differences in the rules of prosody as well as variety of meters. Hence, the multilingual support is still primitive.

3 Evaluation for Error Correction

One of the primary goals of Chandojñānam is to facilitate error detection from the Sanskrit text obtained from various sources. Consequently, we evaluate the ability of the tool to correctly identify the meters from erroneous text.

3.1 Corpus

Evaluation of a meter identification system requires tagged metrical data. As mentioned by Rajagopalan (2020), Meghadūta composed by Kālidāsa (Kale, 2011), being entirely in Mandākrāntā meter, is an ideal corpus for evaluation. The same text, available from various sources, can also differ greatly in terms of encoding, character-by-character comparison and errors present. We use three online sources, namely, Wikisource[16], sanskritdocuments.org[17] and GRETIL[18] to obtain three versions of Meghadūta.

In addition to Meghadūta, we also use texts with more metrical variety. We choose three texts from Wikisource, namely, Śāntavilāsa[19], Śrīrāmarakṣāstotra[20] and Rājendrakarṇapūra[21]. We manually tag meters for each verse from these texts. Together, the 4 datasets contain 1038 verses, exhibiting 17 distinct meters.

Further, to evaluate the proposed use-case of post-OCR correction, we simulate the digitization pipeline. First, we synthetically create a PDF from each corpus in the following manner:

- We open the text file in a text editor. (We use `gedit` with `Sanskrit2003` font.)
- We next trigger the operating system's (Ubuntu 18.04) print dialogue (`Ctrl+P`)
- We use the '*Print to File*' option and save the file as PDF.

A PDF file created in this manner is the best-case scenario for OCR engines, as it contains no noise. Now, we run both the OCR systems and obtain the OCR-ed versions of the text. As a result of this simulation, we can now realistically evaluate the detection and correction of errors introduced in the process of OCR.

3.2 Results

We use the following abbreviations for different versions of the corpora:

- **WS**: Wikisource
- **SD**: sanskritdocuments.org
- **GR**: GRETIL
- **GO**: Google Drive OCR on a synthetically generated PDF
- **TO**: Tesseract OCR on a synthetically generated PDF

We evaluate our Chandojñānam system as well as those by Rajagopalan (2020) and Neill (2022) on each version of the corpora. We evaluate the ability of these systems to identify the chanda of the verse in the presence of errors. Table 3 illustrates the result of this evaluation. Chandojñānam was able to identify the correct meter from the erroneous text in 98.2% of the cases, performing better than the systems by Rajagopalan (2020) (91.9%) and Neill (2022) (80.3%). Corpora, code and results of the experiments are made available with the source code.

[16] `https://sa.wikisource.org/s/1c5`
[17] `https://sanskritdocuments.org/doc_z_misc_major_works/meghanew.html`
[18] `http://gretil.sub.uni-goettingen.de/gretil/1_sanskr/5_poetry/2_kavya/kmeghdpu.htm`
[19] `https://sa.wikisource.org/s/7xr`
[20] `https://sa.wikisource.org/s/7up`
[21] `https://sa.wikisource.org/s/7xq`

		Meghadūta					Śāntavilāsa			Rāmarakṣā			Rājendrakarṇapūra			Total
		SD	GR	WS	GO	TO	WS	GO	TO	WS	GO	TO	WS	GO	TO	
Number of Verses		117	111	123	123	123	36	36	36	39	39	39	72	72	72	1038
Unique Chanda		1	1	1	1	1	12	12	12	9	9	9	4	4	4	17
Erroneous Verses		20	79	2	31	77	13	16	31	1	4	13	12	26	71	396
Correct	Neill (2022)	20	79	2	30	66	11	13	14	0	2	9	12	24	36	318 (80.3%)
Meters	Rajagopalan (2020)	19	79	2	30	75	12	15	24	1	2	9	12	26	58	364 (91.9%)
Identified	Chandojñānam	20	79	2	31	77	13	16	29	1	3	9	12	26	71	389 (98.2%)

Table 3: Error tolerance of meter identification systems. (Versions are WS: Wikisource, GO: Google OCR, TO: Tesseract OCR, SD: sanskritdocuments.org, GR: GRETIL.) Chandojñānam is able to detect correct chanda from erroneous verses 98.2% of the times.

3.3 Error Analysis

We now analyze the errors in a more detailed manner.

Despite the Wikisource version being prepared through manual correction of OCR, Chandojñānam was still able to detect 2 errors from Meghadūta. The errors are described below:

- Line: कालक्षेपं ककुभसुरभौ पर्वते पर्वैते ते (Pāda 3, Śloka 1.23)
- Suggestion: [[['का', 'ल', 'क्षे', 'पं'], ['क', 'कु', 'भ', 'सु', 'र', 'भौ'], ['प', 'र्व', 'ते'], ['प', 'r(र्वै)[L]', 'ते'], ['ते']]]
- Description: The error is due to the incorrect word पर्वैते. It is likely that this was due to an oversight by the curator. It can be seen that the system correctly points to the location where a change is required.
- Line: साभिज्ञानप्रहितकुशलैस्ततद्वचोभिर्ममापि (Pāda 3, Śloka 2.53)
- Suggestion: [[['सा', 'भि', 'ज्ञा', 'न', 'प्र', 'हि', 'त', 'कु', 'श', 'लै', 'd(स्त)', 'त', 'द्व', 'चो', 'भि', 'र्म', 'मा', 'पि']]]
- Description: The error is due to an extra letter present in this line, where an extra त appears in the sandhi of words कुशलैः and तद्वत्, resulting in कुशलैस्ततद्वत् instead of कुशलैस्तद्वत्. The system is able to identify the error, and point out that a syllable needs to be deleted. However, we can see that the system points to an incorrect syllable स्त to be deleted. This can be explained from the fact that both स्त and त are laghu letters, and deletion of either letter results in the correct metrical signature. So, it is impossible for a meter identification based system to correctly say which character is to be deleted without any notion of semantic consideration. Such type of semantic error correction is out-of-scope as of yet.

Majority of the 'errors' in GRETIL stem from the text being written with sandhis being split. Despite not being linguistic errors, from the point of view of Chandaḥśāstra, these indeed are errors as they may change the number of syllables in a pāda and subsequently result in the change or loss of the meter.

It is important to remember that the errors detected are only the errors reported by the Chandojñānam system. Errors that do not result in the breaking of metrical pattern are impossible to be corrected by metrical analysis. It is interesting to note that the fuzzy matching performs better for Google OCR than Tesseract OCR. It can be explained as follows. As the Google OCR system performs better and makes fewer errors per line, the possible deviations are fewer. This results in less false positives. On the contrary, if the OCR system makes numerous errors, the *lg-signature* is farther away from the actual *lg-signature* and, therefore, 'the closest match' of the erroneous *lg-signature* might also be erroneous.

Finally, it can be seen that although the meter identification can be a useful tool for detection of errors in the Sanskrit text, there are several other factors that affect the error rate of such a system.

4 Conclusions

We have presented a Sanskrit meter identification tool that adds many user-friendly features and focuses on tolerance towards erroneous text as well as correction of such text. The features such as meter identification from images are useful for Sanskrit enthusiasts without much programming background. Bulk analysis of text files is a useful aid for digitization of Sanskrit texts using the methodology of post-OCR manual correction.

Future directions for the tool include addition of **mātrā** meters, improvement to meter detection and correction algorithm with the possible use of syntactic and semantic aspects, adding more extensive support for Indian languages that use similar rules of prosody.

The system is available online at `https://sanskrit.iitk.ac.in/jnanasangraha/chanda/` and the source code is available at `https://github.com/hrishikeshrt/chanda/`.

References

Ashwini S Deo. 2007. The metrical organization of classical sanskrit verse. *Journal of linguistics*, 43(1):63–114.

Antti Haapala. 2014. python-Levenshtein. `https://pypi.org/project/python-Levenshtein/`, dec 10. [Online; accessed 2022-04-01].

Moreshvar R Kale. 2011. *The Meghaduta of Kalidasa.* Motilal Banarsidass.

Anthony Kay. 2007. Tesseract: an open-source optical character recognition engine. *Linux Journal*, 2007(159):2.

Matthias Lee. 2022. pytesseract. `https://github.com/madmaze/pytesseract`, feb 19. [Online; accessed 2022-04-01].

Keshav S Melnad, Pawan Goyal, and Peter Scharf. 2013. Meter identification of sanskrit verse. *The Sanskrit Library, USA.*

Anand Mishra. 2007. Sanskrit metre recognizer.

Tyler Neill. 2022. Skrutable: Another step toward effective sanskrit meter identification.

Shreevatsa Rajagopalan. 2020. A user-friendly tool for metrical analysis of sanskrit verse. *Computational Sanskrit & Digital Humanities*, page 113.

Vinodh Rajan. 2018. Aksharamukha. `https://github.com/virtualvinodh/aksharamukha`, jul 23. [Online; accessed 2021-11-03].

Sanskrit-programmers. 2021. Indic-transliteration. `https://github.com/indic-transliteration/`, jul 23. [Online; accessed 2021-11-18].

Hrishikesh Terdalkar. 2022. google-drive-ocr. `https://github.com/hrishikeshrt/google_drive_ocr/`, mar 1. [Online; accessed 2022-04-01].

Development of a TEI standard for digital Sanskrit texts containing commentaries: A pilot study of Bhaṭṭi's *Rāvaṇavadha* with Mallinātha's commentary on the first canto

Tanuja P. Ajotikar[1], **Peter M. Scharf**[2]
[1] Maharishi Vedic University, Vlodrop, The Netherlands
[2] IIIT Hyderabad
tanuja@sanskritlibrary.org, scharf@sanskritlibrary.org

Abstract

Sanskrit commentarial literature is important because it pervades all fields of Sanskrit literature and provides rich information in the form of references, explanation and derivation of specialized vocabulary, explanation of metrical patterns, syntax, figures of speech, etc. This information is invaluable to linguists, philologists, and other humanities scholars. In the digital age, it is possible to identify, extract, and reorganize this information easily if contemporary techniques of digital humanities are employed. The extensible markup language (XML) has emerged as the most widely used method of data-interchange, and the Text-Encoding Initiative (TEI) has become recognized as the source of global guidelines for the production of digital editions of texts. Yet there is a need to develop conventions for employing TEI in standard ways for Sanskrit texts and commentaries to maximize the universal accessibility of these texts. After explicating the structure and elements present in commentaries, we describe templates to encode them in accordance with the TEI guidelines to represent relevant structural and semantic information in addition to document strucure. We employ these templates to encode Mallinātha's commentary on the twenty-seven verses of the first sarga of Bhaṭṭi's *Rāvaṇavadha*. We then develop extensible stylesheet language transformations (XSLT) to extract Mallinātha's rendering of the verse in prose syntax (*anvaya*) and to create a dictionary of synonyms and derivations, and indices to words, citations, and definitions of metrical patterns and figures of speech. Finally, we offer some initial observations on the bearing of Mallinātha's anvaya on Sanskrit syntax.

Keywords: XML, TEI, Sanskrit, commentary, text-encoding, syntax

1 Introduction

Scharf (2018) reviewed the history of the development of the extensible markup language (XML) and the Text-Encoding Initiative (TEI). He noted that the principal purpose of XML is to separate the semantic markup of a digital text from software that implements its presentation digitally or in print. Given that the XML metalanguage permits the development of an unlimited variety of markup languages, TEI provides guidelines to standardize such markup to facilitate reuse and interchange. Given that TEI itself offers numerous alternative methods to encode texts, to maximize the universal accessibility of digital Sanskrit texts, there is a need to develop standards for employing TEI. Scharf (2015) and Scharf (2017) developed a TEI template for the digital descriptive cataloguing of Sanskrit manuscripts. Such a standard template needs to be developed for Sanskrit texts. This task is complicated by the fact that Sanskrit literature is vast and diverse. Each discipline has its own special features that require special handling. Sanskrit literature includes not only base texts but also commentaries and sub-commentaries. This commentarial literature is important because it pervades all fields of Sanskrit literature and provides rich information in the form of references, explanation and derivation of special-

Proceedings of the Computational Sanskrit and Digital Humanities, 18th World Sanskrit Conference 2023, pages 128–145

ized vocabulary, explanation of metrical patterns, syntax, figures of speech, etc. Hence commentaries are filled with quotations, derivations, metrical definitions, syntactic reordering and much more additional information which needs to be properly encoded. In a paper presented at the international conference on the tradition of commentary and the stream of knowledge (*Bhāṣyaparamparā Jñānapravāhaśca*), Ajotikar and Scharf (2020) explicated the structure and elements present in commentaries by examining Mallinātha's commentaries on the first verse of the five principal Sanskrit major poetic works (*mahākāvyas*) and devised preliminary templates in accordance with the TEI guidelines to represent relevant structural and semantic information in addition to document structure. They concluded by outlining procedures to build a library of digital Sanskrit commentarial literature. We review the features of commentary and templates to encode them here and describe our use of them to encode Mallinātha's commentary on the twenty-seven verses of the first sarga of Bhaṭṭi's *Rāvaṇavadha*. We then demonstrate the utility of our encoding for the creation of a dictionary of synonyms and derivations, and indices to words, citations, and definitions of metrical patterns and figures of speech using extensible stylesheet language transformations (XSLT) and for extracting Mallinātha's rendering of the verse in prose syntax (*anvaya*). We conclude by offering some initial observations on the bearing of Mallinātha's anvaya on Sanskrit syntax.

2 Principal features of commentary

Each mahākāvya begins with a benedictory verse. Although the benedictory verses differ in each mahākāvya, after a brief introduction, the commentary on each begins by describing the importance of a benedictory verse. The commentary on the benedictory verse and each subsequent verse begins with the citation of the incipit (*pratīka*) of the verse. The commentary then proceeds to explain each word in the original verse in prose order. At relevant junctures, the commentary explains metrical patterns, figures of speech, and often concludes by summing up the purport of the verse. These explanations include a number of features which are summarized as follows:

1. Most words in the base text are provided with a contextually appropriate synonym (*paryāya*) that may reveal its morphological structure as well as its semantic appropriateness.
2. Most commentaries provide words with a derivation (*vyutpatti*).
3. The metrical patterns (*chandas*) used in poetic works are explicitly named and explained by reference to works in the highly sophisticated discipline of Sanskrit poetics (*chandaḥśāstra*).
4. The figures of speech (*alaṅkāra*) used in poetic works are explicitly named and explained by reference to works in the highly sophisticated discipline of Sanskrit rhetoric (*alaṅkāraśāstra*).
5. In providing derivations and explanations of metrical patterns and figures of speech, as well as discussing more general aspects of the verse or the work as a whole, commentators frequently cite the authoritative works of their predecessors.
6. Commentators generally transform verse into prose in the process of their explanation. Mallinātha explains each verse by reordering the words in the syntactic order in which they would appear in ordinary Sanskrit prose (*anvyaya*).

3 TEI elements and attributes employed

In order to capture all of the information described in the preceding section, a number of TEI elements and attributes are employed. These include particular usage of elements and attributes besides the basic text encoding elements and attributes for verse and prose encoding described by Scharf (2018), Scharf (2020), Scharf (2015) and Scharf (2017) in his explanation of manuscript text transcription. We describe how to encode various types of analysis of the base text and its commentary below.

We analyze the base text morphologically in a separate file. Each inflected word is put in a `w` element. We identify the nominal base (*prātipadika*) of each nominal, and the verbal root (*dhātu*) of each finite verb in a `lemma` attribute, the lexical identifier in a `type` attribute, and the inflectional identifier in a `subtype` attribute. Morphemes are indicated by putting the form of the basic element in subordinate `m` elements and their lexical identifier in a `type` attribute. An analytic paraphrase (*vigraha-vākya*) is provided in a `seg` element with `type="vigraha"` as the first child of each compound. Each `w` and `m` element is given an `xml:id` attribute as is each verse and chapter.

The commentary is entered in a separate file from the base text on which it comments. The commentary on each verse is linked with the verse on which it comments by using identical values of the verse's `xml:id` in the base text file and in the commentary file. The explanation of each major division of the commentary on the verse is put in an `ab` element which is supplied with an `xml:id`. The explanation of each word in the commentary is put in an `ab` element with the `type` attribute given the value `pada` and a `corresp` attribute given the value of the `xml:id` of the sandhi-analyzed word in the morphological analysis file. Each word in the base text commented upon in the commentary is put in a `w` element as a child of this `ab` element and is provided with an `n` attribute indicating the sequence in which the word appears in the commentary. Each word is also provided with an `xml:id` that coincides with its `xml:id` in the morphological analysis file and the `corresp` attribute of its parent `ab` element. If a word is not explicitly mentioned yet is commented upon or supplied with a derivation, it is given a `type` attribute with the value `inferred`. The few words that are neither mentioned explicitly nor commented upon are put in a `w` element in the expected sequence in the commentary with `type="supplied"`.

Where Mallinātha supplies a word with a synonym, the synonym is put in a `seg` element as a sister to the `w` element containing the word. The `seg` element is supplied with the attribute-value pair `type="synonym"` and a `corresp` attribute with the value of the `xml:id` of the `w` element. Where Mallinātha supplies the antecedent of a pronominal, we put the antecedent in a `seg` element with the attribute-value pair `type="antecedent"`.

Where Mallinātha supplies a word with a derivation, the entire derivation is put in a `seg` element as a sister to the `w` element containing the word and is supplied with the attribute-value pair `type="derivation"` and a `corresp` attribute with the value of the `xml:id` of the `w` element. Citations of sūtras are tagged with `ref` elements with `corresp` attributes with the value of the xml:id of the original Pāṇinian rule in the Sanskrit Library's sūtra file. The `ref` element is immediately followed by a `note` element containing a `bibl` element which identifies the exact edition, and which has a `biblScope` element which again identifies the sūtra number in the *Aṣṭādhyāyī*.

All quotations are tagged. The `quote` element is used for long passages, and the `q` element for short passages. We analyze the prosodic changes (*sandhi*) at the beginning and end of the quote and put element tags immediately before and after the quote, i.e., before *iti*. We use the `bibl` element within a `note` element immediately following the quote to identify the source of the citation. The entire phrase containing the quote and its reference is put in a `seg` element where classification of the quotation is added in the `type` attribute. Many quotations occur within longer derivation segments which bear the `type="derivation"` attribute-value pair. Most others are citations from lexicons, so their containing `seg` element bears the attribute-value pair `type="lexicon"`. Until the need arises for greater specificity, the rest, which are citations to dharmaśāstra and literary texts, occur within `seg` elements with the attribute-value pair `type="quotation"`.

Explanations of metrical patterns are tagged within `ab` elements with the attribute-value pair `type="vftta"`. An `ana` attribute names the meter (*chandas*) the commentator specifies in his explanation.

Explanations of figures of speech are tagged within `ab` elements with the attribute-value pair `type="alaNkAra"` and an `ana` attribute that names the figure of speech (*alaṅkāra*).

The incipit (*pratīka*) cited by the commentator at the beginning of the commentary on each verse is put in an `ab` element with the attribute-value pair `type="pratIka"`. Comments made in the commentary that tell the purport of the verse are set in an `ab` element with the attribute-value pair `type="tAtparya"` unless intertwined with the explanation of a word in which case it is set in a seg element with type="tAtparya". Where Mallinātha supplies words not in the verse by stating *iti śeṣaḥ*, we put the phrase in an ab element with the attribute-value pair type="Seza". Other comments that explain aspects of the verse that do not fit in any of these categories are put in an ab element with the attribute-value pair type="vyAKyAna".

We also capture syntactic information provided by the commentators reordering of the verse in ordinary prose. Once we have completed tagging the commentary on a versified text, each word in the original verse appears in a w element with an xml:id attribute indicating the sequence of the word in the original verse, and with an n attribute indicating its sequence in the commentator's reordering of the syntax in ordinary prose. We automatically extract the words of each verse in the commentator's prose order from the commentary file and place them in an s element within a p element in that order in a separate file to obtain a file that shows the words of the verse in the prose order in which they are explained by the commentator. In order to show the variance of the prose syntax from the syntax of the verse, a numbered version of this prose file is created in which each word is supplied with the sequence number of the word in the original verse as indicated by the xml:id. Where words are inferred or supplied they are inserted in square brackets and given an explicit "inferred" or "supplied" tag.

Finally, we use the seg element to encode segments of text subject to textual criticism. Three values of the type attribute distinguish them. The variant value indicates that the segment of text discusses a reading that differs from the reading in the base text. The error value indicates that the editor has erred in establishing the text. Lastly, the interpolation value, while also an editorial error, indicates that the passage is interpolated in the commentary by a later redactor.

4 File preparation procedure

Preparation of the base verse file and commentary file would most efficiently be undertaken in two phases. The first phase consists of data-entry in structured text files that number major text divisions, verses, and, in the base text file, lines of verse. A data-entry specialist types the base text and commentary in separate files in the Sanskrit Library phonetic basic (SLP1) encoding. SLP1 is described by Scharf and Hyman (2011) and more briefly by Scharf (2014). Help pages at https://sanskritlibrary.org/help-text.html describe the basic characters. A Sanskrit scholar analyzes the sandhi in copies of each of the two files. The TEITagger program, described by Scharf (2018), is used to transform these files to TEI-tagged versions. This program employs a driver file of sets of regular expressions and replacement expressions written based upon an analysis of the text file structure to make the transformation to a file that conforms to the Text-Encoding Intitiative guidelines.

The sandhi-analyzed file of the base text is programmatically converted to a shell of the morphological analysis file by putting each word in a w element within its seg element that marks its verse quarter and l element that marks its verse line within its lg element that marks its verse. Each w element is provided with n and xml:id attributes. The n attribute numbers each word in sequence from the beginning of the verse. The xml:id attribute is formed by adding to the corresponding xml:id of the original verse a separator dot followed by a w followed by the sequence number. The TEITagger program also can leave type and subtype attributes with dummy values in the w elements. The Sanskrit scholar then just replaces the dummy values with appropriate lexical identifiers and morphological identifiers.

Alternatively, a work-flow can be designed to utilize the Sanskrit Heritage Site's Sanskrit Reader Companion at https://sanskrit.inria.fr/DICO/reader.fr.html. A Sanskrit scholar can use the site to filter possible solutions and save the correct analysis in the Corpus Manager described by Huet and Lankri (2018). Software described by Goyal et al. (2012) and utilized by Scharf et al. (2015) could be revised to scrape the HTML pages of these saved morphological analyses. This software converts the Sanskrit Heritage lexical and morphological identifiers to Sanskrit Library tag-sets, loads the analysis into a flexible editing interface that permits corrections and writes the morphological analysis to an XML file. While at present the XML file the software writes does not conform to TEI guidelines, it could be revised to do so.

To create the TEI-tagged version of the commentary requires an expert Sanskrit scholar experienced in reading commentaries and familiar with Sanskrit grammatical, lexical, poetic, and rhetorical texts. To assist such a scholar in inserting the appropriate TEI elements and attributes in a copy of the sandhi-analyzed commentary file, an interface could be created that permits the scholar to select appropriate elements and attributes from menus that contain only the contextually appropriate tags.

5 Details of the data preparation

The verses of the entire text of Bhaṭṭi's *Rāvaṇavadha*, as in the edition of Śāstrin (1912), were typed, tagged and morphologically analyzed in a project entitled *Bhaṭṭikāvya-svādhyāya-pariyojanā* at the Rashtriya Sanskrit Sansthan, Ganganath Jha Campus, Prayagraj by Dr. Monali Das under the supervision of Prof. Lalitkumar Tripathi. In that project, Dr. Das manually constructed a prose ordering of words and fed the resulting sentences to the Saṁsādhinī morphological analyzer first described by Kulkarni and Shukl (2009) and most recently by Krishnan and Kulkarni (2019). The analyzer provides lexical and inflectional identifiers to words, analyzes compounds and separates preverbs from verbs. However, in most cases the analyzer failed to produce adequate results, and Dr. Das supplied the analysis by hand. Dr. Das typed the commentary of Mallinātha, as in the edition of Trivedi (1898), in WX encoding and then converted it to SLP1 by using Saṁsādhinī transcoding software. She then encoded the text of the commentary of the first canto in XML in accordance with the TEI guidelines under the supervision of Scharf and Ajotikar who made final revisions. Scharf transcoded the morphologically analyzed text to SLP1 using the Sanskrit Library's TranscodeFile software and restored sandhi to compounds by calling his revision of a Java version of sandhi software, originally written by him in Pascal in 1991, from an XSLT transformation. He added morphemic analysis of compound constituents in `m` elements as children of the `w` element containing the compound and provided them with `xml:ids` so that they could be referred to where needed by linking attributes in the commentary file.

6 Issues in tagging the commentary

6.1 Compound constituent analysis

Mallinātha dissolves compounds while commenting on the verse and provides synonyms and derivations of its constituents. For example, he comments on the compound *vibudhasakhaḥ* in the first verse by separating its constituents and commenting on each separately. His comment with our translation is as follows:

> विशेषेण बुध्यन्त इति विबुधा विद्वांसो देवाश्च। विबुधौ सुरपण्डितौ इति विश्वः ॥इगुपधलक्षणः कप्रत्ययः ॥ तेषां सखा विबुधसखो विद्वत्सेवी देवेन्द्रसहचरश्च विजयसहकारित्वात्तस्येति भावः ॥ राजाहःसखिभ्यष्टच् इति टच् ॥
>
> "Those who especially know are wise (*vibudha*), i.e. knowledgable people (*vidvat*) and deities (*deva*). Viśva says, 'The wise (*vibudha*) are gods (*sura*) and the learned (*paṇḍita*).' The affix ***ka*** is added by *A.* 3.1.135 *igupadhajñāprīkiraḥ kaḥ*. Their friend (*sakhin*) is called *vibudha-sakha* which means the one who serves knowledgable people (*vidvat-sevin*) and is the companion of Indra, the king of the gods (*devendra-sahacara*), because he helped him obtain victory. The compound-final affix ***ṭac*** is provided by *A.* 5.4.91 *rājāhaḥsakhibhyaṣṭac*."

Mallinātha begins his comment on the compound *vibudha-sakha* by implicitly dissolving the first constituent, *vibudha*, into its constituents *vi* and *budha* by providing its meaning in the phrase *viśeṣeṇa budhyante* 'Those who especially know'. He then provides two synonyms for the word *vibudha* 'wise', i.e. *vidvat* 'knowledgeable' and *deva* 'deity' and cites the lexicographer Viśva as evidence for these synonyms. He then gives the derivation of the word *vibudha* by the addition of the affix ***ka*** by citing the rule in Pāṇini's *Aṣṭādhyāyī* that provides the affix after roots with penultimate *i*, *u*, *r*, or *l* as well as after the roots *jñā* 'know', *prī* 'please', and *kṝ* 'skatter'.

He then shows that the compound *vibudhasakha* is a ṣaṣṭhī-tatpuruṣa compound equivalent to the paraphrase *vibudhānāṁ sakhā* by using the pronoun *teṣām* instead of the prior compound constituent itself. He provides two synonyms for the compound *vibudha-sakha*: *vidvatsevin* 'one who serves the knowledgeable' and *devendra-sahacara* 'friend of the king of the gods'. He closes his comment on this word by citing *A.* 5.4.91 which provides the compound-final affix *ṭac*.

This passage in Mallinātha's commentary is encoded utilizing the elements and attributes described in §3 as shown in Figure 1. Since the whole passage concerns the single word *vibudhasakha* in the verse, the entire passage is set in an `ab` element with the attribute-value pair `type='pada'` and `corresp` attribute with the value of the `xml:id` of the word in the morphological analysis file. Segments of the passage that 1. provide an analytic paraphrase (*vigraha-vākya*) of the compound or one of its constituents, 2. give synonyms, 3. cite a lexicon, or 4. provide a derivation are each set in `seg` elements with the value of the `type` attribute indicating its function with the respective keyword: 1. `vigraha`, 2. `synonym`, 3. `lexicon`, 4. `derivation`. For example, *vidvatsevī* and *devendrasahacaraḥ* are put in a `seg` element with the `type` attribute with the value `synonym`. Each of these `seg`s has a `corresp` attribute that bears the value of the `xml:id` of the word or morpheme to which it relates, that is, of the word in the case of the analytic paraphrase of the compound *teṣāṁ sakhā*, and of the morpheme in the cases of the analytic paraphrase, synonym, and lexical citation relating to *vibudha*. The citation from the *Viśvakośa* lexicon is set in the `quote` element. This quote and the references to Pāṇini's *Aṣṭādhyāyī* in the derivations are immediately followed by `note` elements supplied with `bibl` elements indicating the text with `corresp` attributes linking to the bibliographic entry in our TEI file of bibliographic entries, `listbiblfile.xml`. Each of these `bibl` elements has a child `biblScope` element giving the precise reference within the text with a `corresp` attribute with the value of the `xml:id` of the passage cited or referenced. In the case of the *Viśvakośa* of which we do not yet have a digital edition, the `biblScope` and the `corresp` values are dummy values. Finally, the compound word in the text being commented upon (*vibudhasakhaḥ*), which finally appears towards the end of the passage, is set in a `w` element with an `xml:id` matching that of the `w` element in the morphological analysis file.

6.2 Repetition of the base text word in the commentary

Generally Mallinātha cites and explains each word in the base text just once in the commentary; however, occasionally he repeats a word, especially the verb, supplying it again to complete the phrase or clause on which he comments. For example, the sixth verse of the first sarga, the first of three verses describing the city Ayodhyā, consists of a relative clause as follows:

> निर्माणदक्षस्य समीहितेषु   सीमेव पद्मासनकौशलस्य।
> ऊर्द्ध्वस्फुरद्रत्नगभस्तिभिर्या   स्थितावहस्येव पुरं मघोनः ॥६॥
>
> "Which (Ayodhyā) stood, as if the apex of the skill of the lotus-seated (Brahmā) who was expert in the manifestation of his desired aims, as if laughing at the city of Indra, with the rays from its jewels scintillating upwards."
> "(Ayodhyā) which seemed to be the limit of the expertise of the undertaking of the Creator who was careful in (the art of) creating, and stood laughing, as it were, at the city of Indra, with the rays from its jewels scintillating upwards." (Karandikar and Karandikar, 1982, 2)

The past participle *sthitā* serves as the predicate of the long relative clause that comprises the entire verse. The verse contains two similes, one in each line. Mallinātha cites the word twice in his commentary, once with each simile. His commentary on the end of the first line runs as follows:

> सीमा परमावधिः इव स्थिता इत्युत्प्रेक्षा।
> "'...stood as if the border, i.e. supreme limit,' is a simile."

Figure 1: TEI encoding of Mallinātha's commentary on the word *vibudhasakhaḥ*

```
<ab type="pada" corresp="s1.v1.w3" xml:id="s1.v1.ab2">
 <seg type="vigraha" corresp="s1.v1.w3.m1">viSezeRa buDyanta iti vibuDAH</seg>
 <seg type="synonym" corresp="s1.v1.w3.m1">vidvAMso devASca</seg><pc>.</pc>
 <seg type="lexicon" corresp="s1.v1.w3.m1">
  <quote>vibuDO surapaRqitO</quote>
   iti viSvaH..
  <note>
   <bibl corresp="listbiblfile.xml#xxxxx.visvakosa">{v}iSva. <biblScope
       corresp="xxxxx">xxxxx</biblScope></bibl>
  </note>
 </seg>
 <seg type="derivation" corresp="s1.v1.w3">
  <ref target="A3.1.135">igupaDalakzaRaH kapratyayaH..</ref>
  <note>
   <bibl corresp="listbiblfile.xml#panini.astadhyayi">A. <biblScope
       corresp="A3.1.135">3.1.135</biblScope></bibl>
  </note>
 </seg>
 <seg type="vigraha" corresp="s1.v1.w3">tezAM saKA</seg>
 <w n="1" xml:id="s1.v1.w3">vibuDasaKaH</w>
 <seg type="synonym" corresp="s1.v1.w3">vidvatsevI devendrasahacaraH</seg>
 ca
 <s>vijayasahakAritvAttasyeti BAvaH..</s>
 <seg type="derivation" corresp="s1.v1.w3">
  <ref target="A5.4.91">rAjAhaHsaKiByazwac</ref>
  <note>
   <bibl corresp="listbiblfile.xml#panini.astadhyayi">A. <biblScope
       corresp="A5.4.91">5.4.91</biblScope></bibl>
  </note>
  iti wac..</seg>
</ab>
```

He comments on the end of the second line as follows:

हसित्वा इव स्थिता इति पूर्वोत्प्रेक्षया सजातीयया संकरः ॥

"'...stood as if laughing' is mixed with the similar previous simile."

Both comments include the word *sthitā* which occurs just once in the verse but is syntactically understood in both phrases. Here Bhaṭṭi has employed the familiar linguistic structure called *gapping* in which the verbal predicate is elided in one of two parallel phrases. The commentator has supplied the verbal predicate in each in his explanation. Because we would like to utilize the commentator's reordering of the words of the verse in the base text to evaluate ordinary prose syntax, we would like to determine which of the two occurrences represents the original word and which is supplied. In English syntax, generally the verb occurs in second position, immediately after the subject, and could be elided in subsequent parallel phrases where it could be understood, and could be supplied in the exposition of the complex sentence. For example, Gillon (2019, 196) gives as his first example of gapping, *Peter saw the movie, and Susan ____ the play.*[1] Hence in our translation, in accordance with English syntax, we have placed *stood* in the normal position of the verb in English and gapped it in the second simile. In contrast to English, in Sanskrit the verb typically appears at the end of its clause and would be gapped in the preceding phrase. Thus Bhaṭṭi places the verbal predicate *sthitā* in the fourth verse quarter in the second simile and gaps it in the first. We therefore determine that the second occurrence of the word *sthitā* represents the original word in the verse, and that Mallinātha has supplied the first occurrence to fill the ellipsis in the first simile.

It is significant to understand that each word of the base text that occurs in the commentary should carry unique identification in our encoding of the commentary. We achieve the unique identification of the commentator's use of each word in the base text by providing the unique `xml:id` attribute of the `w` element that contains the word in the morphological analysis file of the base text as the value of the unique `xml:id` of the `w` element that contains the word in the commentary file. The same value is given to the `corresp` attribute of the `ab` element that contains the commentary on the word. Two occurrences of the same word should not carry same value. Obviously we cannot eliminate the second occurrence from the commentary; for we would then lose the information that the commentator supplied the word to fill the gap in the clause. In the case where the commentator supplies a word a second time, we need to select just one as the representation of the original word and encode the other in a different manner to prevent duplication. We achieve this by using the attribute `copyOf` in the `w` element of the repeated word provided with the value of the `xml:id` of that word in the morphological analysis file of the base text.

In the case of the word *sthitā* in the commentary on verse six, we represent that the second occurrence is the original, and the first occurrence is the copy supplied by the commentator as follows:

```
<ab type="pada" corresp="s1.v6.w4">
 <w n="6" xml:id="s1.v6.w4">iva</w>
 <w copyOf="s1.v6.w8">sTitA</w>
</ab>
...
<ab type="pada" corresp="s1.v6.w8">
 <w n="12" xml:id="s1.v6.w8">sTitA</w>
iti
</ab>
```

The first occurrence of the word is not numbered: it occurs in the `w` element with the attribute `copyOf` without any `n` attribute so that it will not find any place in the reordering of the words of the verse in prose order.

Another instance in which Mallinātha repeats a word that occurs just once in the verse occurs in his commentary on verse eighteen of the first sarga. The verse runs as follows:

[1] Comma supplied.

ऐषीः पुनर्जन्मजयाय यत्त्वं   रूपादिबोधान्न्यवृतद्य यत्ते ।
तत्त्वान्यबुद्धाः प्रतनूनि येन   ध्यानं नृपस्तच्छिवमित्यवादीत् ॥१८॥

"The king said, 'Your meditation, to which you have resorted for victory over rebirth and which turned back from the experience of (the qualities) color, etc., by which you have known subtle entities, is auspicious?"'

"The king spoke thus: I hope that you are free from hindrances in your meditations intended for the conquest of rebirth which cease after the realization of the Ultimate form, and other things, and through which you grasp the subtlest principles." (Karandikar and Karandikar, 1982, 4)

The word *yena*, instrumental singular of the relative pronoun *yad* 'which', occurs just once at the end of the third verse quarter in a relative clause. In his commentary, Mallinātha takes the word twice in two relative clauses, once in connection with the first verse quarter and again in connection with the third. The pronoun refers to the sage's meditation (*dhyāna*), the term for which occurs in the nominative singular in the fourth verse quarter in the main clause of the sentence. In his commentary on the first verse quarter, Mallinātha, reading *tattvam* for *yattvam*, writes,

ते तव येन ध्यानेन पुनर्जन्मनो जयाय निरासाय अपुनर्भवाय तत्त्वमात्मस्वरूपं त्वमैषीरज्ञासीः ।, ...

"By which meditation of you you have gone to, i.e. you have known, the reality, i.e. the nature of the self, ..."

and in his commentary on the third verse quarter he writes,

येन ध्यानेन प्रतनूनि सूक्ष्माणि तत्त्वानि महदादीन्यबुद्धा अज्ञासीः ।, ...

"By which meditation you have become aware of, you have known, the fine, i.e. subtle, elements, i.e. the great (*mahat*) etc., ...

While the base text in the edition of Trivedi (1898, 14) reads the neuter accusative singular of the relative pronoun in the first quarter ('to which you have resorted'), the commentary in the same edition lacks a relative pronoun there where Mallinātha reads *tattvam*.[2] Due to the absence of a relative pronoun where needed, Mallinātha borrows the instrumental relative pronoun from the third quarter in his paraphrase of the first quarter ('by which meditation ...you ...have known'). The occurrence in the third quarter is clearly the original, so we determine that Mallinātha's first use is a copy and his second use takes the original. We represent these two as follows as described above.

```
<ab type="pada" corresp="s1.v18.w3">
 <w copyOf="s1.v18.w13">yena</w>
 <seg type="antecedent">DyAnena</seg>
</ab>
...
<ab type="pada" corresp="s1.v18.w13">
 <w n="9" xml:id="s1.v18.w13">yena</w>
 <seg type="antecedent">DyAnena</seg>
</ab>
```

The word that is a copy is put in a `w` element with the `copyOf` attribute and without an `n` attribute. The word that takes the original is put in a `w` element with an `xml:id` and `n` attribute. The former being unnumbered will not occur in our extraction of the commentators reordering of the words of the verse in the syntactic order of ordinary prose; the latter will.

6.3 Intertwined commentary on more than one word

Generally Mallinātha comments on one word at a time and explains aspects of the word in a consistent order. First he provides an analytic phrase, then a synonym, and then a derivation

[2]We discuss other cases of variant readings below in §6.5 on page 117.

if all are present, though not all of these three aspects of explanation are always present. He usually provides a synonym (for 251 = 61% of 409 words), a derivation half as often (126/409 = 31%), and an analytic phrase less than a quarter as often (54/409 = 13%). If he provides a synonym based on a thesaurus, the synonym is immediately followed by a citation from the thesaurus. While discussing the derivation of the word in question, the significant rules in the *Aṣṭādhyāyī* are referenced.

However, sometimes he deviates from this procedure and comments on a phrase by providing these aspects of explanation serially for more than one word in the phrase at a time, thereby intertwining the individual words and their explanations. For example, he does so in his commentary on the first two words of the first quarter of verse twenty-five. The verse and its translation are as follows:

> प्रयास्यतः पुण्यवनाय जिष्णो रामस्य रोचिष्णुमुखस्य धृष्णुः ।
> त्रैमातुरः कृत्स्नजितास्त्रशस्त्रः सध्र्यङ्ङ्तः श्रेयसि लक्ष्मणो ऽभूत् ॥२५॥
> "Devoted to (Rāma's) good, the daring Lakṣmaṇa, the son of three mothers, who completely mastered missiles and blades, became the fellow-traveller of the victorious Rāma who had a beaming face and was about to set out for the holy forest."
> "Dedicated to (Rāma's) well-being, the daring Lakṣmaṇa, who had three mothers and had acquired all the missiles and weapons, became the fellow-traveller of the victorious Rāma who had a beaming face and had set out for the holy forest." (Karandikar and Karandikar, 1982, 6)

Mallinātha comments on the first two words of the first quarter in reverse order: *puṇyavanāya prayāsyataḥ*, as follows:

> ततो ऽनन्तरं पुण्यवनाय तपोवनाय प्रयास्यतः तपोवनं गमिष्यतः ॥ गत्यर्थकर्मणि इत्यादिना कर्मणि चतुर्थी ॥ लृटः सद्वा इति शत्रादेशः ॥
> "After that, of the one about to set out for the holy-forest (sacred-forest), (of the one about to go to the sacred-forest). A fourth-triplet nominal termination occurs in the sense of the direct object by *A.* 2.3.12 *gatyarthakarmaṇi dvitīyācaturthyau ceṣṭāyāmanadhvani*. The affix ***śatṛ*** occurs by *A.* 3.3.14 *lṛṭaḥ sadvā* (*bhaviṣyati* 3)."

Mallinātha first provides a synonym for each word, glossing *puṇyavanāya* 'holy forest' as *tapovanāya* 'sacred-forest', and *prayāsyataḥ* 'of the one about to set out' as *gamiṣyataḥ 'of the one about to go'*. Then he discusses the derivation of each word. First he explains why the first of these words, *puṇyavana*, is in the dative case and provides the relevant *sūtra* that provides the fourth-triplet nominal termination to denote the direct object (*karman*) of a verb of locomotion. Then he explains that the second word, *prayāsyat*, is a future active particple by citing the rule that replaces the future indicative affix ***lṛṭ*** with the participle suffix ***śatṛ***. In such cases where the commentary on words is intertwined, we put the commentary on the whole phrase in a single `ab` element and provide its `corresp` attribute with two values matching the values of the `xml:id`s of the two words as shown in Figure 2. The synonym and derivation, and where present the analytic paraphrase, of each of the words is linked to the particular word to which it relates by the correspondence of their `seg` elements' `corresp` attributes with the `xml:id` of the word to which they relate.

6.4 Missing words

Mallinātha comments on almost all of the words in each verse. Of the 409 words in the twenty-seven verses in first sarga, he comments on 369 (90%) by mentioning the word in the commentary explicitly. He comments on another 36 words (9%) by analyzing them without repeating the word, in which case the word may be inferred. On just 4 words (less than 1%), he neglects to comment at all.

Almost all of the inferrable words are compounds where he comments on one of the constituents and repeats the other, or on both of the constituents separately. For example, com-

Figure 2: TEI encoding of Mallinātha's intertwined commentary on words in the phrase *prayāsyataḥ puṇyavanāya*

```
<ab type="pada" corresp="s1.v25.w2 s1.v25.w1" xml:id="s1.v25.ab2">tato
    'nantaraM
 <w n="1" xml:id="s1.v25.w2">puRyavanAya</w>
 <seg type="synonym" corresp="s1.v25.w2">tapovanAya</seg>
 <w n="2" xml:id="s1.v25.w1">prayAsyataH</w>
  tapovanaM
 <seg type="synonym" corresp="s1.v25.w1">gamizyataH</seg><pc>..</pc>
 <seg type="derivation" corresp="s1.v25.w2">
  <ref target="A2.3.12">gatyarTakarmaRi</ref>
  <note>
   <bibl corresp="listbiblfile.xml#panini.astadhyayi">A. <biblScope
       corresp="A2.3.12">2.3.12</biblScope></bibl>
  </note>
  ityAdinA karmaRi caturTI..
  <ref target="A3.3.14">lfwaH sadvA</ref>
  <note>
   <bibl corresp="listbiblfile.xml#panini.astadhyayi">A. <biblScope
       corresp="A3.3.14">3.3.14</biblScope></bibl>
  </note>
  iti SatrAdeSaH..</seg>
</ab>
```

menting on the word *śrutānvitaḥ* 'endowed with Vedic knowledge', an adjective describing king Daśaratha in the second quarter of the first verse, Mallinātha writes,

> श्रुतेन वेदशास्त्रश्रवणेन अन्वितः स्वयं च विद्वानित्यर्थः।
> "Endowed with learning (learning of the science of Veda)."

Here, Mallinātha does not mention the compound *śrutānvitaḥ*. Yet he provides an analytic paraphrase of the compound, with the words *śrutena* 'with that which is heard' ...*anvitaḥ* 'endowed', which shows that it is a tṛtīyā-tatpuruṣa compound. Immediately after the initial compound constituent, he provides the synonym *vedaśāstraśravaṇena* 'with learning (literally 'hearing') of the science of Veda'. As mentioned in §3 on page 107, in cases where the word can be inferred from his analysis, we supply the word in a `w` element with a `type` attribute with the value `inferred`.

There are several instances where the word in the base text can be inferred by syntactic criteria. For example, the first line of verse twenty-two contains a relative clause in the second quarter coordinated with the main clause in the first quarter by the use of the instrumental singular of coordinated masculine singular demonstrative and relative pronouns *tena* ...*yena*. The line reads as follows:

> घानिष्यते तेन महान् विपन्नः स्थायिष्यते येन रणे पुरस्तात्।
> "A great adversary will be slain by him, by whom standing will be done in front in battle."
> "By him, who will stand at the vanguard in the battlefield, (even a) great adversary will be killed." (Karandikar and Karandikar, 1982, 5)

Mallinātha omits the relative pronoun `yena` in his commentary on the second quarter. He writes:

> रामेण रणे पुरस्तादग्रे स्थायिष्यते स्थास्यते
> "By Rāma standing will be done in front (at the fore) in battle."

The appropriate position of the relative pronoun *yena* can be inferred in the commentary, despite Mallinātha's omitting it, by his use of its antecedent *rāmeṇa*. We place the pronoun immediately preceding the antecedent in a `w` element with the attribute-value pair `type="inferred"`.

The few words on which Mallinātha neglects to comment entirely are mostly pronouns or particles, for example, the relative pronoun *yā* at the end of the third quarter of verse six on page 111, and the conjunction *ca* in the second quarter of verse eighteen on page 113. Unusually, he neglects to include the word *rataḥ* 'dedicated' in the fourth quarter of verse twenty-five on page 115. The fact that it is so unusual for Mallinātha to neglect to comment on a word is contributory evidence for understanding his omission of the relative pronoun *yat* 'which' and the second-person singular pronoun *tvam* 'you', which occur at the end of the first quarter of verse eighteen, as due to reading instead *tattvam* 'reality' as remarked in §6.2 on page 114. In order to extract from the commentary the words of the verse transformed into prose order in the commentary, it is necessary to represent every word that occurs in the base text because the transformed syntax would be incomplete if it lacked even a single word that appears in the base text. In this case, we supply the word at the proper place. As mentioned in §3 on page 108, where Mallinātha neglects to comment entirely on a word, we supply the word in a `w` element with a `type` attribute with the value `supplied`. For example, for the pronoun *yā* in verse 6:

```
<w type="supplied" n="1" xml:id="s1.v6.w7">yA</w>.
```

We place this supplied `w` element at the beginning of its clause because Mallinātha has similarly placed other pronominals at the beginning of their clauses in other verses.

6.5 Recording variants

Editions of classical Sanskrit texts vary, critical editions record variant readings, and commentators often record variants known to them. The text of Mallinātha's commentary on the *Rāvaṇavadha* occasionally reveals that he had a version of the base text that differs from the base text in the same edition (Trivedi, 1898). Moreover both occasionally differ from the base text as in the edition Das used for the morphological analysis (Śāstrin, 1912). In addition, Mallinātha records variant readings known to him. As noted by Ajotikar et al. (2018), the variants used and mentioned in commentary are crucial information from the point of view of text-transmission because they usually predate the oldest manuscripts. Hence we take care to record these variants. To do so, we use the attribute-value pair `type="variant"` to identify each variant present in Mallinātha's commentary. Most of these variants occur where Mallinātha simply uses a different word from the word in the base text. For example, in his commentary on the third verse, he uses a different verb from the one that occurs at the end of the first quarter of the verse in both the above-mentioned editions (Trivedi, 1898; Śāstrin, 1912) and in the edition with text and translation by Karandikar and Karandikar (1982). The editions read:

वसूनि तोयं घनवद्व्यकारीत्
He scattered riches just as a cloud does water.

The first quarter of the verse in all three editions has the word *vyakārīt*, aorist third-person singular of the verbal root *kṝ* with the preverb *vi* meaning scatter. In contrast, Mallinātha records the reading of the word *vyatārīt* which is the same form with the same preverb but with a different root, i.e. *tṝ*, meaning bestow. We encode this variant by putting the attribute-value pair `type="variant"` in the `w` element as follows:

```
<ab type="pada" corresp="s1.v3.w4">
 <w n="5" type="variant" xml:id="s1.v3.w4">vyatArIt</w>
</ab>
```

Besides simple cases such as the above where the commentator has a different reading from the editions of the base text, there are cases where the commentator remarks on a variant along with the reading given in the edition of the base text. For example, in the last quarter of verse eleven, the edition with Mallinātha's commentary edited by Trivedi (1898, 9) reads

स कर्मठः कर्म सुतानुबन्धि
"Expert in his work, he (...performed) the sacrifice that would result in sons." (Karandikar and Karandikar, 1982, 3)

After commenting on the last word, *sutānubandhi*, in the commentary in the same edition, Mallinātha mentions and comments on the variant *sutānubandham*, which is the reading adopted in the base text both by Śāstrin (1912, 9) and by Karandikar and Karandikar (1982, 3), Mallinātha writes:

सुताननुबध्नाति सन्तनोतीति सुतानुबन्धमिति वा पाठान्तरम्। कर्मण्यण्।

In this case, after Mallinātha mentions the reading *sutānubandhi* in the base text and provides a derivation for it, including a synonym for the morpheme *sutānubandha*, he proceeds to comment on the variant (*pāṭhāntara*) *sutānubandham*, providing it with the analytic paraphrase *sutān anubadhnāti*, a synonym *santanoti*, and a derivation *karmaṇyaṇ*. The situation complicates the encoding because instead of there being segments of the type `synonym`, `vigraha`, and `derivation` associated with one word, there are two sets of segments of these kinds associated with two words: the adopted reading and the variant, both associated with a single word in the base text. To encode this situation, we incorporate the entire section in a single `ab` associated with the word in the base text by its `corresp` attribute with the value of the `xml:id` of the word in the morphological analysis file as usual, but we segregate all of the information about the variant in a single subordinate `seg` element with the attribute-value pair `type="variant"`. The variant word is put in a `w` element with the attribute-value pair `type="variant"` and an `xml:id` whose value is the `xml:id` of the word in the base text with the suffix `.var` added to it. The segments that provide an analytic paraphrase, synonym, and derivation of the variant reading are encoded in subordinate `seg` elements with the appropriate type attributes, and with `corresp` attributes with the value of the variant word's `xml:id`. The `w` element containing the variant and its `synonym` segment, `vigraha` segment and `derivation` segment are all child nodes of the `variant` segment as shown in Figure 3.

Figure 3: TEI encoding of Mallinātha's commentary on the variant *sutānubandham*

```
<seg type="variant">
 <seg type="vigraha">sutAn anubaDnAti
  <seg type="synonym" corresp="s1.v11.w16.var">santanoti</seg>
   iti
  <w type="variant" n="14" xml:id="s1.v11.w16.var">sutAnubanDam</w>
   iti vA pAWAntaram..
  <seg type="derivation" corresp="s1.v11.w16.var">
   <ref target="A3.2.1">karmaRyaR..</ref>
   <note>
    <bibl corresp="listbiblfile.xml#panini.astadhyayi">A. <biblScope
        corresp="A3.2.1">3.2.1</biblScope></bibl>
   </note>
  </seg>
 </seg>
</seg>
```

7 Interpolation

Trivedi's (1898, 17) edition of Mallinātha's commentary on verse twenty-three includes a portion which cannot possibly have been composed by Mallinātha. The portion reads as follows:

कौमुद्यां तु ततो ऽनुजज्ञ इति पाठमनुसृत्य अनुपसर्गाज्ज्ञः इति शास्त्रप्रातिकूल्यमुद्भाव्य नृप इत्यत्र नृपेणेति विपरिणामं कृत्वा दोषपरिहारः कृतः।

"In the kaumudī, after adopting the reading *anujajñe*, and stating that this form violates *A.* 1.3.76 *anupasargājjñaḥ*, the fault is rectified by changing the reading *nṛpaḥ* to *nṛpeṇa*."

The passage refers to Bhaṭṭoji Dhīkṣita's citation of the second half of verse twenty-three of the *Rāvaṇavadha*, as it appears in the editions of Trivedi (1898, 17), Śāstrin (1912, 16) and Karandikar and Karandikar (1982, 5), in his comment on *A.* 1.3.76. The comment including the citation runs as follows:

> कथं तर्हि भट्टिः
> इत्थं नृपः पूर्वमवालुलोचे ततो ऽनुजज्ञे गमनं सुतस्य॥
>
> इति। कर्मणि लिट्। नृपेणेति विपरिणामः॥ Then how does Bhaṭṭi write,
> "The king previously thought thus, then he approved his son's going."
> "Thus did the king reflect first and then permit the departure of his son." (Karandikar and Karandikar, 1982, 5)
> The verbal termination of the perfect (textitl**iṭ**) occurs to denote the direct object.
> There is alteration of the nominal termination 'by the king (*nṛpeṇa*).

A. 1.3.76 provides that an ātmanepada verbal termination occurs after the verb *jñā* 'know' without a preverb if the result of the action accrues to the agent. The rule accounts for the use of *jñā* in the middle voice only without a preverb not with the preverb *anu* as it occurs in the fourth quarter of verse 23. Bhaṭṭoji Dhīkṣita justifies the form by claiming that the form *anujajñe* is passive rather than middle and that its agent, which appears in the nominative (*nṛpaḥ*) must be understood to be an alteration of the instrumental (*nṛpeṇa*). The passage in the edition of Mallinātha's commentary explains Bhaṭṭoji Dhīkṣita's justification.

While the passage makes a correct observation, it must be a later interpolation. For it is impossible that Mallinātha would quote Bhaṭṭojī Dīkṣita's *Siddhāntakaumudī* because Bhaṭṭojī Dīkṣita (1547–1633 CE Dash (2007, 111b)) is dated a two centuries after Mallinātha (14th century CE (Lienhard, 1984, 39)). Trivedi (1898, Notes 20) leaves the reader in doubt on this point when he comments in his note on verse 23, "But the true reading seems to be the one adopted in the text. Malli. notices it and shews how it is discussed in the *Siddhāntakaumudī*," and allows the reader to be misled by including it in the text of his edition. However, after discussing the identity and date of Mallinātha in detail in his introduction, he (1898, xxviii) concludes regarding this and one other citation from the *siddhāntakaumudī*, "they must be considered as interpolations. They may have been originally marginal notes of some copyist and afterwards inserted into the commentary." Further down the page he notes that the other passage that cites the *Siddhāntakaumudī* is omitted in a manuscript he obtained from the Theosophical Society of Madras, and continues regarding the citation under discussion, "As regards the second reference to the kaumudī (C. I. St. 23) I have secured, ..., a copy of the commentary of Mallinātha from another manuscript at Udamalpet, in which the reference to the kaumudī is omitted." Finally, he (1898, xxviii–xxix) concludes his introduction writing, "I therefore conclude that ...he flourished before Bhaṭṭojī Dīkṣita and that the two references to the Siddhāntakaumudī in the commentary are interpolations." To mark the text as an interpolation, we tag this passage with the attribute-value pair `type="interpolation"`.

8 Utility of the TEI-tagged data

The analysis and tagging of major Sanskrit poetic works and their commentaries in the manner described above leads to a number of useful applications. Several such applications are described below.

- **Dynamic lemmatized index.** In the morphological analysis file described in §3 on page 107, the root of each verb and nominal base of each nominal is provided, as are the word's lexical and morphological identifiers. From this information dynamic indices can be created that can provide access to words and their contexts based on a number of criteria. These indices include an alphabetical list of words (*padas*) and an alphabetical list of lemmas (roots and nominal bases). These lists could be trimmed according to the selection of additional criteria such as various lexical and morphological categories, and text extents.

- **Dictionary of synonyms (*paryāyakośa*).** The commentary provides the synonym of each word in the base text as described in §2 on page 107, and the TEI-tagged commentary file tags these synonyms as described in §3 on page 107. From this information one can programmatically generate a dictionary of synonyms.

- **Index of quotations.** The commentary cites a number of different texts in a variety of disciplines as discussed in §2 on page 107. The highest quality scholarly editions of Sanskrit works enrich their editions with lists of quotations through time-consuming and tedious labor. Many editions lack such useful lists. The TEI-tagged commentary file tags quotations as described in §3 on page 108. From this information one can programmatically generate an alphabetical or searchable index of quotations very easily.

- **Index of derivations.** As described in §2 on page 107, commentaries provide the Pāṇinian derivation of numerous words. This information is significant for Sanskrit readers. Yet it would also be extremely valuable for linguists if systematized. The TEI-tagged commentary file tags such derivations as described in §3 on page 108. One can programmatically generate an index of derivations that provides access to them by the word derived, roots and stems, affixes, and the numbers of sūtras referenced.

- **Index of meters.** Although commentaries identify the metrical patterns commonly found in each chapter of poetic texts as described in §2 on page 107 and these will be tagged in our analysis as described in §3 on page 108, they do not provide the exact sub-type or description of the metrical pattern of each verse. However, TEITagger checks the metrical pattern of each verse in the process of creating the TEI-tagged XML file from the original text file of the base text as mentioned in §5 on page 110 and inserts the specific meter name in the `type` attribute of the `lg` element which houses each verse. TEITagger also identifies the class and general type of the meter, and the metrical pattern of the verse as described by Melnad et al. (2015a), Melnad et al. (2015b) and Scharf (2018), and discovers aberrant cases. From this information, one can programmatically generate an alphabetical or searchable index of meters used in the text.

- **Index of figures of speech.** Commentaries identify figures of speech used in each verse as described in §2 on page 107 and these will be tagged as described in §3 on page 108. From this information, one can programmatically generate an alphabetical or searchable index of figures of speech used in the text.

- **Preparation of a tree-bank of Sanskrit prose.** The file containing the prose sentences in the commentator's reordering of the verse should prove to be extremely useful to those studying Sanskrit syntax. Kulkarni et al. (2015) recently explored the limitations of free word order in Sanskrit, and Scharf et al. (2015) examined differences in Sanskrit prose versus verse word order. The prose word order file links every word with the morphological analysis file where every word is supplied with its lemma, and lexical and inflectional identifiers. Adding relational information to this information could form the basis of a tree-bank of Sanskrit prose.

Scharf wrote extensible stylesheet language transformations (XSLT) that prepare a dictionary of synonyms and derivations, a word index, an index of citations, and indices of passages in which Mallinātha discusses meters and figures of speech. The resultant XML files conform to the TEI guidelines for dictionaries and indices and can easily be utilized to create Web-interfaces for each. Figure 4 shows an entry for the verb *vyatārīt* which occurs in Mallinātha's commentary on the first quarter of verse three as discussed above in §6.5 on page 117. The `etym` element houses the derivation provided by the commentator, and the `def` element, as a child of the `sense` element houses the synomym he provides. The additional `bibl` elements not copied from references in the commentary itself provide links back to the text of the commentary.

Figure 4: TEI encoding of the dictionary entry for the verb *vyatārīt*

```
<entry>
 <form>vyatArIt</form>
 <etym>taraterluNi
  <xr corresp="A8.2.28">iwa Iwi</xr>
  <note>
   <bibl corresp="listbiblfile.xml#panini.astadhyayi">A.<biblScope
       corresp="A8.2.28">8.2.28</biblScope></bibl>
  </note>
   iti sijlopaH.
  <bibl>BhRV.<biblScope corresp="s1.v3.w4"/></bibl>
 </etym>
 <sense>
  <def>vitIrRavAn
   <bibl>BhRV.<biblScope corresp="s1.v3.w4"/></bibl>
  </def>
 </sense>
</entry>
```

9 Syntactic research

Higher-level encoded text can be used to resolve pertinent issues of research. While the encoding of text-structure and document-format in digital text is useful for creating a variety of print and HTML publications from a single document source, higher-level encoding can efficiently be used to investigate various research problems. We plan to use our encoding of Mallinātha's commentary on the first sarga of the *Rāvaṇavadha* to explore his reordering of the words of the verse as evidence of the unmarked syntax of ordinary prose. To this end, Scharf wrote a pair of XSLT transformations that extract each word of each verse in the order in which Mallinātha comments on it and constructs prose renderings of each verse. One version of the transformation preserves the numbering of the order of the words in the original verse and information on whether we inferred or supplied the word; the other omits this information providing a readable prose rendering of the words of each verse. We plan to subject the original verse and Mallinātha's prose to the sort of syntactic analysis conducted by Scharf et al. (2015).

At present the twenty-seven verses of the first sarga of Bhaṭṭi's *Rāvaṇavadha* does not comprise a significant data-set. Tripathi's project described in §5 on page 110 will extend the data-set by a factor of ten. Moreover, Scharf and Tripathi have begun a two-year project entitled, "Digitization and markup of the masterpieces of Sanskrit kāvya and their most essential commentaries." The project will produce TEI editions of the base text and commentaries of five major and minor poetic works. We hope to present some interesting results bearing on Sanskrit syntax in a couple of years.

10 Conclusion

The digital medium provides methods to find information quickly, and contemporary scholars expect to be able to locate the information they seek using these methods. Developments in digital humanities have made it possible to ease the process of making very specific information embedded in texts available in the way that contemporary scholars expect. To make this information available requires careful analysis of the structure and content of the concerned texts. We have analyzed the structure and content of Sanskrit commentarial literature on poetry which provides rich information in the form of references, explanation and derivation of specialized vocabulary, explanation of metrical patterns, syntax, figures of speech, etc. as described above. We have devised templates in accordance with the TEI guidelines to represent all of the relevant information in poetic texts and their commentaries, have written XSLT transformations that prepare dictionaries of and indices to this information, and have outlined procedures to build a library of digital Sanskrit commentarial literature. The employment of these procedures and construction of this library should prove to be invaluable to linguists, philologists, and other humanities scholars.

References

Tanuja P. Ajotikar and Peter M. Scharf. 2020. Development of a tei standard for digital sanskrit texts containing commentaries. In *Proceedings of the international conference on the tradition of commentary and the stream of knowledge (bhāṣyaparamparā jñānapravāhaśca)*. Somnath Sanskrit University.

Tanuja P. Ajotikar, Anuja P. Ajotikar, and Peter M. Scharf. 2018. Enriching the digital edition of the *Kāśikāvṛtti* by adding variants from the *Nyāsa* and *Padamañjarī*. In Huet and Kulkarni (hue, 2018), pages 277–294.

Siniruddha Dash, editor. 2007. *New catalogus catalogorum*, volume 16. University of Madras.

Brendan S. Gillon. 2019. *Natural language semantics*. MIT Press.

Pawan Goyal, Gérard Huet, Amba Kulkarni, Peter Scharf, and Ralph Bunker. 2012. A distributed platform for sanskrit processing. In *Proceedings of COLING 2012*, pages 1011–1028. The COLING 2012 Organizing Committee.

2018. Computational sanskrit and digital humanities.

Gérard Huet and Idir Lankri. 2018. Preliminary design of a sanskrit corpus manager. In Huet and Kulkarni (hue, 2018), pages 259–276.

Maheshvara Ananta Karandikar and Shailaja Karandikar. 1982. *Bhaṭṭikāvyam*. Motilal Banarasidas.

Sriram Krishnan and Amba Kulkarni. 2019. Sanskrit segmentation revisited. In *ICON 2019*. NLP Association of India.

Amba Kulkarni and Devanand Shukl. 2009. Sanskrit morphological analyser. volume 70, pages 169–177.

Amba Kulkarni, Preeti Shukla, Pavankumar Satuluri, and Devanand Shukl. 2015. How free is 'free' word order in sanskrit? In Scharf (sch, 2015), pages 269–304.

Siegfried Lienhard. 1984. *A history of classical poetry*. Number III.1 in A history of Indian literature. Otto Harrasssowitz.

Keshav Melnad, Pawan Goyal, and Peter M. Scharf. 2015a. Identification of meter in sanskrit verse. In Scharf (sch, 2015), pages 325–346.

Keshav Melnad, Pawan Goyal, and Peter M. Scharf. 2015b. Updating meter identifying tool (mit). Paper presented at the 16th World Sanskrit Conference, Bankok.

Yonghui Qiu, Bangwei Wang, George Cardona, Hong Luo, and Peter M. Scharf, editors. 2020. *Saṁskṛtādhvā*.

Vināyaka Śāstrin, editor. 1912. *The Bhaṭṭikāvya of Bhaṭṭi*. Nirṇaya-sāgara Press, 4 edition.

2015. Sanskrit syntax.

Peter M. Scharf and Malcolm D. Hyman. 2011. *Linguistic issues in encoding Sanskrit*. The Sanskrit Library.

Peter M. Scharf, Anuja Ajotikar, Sampada Savardekar, and Pawan Goyal. 2015. Distinctive features of poetic syntax. In Scharf (sch, 2015), pages 305–324.

Peter M. Scharf. 2014. Linguistic issues and intelligent technological solutions in encoding sanskrit. 16(3):15–29.

Peter M. Scharf. 2015. Providing access to manuscripts in the digital age. In Justin Thomas McDaniel and Lynn Ransom, editors, *From Mulberry leaves to silk scrolls*, number 1 in The Lawrence J. Schoenberg Studies in Manuscript Culture, pages 231–271. University of Pennsylvania Libraries.

Peter M. Scharf. 2017. Accessing manuscripts in the digital age. volume 6, pages 131–173. National Mission for Manuscripts.

Peter M. Scharf. 2018. Teitagger. In Huet and Kulkarni (hue, 2018), pages 169–191.

Peter M. Scharf. 2020. Issues in digital sanskrit philology and computational linguistics. In Qiu et al. (Qiu et al., 2020), page xxxxx.

Kamalāśaṅkara Prāṇaśaṅkara Trivedi, editor. 1898. *Rāvaṇavadha*. Government Central Book Depot.

Rāmopākhyāna
a Web-based reader and index

Peter M. Scharf
President, The Sanskrit Library
Adjunct Professor, IIIT Hyderabad
scharf@sanskritlibrary.org
and
DHRUV CHAUHAN
International Institute of Information Technology, Hyderabad

Abstract

Web-based interactive readers integrated with indices provide scholars of Sanskrit a learning environment more responsive to their needs. Advances in Web technology and more stringent security requirements rendered the *Kramapāṭha* reader and indices developed for the *Rāmopākhyāna* two decades ago obsolete and inoperative. A current implementation using state-of-the art encoding and Web-development software revives the reader and its indices.

Keywords: Sanskrit, Mahābhārata, Rāmāyaṇa, text-encoding, XML, TEI

1 Introduction

The story of Rāma is one of the most popular stories in India. Its most ancient extant version is told in Vālmīki's *Rāmāyaṇa*. More than 35 other major Sanskrit works retell it, as do numerous versions in every modern Indian language and those of Southeast Asia. It spread to Tibet, China, and Japan in ancient and medieval times and continues to be appreciated in India in modern performances and television productions. Before the final redaction of the *Rāmāyaṇa* in about 25,000 verses, however, it was summarized in the *Rāmopākhyāna* in the great epic *Mahābhārata* in 704 verses in eighteen chapters comprising chapters 258–275 of the *Āraṇyaka Parvan*. There it is introduced in chapter 257 after the Pāṇḍavas' rescue of their wife Kṛṣṇā from abduction by Jayadratha when the exiled king Yudhiṣṭhira who asks the sage Mārkaṇḍeya who could be more unfortunate than he. Mārkaṇḍeya draws implications for the Pāṇḍavas from Rāma's successful defeat of Rāvaṇa and return to Ayodhyā with the help of the alliances he formed during his exile.

Scharf (2002) produced a Sanskrit reader of the *Rāmopākhyāna* that provides everything a student of Sanskrit would need for the precise understanding of each verse. The text of each verse occurs as in the critical edition (Sukthankar and others, 1933 1959) with minor revisions as described by Scharf (Forthcoming, §IIA) in Devanāgarī and is supplied with a close prose English translation. The explanation of each verse includes Roman transliteration; analysis of sandhi; identification of inflection; a glossary that includes the analysis of compounds, and nominal and verbal derivates; prose Sanskrit sentences paraphrasing the verse, and syntactic and cultural notes. Scharf (2005) and the introduction to the book describe the features of the book in detail. A second edition (Scharf, Forthcoming) will appear imminently.

Simultaneous with the preparation of the first edition of the *Rāmopākhyāna*, Scharf prepared an interactive digital reader and detailed digital indices called *Kramapāṭha*. *Kramapāṭha* consisted of two integrated apps that ran in the browser. The Web-based reader included sound in addition to the features of the printed book. The Web-based indices allowed one to filter a list of lemmata by lexical, inflectional, and text extent parameters, and to see related inflected forms, definitions, and the passages in which they occurred. An index of Pāṇinian sūtras was also included. Created before the availability of Indic Unicode Fonts, *Kramapāṭha* displayed Devanāgarī directly on the users screen using a dynamic font.

Proceedings of the Computational Sanskrit and Digital Humanities, 18th *World Sanskrit Conference 2023*, pages 146–154

Great progress has been made over the past twenty years since the publication of *Rāmopākhyāna* and the development of *Kramapāṭha* in making resources available in digital form on the Web for scholars and students of Sanskrit. High quality Indic Unicode fonts are now widely available. The extensible markup language (XML) has become ubiquitous and integrated with hypertext markup language (HTML). JavaScript has been enriched and made easy to use by the development of numerous programming packages. JavaScript Object Notation (JSON), a lightweight data-interchange format is isomorphic with XML and integrated with powerful databases. However, along with the progress of the last two decades came restrictions. Enhancement of Web security rendered our Web-based version of the *Rāmopākhyāna* and its fabulous indices deployed in the Kramapāṭha reader and index applets obsolete several years ago. The present paper describes the redesign of the *Rāmopākhyāna* source data and reimplementation of the Web-based *Kramapāṭha* that utilizes recent advances in text encoding and Web technology.

2 Data description

The original source data for the *Kramapāṭha* reader was stored in a set of plain ASCII text files with tab-delimited fields that used special characters to mark the position for non-ASCII characters to be displayed in HTML or print such as single and double curly quotes and the root sign, and to designate the beginning and end of Sanskrit text such as proper names in English text fields. Sanskrit text was encoded in a subset of what became the Sanskrit Library Phonetic basic encoding (SLP1) described by Scharf and Hyman (2011). Several years ago Scharf wrapped the tab-delimited fields in these text files in XML tags to check and protect data-validity. Over the past several months he transformed all the data to an XML format that conforms to the Text-Encoding Initiative guidelines by writing XSLT routines and using TEITagger (described by Scharf (2018) and wrote Document Type Definitions (DTD) and Schematron schemas to validate the data. The TEI source now consists of the following parallel files:

1. text.xml. The text of the *Rāmopākhyāna* in SLP1 encoding.
2. ansan.xml. The text with sandhi analyzed.
3. morph.xml. Morphological analysis of each word.
4. morphCheck.xml. The above with the lemma of verbs with preverbs in a single element and the Unicode character entity for the check mark between the preverbs and root.
5. morphEng.xml. The English translation of each word in morph.xml or morphCheck.xml.
6. prose.xml. Sanskrit prose paraphrases of each verse.
7. proseSandhi.xml. The above with sandhi applied.
8. notes.xml. Syntactic and cultural notes.
9. english.xml. The English translation of verses.

Scharf had written a Pāṇinian sandhi program in Pascal in 1991 and revised it in 2000. Jim Funderburk rewrote the program in Perl, Java, and Python since then, maintains these versions in a Git archive at `https://github.com/funderburkjim/ScharfSandhi`, and described them in the `README` file there. In the past couple of months, Scharf revised the Java version to default to certain combinations more commonly expected and to eliminate spaces between preverbs and finite verbs. He used an XSLT routine that called his latest revision of the Java sandhi program to reproduce the sandhied versions of the Sanskrit verses (text.xml) and Sanskrit prose sentences (proseSandhi.xml) from the original sandhi-analyzed source files (ansan.xml and prose.xml). Another XSLT routine produces the file morphCheck.xml from morph.xml.

The data in all of these files is encoded in XML in accordance with the Text-Encoding Initiative Guidelines (Consortium, 2007). The elements and attributes used for basic text encoding are described in instructions on the Search and Retrieval of Indic Texts project (SARIT) website (`http://sarit.indology.info`) as well as by (Scharf, 2018), (Scharf, 2019 2020), (Scharf, 2015), (Scharf, 2017). We review them briefly here. Every file encodes its data in the `body` element which is a child of the `text` element within the `TEI` root element. A single `div` element occurs as a child of the `body` element with a texttttype attribute value set to `parvan`, and an n attribute set to 3. The data of each chapter is encoded in a div element with the textttype attribute value set to aDyAya, and an n attribute numbering the chapter according to its numbering in the *Āraṇyaka Parvan*. Each chapter groups the verses of each speaker in an sp element, the first child of which is a speaker element containing phrases such as जनमेजयः उवाच।, and whose subsequent children are the verses attributed to that speaker. Each verse is encoded in an lg element and each line of verse in an l element. Each speaker element and lg element has an n attribute that numbers the verse within the adhyāya and an xml:id that uniquely identifies the passage within the text by a combination of the parvan number, the adhyāya number within the parvan, and the verse number. Since an xml:id is required to begin with a letter, we use m for *Mahābhārata*. The speaker element of each speech includes an s to distinguish its xml:id from that of the first verse. For example, m3.257.1s is the value of the xml:id of the speaker element at the beginning of adhyāya 257.

The two files text.xml and ansan.xml containing the original text in SLP1, and its sandhi analysis respectively, are encoded with these elements with exactly parallel numbering and xml:ids. The file english.xml is nearly parallel with the exception that it uses the p element for the prose translation of each verse and child s elements for sentences within it. The xml:id of each p element is identical to that of the corresponding verse in the other two files. The files prose.xml, proseSandhi.xml and notes.xml do likewise. In the English and notes files, Sanskrit text is encoded in a foreign element and single and double curly quotes, ellipsis, and the root sign are rendered with the appropriate Unicode entity values.

In the files morph.xml and morphCheck.xml, each element containing Sanskrit text, i.e. the l and speaker elements, encodes each Sanskrit word in a w element. The root of each inflected verb and the stem of each nominal is encoded as the value of the lemma attribute of the w element. Its lexical identifier is encoded as the value of the w element's type attribute, and its inflectional identifier is encoded as the value of its subtype attribute. Each word w element is numbered within the verse lg element or the speaker element in the value of the n attribute and provided with an xml:id that uniquely identifies it. The xml:id is formed by adding .w and the number to the end of the xml:id is ancestor lg element or parent speaker element. For example, the value of the word, janamejayaḥ, which is the first word of the speaker element of the first speech of adhyāya 257 is m3.257.1s.w1. Morphemes of words are encoded in an m element as children of the w element that contains the word in its text node, and each is supplied with a type attribute whose value is its lexical identifier. If a morpheme is an inflected word whose nominal termination has not been deleted in an *aluk-samāsa*, its m element is supplied with a baseForm attribute whose value is its stem, and with a subtype attribute whose value is its inflectional identifier. The analytic paraphrase (*vigraha-vākya*) of a compound is encoded in a seg element, supplied with a type attribute with the value vigraha, as the first child of the w or m element that contains the compound. These m and seg elements are all supplied with n attributes that number them and xml:id attributes with unique ids. In the case of submorphemes of morphemes, these numbers and ids show the hierarchy of the morpheme relative to its ancestor w element. For example, in the first verse in the morphCheck.xml file, the preverb *prāpya* has the morpheme *pra√āp* with the xml:id with the value m3.257.1.w4.1. This morpheme has two children: the preverb *pra* and the root *√āp* which have the xml:ids with the values m3.257.1.w4.1.1 and m3.257.1.w4.1.2 respectively. The m element may contain child seg elements that separate the markers from roots and augments and similar technical grammatical units classified by appropriate values of the type attribute. These are not considered separate morphemes and are not enumerated or supplied with xml:ids. Additional elements such as bibl and its child biblScope identify references to Pāṇini's *Aṣṭādhyāyī*, Amarasiṁha's *Nāmaliṅgānuśāsana*, and other works. The English translation of each word or morpheme, or each analytic paraphrase of a compound, is encoded in the morphEng.xml file in exactly the same structure.

3 Indices and their production

Given the high degree of analysis of the words in the *Rāmopākhyāna* undertaken in the preparation of the *Kramapāṭha* reader, and the intention to make it useful for learning Sanskrit, it was deemed useful and practical to make the text accessible from various angles by the construction of detailed indices. The original index included an index of lemmata consisting of a list of all the lexical bases of nominal and verbal forms as well as their morphemes, and an index of Pāṇinian sūtras. The new indices include a word index in addition. The lemma index can be limited by a number of parameters. First of all, it can be limited to the lemmata of whole words that occur in the text, excluding their morphemes. The list can also be limited by selecting any combination of lexical categories, inflectional categories, and extents of text. For example, one can search for all masculine nominative singular perfect active participles. One finds eight instances, five of which are the form *jaghnivān* from the root *han* 'slay', one of which is the same with the preverb *ā*, and the remaining two of which are the form *sameyivān* from the root *i* with the preverbs *sam* and *ā* 'come together'. If one limited the search to chapter 263 in addition, one would find just one instance: *ājaghnivān*. It is also possible to show the list of all occurring inflected forms of the lemma of any inflected word or the immediate derivatives of any lemma including morphemes.

In order to make the data for these indices accessible for a Web-based index, Scharf wrote XSLT routines to reassemble the data from the files morphCheck.xml and morphEng.xml in three index files: stems.xml, words.xml, and sutras.xml. The first and principal index file is like a dictionary: it gives the lemma, its lexical identifier, and its English translation. Yet it also includes a list of the derivates of that lemma, a list of its inflected forms, and a list of verses in which the lemma occurs including the `xml:id` of the word or morpheme of each occurrence. Each of the inflected forms also includes a list of the verses in which that form occurs with their `xml:id`s of each occurrence. By looking up a derivate in the same index file, one can find the same information for that lemma and so recursively access all of the derivates of any morpheme.

The word.xml file is somewhat similar but simpler. The entry for each word includes its lemma, its lexical identifier and its inflectional identifier, its English translation, and a list of the verses in which it occurs with the `xml:id` of each occurrence. The sutra.xml file has Pāṇinian sūtra numbers as its main entries. An additional file has a list of sūtras with their numbers as in the *Kāśikā*. Each entry in the sutra.xml file includes a list of the lemmata to derive which the sūtra was cited, each of which has a list of the verses in which that lemma occurs, including the `xml:id` of each occurrence. This arrangement allows one to find the lemma in the stems.xml index file if desired. Each entry also includes a the inverse: a list of the the verses in which that sūtra is cited each of which indicates the lemma to derive which it is cited with the `xml:id` of each occurrence. This arrangement permits easy access to the instances of the citation of the sūtra.

4 Web-interface implementation

Using the Oxygen XML editors XML to JSON converter, Scharf produced JSON versions of the reader files:

1. ansan.json
2. english.json
3. morphCheck.json
4. morphEng.json
5. notes.json
6. prose.json
7. proseSandhi.json
8. text.json

and of the index files:

1. stems.json
2. sutras.json
3. sutraOnly.json
4. words.json

Chauhan used the MongoDB database to house these data, Elasticsearch as a secondary database, and the Flask and VueJS application development frameworks. The MondoDB database is a schema-less database in which one can have any type of data in separate documents and the flexibility to store data of different types. ElasticSearch permits speedy, complex searches. Chauhan migrated the data into both databases and used the RESTful APIs made available in the Flask framework to develop the interaction between Elasticsearch and the frontend framework VueJS. The latter is a progressive framework for building user interfaces, promotes modular application structure and provides practical ways to build component-based, dynamic user interfaces where one can manipulate and manage DOM elements in powerful ways. Figure 1 shows a diagram of the architecture of the system.

The *Kramapāṭha* reader display allows one to show any of the information one wishes to see regarding a verse: text, transliteration, sandhi analysis, prose, notes, and translation, by clicking buttons at the right of the window. Figure 2 shows the display of the first two and last three of these six types of information. By clicking any word in the Devanāgarī or Romanization, one can display the information relevant to that word in stages. In the first stage the word's inflectional identifier and lemma are shown. In the second stage its lexical identifier and English translation are shown, and in the third stage its morphemic analysis is shown. Figure 3 shows the display of the first speaker and verse in adhyāya 257 with its Roman transliteration in which the user has clicked the word *naravyāghrāḥ* three times to show all three stages of information relevant to the word.

The index display allows one to select the list of whole words, morphemes, or inflected forms. By selecting one word in the list at the left, its occurrences are shown in the middle. At the right is an interface in which one can select lexical and morphological categories and text extents by which to limit the list at the left. Figure 4 shows the list of inflected forms selected in the index. Here the word *adṛśyam* is selected and its list of occurrences is shown in the middle with its inflectional identifier, its lemma, and its lexical identifier. Beneath this is shown the verses in which it occurs and its English translation. At the right is shown the pane to limit the list by inflectional identifier with the nominal subpane selected but no parameters within it chosen.

Figure 5 shows the list of the lemmata of whole words that occur in the text, here called *free morphemes.* The lemma *antar* has been selected and the list of verses in which it occurs, either independently, as part of a compound, or as a gati with a verbal root, is shown in the middle. At the head of that list is shown the selected lemma in bold with its lexical identifier in parenthesis. Immediately below is shown the independent word in which it occurs and its verse number. Below that is shown the three derivates in which the lemma occurs, and below them is shown the list of verses in which these forms occur. At the tail end of the list is shown its English translation and beneath that the sūtra cited in the derivation of *antarhita.* The pane at the right shows the interface to limit the list by lexical category. Here the pronominal sub-pane has been selected but no parameters within that pane have been selected. At the bottom of the right pane is shown the interface to limit the list by text extent. The very first and last verses of the text are shown by default.

We are still refining the display of items in the interface and their arrangement. The second index figure shown at present appears crowded with too much information of different types shown at once. We expect to have the display finished with a few weeks work.

5 Conclusion

The interactive reader and index permit scholars of Sanskrit to access the information they need as they need it. A printed text can only present a single view, so the printed edition of the

Rāmopākhyāna presents all the information for each verse on a page at once. The Web-based reader, in contrast, more effectively facilitates learning by hiding information until desired by the reader. While the printed text can supply limited indices in appendices, the Web-based indices dynamically interact with the text display to permit the user to navigate the text easily.

Figure 1: The architecture of the *Kramapāṭha* reader and index system design

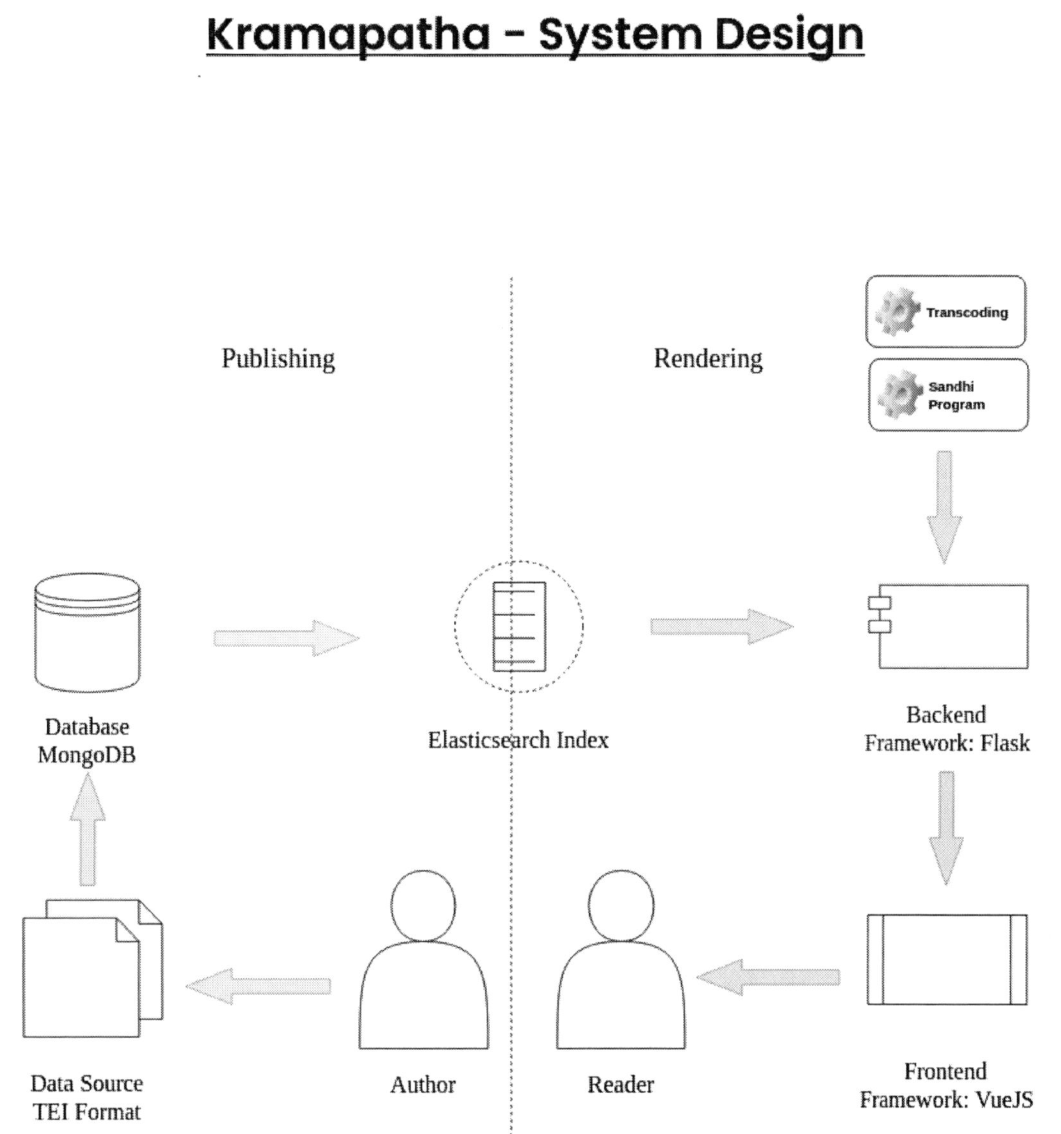

References

TEI Consortium, editor. 2007. *TEI P5*. TEI Consortium.

Peter M. Scharf. 2022. *Rāmopākhyāna—the story of Rāma in the* Mahābhārata. The Sanskrit Library, 2 edition.

Peter M. Scharf and Malcolm D. Hyman. 2011. *Linguistic issues in encoding Sanskrit*. The Sanskrit Library.

Figure 2: The *Kramapāṭha* reader showing the text, Roman transliteration, prose Sanskrit sentences, notes, and translation

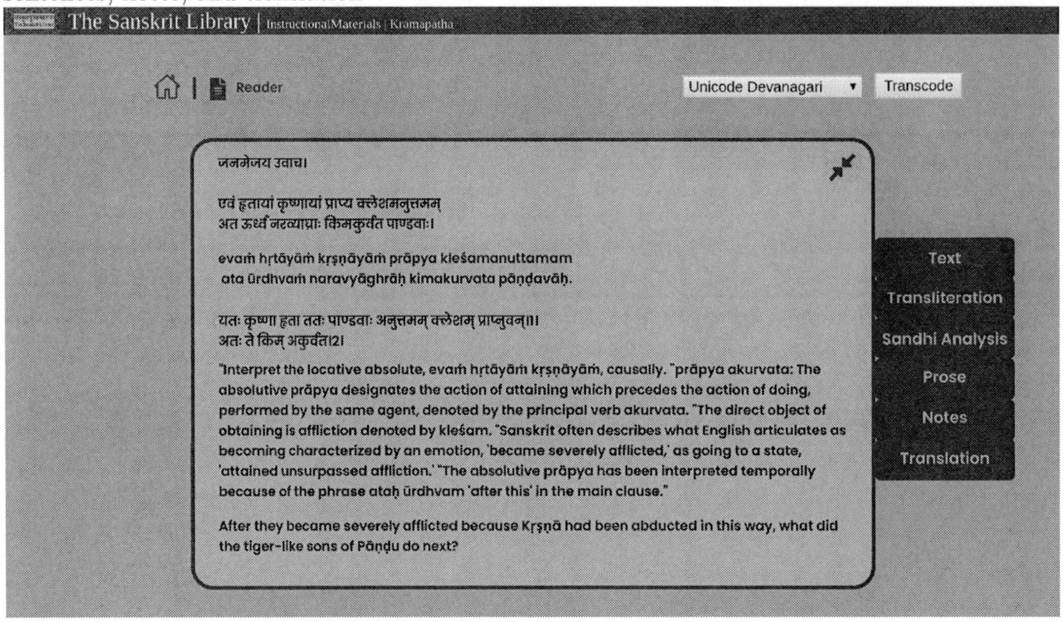

Figure 3: The *Kramapāṭha* reader showing the text, Roman transliteration, and information relating to the word *naravyāghrāḥ*

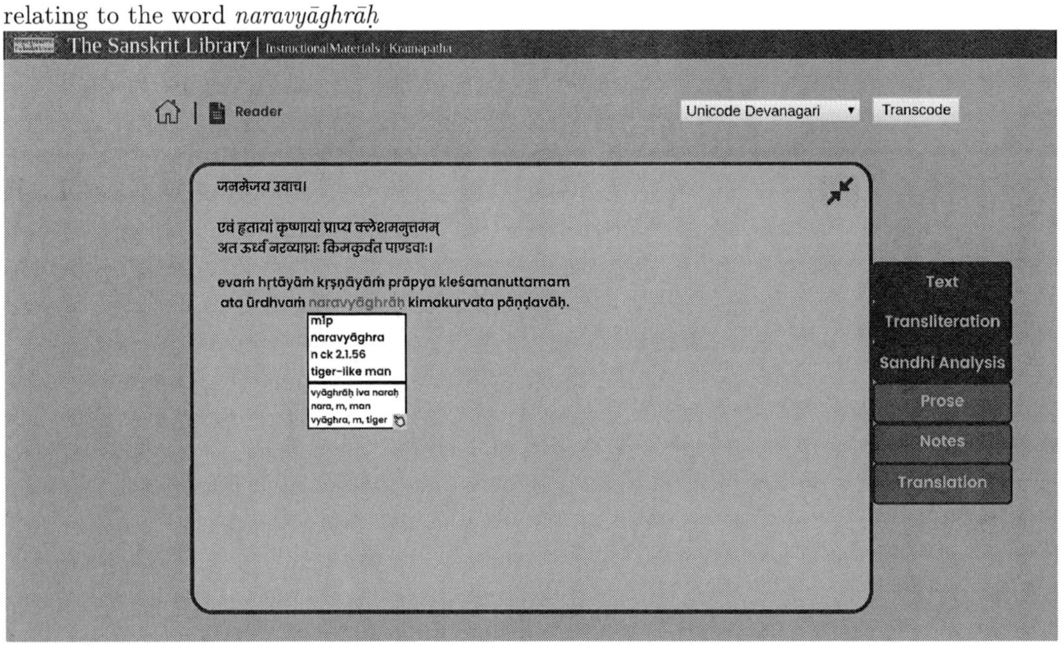

Figure 4: The *Kramapāṭha* inflected forms index

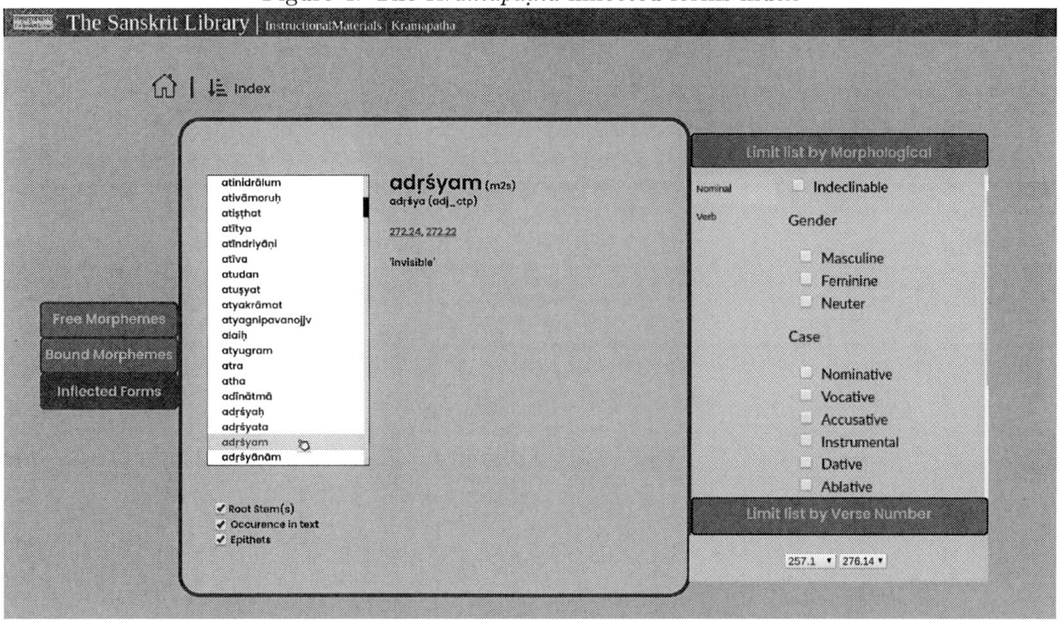

Figure 5: The *Kramapāṭha* lemma index

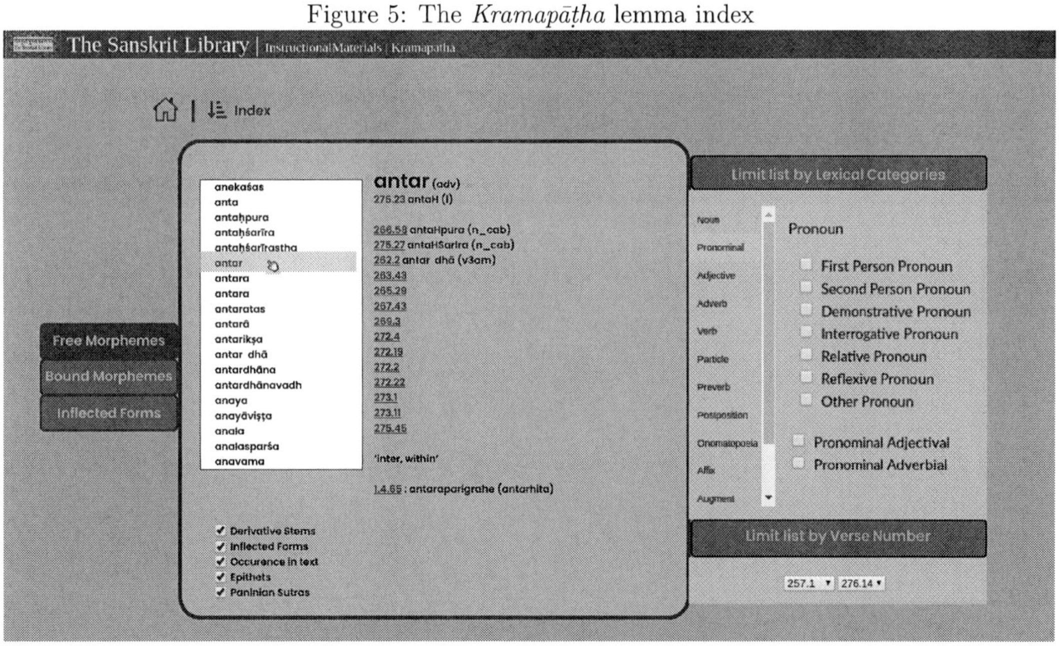

Peter M. Scharf. 2002. *Rāmopākhyāna—the story of Rāma in the* Mahābhārata. RoutledgeCurzon, 1 edition.

Peter M. Scharf. 2005. Rāmopākhyāna: the story of Rāma in the *Mahābhārata*. In T. S. Rukmani, editor, *The* Mahābhārata, pages 49–60. Munshiram Manoharlal. Paper presented at the International Conference on the *Mahābhārata*, 18–20 May 2001, Concordia University, Montreal, Quebec, Canada.

Peter M. Scharf. 2015. Providing access to manuscripts in the digital age. In Justin Thomas McDaniel and Lynn Ransom, editors, *From Mulberry leaves to silk scrolls*, number 1 in The Lawrence J. Schoenberg Studies in Manuscript Culture, pages 231–271. University of Pennsylvania Libraries.

Peter M. Scharf. 2017. Accessing manuscripts in the digital age. volume 6, pages 131–173. National Mission for Manuscripts.

Peter M. Scharf. 2018. Teitagger. In Gérard Huet and Amba Kulkarni, editors, *Computational Sanskrit and Digital Humanities, selected papers presented at the World Sanskrit Conference, University of British Columbia, Vancouver, 9–13 July 2018*, pages 169–191. DK Publishers Distributers.

Peter M. Scharf. 2019-2020. Issues in digital sanskrit philology and computational linguistics. 80:347–375.

Vishnu Sitaram Sukthankar et al., editors. 1933–1959. *The Mahābhārata*. Bhandarkar Oriental Research Institute. Vol. 4, *The Āraṇyakaparvan (part 2)*,1942.

Semantic Annotation and Querying Framework based on Semi-structured Ayurvedic Text

Hrishikesh Terdalkar — hrishirt@cse.iitk.ac.in
Arnab Bhattacharya — arnabb@cse.iitk.ac.in
Department of Computer Science and Engineering,
Indian Institute of Technology Kanpur,
India

Madhulika Dubey — drmadhulikadubey@gmail.com
Ramamurthy S — srmsvn@gmail.com
Bhavna Naneria Singh — bhavnasingh79@gmail.com
India

Abstract

Knowledge bases (KB) are an important resource in a number of natural language processing (NLP) and information retrieval (IR) tasks, such as semantic search, automated question-answering etc. They are also useful for researchers trying to gain information from a text. Unfortunately, however, the state-of-the-art in Sanskrit NLP does not yet allow automated construction of knowledge bases due to unavailability or lack of sufficient accuracy of tools and methods. Thus, in this work, we describe our efforts on manual annotation of Sanskrit text for the purpose of knowledge graph (KG) creation. We choose the chapter Dhānyavarga from Bhāvaprakāśanighaṇṭu of the Ayurvedic text Bhāvaprakāśa for annotation. The constructed knowledge graph contains 410 entities and 764 relationships. Since Bhāvaprakāśanighaṇṭu is a technical glossary text that describes various properties of different substances, we develop an elaborate ontology to capture the semantics of the entity and relationship types present in the text. To query the knowledge graph, we design 31 query templates that cover most of the common question patterns. For both manual annotation and querying, we customize the Sangrahaka framework previously developed by us. The entire system including the dataset is available from `https://sanskrit.iitk.ac.in/ayurveda/`. We hope that the knowledge graph that we have created through manual annotation and subsequent curation will help in development and testing of NLP tools in future as well as studying of the Bhāvaprakāśanighaṇṭu text.

1 Introduction

Sanskrit (संस्कृत, IAST: Saṃskṛta) is one of the most prolific languages in the entire world, and text in Sanskrit far outnumber other classical languages. Consequently, with the advancement of natural language processing with the aid of computers, there has been a surge in the field of computational linguistics for Sanskrit over the last couple of decades. This has resulted in development of various tools such as the *Samsaadhanii* by Kulkarni (2016), *The Sanskrit Heritage Platform (SHP)* by Goyal et al. (2012), *Sanskrit Sandhi and Compound Splitter (SSCS)* by Hellwig and Nehrdich (2018), *Sanskrit WordNet (SWN)* by Kulkarni et al. (2010), etc. for linguistic tasks such as word segmentation, lemmatization, morphological generation, dependency parsing, etc. Despite this, many fundamental processing tasks such as anaphora resolution and named entity recognition that are needed for higher-order tasks such as discourse processing, are either not available or have a long way to go. Combined with the fact that Sanskrit is a morphologically rich language, for tasks such as machine translation, question-answering, semantic

Proceedings of the Computational Sanskrit and Digital Humanities, 18th World Sanskrit Conference 2023, pages 155–173

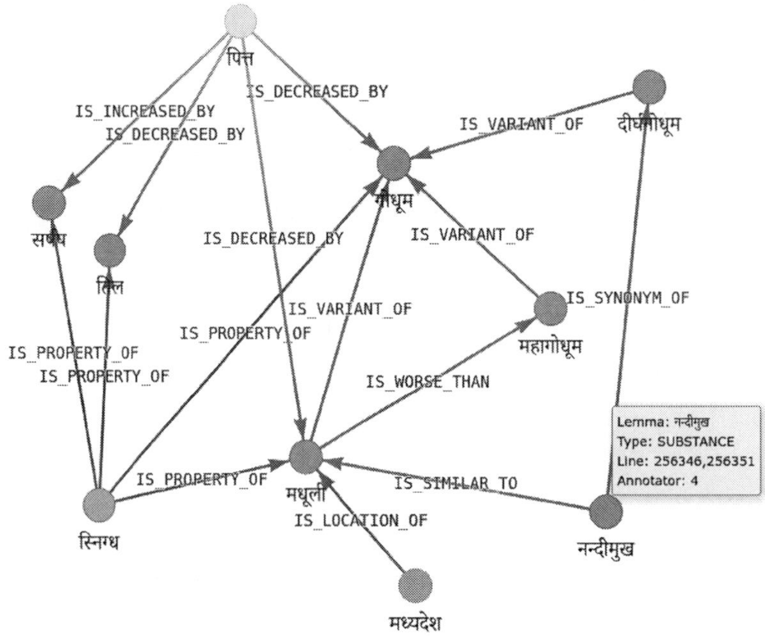

Figure 1: Example of a Knowledge Graph (KG).

labeling, discourse analysis, etc. there are no ready-to-use tools available.

A standard way of capturing knowledge from a text is through the use of *knowledge bases* (KB). It is a form of data repository that stores knowledge in some structured or semi-structured form. A *knowledge graph* (KG) is a particular form of knowledge base that uses the graph data structure to store knowledge. In a KG, nodes represent real-world *entities*, and edges represent *relationships* between these entities. Knowledge about these entities and relationships is typically stored in the form of triplets (*subject, predicate, object*) denoting the relationship predicate a subject has with an object. For example, (Pāṇini, is-author-of, Aṣṭādhyāyī) captures the knowledge nugget 'Pāṇini is the author of Aṣṭādhyāyī'.

An important usage of KGs is automated *question-answering* (QA) where the task is to automatically find answers to questions posed in a natural language. It is an important high-level task in the fields of Information Retrieval (IR) and Natural Language Processing (NLP). Questions can be either from a specific closed domain (such as, say, manuals of certain products) or from the open domain (such as what Google and many other search engines attempt to do). Also, they can be factoid-based (phrase-based or objective) or descriptive (subjective, such as why questions). Since its introduction by Voorhees (1999), one of the main approaches for the question-answering task has been through use of knowledge bases (Hirschman and Gaizauskas, 2001; Kiyota et al., 2002; Yih et al., 2015).

Figure 1 shows an example of (a snippet of) a knowledge graph. The triplets are depicted visually. It contains several nodes (entities) such as madhūlī (मधूली), nandīmukha (नन्दीमुख), pitta (पित्त), snigdha (स्निग्ध), etc. and edges (relationships) including 'is Decreased by', 'is Property of', 'is Variant of', etc. The graph also shows properties associated with the entities and the relationships.

Given a corpus of text, there are many automated ways of constructing knowledge bases from it (Dong et al., 2014; Pujara and Singh, 2018; Mitchell et al., 2018; Wu et al., 2019). These attempts are fairly successful for languages such as English where the state-of-the-art in NLP tools is more advanced. However, due to paucity of such tools in Sanskrit, automated construction of knowledge bases in Sanskrit, to the best of our understanding and knowledge, is only moderately successful. A notable effort is by Terdalkar and Bhattacharya (2019) who attempted to automatically extract all human relationships from Itihāsa texts (Rāmāyaṇa and Mahābhārata) and synonym relationships from an Ayurvedic text (Bhāvaprakāśa). They reported that for an objective natural language query, the correct answer was present in the reported set of answers 50% of the times. They, however, do not report how accurately a triplet is automatically extracted, due to the lack of ground truth for the evaluation.

A more viable and accurate alternative of constructing knowledge bases is through the route of human annotation. *Annotation* of a corpus is the process of highlighting and/or extracting objective information from it. In addition to information extracted from a corpus, the knowledge base may use information that is not directly mentioned in the corpus, such as world knowledge (for example, a person is a living being) or an ontology or a fact specific to the domain of the corpus. Human annotators are typically aware of the domain; although, depending on the task, they need not always be experts in the subject. For example, vāta (वात) has a general meaning as 'wind', but in Ayurvedic context, it refers to the tridoṣa (त्रिदोष) by the name of vāta. This is not directly mentioned in every Ayurvedic text, but any domain expert is aware of this fact.

In this work, we follow the human annotation process of creating a knowledge graph. We choose the chapter Dhānyavarga (धान्यवर्ग) from the Bhāvaprakāśanighaṇṭu (भावप्रकाशनिघण्टु) portion from the Ayurvedic text Bhāvaprakāśa (भावप्रकाश) as the corpus. Bhāvaprakāśa is one of the most prominent texts in Ayurveda, which is an important medical system developed in ancient India and is still in practice. A nighaṇṭu (nighaṇṭu) in the Indic knowledge system is a list of words, grouped into semantic and thematic categories and accompanied by relevant information about these words such as meanings, explanations or other annotations. It is analogous to a glossary in purpose, but differs in structure. In particular, the Bhāvaprakāśanighaṇṭu text, like most of Sanskrit literature, is in padya (verse) form. The text, while loosely following a theme or a structure, is still free flowing. Sanskrit literature contains a large number of such nighaṇṭu texts either as stand-alone books or as parts of other books.

The nighaṇṭu texts, owing to their partial structure are, therefore, amenable to construction of knowledge bases using human annotation. Further, since they contain a wealth of information, they are important resources for building knowledge bases that can be automatically questioned. A benefit of the presence of structure in nighaṇṭu texts is that annotators need not be domain experts as long as the structure is clear.

1.1 Contributions

The contributions of this paper are three-fold.

First, we describe a process of constructing a knowledge graph (KG) through manual annotation. This helps to capture the *semantic information* present in the text that is extremely difficult to do otherwise using automated language and text processing methods. The proposed annotation process also enables capturing relationships with entities that are not named directly in the text. We further discuss the curation process and the optimizations performed during the process of knowledge graph creation from the perspective of querying efficiency.

Second, through careful examination of the different types of entities and relationships mentioned in Bhāvaprakāśanighaṇṭu, we create a suitable ontology for annotating the text. We believe that this can be a good starting point for building an ontology for other Ayurvedic texts, and in particular, glossaries.

Third, we annotate one complete chapter from the text (Dhānyavarga), and create a KG from the annotations. For this purpose, we deploy a customized instance of *Sangrahaka*, an annotation and querying framework developed by us previously (Terdalkar and Bhattacharya, 2021). We also create 31 query templates in English and Sanskrit to feed into the templatized querying interface, that aids users in finding answers for objective questions related to the corpus.

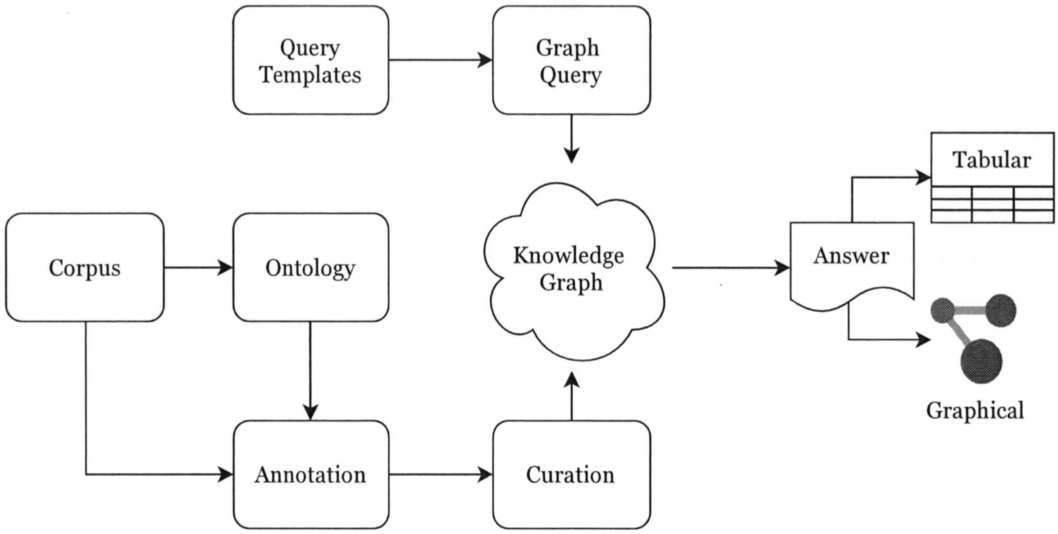

Figure 2: Workflow of semantic annotation for KG construction and querying

The system and the dataset can be accessed at `https://sanskrit.iitk.ac.in/ayurveda/`[1].

1.2 Outline

Figure 2 shows the workflow of our proposed method. The first step after inspection of the corpus is of *ontology* creation. After creating a relevant ontology, i.e., specifying what kinds of relationships and entity types are there in the corpus, annotation is performed. Using the entities and relationships captured through annotation, a knowledge graph is constructed. The knowledge graph can be queried with the help of query templates to retrieve answers for templatized natural language questions. Answers are presented in both tabular and graphical formats.

The rest of the paper is organized as follows. §2 motivates the problem of creating a knowledge graph using manual annotations. §3 describes the annotation and curation process along with the construction of knowledge graph. §4 explains the querying mechanism. We conclude in §5 and discuss future directions.

2 Motivation for Manual Annotation

To the best of our knowledge, the state-of-the-art in Sanskrit NLP and IR is not advanced enough for automatic construction of knowledge bases from text. One of the first efforts towards automatic construction of knowledge graphs from Sanskrit text was made by Terdalkar and Bhattacharya (2019). The framework described does not yield results comparable to state-of-the-art models for English due to errors in various stages of the construction pipeline. As mentioned earlier, the success rate for even single relationships was not very high.

In this section, we discuss the issues with the Sanskrit state-of-the-art linguistic tools and the need for manual annotation for a *semantic* task such as automatic creation of knowledge graphs.

2.1 Word Segmentation

Sanskrit texts make heavy use of compound words in the form of sandhi and samāsa. *Word segmentation*, that splits a given compound word into its constituents is, therefore, an important need in Sanskrit. Notable works in this area are *The Sanskrit Heritage Platform* (SHP) (Huet, 2009; Goyal et al., 2012), *Sanskrit Sandhi and Compound Splitter* (SSCS) (Hellwig and Nehrdich, 2018; Krishna et al., 2016; Krishna et al., 2021).

[1]Please create an account and contact authors requesting access to annotation or querying interface.

Treating the segmentation task as splitting both sandhi and samāsa together, while useful, does not fit well in the pipeline described by Terdalkar and Bhattacharya (2019), where the split output is then passed to a morphological analyzer. An example is splitting of the word maharṣi as mahat + ṛṣiḥ, which while correct as a samāsa-split, if passed to a morphological analyzer as two separate words, produces an analysis[2] of the word mahat independently that does not fit the semantics of the word or the context. Terdalkar and Bhattacharya (2019) applied *SSCS* followed by *SHP*. This results in a word such as rāmalakṣmaṇau getting split into two words rāma and lakṣmaṇau due to *SSCS* resulting in the word rāma getting assigned the vocative case by *SHP*. They used a heuristic to resolve these errors, where the grammatical analysis of the second word was copied to the first word as well. However, this heuristic would change the semantics of the word rāmalakṣmaṇau.

2.2 Morphological Analysis

Sanskrit is a highly inflectional language. In Sanskrit, words are categorized as subanta (noun-like) and tiṅanta (verb-like). *Morphological analysis* is the task of identifying the *stem* (prātipadika or dhātu) of the given word form, along with other relevant linguistic information. Notable works in this area are by Goyal et al. (2012) and Kulkarni (2016). These tools perform the best when the input given is without sandhi. If, however, the input also contains splits of samāsa as generated by tools described in the previous section (§2.1), the morphological analyzers treat it as a separate word, resulting in an analysis of the word that may be correct on the syntactic level, but not so in the context of the sentence.

2.3 Other Linguistic Tasks

A dependency parser for Sanskrit from *Samsaadhanii* (Kulkarni, 2016) expects the sentences to be in an anvaya order (prose form). Further, it is based on a fixed vocabulary and, therefore, when inflected forms of words from outside the vocabulary are encountered, it fails to parse the sentence. For example, a word śālidhānya is not present in the vocabulary, so a sentence containing that word does not get parsed successfully.

Krishna et al. (2021) in their recent work claim to be able to perform poetry-to-prose linearization and dependency parsing. However, we have not been able to obtain the source code or a functional interface to evaluate it for our data (we contacted the authors).

Another hurdle in the poetry-to-prose linearization is that the sentence boundaries are often not clearly marked. In general, a semantically complete sentence may span over multiple verses. On the other hand, at times a verse may contain multiple sentences as well. This can be seen in the sample of 10 verses given in Appendix A. Thus, extracting sentences with proper sentence boundaries is also a difficult task.

2.4 Semantic Information Extraction

Extracting the semantics of a sentence is a very important step in the construction of a knowledge graph. Automatic KG construction frameworks for English such as (Auer et al., 2007; Suchanek et al., 2007) extract semantic information from various information sources including Wikipedia articles and info-boxes. One of the challenges faced in this task is that the same concept can be expressed in English in numerous ways, such as "birthplace" or "place of birth". The issue of expressing a concept in more than one ways is extremely significant and much more severe for Sanskrit due to its semantic richness. In particular, the processes of samāsa and sandhi create long and semantically rich words.

Table 1 highlights this phenomenon. The first column contains the concept while the second column enlists the words used in Dhānyavarga to express that concept. A "concept" captures the semantics of a word or a phrase.

It can be noted that even in the span of 90 verses, there are more than 10 different ways used to express the same concept '(a substance) decreases vāta'. In addition to that, the word vāta

[2] Analysis: mahat `(n. sg. acc. | n. sg. nom.)`

Concept	Words or Phrases
increases bala	balya, balada, balāvaha, balaprada, balakara, balakṛt
increase vāta	vātala, vātakṛt, vātakara, vātajanaka, vātajananī, vātātikopana, vātaprakopaṇa, vātavardhana, vātakopana
decreases pitta	pittaghna, pittapraṇāśana, pittapraśamana, pittahara, pittaghnī, pittajit, pittāpaha, pittajit, pittahṛt, pittanut, pittavināśinī
decreases vāta and pitta	vātapittaghna, pittavātaghna, pittavātavibandhakṛt, vātapitta-hara, vātapittahṛt

Table 1: Semantic variations due to richness of Sanskrit through examples from Dhānyavarga.

itself can be part of another compound, coupled with other words as can be seen in the example 'decreases vāta and pitta'. There are more than 5 usages of this complex concept, which is a superset of the earlier concept. Moreover, these are not the only ways in which the concept of increasing vāta is expressed.

There are numerous other words that can combine with the word vāta in the form of samāsa to indicate the concept of decrement for multiple entities at the same time. Moreover, in such cases, where a samāsa is used, the order of vāta and pitta could be reversed as well. Further, this list for a particular concept is not exhaustive for Sanskrit, and there are practically endless possible ways to denote the same concept.

One can observe that there are some common suffixes used in similar concepts. However, firstly, there is no exhaustive list of suffixes available associated with a particular concept. Second, the suffixes have different concepts in different contexts. For example, the suffix -ghna (-घ्न) in the context of Ayurveda, or specifically of tridoṣa, means 'to decrease', e.g., pittaghna (pittaghna). The same suffix in the context of a person may mean 'to kill', e.g., śatrughna (शत्रुघ्न) – one who kills his enemies (śatru).

Thus, using a fixed set of suffixes may not be a feasible solution.

To the best of our knowledge, there is no existing system for Sanskrit that can extract such semantic information in either a generic sense or in a specific context. Amarakoṣa Knowledge Net (Nair and Kulkarni, 2010) and Sanskrit WordNet (Kulkarni et al., 2010) are also limited in their scope. For example, none of the words listed in the Table 1 to express the concept of 'increasing bala' can be found in either of these two resources.

2.5 Need for Annotation

Issue of compounding errors is relevant to any NLP pipeline, where individual parts of the pipeline have their own error rates. The success rate of the entire pipeline, being a multiplicative factor of the individual success rates (since all the parts have to be accurate for the entire task to be accurate), is significantly lower. Thus, the pipeline for the automated question-answering task that requires modules such as word segmentation, morphological analysis, part-of-speech tagging, dependency parsing, etc. has a very low accuracy. Further, the lack of semantic analysis tools or systems is a major hurdle in semantic tasks such as construction of knowledge graphs. Thus, even if the accuracy of the individual parts are improved significantly, the final semantic labeling remains a bottleneck.

We highlight this fact by taking an example of the first $\sim 10\%$ of the Dhānyavarga, i.e., 10 verses corresponding to 21 lines. We have manually segmented the words in these lines and also converted the sentences to anvaya order. The first 10 verses correspond to a total of 14 prose sentences. The original text in verse format, in the sandhi-split format, and in anvaya format, is given in Appendix A.

There are a total of 35 occurrences of sandhi and 50 occurrences of samāsa in the text. *SSCS* is able to identify 34 of the sandhi (with an accuracy of 0.97) and 34 occurrences of samāsa correctly (with an accuracy of 0.68). However, the tool does not differentiate a sandhi from a samāsa. Therefore, when passed to the *SHP* it is likely to obtain incorrect analysis.

A single word-form in Sanskrit can have numerous valid morphological analyses. If there are N words in a sentence, and every word has a_i analyses possible, then there are $\Pi_{i=1}^{N} a_i$ possible combinations for the correct analysis of the sentence. *SHP* and *Samsaadhanii* both rank these solutions based on various linguistic features, and after pruning the unlikely ones, present the feasible solutions. For automatic processing pipelines, a particular choice of the solution is required, and the solution presented as the *best* by the tools, i.e., the first solution, is a natural choice. Thus, we present the evaluation by choosing the first solution.

We pass the manually created sandhi-split corpus through *SHP* for morphological analysis.[3] There are an average of 9 solutions per line (ranging from 0 to 72) reported. We evaluate based on the first reported solution.

There are 103 words, after manually splitting sandhi. *SHP* could not analyze 21 words, and wrongly analyzed 14 words, resulting in an overall accuracy of 0.66. Further, *SHP* split 34 words, of which 8 were incorrect splits, resulting in an accuracy of 0.76 for samāsa-split.

Additionally, we pass the anvaya-order sentences to the dependency parser tool by Kulkarni (2016). We also manually add missing verbs (adhyāhāra forms such as asti, santi, etc.) due to that being a requirement of the parser. Without samāsa split markers, the dependency parser manages to parse only 1 out of 14 sentences, while with the samāsa markers, it can parse 6 out of 14. Out of the 6 sentences that produce a dependency parse tree, 4 are simple 3-word sentences (sentences 2, 3, 4, 6 in Appendix A). In the other 2 instances (sentences 7, 10), errors were found in the dependency parse trees.

For example, consider a line from śloka 2:

Sanskrit: ⟨ कङ्गादिकं क्षुद्रधान्यं ⟩ ⟨ तृणधान्यञ्च तत्स्मृतम् ⟩
IAST: ⟨ kaṅgvādikaṃ kṣudradhānyaṃ ⟩ ⟨ tṛṇadhānyañca tatsmṛtam ⟩
Meaning: kaṅgu etc. are types of kṣudradhānya. It (kṣudradhānya) is also called tṛṇadhānya.
Anvaya: क्षुद्रधान्यम् कङ्गादिकम् (अस्ति)। तत् तृणधान्यम् च स्मृतम् (अस्ति)।

There are two sentences in this line, as can be seen by the boundary markers and anvaya text. Figure 3 shows the dependency parse for these two sentences. The dependency parse for the first dependency tree is correct. However, even for the sentences that get a correct dependency parse, the dependency relations we get are kartā and kartṛsamānādhikaraṇa which, while grammatically correct, still do not help in capturing the *semantic* concept of the sentence that kaṅgu is a *type* of kṣudradhānya. Also, tat in the second sentence is an *anaphora* of kṣudradhānya from the first sentence. Thus, the intended relation that tṛṇadhānya is a synonym of kṣudradhānya cannot be extracted without a module for *anaphora resolution*. Yet again, to the best of our knowledge, there is no such co-reference resolution system for Sanskrit.

More importantly, no existing tool has a capability of performing *semantic* tasks, which are a requirement for knowledge extraction. Manual annotation, therefore, is the only way to capture the semantic relations. In addition, it bypasses the entire NLP pipeline and, thus, has a high potential for creating a question-answering system that is much more accurate and reliable than a system based on automatically created knowledge graphs.

Another prevalent issue is the lack of datasets for training and evaluation of tasks such as question-answering or creation of knowledge bases. Creation of knowledge bases through manual annotation is, thus, of utmost importance both for the actual task of question-answering and for further research in the field, including automated knowledge base construction since these may act as ground-truth benchmark datasets for evaluation of future automated tools.

[3]We keep a timeout of 60 seconds, within which if the analysis is not found, we report the analysis as missing, i.e., 0 solutions for that line.

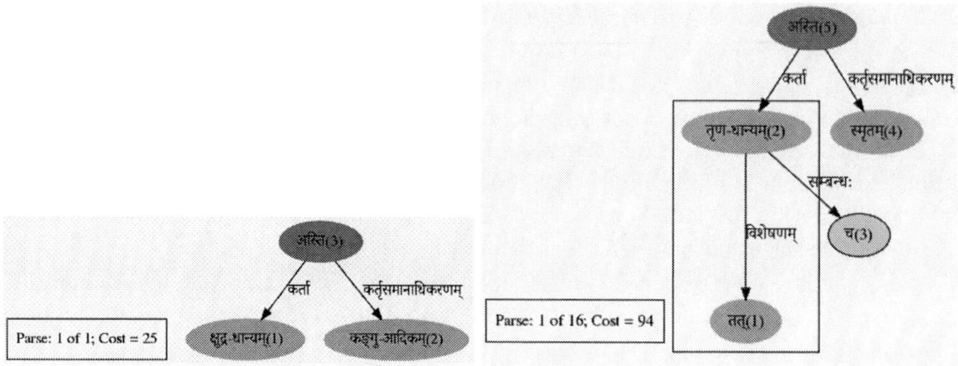

Figure 3: Dependency parse trees for sentences from śloka 2.

Bhavaprakasha Nighantu - धान्यवर्गः

Search

	LINE	TEXT	SPLIT	?
⊙	256381	मसूरो मधुरः पाके संग्राही शीतलो लघुः	मसूरः मधुरः पाके संग्राही शीतलः लघुः	✓

WORD	मसूरः	मधुरः	पाके	सङ्ग्राही	शीतलः	लघुः
ROOT	मसूर	मधुर	पाक	सङ्ग्राहिन्	शीतल	लघु
GENDER	m.	m.	m.	m.	m.	m.
CASE	1	1	7	1	1	1
NUMBER	sg.	sg.	sg.	sg.	sg.	sg.

Figure 4: Sample text from Dhānyavarga with linguistic information

3 Annotation Process

Annotation has been done with the purpose of building a knowledge graph (KG). We fix the unit for annotation to be a line from a verse (śloka). We collect annotations of two types — *entity* and *relation* — described in detail in §3.3 and §3.4 respectively.

The corpus interface from *Sangrahaka* is capable of displaying extra information about each line. We use this feature to display word segmentation and morphological analysis of the text produced by *SSCS* and *SHP*, which can potentially help the annotators. Figure 4 shows a sample text from Dhānyavarga with linguistic information.

An annotator goes through the lines assigned to her and for each line, identifies the entities as well as the relationships between the entities appearing in it.

3.1 Corpus

Bhāvaprakāśanighaṇṭu is the nighaṇṭu portion of Bhāvaprakāśa. It contains a list and description of various medicinally relevant plants, flowers, fruits, animals, grains, animal products, metals, prepared substances, etc. These are divided into 23 chapters called vargas.

A general structure followed in the Bhāvaprakāśanighaṇṭu is as follows,

Entities (25)	Substance, Part of a Substance, Compound Substance, Prepared Substance, Collection of Substances, Tridoṣa, Property, Effect, Disease, Symptom, Product/Waste of Human Body, Part of Human Body, Person, Animal, Plant, Source, Animal Source, Plant Source, Quantity, Method or Preparation, Usage, Location, Time, Season, Others
Relationships (29)	is Synonym of, is Type of, is Variant of, is Property of, is (Not) Property of, is Similar to, is Better/Larger/Greater than, is Worse/Smaller/Lesser than, is Newer than, is Older than, is Best/Largest/Greatest among, is Medium among, is Worst/Smallest/Least among, is Ingredient of, is Part of, is (Not) Part of, is Disease of, is Caused by, is (Not) Caused by, is Benefited by, is Harmed by, is Produced by, is Removed/Cured by, is Increased by, is Decreased/Reduced by, is Preparation of, is (Absence/Lack of) Preparation of, is Location of, is Time of

Table 2: Entity and relationship types in our ontology

- Substances are semantically grouped in chapters. For example, all grains appear in the chapter Dhānyavarga.
- Each chapter contains several virtual sections pertaining to a single substance. Only when a substance has been described in entirety, discussion about another substance starts.[4]
- Each section about a substance has the following information:
  - Synonyms, if any, of the substance
  - Properties, e.g., color, smell, texture
  - Effects, e.g., effect on tridoṣa (vāta, pitta, and kapha)
  - Symptoms and diseases treated or cured by the substance
  - Variants, if any, of the substance
  - Properties of each variant, and their distinguishing characteristics
  - Comparison between the variants, if possible
  - Time and location where the substance is found or grown, if relevant
- The order of information components about a substance within a section may vary.

The entire Bhāvaprakāśanighaṇṭu contains 2087 verses, corresponding to 4201 lines. We have chosen Dhānyavarga, a chapter about grains, which has a wide variety of entity types and relations. It contains 90 verses, corresponding to 183 lines.

3.2 Ontology

We have created an ontology consisting of 25 entity types and 29 relationship types by carefully going through multiple chapters from the Bhāvaprakāśanighaṇṭu including Dhānyavarga. An exhaustive list of them is mentioned in Table 2.

The decision to add a certain entity type or relation type is made based on the importance of the concept, frequency of its occurrence, and nature of frequently asked questions.

For example, the concept of vāta, pitta and kapha, collectively referred to as tridoṣa or fundamental elements (humors) of the body, is central to Ayurveda. Consequently, queries

[4]There is, however, no indication in the original text that a section/substance has ended and a new one has started. It must be inferred by reading the text.

such as "What effect does a substance X have on a (one of the) tridoṣa?" is one of the most fundamental and common information requirement about the substance. Therefore, we have decided to create a category "Tridoṣa" only for these three entities. Therefore, any occurrence of these words or their synonyms, e.g., śleṣma, a synonym of a kapha, results in the creation of an entity of type Tridoṣa.

Similarly, the type of effect any substance has on each of the tridoṣa is either an increment or decrement. Therefore, we have identified relations is Increased by and is Decreased by.

After the ontology has been finalized, the next step is annotation.

3.3 Entity Annotation

Entities correspond to nodes in the knowledge graph. When a word that represents an entity is encountered, its *lemma* (prātipadika) and the entity type it belongs to are identified, and the entity is marked.

As an example, consider the following line from śloka-31 of Dhānyavarga:

> Devanagari: गोधूमः सुमनोऽपि स्यात्त्रिविधः स च कीर्त्तितः।
> IAST: godhūmaḥ sumano'pi syāttrividhaḥ sa ca kīrttitaḥ.
> Meaning: Godhūma (wheat) is also called Sumana, and it is said to be of three kinds.

Here, there are two entities, godhūma and sumana, both of type "Substance". An entity needs to be added explicitly only the first time it is encountered.

In a case where a samāsa is used to indicate an effect on an entity, and the relation fits one of the relationship types, a relevant word (pada) from the segmentation (vigraha) of samāsa is used. For example, consider the following line from śloka-33:

> Devanagari: गोधूमः मधुरः शीतो वातपित्तहरो गुरुः।
> IAST: godhūmaḥ madhuraḥ śīto vātapittaharo guruḥ.
> Meaning: Godhūma is sweet, cold, hard to digest and removes (decreases) vāta and pitta.

Here, vātapittaharaḥ is a single word, which uses samāsa, to indicate that vāta and pitta are reduced by godhūma. Therefore, vātapittahara will not be added as an entity; instead the entities vāta and pitta are recognized.

3.4 Relation Annotation

Relations correspond to edges in the knowledge graph. A relation, which fits one of the relationship types from the ontology, is identified by interpreting the śloka. *Subject* and *Object* for this relation are then identified. Relations, where extra semantic information is known, such as madhura is known to be a rasa, are endowed with that extra information.

Consider the two examples of lines mentioned in the previous section (§3.3), śloka-31 and śloka-33. Following relations are added based on these two lines:

sumana $\vdash$ is Synonym of $\rightarrow$ godhūma
madhura $\vdash$ is (rasa) Property of $\rightarrow$ godhūma
śīta $\vdash$ is Property of $\rightarrow$ godhūma
vāta $\vdash$ is Decreased by $\rightarrow$ godhūma
pitta $\vdash$ is Decreased by $\rightarrow$ godhūma
guru $\vdash$ is Property of $\rightarrow$ godhūma

It should be noted that neither the subject nor the object may be present as words in the line that mentions a relationship about it. Consider, for example, the next line of the śloka-33:

> Devanagari: कफशुक्रप्रदो बल्यः स्निग्धः सन्धानकृत्सरः।
> IAST: kaphaśukraprado balyaḥ snigdhaḥ sandhānakṛtsaraḥ.
> Meaning: (Godhūma) increases kapha, śukra, bala, is snigdha, sandhānakṛt (helps in joining broken bones) and laxative.

Here, the description of properties of godhūma (from previous line) is continued. Therefore, one of the relations added is

kapha ⊢ is Increased by → godhūma

This relation has godhūma as *Object*, although it is not present in the line itself.

3.5 Unnamed Entities

On occasions, it may happen that an entity is referenced by its properties only, and it is not named at all in the text. Consider the following line from śloka-39:

Devanagari: मुद्गो बहुविधः श्यामो हरितः पीतकस्तथा।
IAST: mudgo bahuvidhaḥ śyāmo haritaḥ pītakastathā.
Meaning: Mudga is of various types – black, green, and yellow.

Thus, there are three colored variants of the substance mudga, but they are not named. In such a case, we create three *unnamed entities* (denoted by `X`-prefixed nodes) with entity type "Substance", same as that of mudga to refer to the three varieties. Each of these entities is given a unique identifier. The unique identifier is a combination of the unnamed entity number and the line number it occurs in. Thus, if the line number is 256358, the black variant is given the identifier `X1-256358`. Similarly, the green variant is identified as `X2-256358` while the yellow variant is identified as `X3-256358`.

To describe these variants, three relations are added as well:

śyāma ⊢ is (varṇa) Property of → `X1-256358`
harita ⊢ is (varṇa) Property of → `X2-256358`
pīta ⊢ is (varṇa) Property of → `X3-256358`

The utility of such annotations becomes clear when these unnamed entities are later referred to in another line or another verse.

The next line of śloka-39 reads

Devanagari: श्वेतो रक्तश्च तेषान्तु पूर्वः पूर्वो लघुः स्मृतः ॥३९॥
IAST: śveto raktaśca teṣāntu pūrvaḥ pūrvo laghuḥ smṛtaḥ. ||39||
Meaning: ... white and red. Among them, each is successively easier to digest.

The word teṣām here refers to the five varieties of mudga, and gives a relation between them. So, we get two new unnamed entities in this line, `X1-256359` and `X2-256359` (note how `X1` and `X2` are re-used but with different line numbers).

We also get a total of four new relations to capture the successive ease in digestion properties:

`X1-256358` ⊢ is Better (in property laghu) than → `X2-256358`
`X2-256358` ⊢ is Better (in property laghu) than → `X3-256358`
`X3-256358` ⊢ is Better (in property laghu) than → `X1-256359`
`X1-256359` ⊢ is Better (in property laghu) than → `X2-256359`

For the purpose of querying, the anonymous nodes are treated like any other node.

3.6 Auto-complete Suggestions

We have enhanced the annotation interface from *Sangrahaka* to improve user experience with Sanskrit text by adding transliteration-based suggestions. There are numerous standard schemes for *Devanagari* transliteration[5]. Whenever, a *Devanagari* entity is annotated, we transliterate it using `indic-transliteration` package (Sanskrit programmers, 2021) into all the available schemes. We maintain an index with all the transliterations. Now, when a user enters any text, we query our index and return all suggestions that match with the lower-cased version of the user text. For example, consider a word in Devanagari 'माष', which transliterates into 'mASa' (HK), 'mASha' (ITRANS), 'māṣa' (IAST), 'maa.sa' (Velthuis), 'mARa' (WX) and 'mAza' (SLP1). Now, a user may enter at least 3 starting characters from any of the scheme, e.g., 'mas', 'maa',

[5]`https://en.wikipedia.org/wiki/Devanagari_transliteration`

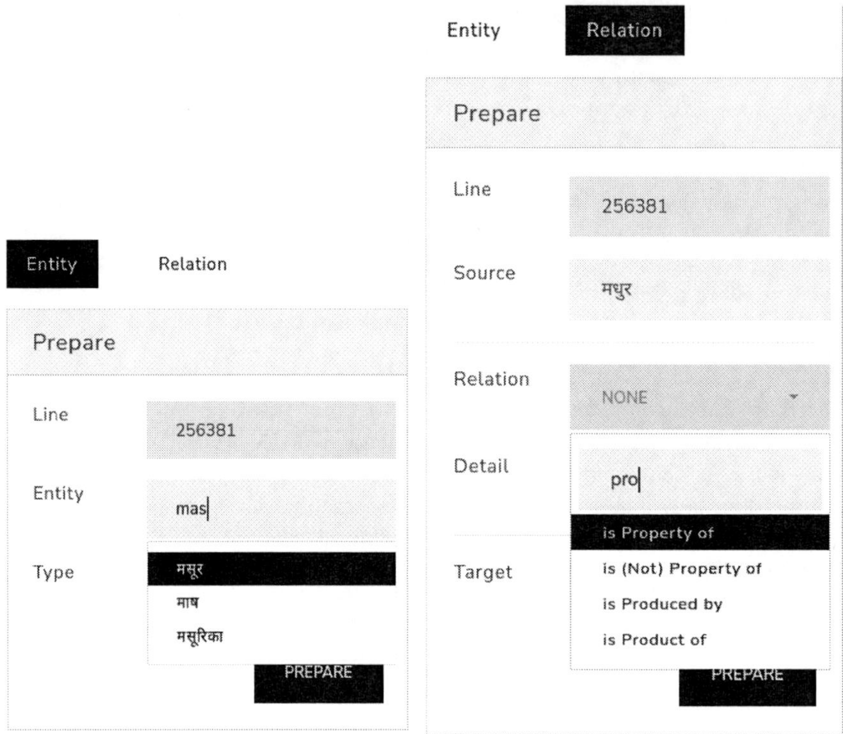

Figure 5: Modified annotation interface with multi-transliteration-based suggestions

'maz', 'mar' etc. and the Devanagari word 'माष' will be suggested. The index is maintained globally. So, once an entity is entered by any annotator, the completions for that entity become available to all annotators.

These suggestions are enabled to all text input fields, namely, entity annotation, relationship annotations and querying interface.

Figure 5 shows the modified annotation interface with auto-complete suggestions.

3.7 Curation

After the annotation step, before construction of the knowledge graph, a thorough curation step is required to resolve errors or inconsistencies that may inadvertently creep up during the annotation process.

3.7.1 Equivalent Entities

The linguistic information that we have added with the corpus is supposed to serve as a guideline for the annotation. However, since this information is generated using automated tools, there might be errors. For example, the word grāhī (ग्राही) refers to substances that have a property of absorbing liquid and increasing digestive power. The reported prātipadika of this word, automatically generated by *SHP*, is grāha (ग्राह) instead of grāhin. An annotator, by oversight, may mark the incorrect lemma. Additionally, for substance names in feminine gender, which also have this property, an adjective grāhiṇī (ग्राहिणी) is used. The correct prātipadika in this case would be grāhiṇī. The node refers to the same property. So, semantically they are equivalent to each other, and ideally should be captured using a single name. These instances are common for properties of substances.

To address this issue, we add a relation is Synonym of between these entities. This, in conjunction with the optimization mechanism described in §3.8, tackles the issue of equivalent entities.

3.7.2 Inconsistent Node Categories

There may be differences of opinions between annotators regarding which category a particular node should belong to. For example, an entity jvara (ज्वर) refers to fever. This entity was marked as a *Symptom* by some annotators and as a *Disease* by the others. Such cases were resolved through discussion among the curators.

3.7.3 Missing Node Categories

The framework allows entities to be mentioned in the relationships without being added as entities. While care was taken to always add entities before marking relationships involving those entities, there may still be instances of human error, where an annotator may forget to mark an entity. We created a set of inference rules to infer as many instances of such occurrences as possible. For example, if an entity is marked as a *source* of the relation is Property of, without having been added as an entity, we can automatically create that entity by assigning the category '*Property*' to it.

3.8 Symmetric Relationships

The relation is Synonym of is symmetric, i.e., if `A` is a synonym of `B`, then, by definition, `B` is also a synonym of `A`. A query can be made using any of the synonyms, and the system should still be able to return the correct answer.

Suppose, $S_1, S_2 \ldots, S_N$ are N synonyms of a substance. If the synonym group is completely captured, then a user should be able to query using any synonym and still get the desired result. Properties of the substance corresponding to this synonym group can also be scattered across S_i's. Say, there are M properties $P_1, P_2, \ldots, P_M$, and some of the relations are P_1 is Property of S_1, P_2 is Property of S_4, P_3 is Property of S_3, and so on. Now, if we want to query whether substance S_2 has property P_1 but we search using the name of the substance as S_2, a direct query will not work, as there is no direct relation between the nodes S_2 and P_1. For the correct answer, we would have to find every synonym of S_2 and check if any of them has the property P_1. This requires a *path query*. A path query involving N synonyms may require as many as $N-1$ edge traversals. Path queries are NP-hard (Mendelzon and Wood, 1995) and are, therefore, computationally expensive.

For example, rājikā, kṣava, kṣutābhijanaka, kṛṣṇīkā, kṛṣṇasarṣapa, rājī, kṣujjanikā, āsurī, tīkṣṇagandhā, cīnāka are all names of the same substance. A relation is added as follows,

uṣṇa $\vdash$ is Property of $\rightarrow$ rājikā

Now, suppose that we want to query for a property of the substance kṣava, which while referring to the same entity as rājikā, does not have a property edge incident upon it.

We, therefore, are forced to use a path query, and the query has to explore all the synonym paths from kṣava to find out if kṣava itself or one of its synonyms has any property edge. The number of such paths can be impractically large, especially for large knowledge graphs.

We perform a simple optimization heuristic to tackle this issue. We first identify a synonym S_K among all the synonyms having the highest degree, i.e., $K \in \{1, .., N\}$, such that $K = \underset{i}{\text{argmax}}\ degree(S_i)$. We treat this as the *canonical name* for that synonym group, and we add a relation is Synonym of from every $S_i, i \neq K$ to S_K. Further, we transfer all the edges (other than the `is Synonym of` edge) from every $S_i, i \neq K$ to S_K. In other words, if S_i was connected to a node V by a relation R, after optimization, S_K will be connected to node V by relation R. Now, every synonym has a direct edge to the canonical name, with all the properties getting attached to the canonical name only. Thus, a query on any synonym has to traverse *at most 1 edge* before reaching the desired node.

At the end of curation and optimization steps, there were 410 nodes and 764 relationships that constitute our knowledge graph.

4 Querying

Although the ideal way of question-answering is by posing queries in natural language, unfortunately, the state-of-the-art in Sanskrit NLP tools does not allow that. Hence, to simulate natural language queries, we use query templates.

The annotation and querying platform that we use, *Sangrahaka*, uses *Neo4j* graph database[6] for the purpose of storing and querying the knowledge graph. *Cypher*[7] is *Neo4j*'s graph query language inspired by SQL, but optimized for graph querying and it makes use of intuitive ASCII-art syntax for querying. The platform utilizes the power of *Cypher* for connecting to the graph database. Natural language queries are simulated using query templates.

4.1 Query Templates

A query template consists of a set of natural language templates and an equivalent graph query template. Each of these templates contain *placeholders*. Values of these placeholders can be filled by choosing the required entity, entity type or relation, to convert the query template into a valid natural language query. The same replacement in the graph query template yields a valid graph query which can be directly used to fetch results from the graph database.

For example, consider a sample query template:

- Sanskrit: के पदार्थाः `{0}` इति दोषस्य वर्धनं कुर्वन्ति।
- English: `Which entities increase the dosha` {0}?
- Cypher:

```
MATCH (dosha:TRIDOSHA)-[relation:IS_INCREASED_BY]->(entity)
WHERE dosha.lemma =  "{0}"
RETURN entity
```

The variable `{0}` here is a word representing an entity of type `TRIDOSHA`. The valid values for the variable in this query are vāta or pitta or kapha or one of their synonyms. So, natural language questions such as "Which substances increase kapha?", etc. can be realized using this query template.

In order to increase the number of the questions that can be answered, we have created a set of *generic* queries which help model *any* query up to a single relation. It contains the following three query templates:

- Which entity is related to entity `{0}` by relation `{1}`?
- How is entity `{0}` related to entity `{1}`?
- Show all matches where an entity of type `{0}` has relation `{1}` with an entity of type `{2}`.

We have a total of 31 *natural language query templates* in Sanskrit[8] to represent the most relevant queries. We have classified these templates semantically into 12 categories. Classification helps to locate an intended query template faster. An exhaustive list of these query templates and their categories is in Appendix B.

4.2 Query Answers

Result of graph queries are also graphs. The querying interface from *Sangrahaka* consisted of a graphical and a tabular display. Figure 6 shows a sample output using the query interface. In the graph, hovering a node lets the user see the properties associated with the node by hovering over

[6] `https://neo4j.com/`

[7] `https://neo4j.com/developer/cypher/`

[8] We also have their English translated versions in the system.

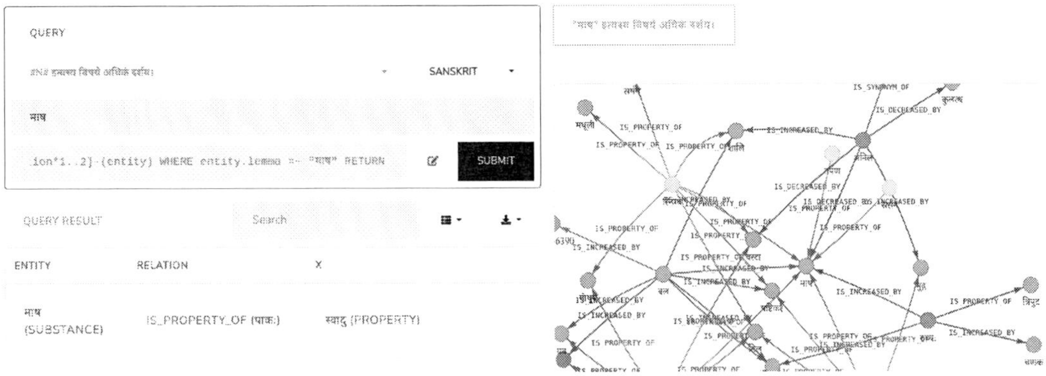

Figure 6: Sample output using query interface featuring Sanskrit query templates

the node in the graph. Each node label is a *lemma* (word-stem) associated with that node. In addition, provenance of the node such as which line from the corpus does that node correspond to, and the identifier of the annotator(s) who added that entity are also mentioned. The nodes are color-coded in such a way that nodes referring to entities of same type get the same color[9].

5 Conclusions and Future Work

Current state of Sanskrit NLP makes manual annotation a necessity for semantic tasks. We propose a construction of a knowledge graph (KG) through manual annotation process with a special focus on capturing semantic information. We also introduce a mechanism to handle unnamed entities in a knowledge graph.

The deployed instance of the framework used for the purpose of annotation and querying can be accessed at `https://sanskrit.iitk.ac.in/ayurveda/`.

As a proof-of-concept, we have selected a chapter from the nighaṇṭu text Bhāvaprakāśanighaṇṭu, carefully created an ontology, and performed semantic annotation to construct a knowledge graph. Our methodology is extensible to other nighaṇṭu texts.

In future, we plan to complete the annotation of the rest of the Bhāvaprakāśanighaṇṭu. We also plan to explore more classical texts such as Rāmāyaṇa and Mahābhārata for annotating other kinds of relationships.

We also hope that the dataset created in the process will prove useful for further research efforts in the area of NLP in Sanskrit. We make the ontology and the dataset available at `https://sanskrit.iitk.ac.in/ayurveda/dataset/`.

Acknowledgements

We thank Anil Kumar Gourishetty from IIT Roorkee for his help in connecting us with Sanskrit volunteers.

[9]Colors are not fixed. Thus, the color *yellow* is not indicative of a specific entity type. It only ensures that for a particular query answer, all yellow nodes will have the same entity type.

References

Sören Auer, Christian Bizer, Georgi Kobilarov, Jens Lehmann, Richard Cyganiak, and Zachary Ives. 2007. DBpedia: A nucleus for a web of open data. In *The Semantic Web*, pages 722–735.

Xin Dong, Evgeniy Gabrilovich, Geremy Heitz, Wilko Horn, Ni Lao, Kevin Murphy, Thomas Strohmann, Shaohua Sun, and Wei Zhang. 2014. Knowledge vault: A web-scale approach to probabilistic knowledge fusion. In *KDD*, pages 601–610.

Pawan Goyal, Gérard Huet, Amba Kulkarni, Peter Scharf, and Ralph Bunker. 2012. A distributed platform for Sanskrit processing. In *COLING*, pages 1011–1028.

Oliver Hellwig and Sebastian Nehrdich. 2018. Sanskrit word segmentation using character-level recurrent and convolutional neural networks. In *EMNLP*, pages 2754–2763.

Lynette Hirschman and Robert Gaizauskas. 2001. Natural language question answering: the view from here. *Natural Language Engineering*, 7(4):275.

Gérard Huet. 2009. Sanskrit segmentation. *South Asian Languages Analysis Roundtable XXVIII, Denton, Ohio (October 2009)*.

Yoji Kiyota, Sadao Kurohashi, and Fuyuko Kido. 2002. "Dialog Navigator": A question answering system based on large text knowledge base. In *COLING*.

Amrith Krishna, Bishal Santra, Pavankumar Satuluri, Śasi Prasanth Bandaru, Bhumi Faldu, Yajuvendra Singh, and Pawan Goyal. 2016. Word segmentation in sanskrit using path constrained random walks. In *COLING*, pages 494–504.

Amrith Krishna, Bishal Santra, Ashim Gupta, Pavankumar Satuluri, and Pawan Goyal. 2021. A graph-based framework for structured prediction tasks in sanskrit. *Computational Linguistics*, 46(4):785–845.

Malhar Kulkarni, Chaitali Dangarikar, Irawati Kulkarni, Abhishek Nanda, and Pushpak Bhattacharyya. 2010. Introducing Sanskrit WordNet. In *Global Wordnet Conference (GWC)*, pages 287–294.

Amba Kulkarni. 2016. Samsaadhanii: A Sanskrit computational toolkit.

Alberto O Mendelzon and Peter T Wood. 1995. Finding regular simple paths in graph databases. *SIAM Journal on Computing*, 24(6):1235–1258.

Tom Mitchell, William Cohen, Estevam Hruschka, Partha Talukdar, Bishan Yang, Justin Betteridge, Andrew Carlson, Bhanava Dalvi, Matt Gardner, Bryan Kisiel, et al. 2018. Never-ending learning. *Communications of the ACM*, 61(5):103–115.

Sivaja S Nair and Amba Kulkarni. 2010. The knowledge structure in Amarakośa. In *International Sanskrit Computational Linguistics Symposium (ISCLS)*, pages 173–189.

Jay Pujara and Sameer Singh. 2018. Mining knowledge graphs from text. In *WSDM*, pages 789–790.

Sanskrit programmers. 2021. Indic-transliteration, jul 23. [Online; accessed 2021-11-18].

Fabian M. Suchanek, Gjergji Kasneci, and Gerhard Weikum. 2007. YAGO: A core of semantic knowledge. In *WWW*, pages 697–706.

Hrishikesh Terdalkar and Arnab Bhattacharya. 2019. Framework for question-answering in sanskrit through automated construction of knowledge graphs. In *International Sanskrit Computational Linguistics Symposium (ISCLS)*, pages 97–116.

Hrishikesh Terdalkar and Arnab Bhattacharya. 2021. Sangrahaka: A tool for annotating and querying knowledge graphs. In *ESEC/FSE 2021*, pages 1520–1524.

Ellen M Voorhees. 1999. The TREC-8 question answering track report. In *Trec*, volume 99, pages 77–82.

Xindong Wu, Jia Wu, Xiaoyi Fu, Jiachen Li, Peng Zhou, and Xu Jiang. 2019. Automatic knowledge graph construction: A report on the 2019 ICDM/ICBK contest. In *ICDM*, pages 1540–1545.

Scott Wen-tau Yih, Ming-Wei Chang, Xiaodong He, and Jianfeng Gao. 2015. Semantic parsing via staged query graph generation: Question answering with knowledge base. In *IJCNLP*, pages 1321–1331.

A Dhānyavarga Sample

A.1 Sample of Text

We present here an extract from Dhānyavarga used in §2. Table 3 contains the first 10 verses from Dhānyavarga and a version with sandhi resolved. The sentence boundaries are denoted using '⟨' and '⟩' markers.

Original Text	Sandhi **Split**
⟨ शालिधान्यं व्रीहिधान्यं शूकधान्यं तृतीयकम् शिम्बीधान्यं क्षुद्रधान्यमित्युक्तं धान्यपञ्चकम् १ ⟩	शालिधान्यम् व्रीहिधान्यम् शूकधान्यम् तृतीयकम् शिम्बीधान्यम् क्षुद्रधान्यम् इति उक्तम् धान्यपञ्चकम् १
⟨ शालयो रक्तशाल्याद्या ⟩ ⟨ व्रीहयः षष्टिकादयः ⟩ ⟨ यवादिकं शूकधान्यं ⟩ ⟨ मुद्गाद्यं शिम्बिधान्यकम् ⟩ ⟨ कङ्ग्वादिकं क्षुद्रधान्यं ⟩ ⟨ तृणधान्यञ्च तत्स्मृतम् २ ⟩	शालयः रक्तशाल्याद्याः व्रीहयः षष्टिकादयः यवादिकम् शूकधान्यम् मुद्गाद्यम् शिम्बिधान्यकम् कङ्ग्वादिकम् क्षुद्रधान्यम् तृणधान्यम् च तत् स्मृतम् २
⟨ कण्डनेन विना शुक्ला हैमन्ताः शालयः स्मृताः ३ ⟩	कण्डनेन विना शुक्लाः हैमन्ताः शालयः स्मृताः ३
⟨ रक्तशालिः सकलमः पाण्डुकः शकुनाहृतः सुगन्धकः कर्दमको महाशालिश्च दूषकः ४	रक्तशालिः सकलमः पाण्डुकः शकुनाहृतः सुगन्धकः कर्दमकः महाशालिः च दूषकः ४
पुष्पाण्डकः पुण्डरीकस्तथा महिषमस्तकः दीर्घशूकः काञ्चनको हायनो लोध्रपुष्पकः ५	पुष्पाण्डकः पुण्डरीकः तथा महिषमस्तकः दीर्घशूकः काञ्चनकः हायनः लोध्रपुष्पकः ५
इत्याद्याः शालयः सन्ति बहवो बहुदेशजाः ⟩ ⟨ ग्रन्थविस्तरभीतेस्ते समस्ता नात्र भाषिताः ६ ⟩	इत्याद्याः शालयः सन्ति बहवः बहुदेशजाः ग्रन्थविस्तरभीतेः ते समस्ताः न अत्र भाषिताः ६
⟨ शालयो मधुराः स्निग्धा बल्या बद्धाल्पवर्चसः कषाया लघवो रुच्याः स्वर्या वृष्याश्च बृंहणाः अल्पानिलकफाः शीताः पित्तघ्ना मूत्रलास्तथा ७ ⟩	शालयः मधुराः स्निग्धाः बल्याः बद्धाल्पवर्चसः कषायाः लघवः रुच्याः स्वर्याः वृष्याः च बृंहणाः अल्पानिलकफाः शीताः पित्तघ्नाः मूत्रलाः तथा ७
⟨ शालयो दग्धमृज्जाताः कषाया लघुपाकिनः सृष्टमूत्रपुरीषाश्च रूक्षाः श्लेष्मापकर्षणाः ८ ⟩	शालयः दग्धमृज्जाताः कषायाः लघुपाकिनः सृष्टमूत्रपुरीषाः च रूक्षाः श्लेष्मापकर्षणाः ८
⟨ कैदारा वातपित्तघ्ना गुरवः कफशुक्रलाः कषायाश्चाल्पवर्चस्का मेध्याश्चैव बलावहाः ९ ⟩	कैदाराः वातपित्तघ्नाः गुरवः कफशुक्रलाः कषायाः च अल्पवर्चस्काः मेध्याः च एव बलावहाः ९
⟨ स्थलजाः स्वादवः पित्तकफघ्ना वातवह्निदाः किञ्चित्तिक्ताः कषायाश्च विपाके कटुका अपि १० ⟩	स्थलजाः स्वादवः पित्तकफघ्नाः वातवह्निदाः किञ्चिद् तिक्ताः कषायाः च विपाके कटुकाः अपि १०

Table 3: First 10 verses from Dhānyavarga of Bhāvaprakāśanighaṇṭu

A.2 Poetry-to-Prose Conversion of Verses from Table 3

We next list the prose version of the verses listed in Table 3 above.

1. शालिधान्यम् व्रीहिधान्यम् तृतीयकम् शूकधान्यम् शिम्बीधान्यम् क्षुद्रधान्यम् इति धान्यपञ्चकम् उक्तम् (अस्ति)।
2. शालयः रक्तशाल्याद्याः (सन्ति)।
3. व्रीहयः षष्टिकादयः (सन्ति)।
4. शूकधान्यम् यवादिकम् (अस्ति)।
5. शिम्बिधान्यकम् मुद्गाद्यम् (अस्ति)।
6. क्षुद्रधान्यम् कङ्ग्वादिकम् (अस्ति)।
7. तत् तृणधान्यम् च स्मृतम् (अस्ति)।

8. कण्डनेन विना शुक्लाः हैमन्ताः (च) शालयः स्मृताः (सन्ति)।

9. शालयः रक्तशालिः सकलमः पाण्डुकः शकुनाहृतः सुगन्धकः कर्दमकः महाशालिः दूषकः पुष्पाण्डकः पुण्डरीकः महिषमस्तकः दीर्घशूकः काञ्चनकः हायनः लोध्रपुष्पकः च तथा इत्याद्याः बहवः बहुदेशजाः सन्ति।

10. ग्रन्थविस्तरभीतेः ते समस्ताः अत्र न भाषिताः (सन्ति)।

11. शालयः मधुराः स्निग्धाः बल्याः बद्धाल्पवर्चसः कषायाः लघवः रुच्याः स्वर्याः वृष्याः बृंहणाः अल्पानिलकफाः शीताः पित्तघ्नाः तथा मूत्रलाः च (सन्ति)।

12. दग्धमृज्जाताः शालयः कषायाः लघुपाकिनः सृष्टमूत्रपुरीषाः रूक्षाः श्लेष्मापकर्षणाः च (सन्ति)।

13. कैदाराः (शालयः) वातपित्तघ्नाः गुरवः कफशुक्रलाः कषायाः अल्पवर्चस्काः मेध्याः बलावहाः च एव (सन्ति)।

14. स्थलजाः (शालयः) स्वादवः पित्तकफघ्नाः वातवह्निदाः किञ्चिद् तिक्ताः कषायाः विपाके कटुकाः च

B Query Templates

Category	Sanskrit Template	English Template	Input Type
सूचि (Contents)	पदार्थानां के प्रकाराः।	What are all the entity types?	
सूचि (Contents)	पदार्थेषु के सम्बन्धाः।	What are all the relationships?	
सूचि (Contents)	के के द्रव्याः।	What are all the substances?	
सूचि (Contents)	के के पदार्थाः।	What are all the entities?	
वर्णन (Detail)	{0} इत्यस्य विषये दर्शय।	Show some details about {0}.	Entity
वर्णन (Detail)	{0} इत्यस्य विषये अधिकं दर्शय।	Show some more details about {0}.	Entity
प्रकार (Type)	{0} इत्यस्य प्रकारः कः।	What is the type of {0}?	Entity
प्रकार (Type)	सर्वे {0} इति प्रकारस्य पदार्थाः चिनु।	Find all the entities of type {0}.	Entity-Type
गुण (Property)	केषां द्रव्याणां {0} इति गुणः अस्ति।	Which substances have a property {0}?	Entity
द्रव्य (Substance)	{0} इत्यस्य गुणाः के।	What are the properties of {0}?	Entity
द्रव्य (Substance)	{0} इति द्रव्यस्य प्रकाराः के।	What are the types/variants of the substance {0}?	Entity
समानार्थक (Synonym)	{0} इत्यस्य अन्यानि नामानि कानि।	What are the synonyms of {0}?	Entity
सम्बन्ध (Relation)	{0} इति सम्बन्धेन बद्धं सर्वं दर्शय।	Find all entities related by the relation {0}.	Relation
सम्बन्ध (Relation)	{0} {1} एतयोः मध्ये कः सम्बन्धः।	What is the relation between {0} and {1}?	Entity, Entity

Category	Sanskrit Template	English Template	Input Type
त्रिदोष (Tridoṣa)	के पदार्थाः {0} इति दोषस्य वर्धनं कुर्वन्ति।	Which entities increase the dosha {0}?	Entity
त्रिदोष (Tridoṣa)	के पदार्थाः {0} इति दोषस्य ह्रासं कुर्वन्ति।	Which entities decrease the dosha {0}?	Entity
त्रिदोष (Tridoṣa)	के पदार्थाः {0} इति दोषस्य वर्धनं {1} इति दोषस्य ह्रासं च कुर्वन्ति।	Which entities increase the dosha {0} and decrease the dosha {1}?	Entity, Entity
त्रिदोष (Tridoṣa)	के पदार्थाः {0} {1} एतयोः दोषयोः वर्धनं {2} इति दोषस्य ह्रासं च कुर्वन्ति।	Which entities increase the doshas {0} and {1} and decrease the dosha {2}?	Entity, Entity, Entity
त्रिदोष (Tridoṣa)	के पदार्थाः {0} इति दोषस्य वर्धनं {1} {2} एतयोः दोषयोः ह्रासं च कुर्वन्ति।	Which entities increase the dosha {0} and decrease the doshas {1} and {2}?	Entity, Entity, Entity
रोग (Disease)	के पदार्थाः {0} इति रोगं कुर्वन्ति।	Which entity causes the disease {0}?	Entity
रोग (Disease)	के पदार्थाः {0} इति रोगं हरन्ति।	Which entity cures the disease {0}?	Entity
प्रभाव (Effect)	के पदार्थाः {0} एतं विकुर्वन्ति।	Which entities affect {0}?	Entity
प्रभाव (Effect)	के पदार्थाः {0} एतस्मै लाभप्रदाः।	Which entities benefit {0}?	Entity
प्रभाव (Effect)	के पदार्थाः {0} एतस्मै क्षतिप्रदाः।	Which entities harm {0}?	Entity
प्रभाव (Effect)	के पदार्थाः {0} इत्यस्य वर्धनं कुर्वन्ति।	Which entities increase {0}?	Entity
प्रभाव (Effect)	के पदार्थाः {0} इत्यस्य ह्रासं कुर्वन्ति।	Which entities decrease {0}?	Entity
अधिकरण (Space-Time)	{0} इति पदार्थः कदा जायते।	When does {0} grow?	Entity
अधिकरण (Space-Time)	{0} इति पदार्थः कुत्र लभ्यते।	Where is {0} found?	Entity
साधारण (Generic)	के पदार्थाः {0} इति पदार्थेन सह {1} इति सम्बन्धेन सम्बन्धिताः।	Which entity is related to {0} by relation {1}?	Entity, Relation
साधारण (Generic)	{0} इति पदार्थः {1} इति पदार्थेन सह कथं सम्बन्धितः।	How is {0} related to {1}?	Entity, Relation
साधारण (Generic)	{0} इति प्रकारस्य पदार्थैः सह {1} इति सम्बन्धेन बद्धाः {2} इति प्रकारस्य पदार्थान् दर्शय।	Show all matches where an entity of type {0} has relation {1} with an entity of type {2}.	Entity-Type, Relation, Entity-Type

Shaastra Maps: Enabling Conceptual Exploration of Indic Shaastra Texts

Sai Susarla[1], Suryanarayana Jammalamadaka, Vaishnavi Nishankar, Siva Panuganti, Anupama Ryali, and Sushrutha S
[1] Vedavaapi Foundation, Bangalore
MIT School of Vedic Sciences, MIT-ADT University, Pune
sai.susarla@gmail.com, jam.narayana@gmail.com, r.vaishnavi.rao@gmail.com, panugantisiva@gmail.com, anupamaskt@gmail.com, ayrveda1984@gmail.com

Abstract

Indic shaastra texts employ a rigorous, structured style of discourse that adheres to well-laid out conventions of Nyaaya and Mimaamsa. As a result, unlike modern scientific treatises which use free form natural language for their discourse, Indic shaastra texts are more amenable to mechanized navigation and interpretation. Such a facility also simplifies their study by novice readers via creating custom dynamic views on demand for rapid drill-down and assimilation.

This paper contributes a conceptual network representation of Indic shaastra texts called *Shaastra Map* along with a graph query scheme called *ShaastricQL*[1] that together provide these benefits. At its core, ShaastraMap is an overlay directed graph of sentences and sections of one or more Shaastra texts linked via relations widely employed by shaastra authors and experts such as *tantrayuktis* and *padaartha sambandhas*. This representation directly mimics shaastric discourse structure and hence makes the author's intent more explicit to reduce learning barrier. Moreover, ShaastriQL offers primitives to help generate the following custom views of a shaastra text:

- Glossary: Show all the technical terms used in the text along with their definitions, illustrative examples and explanations ·
- Category Hierarchy: Given a conceptual category, show its recursive hierarchy of attributes and sub-categories. ·
- Discourse by topic: Given a topic, show its complete analysis in the text to a given level of detail. ·
- Summary: Show a high-level summary of the text with an incremental drill-down view of details.

We have built a web-based ShaastraMap editor that lets users (i) mark up a shaastra text to describe its structural layout upto individual sentences, (ii) tag the sections and their inter-relationships using well-formed 7-layer shaastric categories based on Nyaaya and Mimaamsa principles of text interpretation, and (iii) explore the text via the above custom views. This paper outlines these capabilities and our experience in the context of mapping four diverse shaastra texts.

1 Introduction

India's traditional scientific knowledge is articulated in numerous shaastra texts in a wide variety of disciplines, e.g., Ayurveda, Jyotisha, Vaastu, Yoga, Aesthetics, Dharma and Artha shaastras to name a few. There is untapped knowledge in the shaastras which can potentially address several prevailing issues in the world. There are areas in modern disciplines which can be augmented with shaastric insights. For these reasons, there is growing curiosity among the younger generation to explore Indic shaastras. Moreover, encoding knowledge for machine processing is

[1] *We recommend pronouncing ShaastriQL as Shaastric-quel.*

Proceedings of the Computational Sanskrit and Digital Humanities, 18th *World Sanskrit Conference 2023*, pages 174–187

crucial for leveraging Indic knowledge for contemporary uses at scale. Some examples of useful applications include an automated tool for Ayurvedic diagnostics assistance, Vaastu compliance checking, and symptom-based herbal remedies. However, due to their highly technical nature and unfamiliar style of discourse for modern seekers, Indic shaastra texts require special training to navigate, grasp and utilize.

1.1 Challenges in exploring Shaastra Texts

There are a number of issues that a novice seeker faces in studying shaastra texts in their current format. The exposition style looks too detailed for first reading as key points often get interspersed with detailed commentaries and nuanced arguments. The definitions of terms and examples of concepts seem hard to locate in flat text. The long compounds and sandhis are difficult to parse and cross-references of concepts drawn from other shaastras are hard to find. The novice cannot benefit from shared community experience from prior readers and more often than not, deep experts of shaastras are hard to obtain.

1.2 Approach to a Solution

An insight into how to make Indic texts more accessible to modern seekers can come from understanding how a traditional scholar digests them, uses cross-references and presents them to his/her students. We explore this further in Section 3. To effectively leverage Indic scientific knowledge for contemporary uses, we need to reduce the didactic burden of scholars for training large numbers of students and also encode the knowledge contained in Indic texts for machine-assisted cognition and mining. Both the objectives can be achieved by encoding shaastra text content as a multi-dimensional concept network with a standard schema for navigation.

In this paper, we present a novel way of representing shaastric content that is amenable to drill-down exploration and topic-based consultancy, by using the inherent structuring schemes of shaastras, specifically Tantrayuktis Lele (1981) and Nyaaya-sambandhas Jha (2010). Section 3 gives further details about Tantrayuktis. We have developed a web-based editor for experts to collaboratively overlay a shaastra text and/or its commentary with a concept map representation. It includes a graph-based concept browser that supports drill-down exploration and summary views. We have evaluated the expressive power of Shaastra Map's representation scheme by applying it to diverse, popular shaastra texts including Tarka sangraha, Saankhya kaarika, KaavyaprakaaSa, Kshemakutuhala, AshtaangahRdaya etc.

The rest of the paper is organized as follows. Section 2 discusses prior work in relation to ours. Section 3 gives the organisation of discourse structure used in the shaastras that inspired our solution. Section 4describes our core contributions, namely, shaastra maps, their definition, creation and knowledge representation structures. Section 4.3 illustrates through actual examples from diverse shaastras, the expressive power of our representation - *tarka sangraha*, *Kaavya prakaasha* and *Saankhya kaarikaa*. Section 4.4 introduces a query scheme for conceptual search using a shaastra map, and how several higher-level views can be expressed using it. Section 5 outlines the implementation details and current status of this work. Section 6 outlines lessons learnt from our experience and suggest directions for further work. Section 7 summarizes the paper's contributions and key takeaways.

2 Related Work

The idea of shaastra maps is inspired by the success of mind maps. The value of mind maps to organize and present knowledge has been well-studied Beel et al. (2019). The proliferation of mind mapping tools (both free and commercial) is a testimony to their effectiveness. However, our unique contribution is in devising a standard schema for semantic networking of Indic text content that allows automated navigational queries. Semantic web is a methodology to represent and organize web content to support sophisticated knowledge processing and visualization. The natural language processing community has developed numerous tools Goyal et al. (2012; Hellwig

(2009; Kulkarni (2016) for automatically inferring semantic linkages among multiple sentences in a paragraph Srinivasan and Parthasarathi (2011). Such tools can be leveraged to infer some of the semantic tags identified in this paper, and hence are complementary. Brat Brat (2016) is a text annotation tool that provides a user-interface for concept mapping, but leaves the higher-level annotation and tagging strategy to the user.

A prior position paper Susarla et al. (2017) has made a strong case for concept mapping of Indic shaastras and proposed a representation scheme for exploiting their inner structure for machine processing. Our paper improves on that work in two ways. First, we propose tantrayuktis and padaartha sambandhas as a sounder basis for shaastra mapping due to their comprehensive and nuanced coverage of shaastric discourse concepts. Second, we offer a query mechanism on shaastra maps to support sophisticated knowledge search and navigation.

3 Organization of Shaastraic Discourse

A traditionally trained shaastric scholar eases the understanding of a shaastric discourse for any audience by (i) mapping the content of a shaastra to suit their audience, (ii) focusing on some concepts and glossing over others, (iii) bringing in relevant external references, etc. based on the objective of the study. This is because a shaastra expert uses his/her familiarity to mentally build a concept map of the flat text along with relevant works, and uses it to assist students in imbibing the concepts without getting overwhelmed.

We view a shaastric discourse as consisting of three aspects, viz.,

1. The categories of entities defined as technical terms specific to the shaastra. Shaastra has specific conventions to enumerate, define, categorize and analyze them.

2. The relations between the categories and postulates that aid in well-formed classification, logical evaluation and conclusion of the shaastric theories

3. The discourse involving logical and rational flow of thought based on the reasoning tenets of Nyaaya through topical discussions, cross-referencing and addressing objections and prima facie views leading to conclusive theorization.

The conventions available in the shaastras for describing these aspects can be broadly identified as follows:

Tantrayuktis – Between 32-43 tantrayuktis are used in celebrated Shaastra texts. Tantrayukti denotes a category of sentence or inter-sentence relationships that denotes their role in a coherent logical discourse. The following elementary and standard structures are found in most shaastra texts.

- UddeSa, LakshaNa, pariikShaa and nirNaya - enumeration, definition, examination of definition and conclusion – the basic navigation structures.
- adhikaraNa, sangati and taatparya-lingas – topicalization, logical succession of discussion and pointers to arrive at conclusions. Each of these have subcomponents that are applied in the discourse as relevant to the context. For instance, adhikaraNa comprises of vishaya, viSaya, poorvapaksha, uttarapaksha, nirNaya – topic, doubt, prima facie view, proponent's view, conclusion. They, in turn use other elements such as hypothesis (pratijnaa), hetu (reason), udAharaNa (illustration), tarka (proof by contradiction), means of proof (perception, inference etc), previous / forward reference, extension of application etc.

Different shaastras employ different subsets of these constructs in their discourse as needed. We find that tantrayuktis cover a superset of these structures, and hence are useful to adopt for the purpose of creating shaastra maps.

Nyaaya-sambandhas – Relations between the categories and concepts that form part of shaastra discourse, e.g., lakshya-lakshaNa-bhaava (defined-definition), dharma-dharmi-bhaava (property-holder), saamaanya-viSesha-bhaava (class-type), avayava-avayavi-bhaava (whole-part) and so on.

Figure 1 enumerates 7 dimensions of concept categorizations used in shaastric discourse with values in each dimension. Our study of these dimensions revealed that many of the categories under Topic, commentary, gist, concept and treatise dimensions are covered under tantrayukti. Hence we believe that tantrayuktis can be used to adequately characterize a shaastra's sections and their linkages. However, capturing inter-concept relations requires, in addition, the padaartha sambandhas listed in the last column of the figure.

	A	B	C	D	E	F	G
1	Tantrayukti_tag वाक्य-स्तरे (तन्त्रयुक्तिः)	Topic_tag अधिकरण-स्तरे	Commentary_tag व्याख्यान-स्तरे	Gist_tag तात्पर्य-स्तरे	Concept_tag विषय-स्तरे	Treatise_tag ग्रन्थ-स्तरे	Relation_tag पदार्थ-संबन्धः
2	-	-	-	-	-	-	-
3	अतिक्रान्तावेक्षणम् retrospection	विषयः Topic	पदच्छेदःdivision of wor	उपक्रमःbeginning	उद्देशः (लक्ष्यम्)illustration	अधिकारीthe qualified student	निरूप्य - निरूपक-भावः
4	अतिदेशः extrapolation	विशयःambiguity / doubt	पदार्थोक्तिःmeaning of wor	उपसंहारःconclusion	लक्षणम्definition	विषयःthe theme	धर्म - धर्मि-भावः
5	अधिकरणम् Topic	उपोद्घातः-सङ्गतिःintroduction	विग्रहःanalysis of gram	अभ्यासःrepetition	परीक्षाverification	प्रयोजनम्result	अवच्छेद्य - अवच्छेदक-भावः
6	अनागतावेक्षणम् forward reference	पूर्वपक्षः adversary argument	वाक्ययोजनाprose-renderi	अपूर्वताnovelty		अधिकारी-विषय-संबन्धःthe qua	उपादान - उपादेय-भावः
7	अनुमतम् agreement	उत्तरपक्षः rebuttal	आक्षेपःobjection	फलम्purpose		विषयः-प्रयोजन-संबन्धःthe them	नियाम्य - नियामक-भावः
8	अपदेशः/हेत्वर्थः reason	प्रसङ्गः-सङ्गतिःcontext	समाधानम्answer	अर्थवादःdescription		अधिकारी-प्रयोजन-संबन्धःthe qu	निरूप्य - निरूपक-भावः
9	अपवर्गः exception	हेतुता-सङ्गतिःargumentation		उपपत्तिःcogency		अधिकारी-विषय-प्रयोजन-संबन्धः	प्रतिपाद्य - प्रतिपादक-भावः
10	अर्थापत्तिः implied meaning	अवसरः-सङ्गतिःscope					आधार - आधेय-भावः
11	उत्तरपक्षः Refutation	निर्वाहकैक्य-सङ्गतिःoneness performing					कार्य - कारण-भावः
12	उद्देशः concise summary	कार्यैक्यम् (एकफलकत्वम्)-सङ्गतिःoneness result					नियोज्य - नियोजक-भावः
13	उपदेशः advisory guidance	दृष्टान्तः-सङ्गतिःexemplification					प्रकार - प्रकारि-भावः
14	उपमानम् analogy	प्रत्युदाहरणम्-सङ्गतिःre-answer					प्रतियोगि - अनुयोगि-भावः
15	ऊह्यम् deduction	आक्षेपः-सङ्गतिःobjection					उद्देश्य - विधेय-भावः
16	एकान्तः exclusive statement						गुरु - शिष्य-भावः
17	निदर्शनम्/दृष्टान्तः example						पति - पत्नी-भावः
18	नियोगः Dictate						पितृ - पुत्र-भावः

Figure 1: Conceptual structures used in Shaastra texts

4 Shaastra Maps

Based on the understanding of shaastric structures in Section 3, we have designed a conceptual network representation of shaastra texts. We describe that in this section.

We define a *Shaastra Map* (hereafter referred to as *SMap*) as a directed graph representation of the content of one or more Indic scientific treatises or shaastra texts. An SMap captures the physical sectional hierarchy, conceptual category hierarchies, logical network of sentences, arguments etc. that constitute a coherent discourse. While discourse analysis in general is a well-developed field with its own knowledge representation conventions, we have designed SMap to specifically encode the common methods and schemas employed in Indic shaastric treatises (e.g., Ayurveda, Artha shaastra, Natya shaastra and Jyotisha, etc.). An SMap makes explicit a shaastra's inherent conceptual network that is normally implicitly understood and mentally navigated by a well-versed traditional shaastra expert. Its purpose is twofold: 1) to simplify the navigation of shaastra texts by novices by giving them access to expert-level insights, 2) to enable machine-navigation, search and mining of Indic shaastra texts at scale. Figure 2 shows the full SMap of tarka sangraha text. The nodes with high fanout indicate clustering of the discourse around a few concepts and branches and long chains indicate their elaboration.

4.1 Anatomy of an SMap

An SMap comprises a set of text segment objects and a set of relation objects. Each *text segment* in an SMap is either an individual sentence (vaakya), verse (shloka), chapter (adhikarana) or entire book (grantha). A *relation* (sambandha) is a labelled directed edge between two segments that captures one of several types of connections identified in Indic shaastraic conventions –

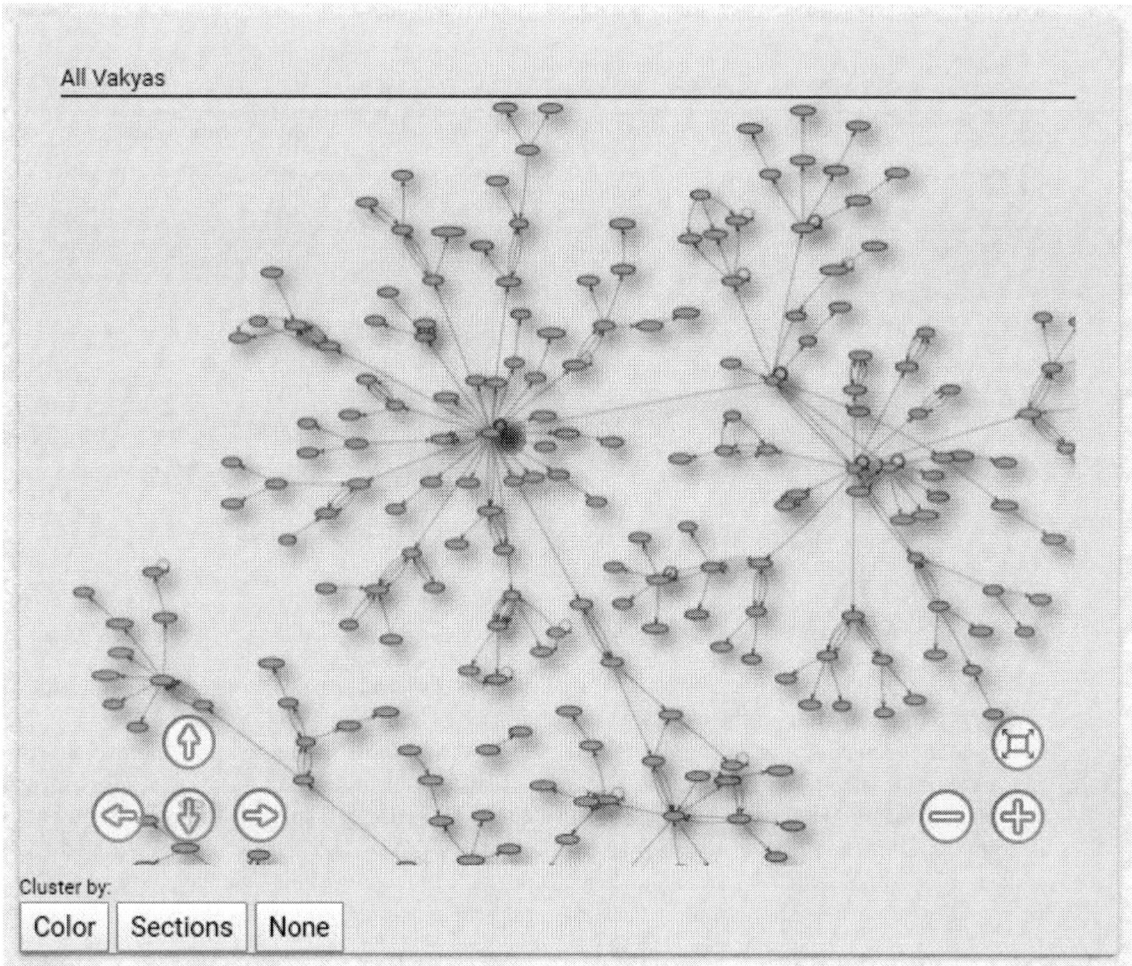

Figure 2: Full SMap graph of Tarka Sangraha text.

specifically *tantrayuktis* and *nyaaya sambandhas* for the purpose of this paper. We plan to include 6 other types of relations in the future. An SMap relation object is a quintuple:

- [Source segment, source anchor phrase*, relation tag (key=value), target anchor phrase*, target segment]

The scope of our SMap work is to encapsulate information at the level of sentence and above, and not intra-sentence linguistic analysis which is the subject matter of *shaabda-bodha.* There is a large body of existing work devoted to language-level syntactic and semantic analysis within a sentence that can be incorporated into an SMap framework, but is outside the scope of this paper. Since an SMap doesn't tag individual words / phrases as first-class entities below the sentence level, we use anchor phrases in relations to identify technical terms or concept / topic names employed in a shaastra. This reduces the tedium of shaastra mapping process while enabling concept-based search.

Tantrayukti_tags can be used to tag both text segments and relations of an SMap, while Nyaaya padaartha sambandhas, also called Relation_tags are used only to tag relations. In case of segments, tantrayukti tag indicates the type of exposition used in a vaakya or adhikarana, such as term-defining, exemplifying, rebuttal, forward / backward reference, enumerating, concluding, elaborating, commenting etc. Figure 5 shows an 'Uhyam' tantrayukti example in *Kshema kutuhalam* text on culinary science.

Each relation involves an optional anchor phrase of a text segment that conceptually connects it with an anchor phrase in the target segment. Thus, the relations bind together individual sentences into a coherent discourse. For instance, when a sentence uses a technical term defined in another sentence, a relation mentions the term used as the source anchor phrase, sets the relation_tag to *lakshya-lakshana bhaava.* Figure 3 illustrates it with an example from tarka sangraha text.

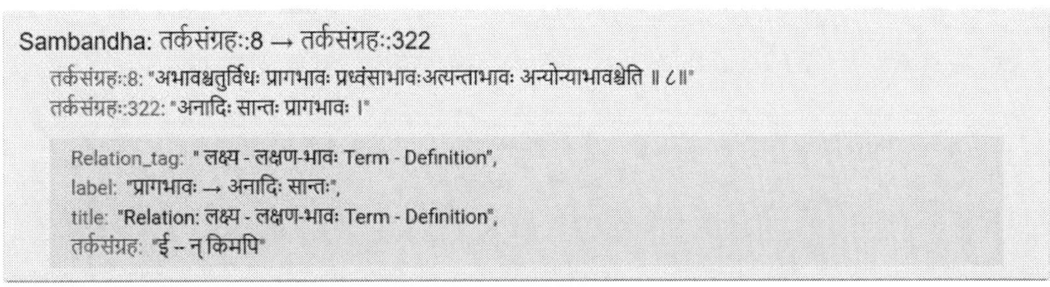

Figure 3: Capturing term definition and use in tarka sangraha SMap.

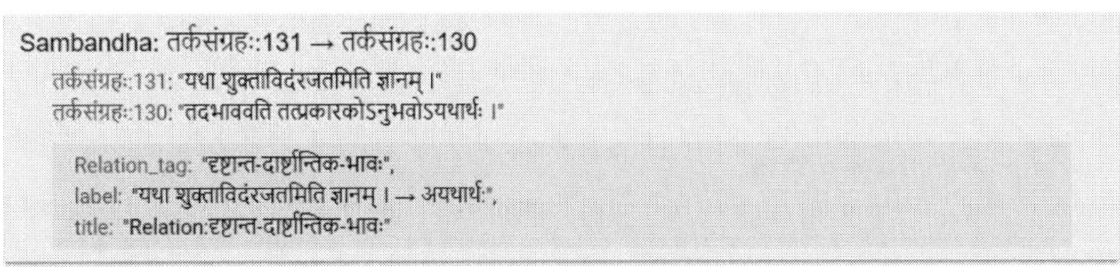

Figure 4: Capturing a concept and its example in tarka sangraha SMap.

4.2 Creating an SMap

SMap creation from a raw shaastra text is currently a manual process since it involves proficiency in identifying deep shaastraic concepts. However, we have defined the structure and schema of

Figure 5: Tantrayukti tag for a vaakya in Kshema kutuhalam text.

SMaps and developed software tools for visualization and editing of SMaps as well as a powerful query mechanism to perform knowledge queries on SMap content. Transforming one or more shaastra texts into an SMap involves the following manual steps:

- Markup the text to identify the various structural entities - chapters, sections, verses, sentences - with unique IDs so they can be explicitly tagged and referred in relations.
- Tag the entities with SMap-defined entity attributes and their values.
- Create inter-entity relations with SMAP-defined relation types.

We provide a facility to export and edit an SMap in a spreadsheet containing a vaakya sheet and sambandha sheet for tagging purpose. We have built a web-based SMap UI editor that includes a text editor for markup, structural viewer and an SMap explorer that enables specific canned views of shaastra texts described in Section 4.4.

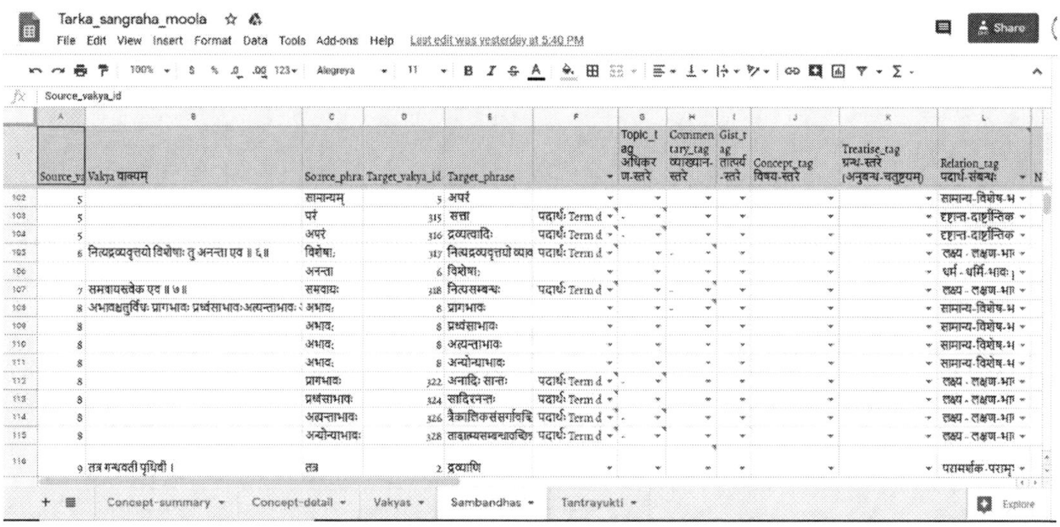

Figure 6: SMap spreadsheet of Tarka Sangraha for editing relations.

Markup of a Shaastra Text

The first step to creating a shaastra map is to identify the meaningful units of a treatise, the smallest being a vaakya. To facilitate this, we have devised a simple markup scheme that enables a shaastra text's unique structural hierarchy to be expressed without too much verbosity unlike XML. It allows a shaastra text's verses to be resplit into sentences, which is essential for tagging. We are open to replacing this markup with other more standardized / sophisticated markup schemes if found suitable.

Figure 7 shows the markup created in SMap structural editor for *KaavyaprakaaSa* a seminal saahitya-shaastra text by Mammata. Figure 8 illustrates how the resultant structure is visualized using the SMap structure viewer:

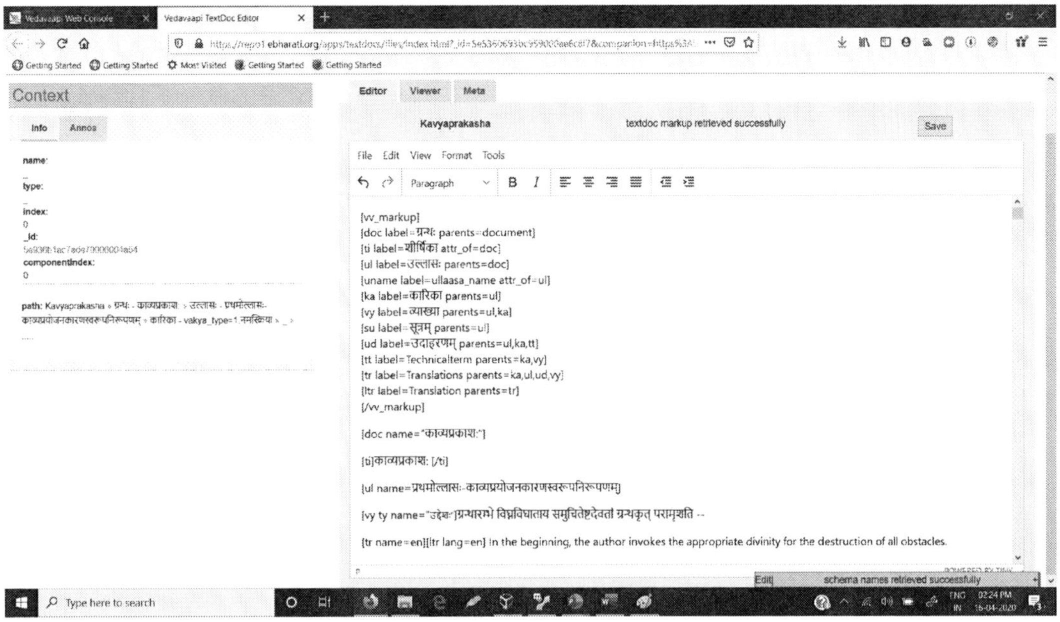

Figure 7: Specifying a shaastra text's structural hierarchy via custom markup.

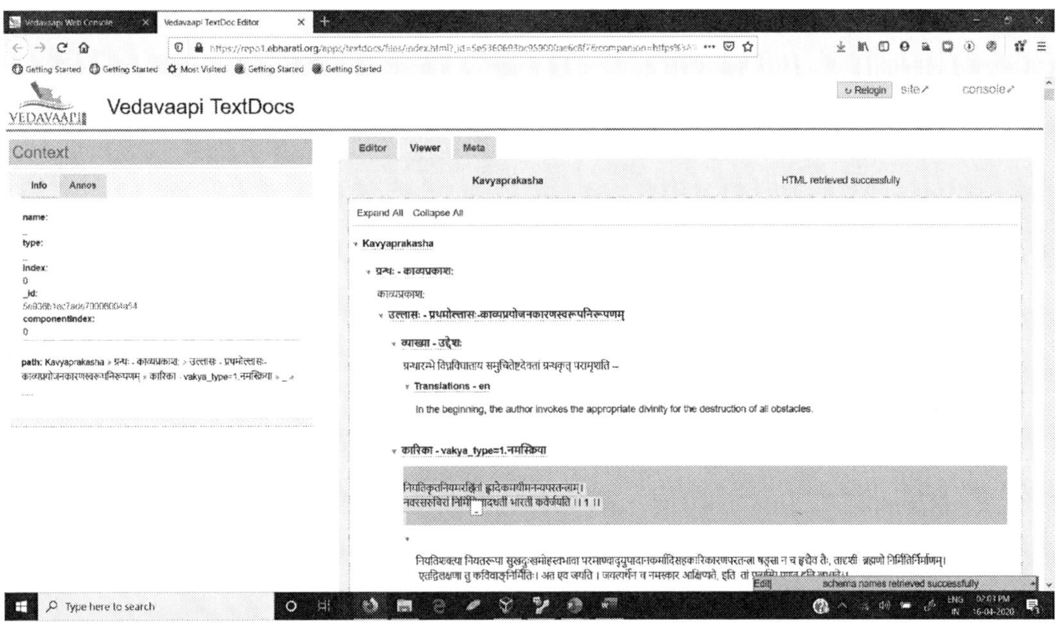

Figure 8: SMap Structure viewer

4.3 Shaastra Mapping Examples

In this section, we illustrate the SMap tagging process via examples from four shaastra texts that employ diverse discourse styles, tantrayuktis and relations. Our objective is to evaluate how well the diversity of exposition is covered by the SMap tag set.

4.3.1 Tarka sangraha

Tarka sangraha text is an elementary text on Navya Nyaaya that is widely studied by junior students. It describes ontological categories and sub-categories extensively.

Identifying type of the sentence according to tantrayukti

- Example 1: 'अभावश्चतुर्विधः प्रागभावः प्रध्वंसाभावःअत्यन्ताभावः अन्योन्याभावश्चेति'(Vk id_8): this sentence is tagged as 'उद्देशः' because it is concise summary for further elaboration.

- Example 2: 'असाधारणं कारणं करणम्' (Vk id_137): this sentence is tagged as 'पदार्थः' because it is a definition of a term.

- Example 3: 'यथा शुक्ताविदंरजतमिति ज्ञानम्' (Vk id_131): this sentence is tagged as निदर्शनम्/दृष्टान्तः' because it states an example of a false knowledge.

- Example 4: चक्षुः संयुक्ते घटे रूपस्य समवायात्' (Vk id_158): this sentence is tagged as व्याख्यानम् because it explains why samyukta-samavaaya is the relation to perceive colour of the pot.

Relating the source and the target phrase

- Example1: सामान्य-विशेष-भावः (Type-subtype) In Tarkasamgraha Experience is classified into four. The relation between Experience and its types is सामान्य-विशेष-भावः (Type-subtype). From the sentence यथार्थनुभवश्चतुर्विधः(Vk id_133) the phrase यथार्थनुभवः is targeting प्रत्यक्षानुमित्युपमितिशाब्दभेदात् (Vk id_134) with the relation tag सामान्य-विशेष-भावः (Type-subtype).

- Example 2: लक्ष्य - लक्षण-भावः Term - Definition In Tarkasamgraha Perceptive cognition is defined in the sentence इन्द्रियार्थसंनिकर्षजन्यं ज्ञानं प्रत्यक्षम्(Vk id_149), here the phrase प्रत्यक्षम् is targeting इन्द्रियार्थसंनिकर्षजन्यं ज्ञानं with the relation tag लक्ष्य - लक्षण-भावः Term - Definition.

- Example 3: दृष्टान्त-दार्ष्टान्तिक-भावः In Tarkasamgraha Pruthivi is defined as one of the types of Dravya. And further it is divided into three. Each type of Pruthivi has an example. In this sentence पुनस्त्रिविधा शरीरेन्द्रियविषयभेदात्(Vk id_13) शरीर, इन्द्रिय, विषय are stated as three types. So, each phrase is targeting अस्मदादीनाम्(Vk id_14), गन्धग्राहकं घ्राणम्(Vk id_15) andमृत्पाषाणादिः(Vk id_17) respectively with दृष्टान्त-दार्ष्टान्तिक-भावः relation tag.

- Example 4: धर्म - धर्मि-भावः property - holder In Tarkasamgraha Rupam (colour) is divided into seven and each is an attribute to different objects. In particular Pruthivi is attributed with all the types of colours. In the sentence तत्र पृथिव्यां सप्तविधम् (Vk id_63) the source phrase पृथिव्यां is targeting सप्तविधम् with the धर्म - धर्मि-भावः property - holder relation tag.

4.3.2 Kaavyaprakaasha

kaavya prakaasha is a seminal text on Indic theory of poetics - saahitya shaastra - this is compulsory for Master's students in Sanskrit throughout India. Unlike tarka sangraha, this text is more descriptive with lot of examples of concepts and their commentary. Figure 9 shows an example of concept-example relation in this text as shown in its SMap viewer.

Identifying type of the sentence according to tantrayukti

- Example 1:इति हेतुस्तदुद्भवे (Vk id_1.2.8)' this sentence is tagged as 'उद्देशः' because it is concise summary for further elaboration.

- Example 2: तददोषौ शब्दार्थौ सगुणावनलङ्कृती पुनः क्वापि।(Vk id_1.3.2)' this sentence is tagged as 'पदार्थः' because it is a definition for a term.

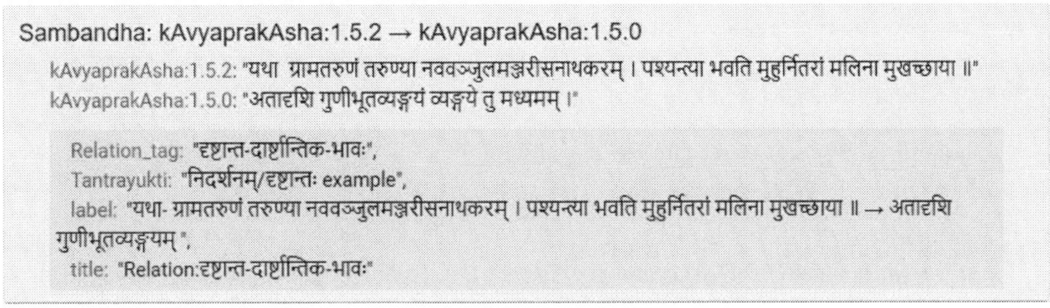

Figure 9: Concept-example relation in Kavyaprakaasha text.

- Example 3: काव्यं कर्तुं विचारयितुं च ये जानन्ति तदुपदेशेन करणे योजने च पौनःपुन्येन प्रवृत्तिरिति |(Vk id_1.2.7) ' this sentence is tagged as व्याख्यानम् because it explains why samyukta-samavaya is the relation to perceive colour of the pot.

Relating the source and the target phrase

- Example: सामान्य-विशेष-भावः (Type-subtype) In Kāvyaprakāśa, Avarakāvya-type is classified into two. The relation between avarakāvya and its types is सामान्य-विशेष-भावः (Type-subtype). From the sentence शब्दचित्रं वाच्यचित्रम् अव्यङ्ग्यं त्ववरं स्मृतम् ॥(Vk id_1.6.0) the phrase अवरं is targeting two subtypes शब्दचित्रं andवाच्यचित्रम् (Vk id_1.6.1) with the relation tag सामान्य-विशेष-भावः(Type-subtype).

4.3.3 Saankhya Karika

Saankhya kaarika has a mix of ontological discourse and philosophical reasoning. It is a widely studied root text on Saankhya system of Indian philosophy.

- Example 1: 'दृष्टम्-अनुमानम्-आप्तवचनं च(Vk id_4.1a)' is tagged as 'उद्देशः' because it is concise summary of the list of epistemological tools, which will be elaborated later.

- Example 2: महत्-आदि तच्च कार्यं प्रकृति-विरूपं सरूपं च (Vk id_8.2) is tagged to निर्देशः for.this sentence detailed enumeration of Mahat etc fromमहद्-आद्याः प्रकृति-विकृतयः सप्त (Vk id_3.1b) sentence.

- Example 3: एकान्त-अत्यन्ततः-अभावात्(Vk_1.2c) is tagged as अपदेशः/हेत्वर्थः as it is explaining the reason for why one has to enquire into Anumana, rather completely depending upon sensory perception and Vedas.

- Example 4: सत्कार्यम् (Vk id_9.2c) is tagged as निर्णयः type of sentence because it is concluding that the effect / product exists in the cause, after explaining all the valid reasons.

- Example 5: सङ्कल्पकमिन्द्रियं च (VK id_27.1b) is tagged as योगः as it adds one more characteristic of mind as a continuation from the previous statement which defines the ''Manas''

- Example 6: युगपत् चतुष्टयस्य तु वृत्तिः क्रमशश्च तस्य निर्दिष्टा(VK id_30.1) is tagged as अतिक्रान्तावेक्षणम् because it is retrospecting what is said earlier regarding Indriya and Antahkarana. }

4.3.4 Ashtanga Hrdayam

Ashtanga Hrdayam is a popular foundational text of Ayurveda studied by most practitioners. It has highly structured descriptions of herbs and their properties.

Identifying type of the sentence according to tantrayukti

- Example: In Asthanga Hridaya, there is a separate chapter for medicinal data that starts with the vaakya अथौषधवर्गः (Vk id_1), this is tagged as 'अधिकरणम्' .

Relating the source and the target phrase

All the following examples are in relation to the sentence, 'नागरं दीपनं वृष्यं ग्राहि हृद्यं विण्मबन्धनुत् // रुच्यं लघु स्वादुपाकं स्निग्धोष्णं कफवातजित् (Vk id_43)

- Example 1: नागरं is source phrase and अथौषधवर्गः (Vk id_1) is target phrase with विषय - विषयि-भावः relation tag.
- Example 2: नागरं is source phrase and दीपनं, वृष्यं, ग्राहि, हृद्यं, विबन्धनुत्, रुच्यं, कफवातजित् are target phrases with धर्म - धर्मि-भावः relation tag. According to this tag, the karma (action of drug) properties of nagara can be extracted.
- Example 3: नागरं is source phrase and लघु and स्निग्ध are target phrases with गुण-गुणि-भावः relation tag. According to this tag, the guna (physical quality) properties of nagara can be extracted.
- Example 4: नागरं is source phrase and स्वादुपाकं is target phrase with गुण-गुणि-भावः relation tag. According to this tag, the rasa (taste) properties of nagara can be extracted.
- Example 5: नागरं is source phrase and उष्णं is target phrase with गुण-गुणि-भावः relation tag. According to this tag, the virya (potency) property of nagara can be extracted.

Overall, by using धर्म - धर्मि-भावः, गुण-गुणि-भावः, the rasapanchaka (rasa, guna, virya, vipaaka, karma) of a drug or a dravya is easily extracted from Ayurveda texts or lexicons. Note that though uShNa-tvam, svaadu-tvam, laghu-tvam, diipanam etc. are guNas / properties of Naagara, they are visheshas of different saamaanya categories (or classes), namely, viirya, rasa, guna and karma respectively and need to be connected as such to reconstruct the schema of oshadhis from text.

4.4 ShaastriQL: A Shaastric Query Library for Conceptual Search using SMaps

To facilitate an extensible set of services using SMap, we devised a powerful recursive graph query library in Python and Javascript that yields a subset of the given SMap based on the following filtering criteria.

- A starting segment selector: Select the starting text segments for navigation based on their properties,
- A sequence of one or more hop selectors: Navigate from chosen segments to their neighbors based on the attributes of the linking relation as well as of the target segment reached, ·
- Number of hops to traverse (-1 means unlimited hops), and
- Inclusion criteria: Select which segments and relations to include in the resultant subset of SMap, regardless of which were traversed during query processing.

Result_smap = mySMap.filter(start_node_selector, hop_selectors, nhops, inclusion_criteria)

In ShaastriQL, we aim to support functional chaining paradigm similar to JavaScript, i.e., lazy execution of queries, programmatic iteration over their results and feeding them to subsequent operations to generate sophisticated views of a shaastra text. Towards that end, we support the following primitive operations on an SMap:

SMap.filter(start_nodes=[], hop_selectors[], nhops=-1,inclusion_criteria=None): A generic ShaastriQL query that returns a filtered, iterable SMap object to enable functional chaining. Default parameter values are mentioned in the function signature.

SMap.segments(filter=None): Provide the text segment objects of given SMap as an iterable list.

SMap.relations(filter=None): Provide the relation objects of given SMap as an iterable list.

Using these operators, a variety of canned views can be created on an SMap:

SMap.terms(): Provide a glossary of technical terms / concepts defined in the treatise as iterable list. This involves querying for vaakyas with padaartha tantrayukti. To retrieve the terms being defined, hop_selector can be set to retrieve lakshya-lakshana bhaava relations. The source anchor phrase denotes the term. Figure 10 show the Glossary of term definitions generated in SMap viewer for *Vedaanta saara* text.

SMap.properties(dravya): List properties (guNas) of a dravya mentioned in the treatise. This involves search for *dharma-dharmi bhaava* and *guNa-guNi bhaava* relations where the target anchor phrase is the dravya name. Then traverse the guNa-guNi relations recursively to retrieve its property hierarchy.

SMap.examples(concept): Retrieve examples of a concept mentioned in the treatise. This involves retrieving drshTaaanta-daarShTaantika bhaava relations whose target anchor phrase is the concept name, along with their source segment, which is the example sentence.

SMap.type_hierarchy(term): Recursively enumerate the type-subtype hierarchy of a term. This involves starting with the nirdesha vaakya of given term (enumerating tantrayukti).

SMap.table_of_contents(): Show the section hierarchy of the treatise (chapters, sections, subsections etc.). This involves navigating the avayava avayavi relations recursively starting with the adhikaraNa vaakyas.

SMap.summary(N): Create an N-sentence summary of the treatise. This involves starting with vaakyas tagged as adhikaraNa tantrayukti (i.e., head sentences), and retrieving their neighboring vaakyas until the target of N vaakyas is reached.

SMap.discourse(concept): Retrieve the entire hierarchy of sentences on given topic and its analysis, in depth-first or breadth-first order.

SMap.sahadharmis(dravya): Retrieve dravyas with similar properties to given dravya. This involves the following steps:

- First, we retrieve saamaanya-vishesha siblings of given dravya. To do this, we first retrieve saamaanya-vishesha relations whose target phrase is dravya name and source phrase denotes its class name, followed by segments reachable from the class name by one hop via saamaanya-vishesha relation.
- Then we retrieve all the dharmas / guNas of given dravya via SMap.properties(dravya).
- Finally, we select those siblings of dravya whose guNa set maximally overlaps its guNa set.

5 Implementation Status

We have implemented Shaastra maps as an application on a scalable annotated object store based on MongoDB JSON object database Susarla and Challa (2019). All entities and relations are stored as objects in the object store, and the ShaastriQL graph traversal API is built on MongoDB's query language. We have implemented a web-based SMap editor (Figure 8 provides a screenshot) and an SMap navigation tool (Figure 10 shows a screenshot). We are in the process of integrating SMap network editing UI (for segment and relation tagging) into the SMap editor. Since ShaastraMap functionality has humans in the loop and does not interpret the language of the text directly, its paradigm is applicable not only to shaastra texts but contemporary applications where plain text needs to be converted into knowledge maps for mining. How well the shaastraic paradigms of SMap ecosystem apply to contemporary text mining is an open question worth exploring.

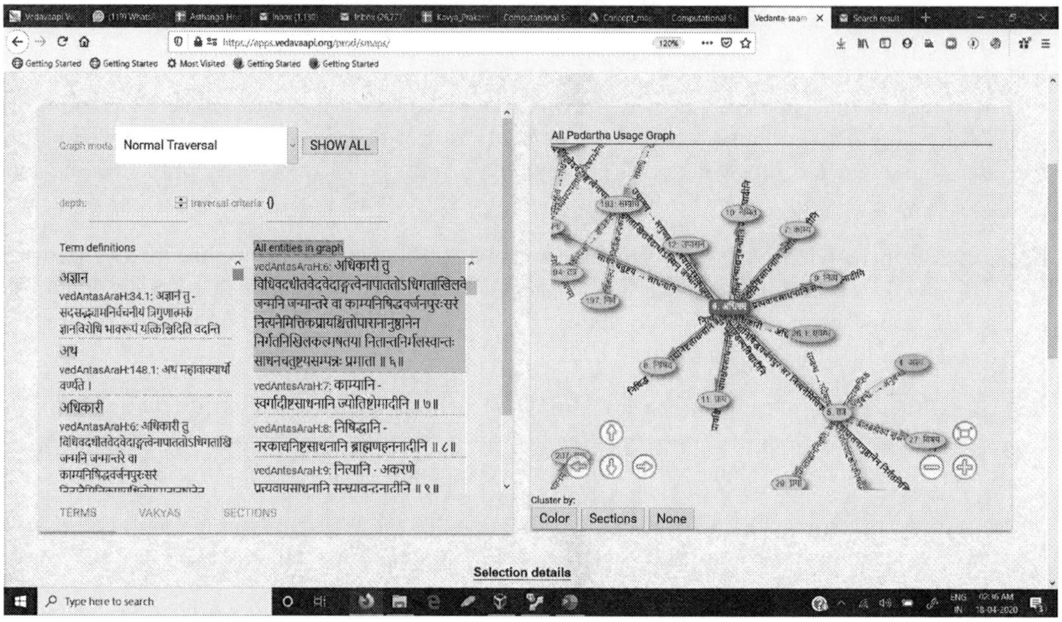

Figure 10: Glossary browsing of *Vedaanta-saara* text in SMap viewer.

ShaastriQL is currently available as a Python API library, and is in use to support the SMap application. We are building a Javascript version and hope to enrich it into a domain-specific functional language with a JavaScript substrate to enable powerful E-reader UI tools for Sanskrit texts.

We have created SMaps of substantial portions of a dozen Sanskrit treatises so far, with a combined size of more than 4000 sentences and 7000 relations. We have designed and delivered a training and certification course on shaastra mapping[2] to 160 Sanskrit scholars across India, and have initiated projects to map 6 major Sanskrit works including Patanjali Mahabhashyam, Yogasutra with Vyaasa bhaashya, Shukraniiti, Artha shaastra, Ashtaanga Hrdayam and a few introductory Jyotisha and Vaastu texts. All the SMap templates and the tools created so far are publicly available at `https://apps.vedavaapi.org/smaps`. For further queries, please contact info@vedavaapi.org.

6 Lessons Learnt and Future Directions

Our experience with Shaastra mapping is that it requires more than academic understanding of Nyaaya and mimaamsa texts. It requires the ability to apply their principles to identify Shaastric knowledge structures in other disciplines. As a result, initial training of traditional scholars to identify Tantrayuktis and sambandhas accurately has been quite tedious and intellectually challenging and forced us to gain nuanced understanding of their semantics. However, we now managed to train more than 160 scholars and have a dozen manually tagged SMaps. A possible avenue of research would be to combine training data with machine-learning for human-assisted annotation of Shaastra map categories in texts. This will greatly accelerate Indic knowledge mining for contemporary utility.

A second avenue is to explore enriching ShaastriQL into a full-blown knowledge processing language and compare its expressive power to prevailing knowledge representation and query paradigms such as Semantic Wikipedia. How well can SMap representation and ShaastriQL support mining of contemporary non-shaastra texts?

[2]https://mitvedicsciences.edu.in/announce/shaastric-modeling/

A third avenue is to explore the synergy of Shaastra mapping with sentence-level and word-level linguistic analysis tools to create an end-to-end knowledge transformation pipeline. Can knowing the tantrayukti of a sentence help resolve the ambiguities that cause hurdles for shaabda-bodha? For instance, can we build custom sentence parsers to automatically extract ontologies from Indic texts based on tantrayukti hints like "enumeration, term-defining sentence" etc.? A fourth avenue is to explore how Mimaamsa nyaayas can be used for effective knowledge mining and robotic intelligence. A fifth avenue is to take knowledge mining towards building deployable Indic models to enrich contemporary knowledge with shaastric insights.

7 Conclusion

In this paper, we presented ShaastraMaps, a knowledge representation and query scheme based on Indic shaastraic paradigm for easy assimilation and machine-processing of Indic scientific texts. While extensive work happened in language processing of Sanskrit at or below sentence level, this paper hints at the feasibility of exploiting Indic knowledge science constructs to enable higher-order meaning processing of Indic knowledge treatises at scale. To exploit this opportunity requires Sanskrit / shaastra scholars and computing professionals to work across boundaries towards application-oriented study of shaastras.

References

Joeran Beel, Bela Gipp, and Jan Olaf Stiller. 2019. Information retrieval on mind maps - what could it be good for? In *5th International Conference on Collaborative Computing (CollaborateCom'09)*, Nov.

Brat. 2016. Brat: Brat Rapid Annotation Tool. http://brat.nlplab.org/.

Pawan Goyal, Gérard Huet, Amba Kulkarni, Peter Scharf, and Ralph Bunker. 2012. A distributed platform for Sanskrit processing. In *24th International Conference on Computational Linguistics (COLING), Mumbai.*

Oilver Hellwig. 2009. Extracting dependency trees from sanskrit texts. *Sanskrit Computational Linguistics 3, LNAI 5406*, pages 106–115.

Ujjwala Jha. 2010. *A Primer of Navya Nyaya Language and Methodology (Navya-Nyaya-Bhasha-Pradipa of MM Mahesha Chandra Nyayaratna) - English Translation.* The Asiatic Society Kolkata.

Amba Kulkarni. 2016. Samsaadhanii: A Sanskrit Computational Toolkit. http://sanskrit.uohyd.ac.in/.

W.K. Lele. 1981. *The Doctrine of the Tantrayuktis.* Chaukhamba Surabharati Prakashan Varanasi.

Bama Srinivasan and Ranjani Parthasarathi. 2011. Mimamsa inspired representation of actions (mira). In *5th International Conference on Artificial Intelligence (IICAI).*

Sai Susarla and Damodar Challa. 2019. Vedavaapi: A platform for community-sourced indic knowledge processing at scale. In *6th International Symposium on Sanskrit Computational Linguistics (ISCLS), IIT Kharagpur.*

Sai Susarla, M.A. Lakshmithathachar, and M.A. Alwar. 2017. Concept maps of indian shaastra texts: Simplifying the study and mining of indic knowledge. In *1st International Conference on New Frontiers in Sanskrit and Indic Knowledge Systems (NFSI), Veliyanad.*

The Vedic corpus as a graph. An updated version of Bloomfield's Vedic Concordance

Oliver Hellwig
Heinrich-Heine-Universität Düsseldorf
Oliver.Hellwig@uni-duesseldorf.de

Sven Sellmer
Heinrich-Heine-Universität Düsseldorf
Adam Mickiewicz University Poznań
sellmer@uni-duesseldorf.de

Kyoko Amano
Kyoto University
amano.skskrt@kcn.jp

Abstract

Bloomfield's *Vedic Concordance* is a valuable resource for understanding the history of Vedic literature, but its structure, which is designed for human readers, prevents its straightforward application in quantitative studies. This paper introduces a new version of the *Vedic Concordance* representing Bloomfield's text in an XML structure that facilitates the programmatic access to this data. We describe the steps necessary for creating the new representation and report about the ongoing extension of the Concordance with late Vedic material. In addition, we present four case studies that illustrate how the new version of the *Vedic Concordance* can be utilized in textual studies.

1 Introduction

The Vedic corpus is thematically largely restricted to a single topic, namely the Vedic sacrifice.[1] While the early metrical Saṃhitās can best be understood as hymns accompanying various sacrifices, the later Vedic prose explains these sacrifices and prescribes how they should be performed. An important trait of these exegetical texts is the frequent citation of mantras from the earlier metrical texts: For a sacrifice to be successful it is crucial to recite the appropriate mantras, which alone guarantee that the sacrifice achieves its purpose (see e.g. Staal (1996) and Patton (2006)). As a consequence, the Vedic literature abounds in mantras quoted in full, in parts and with different degrees of variation. In addition to these citations, the early metrical Saṃhitās share a large number of mantras and pādas that occur with different degrees of variation, a phenomenon that Witzel (1989) explains with a pre-Rigvedic reservoir of "floating mantras".

The importance of mantra citations for reconstructing the history of the Vedic literature has been understood early in Vedic studies, and in 1906 Maurice Bloomfield published the *Vedic Concordance* (VC), a systematic collection of all mantra citations found in the texts edited at that time (Bloomfield, 1906). The VC was re-published in digital form by Marco Franceschini (Franceschini and Bloomfield, 2007), who also extended the inventory of mantras on the basis of several texts published in the meantime. Since its first publication, Bloomfield's Concordance has been used extensively in scholarly research, but only, so to say, on a micro-level: While numerous research papers from the fields of Vedic Studies or Linguistics have based their argumentation on individual entries of the VC, no paper has so far studied what these data as a whole can tell us about the history and structure of the Vedic corpus. Apart from the fact that quantitative methods such as network analysis and graph theory that can provide a global view of Bloomfield's data are rarely applied in this field, there is one very practical reason for this obvious shortcoming: In its present form, the VC is human-, but not machine-understandable. Consider, as an example, line 1,676 of the electronic version of the VC:

```
agne prehi prathamo devayatām (AVŚ. devatānām; MS.KS. devāyatām) #
AVŚ.4.14.5a; AVP.3.38.3a; VS.17.69a; TS.4.6.5.2a; 5.4.7.1; MS.2.10.6a:
```

[1] We use the abbreviations given by Bloomfield when discussing examples from the Vedic Concordance, and those given by Griffiths (2009, 453-456) in all other cases. Citations from the VC are printed in typeface.

Proceedings of the Computational Sanskrit and Digital Humanities, 18th *World Sanskrit Conference 2023*, pages 188–200

`138.4; KS.18.4a; 21.9; ŚB.9.2.3.28. P: agne prehi Vait.8.17; 15.9; Kauś.63.9; 137.27.`

Bloomfield admittedly formatted this entry with maximum brevity in mind, but the reader must replace *devayatām* with *devatānām* for constructing the text of the AVŚ, and with *devāyatām* for constructing that of the MS and KS, as indicated by the content of the round brackets inserted into the mantra text. In addition, the second mantra variant occurs twice in the KS. This must be inferred from the semicolon-separated string `KS.18.4a; 21.9`, which must be resolved into KS 18.4a and KS 21.9. The occurrences of the pratīka `agne prehi` are encoded analogously without giving full citations.

While these steps are mostly not problematic for a human reader (with some important exceptions, on which see Sec. 2.1), this format is clearly not suited for automatic processing, which may explain why Bloomfield's data have not been used for a network analysis of Vedic texts so far. In this paper, we present a new machine-understandable version of the VC and give some initial pointers as to how the transformed data can be used for studying the development of the Vedic corpus.

In Sec. 2, we describe the new storage logic of the VC and the steps required for transforming the current digital version into this new format (2.1, 2.2). We report about ongoing work in expanding the coverage of the VC with texts from the late Vedic period (2.3) and give an overview of basic properties of the co-occurrence graph constructed from the data (2.4). Section 3 presents the results of four case studies that demonstrate which research questions can be addressed when using the new form of the VC and how the data can be visualized. Section 4 summarizes the paper. – The new version of the VC is available for download at `https://github.com/OliverHellwig/sanskrit/tree/master/papers/2023wsc`.

2 Transforming and extending the Vedic Concordance

As the example on page 1 has shown, parsing the VC in the form published by Franceschini and Bloomfield (2007) requires implicit knowledge that is not encoded in its structure. In this section, we describe how such implicit information is transformed into explicit one (Sec. 2.1). In addition, we introduce the new data structure (Sec. 2.2), report on the ongoing extension of the VC (Sec. 2.3) and describe basic properties of the co-occurrence graph (Sec. 2.4). We used standard software and short Python scripts for carrying out the steps described in this section. All transformations described in the following were carried out on the data published electronically by Franceschini and Bloomfield (2007).

2.1 Transforming the data

Each entry of the VC offers information about various facets of a mantra. This section describes these facets and their computational processing. – The strong variability of Vedic mantras is well known in Vedic Studies, and Bloomfield himself was often sceptical which form of a mantra should be accepted as its **basic form** (Bloomfield, 1906, xiv-xv). In the new version, the basic form is the mantra text of Bloomfield's entry, from which all variant information (in round brackets, see below) has been removed. If a mantra occurs in more than one text, its basic form is the one found in the oldest text according to Bloomfield's temporal arrangement of the Vedic literature (Bloomfield, 1906, xvi). This arrangement is certainly correct in most cases, esp. in those involving the RV and other early Saṃhitās, but needs a critical revision given the full graph emerging from the VC. We are currently working on a mathematical formulation of this problem.

Regarding the **citations** of a mantra, we face the challenge that the name of the text is only given once even if a mantra occurs more than one time in a text (see the example on p. 1). We solve this issue by repeatedly applying regular expressions to the original version of the VC. Citations of the form 'VS.8.4d; 33.68d' are, for example, resolved by a regular expression of the form

```
([^0-9 \.]+)\.([0-9]+\.[0-9]+[a-z]*); ([0-9]+\.[0-9]+[a-z]*)([\.;])\b
```

with replacements

```
\1\2; \1.\3
```

This regular expression leaves the first citation 'VS.8.4d' unchanged, but generates 'VS.33.68d' from the part after the semicolon. A few hundred cases that could not be handled using this approach (mostly due to inconsistencies in the encoded data) were resolved manually.

Minor variants of mantras that do not change the alphabetical order of an entry are certainly the most problematic part of the previous version of the VC. Having access to the full form of variants is, however, important for obtaining a clearer picture of the history of the Vedic corpus because they throw light on the processes of textual transmission. As shown in the example on p. 1, such variants are enclosed between round brackets in the main text of a mantra. Contrary to what Bloomfield claims (Bloomfield, 1906, xiv-xv), reconstructing the text of such variants can be challenging even for a human reader without knowledge of Vedic Sanskrit. Consider, for instance, line 70442: `vājajic ca bhava (VSK. caidhi)` ..., where the two strings *ca bhava* must be replaced with one sandhied string *caidhi* (also note that the verb changed from *bhū* to *as*); or line 57802: `mā no agne'va (MG. vi)` where the sandhied preverb *ava* must be replaced with *vi*, resulting in two strings instead of one (*mā no agne vi ...*). We distinguish the following conventions used in the VC (uppercase letters A, B stand for text names):

- ...(A.B x): One or multiple strings to the left of the round bracket are replaced with string(s) x in texts A, B. The encoding does not indicate which strings must be replaced, the surface forms can vary significantly, and sandhi can change the number of strings involved. Manual intervention is required for resolving these cases.
- ...(A.B @x) or ...(A.B x@): A suffix or prefix of a word to the left of the bracket must be replaced with x in texts A, B. The same precautions as in the preceding case apply.
- ...(A.B add x): One or more strings must be inserted in place of the bracket.
- ...(A.B. omit(s) x): String(s) x must be deleted to the left of the round bracket. Note that this encoding is not consistent, even inside a single mantra: ... `devo daivyo (omitted in ApŚ, BaudhŚ., ApŚ, HirŚ)` ... `amuvad amuvat (ŚB. omits amuvad amuvat)` (line 999).

Fuzzy string matching algorithms such as Smith-Waterman could solve many, though not all of these cases, because Bloomfield's notation is not consistent and the scopes of some round brackets are unclear even for a human reader. In order to make the resource as accurate as possible, we therefore decided to manually process a csv file created in the following way:

- We extract the text names from the round brackets and add one line for each text name to the csv file.
- If the replacement x is a single string and if the string preceding the bracket does not contain a visarga, we replace the string to the left of the bracket with x for all texts mentioned in the bracket. The resulting string is written into the respective line of the csv file.
- In all other cases, the content of the round bracket without the text names is copied verbatim in the respective line of the csv file.

One author of this paper manually corrected the resulting csv file, paying special attention to the correct resolution of the variant information.

Apart from these minor variants, the VC features **cross-references** between "variants involving more than one alphabetic entry", which are introduced using the keywords 'See' and 'See under' (see Bloomfield (1906, xv) for details). Finding the targets of such cross-references poses similar problems as the resolution of minor variants because active knowledge of Vedic is again required in many cases. We generate another csv file that contains such cross-references and manually resolve cases in which a unique target line could not be determined automatically. While the original VC contains, for example, the entry `aṃhārir asi bambhāriḥ # ŚŚ.6.12.20. See aṅghārir`, making it necessary that the reader looks up a mantra starting with the word *aṅghārir*, the new XML version maps `See aṅghārir` to the correct line *aṅghārir asi bambhāriḥ* (line 2305).

The VC also features **pratīkas**, i.e. abbreviated citations of a mantra used preferably when an author cites from a Saṃhitā of his own school (Renou, 1947, 26-68). One of the nearly 8,000 pratīkas in the VC is found in line 79,937 where the mantra *saṃ te payāṃsi sam u yantu vājāḥ* (RV 1.91.18a) is abbreviated as *saṃ te payāṃsi* in ŚāṅkhŚS 1.15.4. Pratīkas are introduced with P in the VC and followed by a list of their occurrences which is structured in the same way as that of standard occurrences (see above). After resolving citation information in the same way as for the basic form, pratīkas are extracted automatically using regular expressions.

The (digital version of the) VC contains further pieces of information such as cross-references introduced by 'Cf.' (loose parallels), variae lectiones and occasional pointers into the secondary literature. This supplementary information, which is not central for understanding the structure of the Vedic corpus, has not been included in the present updated version of the VC, but could easily be integrated in future releases of the resource.

2.2 The new storage format

The transformations described in the preceding section modify the original plain text file of the VC (citations) or generate new files (variants). We now need to merge these data into a format that is platform independent and easily processed by a wide range of programming languages. Each entry in the VC can be thought of as a hierarchical structure combining global information (e.g. the original line, the text of the mantra) with a varying number of occurrences in the Vedic corpus, of variants and of cross-references to other lines of the VC. Due to this hierarchical structure, XML recommends itself as storage format, but other structured representations such as JSON would be equally feasible. Using standard libraries of popular programming languages, transforming the XML representation into other formats poses no difficulties.

The following list gives an overview of the new structure and its elements whose names are printed in bold. Indentation indicates hierarchy levels in the resulting XML file, data types are printed in italics, asterisks (*) mark optional elements, and the names of XML attributes start with @:

original-text [*string*] The original line as given in Franceschini and Bloomfield (2007)

number [*integer*] The line number in the text file published by Franceschini and Bloomfield (2007)

mantra [*string*] The basic form of a mantra (see p. 2 of this paper).

citations [*list*] The list of citations, each of which has the following data members:

- **@type** : 'default' (i.e. identical with the basic form), 'variant', 'pratika'
- **@source** This attribute distinguishes between entries found in Franceschini and Bloomfield (2007) and new occurrences added by authors of this paper: 'F(ranceschini)', 'HS' (Hellwig, Sellmer).
- **text** [*string*] The source text that contains the citation
- **chapter** [*string*] Where the mantra is found in the text. For 'AŚ.2.16.19a', for example, `text` is set to 'AŚ' and `chapter` to '2.16.19a'.
- ***string** [*string*] If the occurrence is a variant or a pratīka, this member gives its full text.

***see** [*list*] The list of mantra variants that change the alphabetic order.

- **targetNumber** [*integer*] The line number of the cross-referenced entry.
- **@type** [*string*] 'child' (introduced with 'See under' in Bloomfield (1906) or the second entry of a binary cross-reference), 'parent'

2.3 Extending the Vedic Concordance

We are extending the VC with material from late Vedic texts. We started with the mantras in the BhārŚS for which we performed the following steps:

- From a digital version of BhārŚS 1-12 that encloses mantra citations in pointed brackets[2] we extracted all strings marked as mantras.

[2] Many thanks to Francois Voegeli for providing this text.

Mantras	87,885
Occurrences	212,908
Mantras with more than one occurrence	38,606
Pratīkas	10,762
Minor variants	15,398
Cross-references	6,718

Table 1: Composition of the Vedic Concordance

- We searched the strings thus obtained in our version of the VC using the Levenshtein algorithm for string comparison. If the mantra in the BhārŚS is identical with the basic form of a mantra contained in the VC, its occurrence was added automatically to the VC. All other mantras and their context were written in a csv file.
- Two authors of this paper revised the entries in the resulting csv file, labelling each one either as a variant or a pratīka of an existing mantra, or adding a new mantra to the VC. As in the case of variant resolution (see above), this manual approach was chosen to create a resource as accurate as possible, and extensions using machine learning methods are easily conceivable.

In the same way we added the citations found in the complete BaudhŚS, which increased the number of occurrences by more than 4%.

In order to facilitate the manual revision, we designed a lean user interface based on PHP and XPath that can be used for querying and extending the XML version of the VC. Here the user can search for mantras either in their basic forms, in variants or in both. The retrieved mantras are presented as a list, each entry being formatted with a hyperlink for editing the information associated with it. By clicking on such a link a dialog window is opened in which the type and text of a mantra can be changed manually. This interface can be extended in multiple ways, e.g. by implementing fuzzy string search or searching for further types of information. The source of this UI is published along with the XML version of the VC so that such changes can be implemented by interested users.

2.4 Properties of the VC and its citation graph

Table 1 gives the frequencies of some important elements of the updated VC. The mere size of almost 88,000 entries is impressive, especially when we keep in mind that Bloomfield collected this material without the help of a computer, a fact also emphasized by Jamison (2010). However, only 37,877 from among these entries occur more than once in the extant Vedic canon. The number of entries would also be reduced considerably if full text lines would be considered instead of pādas, as was done by Bloomfield. Updating the VC with such text-line information should not be too challenging because occurrences of pādas are terminated with lowercase letters (e.g. `1.36.17c`).

The order in which Bloomfield recorded the occurrences of a mantra reflects how he understood the chronology of the Vedic corpus, the first occurrence given usually indicating the source of the mantra in Bloomfield's opinion. While it is possible to create a directed graph based on this arrangement, the actual transmission history of individual mantras is far less certain than suggested by these arrangements. For a substantial number of mantras, Bloomfield's ordering is nothing more than an educated guess.[3] To better understand the structure of the VC, we therefore construct an undirected co-occurrence graph. Instead of dividing the texts into citing and cited ones, all texts in which a given mantra appears are indiscriminately connected to each other by this co-occurrence. Let us now have a look at some basic properties of the resulting undirected graph, some of which are expected, others perhaps less so. The graph consists of 121

[3]See e.g. line 22,368 of the VC which records a mantra that is shared by three Gṛhysūtras with unclear chronological relationship: `ūrjaṃ prajām amṛtaṃ dīrgham āyuḥ (AG. amṛtaṃ pinvamānaḥ) # AG.2.4.14c; PG.3.3.6c; MG.2.8.6c..`

Text 1	Text 2	Weight
MS	KS	6058
TS	MS	4986
VS	MS	4898
TS	KS	4775
RV	AVŚ	4678

(a) Highest edge weights (i.e. numbers of mantras shared by two texts) in the undirected co-occurrence graph built from the new version of the VC

Text	Betweenness
AVŚ	385
RV	302.3
TA	235.9
VS	213
GDh	153.9
GB	139.3
MahānU	134.5
ŚvetU	117.4
ApŚ	108.5
MŚ	108.3

(b) Highest betweenness centrality values

Table 2: Graph-theoretical properties of the VC network

vertices that represent the texts included in the VC and 3270 edges that can represent any of the possible connections discussed in Sec. 2.1 (exact citation, variant, or pratīka). The weights of the edges in this graph, i.e. the number of co-occurrences linking two given texts, vary strongly. The four highest values are assigned to edges between Saṃhitās of the Black and White Yajurveda, the fifth to the edge linking the RV and the AVŚ (see Table 2a). Notably the *Ṛgveda-Saṃhitā* is only part of the fifth pair, which shows that it does not have the same privileged position in an undirected graph as it would in a directed one. The edge weight distribution is heavily left-skewed, so that there is a very high number of low-weight edges (as many as 2856 with a weight < 100). This fact is largely due to the small size of many of the texts involved, e.g. most Upaniṣads. In order to nevertheless save the information contained in these weight attributions, which tends to be marginalized by the highest few percent, we employ the natural logarithm of the weight values for tasks such as community detection. In this way, the skew is sufficiently minimized, so as to allow finer structures to emerge.

The most basic property of the vertices is their degree, i.e., the number of edges they possess. Because the VC graph is undirected, among the ten vertices with the highest degrees (between 100 [RV and VS] and 94 [AVŚ]) there are both texts that are predominantly, or even exclusively—as is the case of the RV—*cited*, and such, typically long and younger ones, that contain many citations taken from other texts. To the first category belong RV, VS, MS, TS, KS, and AVŚ, to the latter one ApŚS, MŚS, ŚB, and BaudhŚS. A more sophisticated measure of the importance of a vertex is obtained by applying the PageRank algorithm (Brin and Page, 1998), which considers the degree of a given vertex as well as those of its neighbors, so that it more adequately shows the real influence of a vertex in a graph. Although a high degree does not necessarily correspond to a high PageRank count, in our case the top ten texts according to both measures are in fact almost identical. Notably the AVŚ takes second place just after the RV according to PageRank, whereas in the degree ranking it comes only at position no. 9, which can be attributed to the large number of mantras linking it to the first-placed RV.

Another interesting measure of centrality is the so-called betweenness (Freeman, 1977), for which the number of edges of a vertex is not decisive. Instead, betweenness favors vertices that lie on the shortest path between many other vertices, that is, in functional terms, vertices that act as a kind of bridge between different communities in a network. The texts with the ten highest betweenness centrality values in the unweighted graph are given in Table 2b. Here, the two oldest texts of the Vedic corpus, the Saṃhitās of the RV and AV, occupy the top two positions. Such a result could be expected because RV and AVŚ are cited by numerous other texts from different traditions and thereby constitute a link between them. More remarkable is the quite high betweenness value of a very late (and rather short) text like the *Śvetāśvatara-Upaniṣad.*[4] It can be explained by the syncretic character of this Upaniṣad, which becomes apparent in the wide range of sources on which it draws.

3 Research problems and applications

3.1 Pratīkas

In order to convey an idea of which questions can be addressed with the new format of the VC, let us assess a hypothesis about the usage of mantras in Vedic texts that was brought forward by Gonda (1977, 505-506). Gonda claims that younger Sūtra texts preferably cite mantras as pratīkas, although exceptions to this rule are widely found in Vedic literature. Such a claim can be tested by making use of the new structure of the VC. We extract mantra citations found in all Śrautasūtra texts contained in the VC and record if each mantra is cited in full or as a pratīka.[5] We order the resulting list of texts by increasing pratīka ratios, i.e. by the proportion $\frac{\#\text{pratīka}}{\#\text{full}+\#\text{pratīka}}$ per text. Next, we perform pairwise G-tests (Agresti, 2007) that compare the counts of full and pratīka citations in texts i and $j : j > i$. If such a test gets significant at a level of 0.01 (1%), we consider the pratīka ratio of i as significantly lower than that of j and derive a pairwise ordering $i < j$ from the test result. These partial orderings are used to construct a directed acyclic graph (DAG) whose acyclicity results from the fact that the texts were initially ordered by increasing pratīka ratios and from $j > i$. A topological ordering of the nodes of this DAG produces the following arrangement of Śrautasūtras where a colored box around multiple texts indicates that the G-test did not become significant and that therefore no partial ordering could be induced for the respective group:

BhārŚ < [BaudhŚ HirŚ ApŚ] < MŚ < AŚ < [Vait ŚŚ LŚ KŚ]

This arrangement agrees in parts with the temporal order considered probable by Gonda (1977, 482-483), who claims that BaudhŚS < BhārŚS < ĀpŚS < HirŚS, that KātyŚS and ĀśvŚS are not among the oldest texts, and that the ŚāṅkhŚS is from about the same time as the ĀśvŚS. The graph-based evaluation of pratīka citations thus provides another piece of evidence that helps to understand the history of the late Vedic literature.

3.2 The Random Kavi model

In the second case study we throw a look on what the graph structure of the VC can tell us about the relationship between the early Saṃhitā texts. Witzel (1989, §4.3.2-3) brought up the idea that the Saṃhitās drew their texts from a repository of "floating mantras". In an admittedly over-simplistic setting, such a process can be approximated using a probabilistic urn model without replacement. We think of the whole VC as one huge urn containing $N = 87,885$ mantras (see Tab. 1) from which one Kavi randomly draws mantras for composing his text A;[6] just to repeat, this is an over-simplification. After this Kavi has drawn his $|A|$ mantras, all mantras are placed back in the urn, and the second Kavi draws $|B|$ mantras for his text B. The probability that two sets A, B drawn in this way have k elements in common follows a hypergeometric distribution that can be derived from the Venn diagram in Fig. 1a:

$$p(A, B, k, N) = \frac{\binom{|A|}{k} \cdot \binom{N-|A|}{|B|-k}}{\binom{N}{|B|}} \tag{1}$$

The probability of drawing text B in its transmitted form is the inverse of the binomial coefficient $\binom{N}{|B|}$. Taking the composition of A as given, there are $\binom{|A|}{k}$ ways to choose a subset of k mantras from its $|A|$ mantras. The second term in the numerator of eq. 1 gives the number of choices

[4] The equally late *Mahānārāyaṇa-Upaniṣad* is a special case as it largely is identical with TĀ 10.

[5] Note that variants are counted as full citations and that we only consider citations from texts of the same school.

[6] The term mantra is used somehow sloppily here as most entries of the VC are actually pādas.

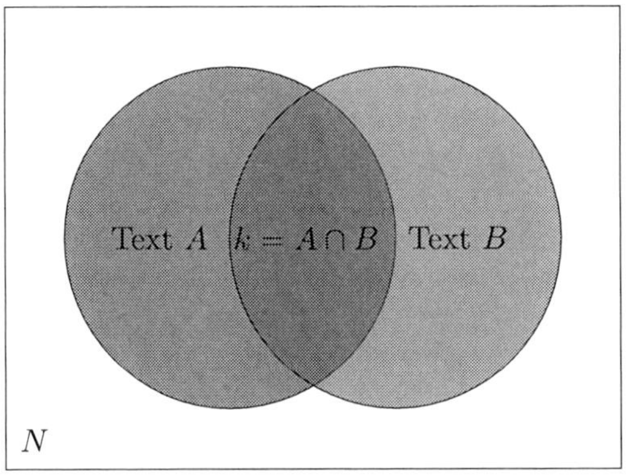

(a) Venn diagram for the Random Kavi model

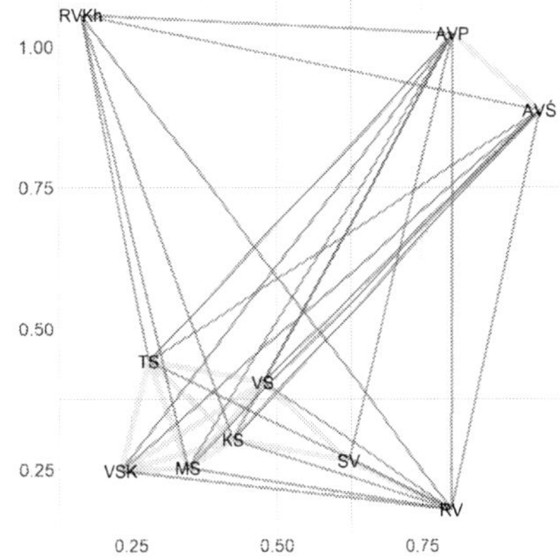

(b) Results of the Random Kavi model for the Saṃhitās. Green: right tail; red: left tail. The distance between a pair of texts is approximately proportional to $1 - p(x \geq k)$.

Figure 1: The Random Kavi model: Venn diagram and results for the Saṃhitās

the second Kavi has after the first one has chosen his $|A|$ mantras: Kavi number two can choose from among $N - |A|$ mantras, and he chooses only $|B| - k$ mantras, because the intersection k is already contained in text A. The distribution in eq. 1 has one free parameter, which is the size of the intersection k. To obtain a proper probability distribution we form the sum of eq. 1 for all sizes of intersections $0 \leq x \leq \min(|A|, |B|)$ (the intersection k can maximally have the size of the shorter of the two texts) and divide eq. 1 by this sum. The probability of obtaining an intersection equal to or larger than k is $p(x \geq k) = \sum_{x=k}^{\min(|A|,|B|)} p(A, B, x, N)$. If this probability is less than 0.001,[7] we assume that the involved texts A, B share many more mantras than could be expected under the Random Kavi model and that they are therefore closely related to each other. Inversely, if $p(x < k) = \sum_{x=0}^{k-1} p(A, B, x, N)$ is less than 0.001, we assume that texts A, B share much less mantras than could be expected under the hypergeometric model.

Figure 1b visualizes the resulting probabilities for the early Saṃhitā texts, indicating the right tails by green lines (size k is larger than expected) and the left tails by red ones. The most obvious feature of this figure is the close connection between the texts of the Yajurvedic schools the texts of which share much more material than expected under the Random Kavi model. Such a result is not surprising given the close connections between these texts in terms of their internal structure, content and ritual application. The SV is loosely connected to this cluster and forms the only strong connection with the RV – again, this result is not surprising when one considers the nature and school association of these two texts. The two recensions of the AV are strongly associated with each other, but do not share strong connections with any of the other Saṃhitās. This special position reflects the status of the AV in comparison to the three other Vedic schools (on which see e.g. Gonda (1975, 267-270)). In our opinion, Fig. 1b thus highlights the fact that the Vedic schools separated early in the history of Vedic literature and that the Atharvaveda Saṃhitās occupy a special position in the early history of the Vedic corpus although they share a substantial amount of mantras with other early texts.

[7] We choose a very small threshold of 0.1% to obtain conservative results.

3.3 Citations from the RV

Citations of RVic mantras occur throughout the Vedic literature, and the importance of the RV as a source of mantras has been emphasized repeatedly in previous research; see e.g. Gonda (1975, 368-370) on the use of RVic mantras in the Brāhmaṇas. It is known that different schools cite from different parts of the RV as, for instance, the Sāmaveda preferably uses material from the Soma hymns in RV 9 (see the large rectangle in the first row of Fig. 2a). Such school-specific preferences interact with text-specific ones which may arise from the topic of a text or the preferences of its author(s). Given that a single text may cite hundreds or even thousands of RVic mantras, distinguishing between text- and school-specific preferences is tedious and time consuming when done in a traditional philological way. We therefore propose a latent variable admixture model that disentangles text- and school-specific contributions to the 60,675 citations of RVic passages found in the VC.[8]

The design of this model is inspired by Latent Dirichlet Allocation (Blei et al., 2003). It considers each citation from one of the ten books of the RV as an atomic feature whose presence is due either to citation habits of the school of a text or to special preferences of the text itself. More formally, there are N mantra citations m_i from the ten books of the RV, $m_i \in \{1, 2, \ldots, 10\}$. For each observed data point m_i we have the citing text $t_i \in T$ and its school $s_i \in \{\mathrm{RV}, \mathrm{YV}, \mathrm{SV}, \mathrm{AV}\}$. Each text t is associated with a text-specific Bernoulli distribution $\mathrm{Bern}(\mu_t)$. The latent variable z_i is drawn from the text-specific Bernoulli distribution $\mathrm{Bern}(\mu_{t_i})$. If $z_i = 1$, the observed RVic book is drawn from a text-specific multinomial distribution $\mathrm{Cat}(\boldsymbol{\Theta}_{t_i})$, $\boldsymbol{\Theta}_t \in \mathbb{R}^{10}$; if $z_i = 0$, the RVic book is drawn from a school-specific multinomial with parameters $\boldsymbol{\Phi}_{s_i} \in \mathbb{R}^{10}$. Using a beta prior with uniform hyperparameters $\boldsymbol{\alpha}$ for the Bernoulli distributions and Dirichlet priors with flat hyperparameters $\boldsymbol{\beta}$ for the text- and school-specific multinomials, we obtain the following joint distribution of this model:

$$p(\mathbf{m}, \mathbf{z}, \boldsymbol{\mu}, \boldsymbol{\Theta}, \boldsymbol{\Phi} | \mathbf{t}, \mathbf{s}, \boldsymbol{\alpha}, \boldsymbol{\beta}) = \prod_{t \in T} \mathrm{Beta}(\mu_t | \boldsymbol{\alpha}) \cdot \prod_{t \in T} \mathrm{Dir}(\boldsymbol{\Theta}_t | \boldsymbol{\beta}) \cdot \prod_{s \in S} \mathrm{Dir}(\boldsymbol{\Phi}_s | \boldsymbol{\beta}) \cdot \prod_{i}^{n} \Big[\mathrm{Bern}(z_i | \mu_{t_i}) \cdot (z_i \cdot \mathrm{Cat}(m_i | \boldsymbol{\Theta}_{t_i}) + (1 - z_i) \mathrm{Cat}(m_i | \boldsymbol{\Phi}_{s_i})) \Big] \quad (2)$$

With $\mathbb{I}[.]$ denoting the Dirac delta function, let $a_{t1} = \sum_j^N \mathbb{I}[t_j = t, z_j = 1]$ (number of cases in which a citation in text t_i is labelled as text-specific), $a_{t0} = \sum_j^N \mathbb{I}[t_j = t] - a_{t1}$, $b_{tm} = \sum_j^N \mathbb{I}[t_i = t, z_i = 1, m_i = m]$ (number of cases in which a citation of the RVic book m_i is labelled as text-specific in text t_i), $c_{tm} = \sum_j^N \mathbb{I}[t_i = t, z_i = 0, m_i = m]$, and a_{t1}^{-i} denote the value of a_{t1} excluding the current data point i. Using this notation, we can derive the following collapsed Gibbs sampler:

$$p(z_i = k | \mathbf{z}^{-i}, \mathbf{m}^{-i}, \mathbf{t}^{-i}, \mathbf{s}^{-i}, \boldsymbol{\alpha}, \boldsymbol{\beta}) \propto \begin{cases} (a_{t1}^{-i} + \alpha) \cdot \frac{b_{t_i m_i}^{-i} + \beta}{\sum_u^{10} b_{t_i u}^{-i} + \beta} & \text{if } z_i = 1 \\ (a_{t0}^{-i} + \alpha) \cdot \frac{c_{t_i m_i}^{-i} + \beta}{\sum_u^{10} c_{t_i u}^{-i} + \beta} & \text{if } z_i = 0 \end{cases} \quad (3)$$

The sampler from Eq. 3 is run for 30,000 epochs. After a burn-in period of 10,000 epochs we record the state of the hidden variables $\mathbf{z}$ after each 1,000th epoch in order to obtain uncorrelated samples. We use the sampled values of $\mathbf{z}$ for calculating posterior estimates of the variational parameters $\boldsymbol{\Theta}, \boldsymbol{\Phi}$. The values of the hyperparameters often exert a strong influence on the result. We therefore search for good values of $\boldsymbol{\alpha}, \boldsymbol{\beta}$ using posterior predictive checks (Mimno et al., 2015). For a given pair α, β, we run the sampler as described above, calculate the posterior estimates of $\boldsymbol{\Theta}, \boldsymbol{\Phi}$, and randomly draw $N = 60,675$ samples from the model described in Eq. 2. We obtain a probability distribution q over the ten books of the RV by normalizing the counts

[8]This number of citations does not contradict the number of 38,606 mantras with more than one occurrence reported in Tab. 1 because individual RVic mantras are often multiply cited in more than one text.

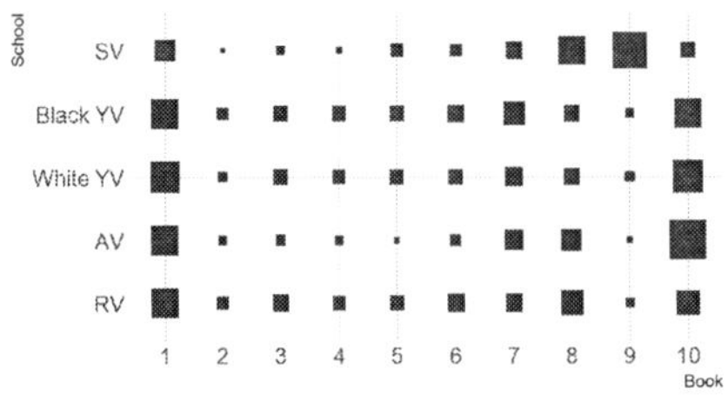

(a) Proportional frequencies of citations from the ten books of the RV (x-axis) in the five Vedic schools (y-axis).

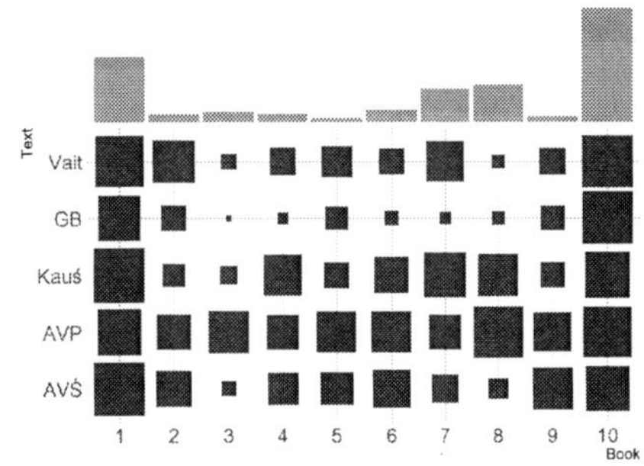

(b) Proportions of RVic citations (x-axis) labelled as school-specific in major Atharvavedic texts (y-axis). The smallest square represents 2.2% and the largest one 91.7%. The stacked bar plots on top visualize the marginal proportions with which each RVic book is cited (blue: school-, red: text-specific).

Figure 2: Citations from the RV in the Vedic literature. Left: Observed values. Right: Results of the admixture model defined in eq. 2 for the Atharvanic texts in the VC.

in the sample, and compare q with the observed global distribution p using the Kullback-Leibler (KL) divergence. When increasing the values of α, β in exponential steps in a grid search, the lowest values of $\text{KL}(p, q)$ (i.e. the best generative results) are obtained for $\alpha = 1, \beta = 10$.

Figure 2b shows the model output for major Atharvanic texts when the optimal hyperparameter values are applied. The x-axis of the plot lists the ten RVic books, and its y-axis shows texts from the AV tradition that use mantras from the RV. The squares in the main plotting area visualize the proportions of data points m_i that are labelled as school-specific for each combination of citing text t and cited RVic book m, the edge lengths of the squares being proportional to $\frac{c_{sm}+\alpha}{b_{tm}+c_{sm}+2\alpha}$. These proportions are in general highest for the first and the tenth books of the RV, this means those RVic books that contain most of the material considered as Atharvanic (see e.g. Arnold (1897); Bloomfield (1899b, 45ff.); Gonda (1975, 28)). Contrary to that, the model tends to explain citations from RV 2-9 by text-specific citation preferences. Such preferences can, for instance, be observed for mantras from RV 8 cited in the AVŚ (see the respective tiny rectangle in the bottom row of Fig. 2b), but they are most obvious for the *Gopathabrāhmaṇa* (GB) which displays a very peculiar style of citing from the RV. This may be another indication of the late date and syncretistic character of this text (see e.g. Bloomfield (1899a, 101-104)) whose author(s) may have had access to the fully canonized version of the RV.

3.4 Rituals and internal structure in the MS

As the fourth case study we present a web-based interface that visualizes mantra co-occurrences in the Vedic corpus. This visualization system which is accessible at `http://34.146.175.179/` is implemented using standard web technologies (HTML, CSS, Javascript) and D3.js. Data are obtained from a relational SQLite database which currently contains mantra occurrences in nineteen Vedic texts, as recorded in the VC. As an example of what can be achieved with such a system, let us have a look at the *Maitrāyaṇī-Saṃhitā* (MS), a foundational text of the Black Yajurveda. The MS groups rituals in dedicated chapters, and each chapter shows its own peculiarities of language and style (Amano, 2020). This state of affairs probably is due to the fact that the development of the rituals and the composition of the respective chapters took place in chronologically and culturally different circumstances.

To see how mantra co-occurrences can help us to understand these processes and especially

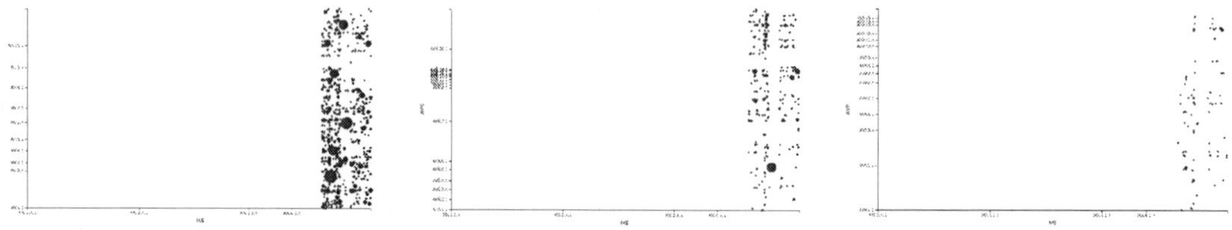

(a) RV (b) AVŚ (c) AVP

Figure 3: The mantra citations from RV, AVŚ, and AVP (y-axes) in the MS (x-axis) *yājyānuvākyā* chapter

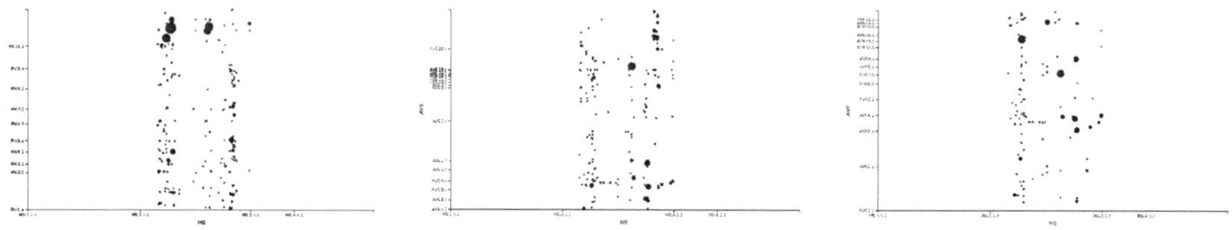

(a) RV (b) AVŚ (c) AVP

Figure 4: The mantra citations from RV, AVŚ, and AVP in the MS *agniciti* chapter; see Fig. 3

the relationship between the MS and the early metrical Saṃhitās (RV, AVŚ, AVP), we focus on two rituals:

1. The *agniciti* (MS 2.7–13) is the ritual of building a huge fire altar. This ritual is extended by numerous, partly esoteric ritual components. As a whole, it has probably been composed in the middle period of the MS editing process.
2. The *yājyānuvākyā* (MS 4.10–14) collects hymns recited by the *hotṛ* priest. This part of the MS has probably been composed in the late period of MS editing.

Figures 3 and 4 show visualizations generated with the web interface. One text is shown along the vertical axis and the other along the horizontal axis, and the corresponding frequencies of co-occurring mantras are displayed as a scatter plot, with sizes of points being proportional to the number of co-occurring mantras. Figure 3 shows where the mantras found in the *yājyānuvākyā* chapters of MS co-occur in RV, AVŚ, and AVP. The plots show that the MS incorporates many mantras from the RV, fewer from the AVŚ, and even fewer from the AVP. Figure 4 shows the co-occurrence frequencies of mantras from RV, AVŚ and AVP in the *agniciti* chapters of MS. From this plot it becomes apparent that the sources of such mantras are much more balanced than in the case of the – presumably late – *yājyānuvākyā* (see Fig. 3) because mantras from all three Saṃhitās are taken over to almost the same extent, thereby increasing the relative importance of the Atharvaveda material. A recent paper dealing with the influence of the Atharvaveda on rituals of the MS also emphasizes the significant impact that the Atharvaveda exerts on the *agniciti* ritual and that is visible in Fig. 4 (Amano, 2022). A detailed comparison of the RV-MS relationship in the *yājyānuvākyā* (Fig. 3) and the *agniciti* (Fig. 4) also shows that the *yājyānuvākyā* chapters contain many quotations from RV 1–8, whereas the influence of RV 10 is prominent in the *agniciti* chapters; note that a similar general preference for using material from RV 10 also becomes apparent in Fig. 2, where the late Gopatha-Brāhmaṇa (GB) draws freely from all parts of the RV. Considering the different sources of the mantras in each chapter of the MS thus yields insights into the history of the formation of the MS. At the same time such an approach is also helpful in understanding the processes involved in the formation and dissemination of the old metrical Saṃhitās.

4 Summary

In this paper, we have described an updated and extended version of Bloomfield's *Vedic Concordance* which was transformed from a weakly structured text-based format into strict XML. This new storage format makes it possible to explore Bloomfield's data from the perspective of graph and network theory and thereby gain insights into the structure and development of the Vedic corpus. We presented three case studies of this kind in Sec. 3 that are primarily meant to demonstrate how to utilize the resource and thus to stimulate network-based studies of the Vedic canon. In addition, this chapter also demonstrates how to visualize Bloomfield's data dynamically in an easily accessible user interface that can serve as a starting point for in-depth textual studies of post-Rigvedic Sanskrit. While we have mainly considered plain co-occurrence information in this paper, possible research applications multiply when additional aspects of the VC are taken into account. Future research could, for example, study what the types of the links (citations, variants, pratīkas) reveal about the relationship between Vedic texts and schools; or it could try to infer the direction of the edges in the graph which could provide a clearer picture of how the Vedic corpus has evolved over time.

Acknowledgments

Oliver Hellwig and Sven Sellmer were funded by the German Federal Ministry of Education and Research, FKZ 01UG2121, when doing research for this paper. Kyoko Amano was funded by JSPS KAKENHI Grant Number 21KK0004.

References

Alan Agresti. 2007. *An Introduction to Categorical Data Analysis.* John Wiley and Sons, Hoboken, New Jersey.

Kyoko Amano. 2020. What is 'knowledge' justifying a ritual action? Uses of yá evám̥ véda / yá evám̥ vidvā́n in the Maitrāyaṇī Saṃhitā. In Céline Redard, editor, *Aux sources des liturgies indo-iraniennes, Collection Religions, Comparatisme - Histoire - Anthropologie*, pages 39–68. Presses Universitaire de Liège, Liège.

Kyoko Amano. 2022. Influence of the Atharvaveda on rituals in the Maitrāyaṇī Saṃhitā. In *The Atharvaveda and its South Asian Contexts: 3rd Zurich International Conference on Indian Literature and Philosophy (ZICILP).*

Edward V. Arnold. 1897. Sketch of the historical grammar of the Rig and Atharva Vedas. *Journal of the American Oriental Society*, 18:203–353.

David M. Blei, Andrew Y. Ng, and Michael I. Jordan. 2003. Latent Dirichlet Allocation. *Journal of Machine Learning Research*, 3:993–1022.

Maurice Bloomfield. 1899a. *The Atharva-Veda and the Gopatha-Brāhmaṇa.* Trübner, Strassburg.

Maurice Bloomfield. 1899b. *The Atharvaveda.* Verlag von Karl J. Trübner, Strassburg.

Maurice Bloomfield. 1906. *A Vedic concordance, being an alphabetic index to every line of every stanza of the published Vedic literature and to the liturgical formulas thereof, that is, an index to the Vedic mantras, together with an account of their variations in the different Vedic books.* Harvard University Press, Cambridge, Mass.

Sergey Brin and Larry Page. 1998. The anatomy of a large-scale hypertextual web search engine. In *Proceedings of the 7th World-Wide Web Conference, Brisbane, Australia, April 1998.*

Marco Franceschini and Maurice Bloomfield. 2007. *An updated Vedic concordance: Maurice Bloomfield's A Vedic Concordance enhanced with new material taken from seven Vedic texts.* Harvard University Press, Cambridge, Mass.

Linton C Freeman. 1977. A set of measures of centrality based on betweenness. *Sociometry*, pages 35–41.

Jan Gonda. 1975. *Vedic Literature (Saṃhitās and Brāhmaṇas).* Otto Harrassowitz, Wiesbaden.

Jan Gonda. 1977. *The Ritual Sūtras.* Otto Harrassowitz, Wiesbaden.

Arlo Griffiths. 2009. *The Paippalādasaṃhitā of the Atharvaveda. Kāṇḍas 6 and 7. A New Edition with Translation and Commentary.* Egbert Forsten, Groningen.

Stephanie W. Jamison. 2010. Review of: Marco Franceschini: An Updated Vedic Concordance: Maurice Bloomfield's A Vedic Concordance Enhanced with New Material Taken from Seven Vedic Texts. *Indo-Iranian Journal*, 53(1):35–36.

David Mimno, David M. Blei, and Barbara E. Engelhardt. 2015. Posterior predictive checks to quantify lack-of-fit in admixture models of latent population structure. *Proceedings of the National Academy of Sciences*, 112(26):E3441–E3450.

Laurie L. Patton. 2006. *Bringing the Gods to Mind: Mantra and Ritual in Early Indian Sacrifice.* University of California Press, Berkeley.

Louis Renou. 1947. *Les Écoles Védiques et la Formation du Veda.* Imprimerie Nationale, Paris.

Frits Staal. 1996. *Ritual and Mantras. Rules without meaning.* Motilal Banarsidass Publishers, Delhi.

Michael Witzel. 1989. Tracing the Vedic dialects. In Colette Caillat, editor, *Dialectes dans les littératures indoaryennes*, pages 97–265. Collège de France, Paris.

The transmission of the Buddha's teachings in the digital age

Sumachaya Harnsukworapanich and Phatchareporn Supphipat
Dhammachai Institute

Abstract

The objective of this paper is to report on and delineate the creation of an online version of the Dhammachai Tipiṭaka Edition, named D-Tipitaka, which has been in development since 2012 by the Dhammachai Tipiṭaka Project (DTP), Thailand. D-Tipitaka is a web page giving access to a series of Pāli texts from the Dhammachai Tipiṭaka Edition(De). It also provides an easy access to manuscript images and other relevant evidence by clicking key words. From over 10,000 digitized Pāli Tipiṭaka manuscripts from Sinhalese, Burmese, Khom, and Tham traditions, the D-Tipitaka displays digital images of 21 sets, totaling approximately 5,000 folios, of selected manuscripts utilized in the creation of the first volume in the series. Their readings were transcribed into Roman script to produce a digital text database which has been emended by researchers. With the help of a state-of-the-art text alignment and editing program, the text has been examined, and critically edited using the academic methods of modern philology. Finally, the edited text and their respective manuscript images are shown on the D-Tipitaka online version. Thus, this developed tool will serve as an alternative and convenient platform to consult Buddhist teachings along with the primary source.

1 Introduction

Buddhist tradition holds that after the Buddha's time, devoted disciples preserved and transmitted the Dhamma originally by means of oral recitation. This made it possible for the authentic and authoritative teachings of the Buddha to be accurately handed down word for word in its original state. After the Buddha attained Nirvana, this form of oral transmission continued to be used in the first three Buddhist Councils. Until approximately 400 B.E., the method of writing was introduced in the Fourth Buddhist Council where canonical text divided into three parts known as Tipiṭaka was written down on palm leaves for the first time in Sri Lanka during the reign of King Vaṭṭa Gāmaṇī Abhaya. Since then, the written transmission has been maintained by many Theravada countries in which palm-leaf manuscripts were inscribed in increasingly different local scripts. In present, the extant palm-leaf manuscripts can be divided into at least four major traditions: Sinhalese, Burmese, Khom, and Tham scripts. Despite their immense historical and cultural value, palm-leaf Pāli manuscripts are susceptible, over time, to many factors, such as climate, insects, ignorance of people, and adverse storage. Taking this matter into consideration, Wat Phra Dhammakaya launched the Dhammachai Tipiṭaka Project (DTP) in 2010 with the aims to preserve the existing palm-leaf manuscripts of various traditions, and to create digitalized and computerized databases of a new critical edition of the Pāli canon (D-Tipitaka) in order to support Buddhist studies. The work is classified into 4 steps as follows: collecting and digitizing the palm-leaf manuscripts, creating databases of digitized images and readings, text analyzing and editing, and finally publishing the critical edition of the Pāli canon. To effectively achieve the Project's goal, the Digital Humanities Center (DHC) of the DTP has developed several computer programs to support the work in every step. This paper will explain the process and the programs created in the production of the first section of the Dīghanikāya, the Sīlakkhandhavagga (DN1).

Proceedings of the Computational Sanskrit and Digital Humanities, 18th *World Sanskrit Conference 2023*, pages 201–212

2 Collecting and digitizing Pāli Tipiṭaka palm-leaf manuscripts

The initial step of the work is to preserve large amounts of palm-leaf manuscripts from various countries in digital format. These color digital images safeguard the primary sources against deterioration over times and permit display or reproduction with image fidelity. Since 2010, the project has digitized over 10,000 bundles from the Sinhalese, Burmese, Khom, and Tham Pāli traditions. The criteria for selection for digitizing are: monolingual Pāli canonical texts, physical condition, completeness of content, age over 100 years old, historical value, and regional diversity. Based on these criteria, the collection of digital images are primarily given to Pāli Canon of Theravada Buddhism and secondarily to other canonical Buddhist literatures. According to DTP's manuscript data the average age of digitized manuscripts is approximately 260 years old, and the oldest dated manuscript is Sinhalese script manuscript of Saṃyutta Nikāya created in the 7th century. Besides yielding preservation benefit, an extensive collection of palm-leaf manuscripts greatly helps in the creation of the critical edition of the Pāli canon as the more digitized manuscripts we have in hand, the clearer lineage within and across manuscript traditions we can establish. The preservation process includes manuscript selection, manuscript registration, colophon reading and age determination, cleaning, page order sequencing, and digitization. To support digitization work, the DHC has developed 2 online programs: "Manuscript Journey" (MSJ) and "Application of Palm-leaf Manuscript Segmentation" (APMS). MSJ has been specifically designed to create metadata describing features of palm-leaf manuscripts. In the registration process, instead of filling in a paper-based information card, MSJ enables staff members to systematically record metadata schemas including bibliographic information (e.g. title, date of inscription, name of donor, name of scribe, etc.), physical characteristics (e.g. script, language, number of pages, size, condition, etc.), and administrative information (e.g. original registration code, location, date of digitization, legibility, etc.). These electronic information cards are useful for long-term management and enable searching and sorting for the rapid retrieval of information. The second program of APMS is developed under the Lanna OCR Project , a cooperation between the DTP and the Department of Computer Science, Chiang Mai University (CMU). It is a palm-leaf segmentation tool, which automatically cuts a single five-folio digital image file into five separated one-folio digital image files. It then renames and sequences the files according to manuscript page numbers and inserts descriptive labels on images. So far, over 10,000 manuscripts have been segmented into an estimated 2,000,000 one-folio image files. The information contain in the MSJ and APMS programs is essential for the on-going development of an online palm-leaf manuscript index database and a digital library. These programs also provide easy access to publicly available collections from any location thereby facilitating the study of Buddhist heritage without traveling to manuscript repositories.

3 Creating databases of digitized images and readings

The work in this step is to create databases of selected manuscript images collected in the previous steps and their readings. On average, in the production of a book in the series, at least 5 sets of the best representatives of palm-leaf manuscripts from each tradition are selected. For the creation of Dīghanikāya Sīlakkhandhavagga (DN1), Suttantapiṭaka, a total 20 sets of palm-leaf manuscripts from four main traditions plus one set of a rare palm-leaf manuscript from the Mon tradition have been used. Almost 5,000 one-folio image files from these 21 manuscripts were assigned to local staff members in Thailand, Sri Lanka, Myanmar, and Cambodia. Each local office has the responsibility to transliterate the Tham, Sinhalese, Burmese, and Khom readings into Roman. To support the distribution of the very large image files to different locations, and the centralization of input digital text across locations to the main server in Thailand, the DHC has developed an Online Data Entry of Manuscripts (ODEM) program [Figure 1]. It makes palm-leaf manuscript images available online page by page for staff members to read and then convert to Roman script. The program uses as a base text the Burmese Pāli text (Be) of the Chaṭṭha Saṅgāyana Tipiṭaka. It serves as a preliminary text for staff members to read, check,

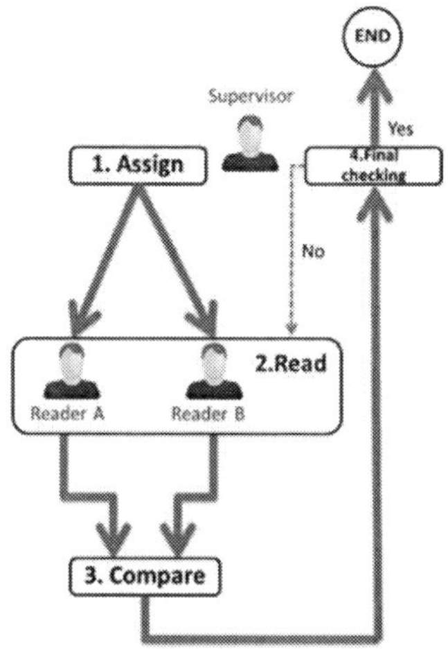

Figure 1: Data Flow of ODEM

alter, and edit in accordance with the text as appeared on the palm-leaf manuscript images by the principle of "Key as You See". In other words, staff members, without taking Pāli grammar into consideration, simply read the Pāli manuscripts and input their reading into the database by altering Burmese Pāli text (Be) of the Chaṭṭha Saṇgāyana Tipiṭaka. To assure accuracy, ODEM allows paired-work in which 2 staff members, called readers, can simultaneously work on the same image files and compare their input data until the result indicates "zero difference" meaning that the transliterated work is exactly the same. Furthermore, for the ultimate accuracy, ODEM allows a third person with Pāli and IT code knowledge, called the final checker, to ascertain that it is 100 % correct and technical symbols have been thoroughly applied.

4 Text analyzing and editing

The work in this step involves textual aligning and computer-based editing. To facilitate its critical editing by Buddhist scholars, the textual database is transferred into a software system developed by DHC named Indic Text Analysis Program (ITAP) and Editing Page (EP). Applying the idea from CollateX, one of the most well-known programs for collating textual sources, the DHC has designed ITAP with Matching and Editing Page (EP) features: Matching helps automatically collate and split transcribed textual data obtained from ODEM at the word level. After that the segmented words will be aligned and all variant readings from every palm-leaf manuscript will be dynamically arranged in a synoptic table along with links to relevant manuscript images. However, due to the complexity of canonical Pāli texts, this automatic variant alignment done by the program reaches only 80 % accurate; human involvement is required to manually adjust the text into a synoptic form. Next, this well-aligned text is transferred to the Editing Page (EP), in which the text is rearranged in a conveniently editable format; it is here that the Pāli text can be critically edited. After the editing process, the selected readings or, in some cases, emendations are kept into EP database together with their annotation, if any. In the final process, EP generates the entire edited text into format ready for the publication of the critical edition of Pāli canon in printed edition and online version. The printed edition will contain the critically established texts and selected critical apparatus showing only variant readings of historical and grammatical value. The online version will contain three selective displays (Text View, Book View, and Synoptic View) of the critically established text. Moreover, it can link to manuscript digital images together with other printed references and a list of every single word appearing in both the critically established texts and critical apparatus.

5 Publishing critical edition of Pāli canon

5.1 Introduction

After researchers have finished editing the text, the final text will be sent to create text layout using Adobe InDesign, a publishing and typesetting software. The program will produce the printed and digital editions in PDF and EPUB formats. The EPUB format is utilized to display the online version of Dhammachai Tipiṭaka called D-Tipitaka because it supports many e-readers and is compatible with software and applications available in most devices, such as smartphones, tablets, and computers. Moreover, instead of creating a Windows-Based Application requiring program installment, the Web-Based Application format will be able to be conveniently accessed via the internet anywhere and anytime without installing any program.

5.2 Algorithm

The process of data preparation of the D-Tipitaka starts from importing the edited text from researchers from the Editing Page (EP) into Microsoft Word (MS Word) for a chief editor to make final amendments. The PDF file alone is used for the publication of the Dhammachai Edition (De) printed edition, while both PDF and EPUB files are imported into the database of D-Tipitaka through Linking Process. It uses EPUB to generate XML and HTML tags with diverse attributes, e.g. idword, idgroup, and span. The encoded data preserves character format (e.g. upper case, italicized, superscript, or bold text), document format (page layout), and paragraph format (e.g. indentation, line spacing, or alignment) of printed edition. However, the formatting tags alone are insufficient as they indicate position PX not text line number. Therefore, PDF is necessary to locate line number and to encapsulate all formats. Through the collaborative performance of EPUB and PDF, the data of text line number and text position are combined. The illustration below [Figure 2] shows the overall process of data preparation.

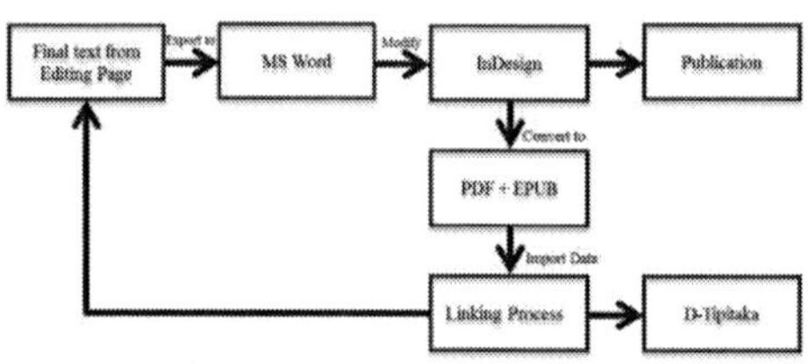

Figure 2: The Process of Data Preparation

The illustration number [Figure 3] reveals the database flow. The ITAP and EP databases operate using Microsoft SQL Server (MSSQL) while Linking and D-Tipitaka databases using PostgreSQL (PGSQL). The reason for using duo databases instead of single database is the enhancement of processing capabilities. MSSQL has been used since the beginning of the project and later PGSQL was utilized for its claim to be the world's most advanced open-source database, and for its safety of server connection and capacity of complicated analytical processes. Using two databases enable users to achieve abrupt analytical response which expedites overall workflow of D-Tipitaka.

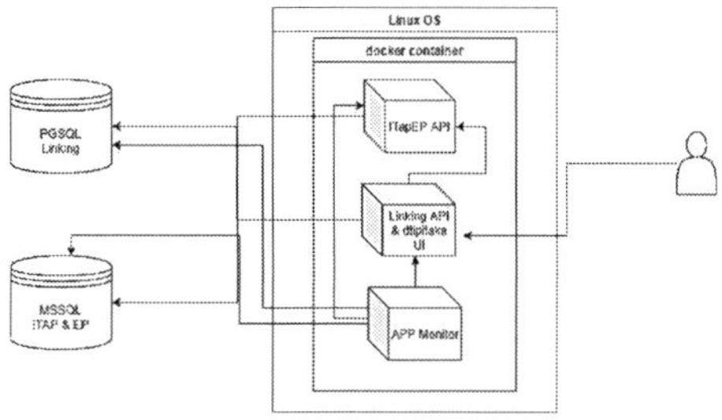

Figure 3: D-Tipitaka Database Flow

5.3 Main Functions of D-Tipitaka

D-Tipitaka consists of 3 main functions: display, manuscript and printed edition link, and search.

5.3.1 Display

- `Text View Function`
  The Text View displays [Figure 4] the content of a selected Sutta of the Dīghanikāya Sīlakkhandhavagga (DN1) divided in units. They are systematically identified by unit numbers and sub-heading names. There are 2 types of words in Text View: non-problematic words and problematic words. Both types are clickable to access a table showing the manuscript and printed edition abbreviations. Each abbreviation links to a manuscript image or an image from the printed editions [See Appendix A]. However, only the underlined problematic words are linked to critical apparatus; by hovering the mouse pointer over any underlined words, a Tool Tip pops up. A click on it leads to the critical apparatus showing all variants and abbreviations, which link to original manuscript images or printed editions. Further details regarding manuscript images and printed edition links are discussed in topic no. 5.3.2.

Figure 4: Text View of D-Tipitaka

- `Synoptic View Function`
  D-Tipitaka also provides Synoptic View function [Figure 5] for easy comparison across manuscript traditions and printed editions. Users firstly select a Sutta and its paragraph number. The program will automatically align all variant readings of that selected paragraph in a table showing 10 columns at a time. The first row of the table is a header row containing the edited text of the Dhammachai Edition (De) followed by rows of variant readings from the different manuscript traditions and printed editions. Every word on the table is clickable and linked to images of the manuscript and printed editions. For easy comparison, variant readings deviating from the header can be highlighted in different colors if users click on "diff" menu.

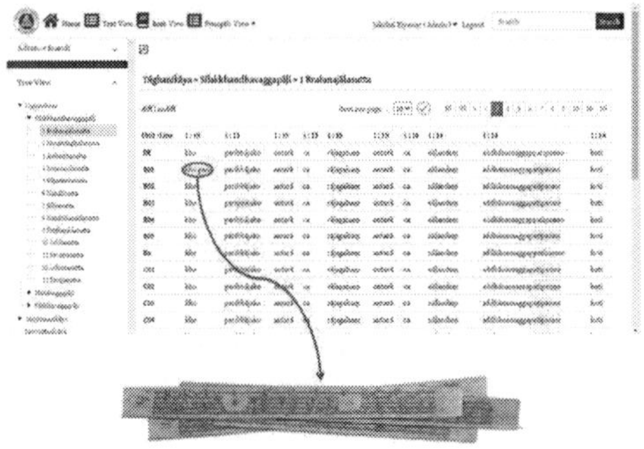

Figure 5: Synoptic View of D-Tipitaka

- `Book View Function`
  The last display of D-Tipitaka is Book View function [Figure 6]. It offers users the convenient experience of reading the electronic version of the Dhammachai Edition page by page plus user friendly features, such as a page turning effect, bookmarks, etc. The main components of Book View are paragraphs and critical apparatus.

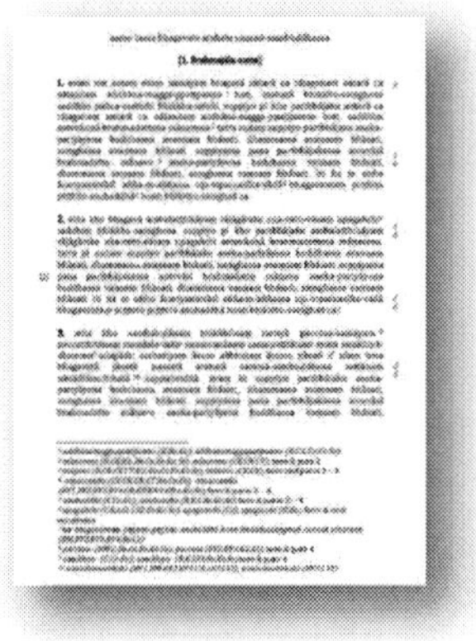

Figure 6: Book View of D-Tipitaka

Paragraphs contain non-problematic and underlined problematic words. Clicking on any word in the paragraph locates its page and paragraph number in the status bar on top of the page and leads to a table of variants which links to images of the manuscripts and printed editions. Similar to Text View, only the underlined problematic words are linked to the critical apparatus, which is revealed by hovering a mouse pointer over any underlined words, causing Tool Tip to pop up leading to the variants of the critical apparatus. In addition, the paragraph part includes unit numbers linking with Chaṭṭhasaṅgīti and PTS (Pali Text Society) printed editions. According to the Dhammachai Edition's superficial study 94 % of the text consists of non-problematic words, while only 6 % of text is problematic. However, less than 6 % of problematic words have been critically analyzed in the Dhammachai Edition.

5.3.2 Manuscript and printed edition link

Another main function of the D-Tipitaka is the linkage to images of selected manuscripts and printed editions [Figure 7]. The linkage is divided into 2 types: single-step access and double-step access. The single-step access applies to the linkage to both manuscript images and printed editions by clicking on any required word on the Synoptic Table or in the critical apparatus of the Book View. It also applies to direct linkage to the Chaṭṭhasaṅgīti and PTS Editions by clicking on a paragraph number of the Chaṭṭhasaṅgīti Edition and a page number of the PTS Edition in Book View. The double-step access means users need to perform 2 steps to access images. In Text View and Book View, clicking on a word will bring users to a variant table where they have to choose an abbreviation to access required manuscript images or printed editions. In short, single-step access shows images right after users click on a word while double-step access requires users to select words from text followed by abbreviation from the variant table.

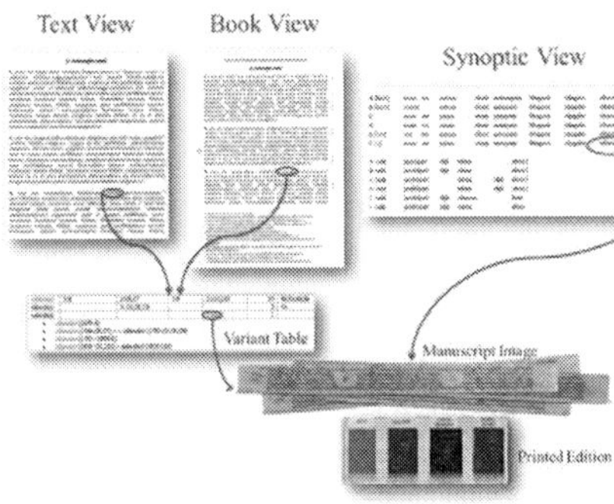

Figure 7: Manuscript images and printed editions link of Text View, Book View, and Synoptic View in D-Tipitaka

The retrieval of text data and image data is shown in the picture below [Figure 8].

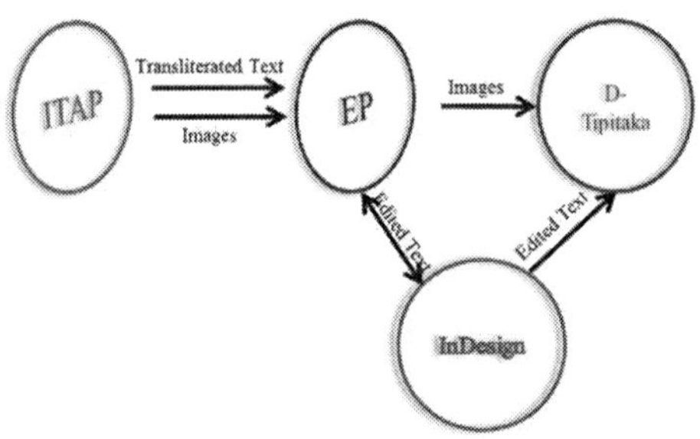

Figure 8: The retrieval of text data and image data

- `Image Data`
  The data of palm-leaf manuscript images and printed editions stored in the Directory are retrieved and displayed on D-Tipitaka through a communication process among 3 programs. Firstly, ITAP reports picture name and address of required images to EP, which then relays all information to the D-Tipitaka program. In other words, EP acts as a medium of communication between ITAP and D-Tipitaka.
- `Text Data`
  Text Data are classified into transliterated text and edited text.
  - The transliterated text data created by readers, who are responsible for producing the Romanized Pāli text from manuscripts written in local scripts (as mentioned earlier). The transliterated data from 4 Pāli traditions is stored in ITAP and sent to EP program for researchers to edit.
  - Edited text data refers to data of text edited in EP programs onwards.
    * Transliterated text data is used to generate the tables used in text alignment suitable for editing. Researchers then examine the text and make critical decisions.

This edited text is then exported from EP Program to MS Word (.DOC) for a chief editor to finalize.

* Edited text data in InDesign: The chief editor will deliberately go through edited work once again. After being emended, this final edited text along with design features, e.g. stylish typography and rich graphics, images and tables, etc., will be sent to update EP database and to D-Tipitaka program for publication.
The commands used for text and data retrieval are as follows:

- The command to get names of manuscript images and printed editions $this.subscription.add(this.http.get < EditionTextItap[] > (this.APIEndpoint +' /ws/api/ieps/editiontext/findbyfcrid/' + this.fcbaseid, headers : this.httpHeaders)$
- The command to get directory of manuscript images and printed editions $this.subscription.add(this.http.get < Picture > (this.APIEndpoint +' /ws/api/ieps/editiontext/findfcpicture?picturename =' +fcedition +' /' + filename, headers : this.httpHeaders)$
- The command to demonstrate manuscript images and printed editions $this.tipitakaImage = this.getBypassSecurityTrustResourceUrl(encodeURI('data : image/jpeg; base64,' +this.picture.binaryfile));$

5.3.3 Search

The D-Tipitaka provides users with 3 searching methods:
1. Search by using search box [Figure 9]
2. Search by clicking on variant readings in De (to compare with relevant witnesses including manuscript images and printed editions)
3. Search by using PTS page number and Chaṭṭhasaṇgīti paragraph number

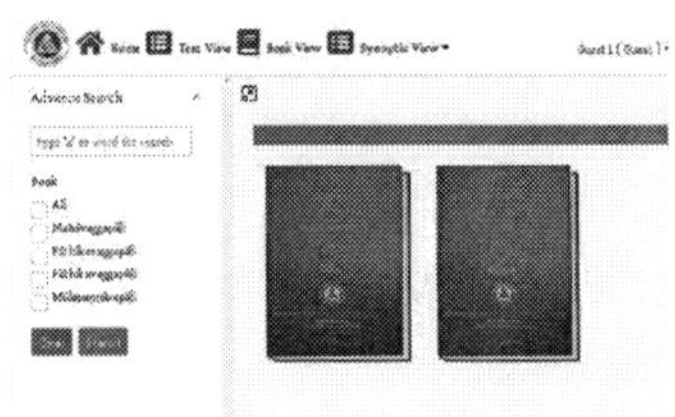

Figure 9: Search Function of D-Tipitaka

- `Search by using search box:`
The search box in D-Tipitaka provides users with 2 options: "partial matches searching" and "exact matches searching".
  - `Partial matches searching` is the default of the system. It lets users enter part of a query word, and the program will automatically show related results. For example, if the desired word contains "Puri", once a user types "P", the related results started with "P" will be automatically shown, and when any syllable or vowel is added after "P", the related results will be shown continuously. Until a user types "Puri", the searching will show the desired word along with others related results such as Purisa, Purise, Purisasa, etc.
  - `Exact matches searching` is an alternative feature that helps users to find only a query word by selecting the EXACT check box. For example, if the target word "Pura" is entered into the search box and the exact check box is ticked, on top of the navigation panel will show the total number of occurrences in D-Tipitaka and in the panel displays all occurrences of the query word along with a couple of surrounding sentences. Each

occurrence is highlighted, and its Sutta heading, unit number, and page are identified. Users can jump directly to any location by clicking on the tab.

- `Search by clicking on variant readings in De:`
  The Book View feature provides a book shelf for users to select any volume to read. It shows all pages exactly the same as those of the printed version divided into the main text and the critical apparatus. The variant readings of the main text can be accessed by double clicking on a word, and then the variant reading table will appear on a new page as shown in [Figure 10] . The first column is a variant reading part arranged as follows. The critical word of the main text appears on top of the list followed by different manuscript readings in a systematic order based on deviation from the critical reading. After each reading, the manuscripts which contain it are arranged in alphabetical order by abbreviations of different traditions (B: Burmese, C: Ceylon, K: Khom, M: Mon, T:Tham). This is a default order of the program.

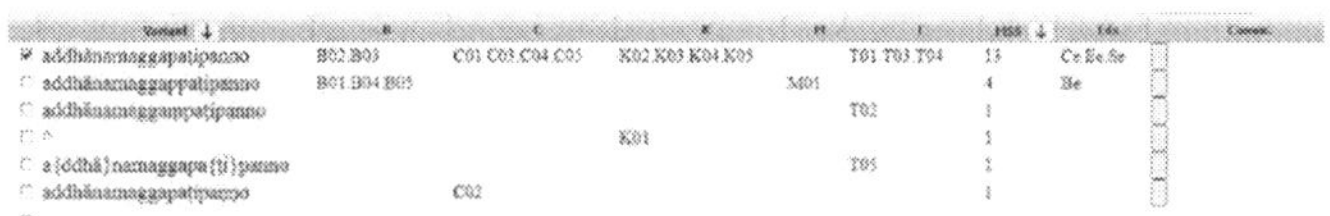

Figure 10: Variant Table

  The columns of manuscript evidence are followed by a column showing the total number of manuscript evidence from all traditions that can be sorted in ascending or descending order. The last column indicates printed editions containing the word, shown in alphabetical order (Be: Burmese Edition, Ce: Ceylon Edition, Ee: European Edition, Se: Syāmaraṭṭhassa Edition) in the "Eds" column. When users click on any manuscript abbreviation, manuscript image will be popped up.

- `Search by using PTS page number and Chaṭṭhasaṅgīti paragraph number`
  In book view, the D-Tipitaka supports the comparison with two well-known printed editions, the PTS or European Edition (Ee) and the Chaṭṭhasaṅgīti or Burmese Edition (Be). The consultation of any De paragraph can be done by clicking on the PTS page number or Chaṭṭhasaṅgīti paragraph number on the outer margin. The PTS page number is on the furthest margin without brackets while the Chaṭṭhasaṅgīti paragraph number is in the square brackets. Clicking these brings up a new window showing pages of the printed edition and its transliterated text.

5.4 Conclusion / Limitation

D-Tipitaka is an on-going program development divided into 6 main parts including Login and Registration feature, Text View, Synoptic View, Book View, manuscript and printed editions link, and search. The development of every part except "Book View" has been accomplished over 80 %; Book View is only 30 % developed. Thus, the overall accomplishment marks up to approximately 60 %; completion is expected by mid 2022. However, as the project is dealing with newly designed programs and a massive database, unexpected problematic are bound to be encountered.

5.4.1 Login and Registration Feature

The Login and Registration feature is 100 % complete and allows user access in 3 levels: standard, registration, and restricted levels. Standard Level allows a user to use the search box and read text in 3 displays (Text View, Synoptic View, and Book view). Registration is not required. Registration Level allows users to search and link text with all evidence excluding palm-leaf manuscript images, and to utilize additional options for reading e.g. give feedback on a word, insert bookmark, highlight text, etc. Restricted Level permits certain groups of users unlimited access to all evidence including palm-leaf manuscript images. Registration and permission are required. The process of login and registration of all user levels is outlined in the picture below [Figure 11].

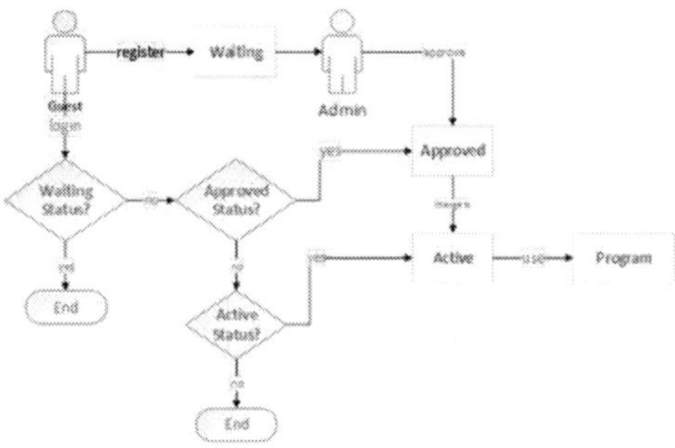

Figure 11: D-Tipitaka login and registration of all user levels process

5.4.2 Synoptic View

The development of Synoptic View is roughly 80 % completed. The cause of 20 % of incomplete work primarily lies on the discrepancy between computer and electronic devices display capacity and the needs of users and secondarily the constant adjustment to serve users' needs. For example, the Synoptic Table was initially designed to show 7 columns per page display as requested by users. After trial, users found them too fragmented to continuously read on computer or electronic device screen and requested programmers to increase columns from 7 to 15 which seemed impossible in terms of program design. The reconciliation between programmers and users is 10 columns per pages. The equipment's capacity limitation and constant adjustments consumed time on recoding and layout rearranging.

5.4.3 Text View

The Text View is almost finished, but has been delayed because of the difficulty in finding the best method to present the critical apparatus along with the canonical text. Unlike the critical apparatus of a printed book appearing at the bottom of the page, the critical apparatus of e-book version should appear in view of text, when scrolling up or down. To fulfill users' needs, programmers spent time on gathering examples from other electronic reading materials to get some ideas and to design several possible critical apparatus displays, each of which possesses a unique code writing and layout design. Users also spent time on testing and finding pros and cons of real-life use. Once the most suitable critical apparatus display was identified, programmers continued adjusting and designing until the critical apparatus display came to satisfied completion.

5.4.4 Book View

Among 3 displays, Book View gains least progress with roughly 30 % of completion due to internal and external factors. The internal factor is the unfamiliarity of users within the project in using a newly-designed program when editing. The whole process from editing until preparing publication artwork had been designed to take place in Editing Page (EP). But in practice, users felt more comfortable working with MS Word (.DOC) than in EP. Amendments in MS Word outside of the program have to be imported back to EP database to make EP and D-Tipitaka equal. This causes an external factor of difficulty in finding an accurate and consistent method to maintain the amended version in MS Word (.DOC) format when being processed in the EP program. To deal with this external factor, programmers tried multiple methods to find the stable format, such as .XML tag from Microsoft Office, .PDF, .PDF plus .IDML, and .PDF plus .EPUB. Eventually, after 3 years of attempts, they came to the conclusion of using the program

InDesign which can export .PDF and .EPUB. The use of these file types together help maintain accuracy and consistency of content, logical structure and formatting information when sent to EP to update the database and to D-Tipitaka for publication. Furthermore, another external factor relating to the database arose. The first database of MSSQL that had been used since the beginning of the project could not work at its maximum speed when operated with the D-Tipitaka program, due to massive text analysis and image links. To expedite speed, a new database of PGSQL was added. The implementation of a new database caused programmers to redesign databases and programs to make co-operating of MSSQL and PGSQL compatible. It can be concluded that the unfamiliarity that users will face with a newly developed programs will take several attempts to find qualified/specific file types, as well as engaging with a new database are the key factors that hinder the progress of the Book View development.

5.4.5 Manuscript and printed edition link

The work on manuscript and printed edition link is 80 % complete; the 20 % of unfinished work is the user interface. So far, we have succeeded in retrieving and presenting images relevant to text, but the interaction between images and users is limited. To make it user-friendly, programmers will build an interface enabling users to have more interaction with the palm-leaf manuscripts and printed edition images, such features as zooming in and out, and pan or scroll from one part of the image to another. It might be possible to incorporate a whole page of text alongside any particular image, but it might be too intricate. Thus, in the meantime we are focusing on improving user interface and leave text incorporation for the next version.

5.4.6 Search by using search box

As explained earlier, the D-Tipitaka provides partial matches searching and exact matches searching. At the moment, the completion of work in this part is more than halfway. Now, users can type part of word or exact word in the search box which seems to work perfectly for searching. However, we plan to provide a short cut of searching by adding “partial search” and “exact search” buttons. This part has not been commenced yet, not because of the complexity of work but time constraint and work prioritization, that requires programmers to focus on crucial work in Book View display.

In conclusion, since 2010 Digital Humanities Center (DHC) of DTP has developed several computer programs, ODEM, ITAP, EP, and D-Tipitaka to support work in every step from palm-leaf manuscript preservation until the publication of the Dhammachai Edition. The database of the previous program has been designed to be used as the database of the consecutive program. At present, the first 3 programs work effectively with minor adjustment according to the users' additional requests or program revisions as effected by web-browser updates. Now, we are in the process of developing our latest program of D-Tipitaka, which has been found to be challenging. Emphasizing on creating a user-friendly interface, dealing with immeasurable palm-leaf manuscript and printed edition image retrieval, and finding a consistent and effective method for accurate electronic output are time consuming. Although we are confronted with several unexpected internal and external factors, which obstruct the achievement of the D-Tipitaka webpage in a timely fashion, we are determined to complete the D-Tipitaka webpage promptly to make it as an alternative and convenient platform for the transmission of the Buddha's teachings in the digital age.

A Abbreviation

ABBR	DCI Code	Location	AD	No.of folios
B01	MM_04_01_006_00	Universities'Central Library, Yangon	1679	435
B02	MM_03_01_001_01	Bakara Temple, Amarapura	1768	237
B03	MM_04_01_001_00	Universities'Central Library, Yangon	1774	240
B04	MM_04_01_005_00	Universities'Central Library, Yangon	1792	301
B05	MM_04_01_008_01	Universities'Central Library, Yangon	1806	228
C01	SR_99_01_003_01	Ridīvihāraya, Kurunegela, Sri Lanka	1744	140
C02	SR_05_01_001_01	Sri Vijayasundarārāma Vihāraya, Kadihāre, Kurunegela, Sri Lanka	1783	214
C03	SR_11_01_001_01	Koṭikāgoda Rajamahavihāraya, Walgama, Mātara	1832	193
C04	SR_02_01_001_12	Sri Narendrasingha Rajamaha Viharaya, Kuṇḍasāle	1855	172
C05	SR_01_01_007_01	Sri Daladā Maligāva Oriental Library, Kandy	Unknown	235
K01	TH_05_01_003_00	National Library, Bangkok	1777	535
K02	TH_05_01_002_00	National Library, Bangkok	(1782-1809)	551
K03	TH_04_01_001_00	Wat Pho, Bangkok	(1824-1851)	591
K04	TH_05_01_006_00	National Library, Bangkok	(1851-1868)	561
K05	TH_03_01_001_00	Wat Hongrattanaran, Bangkok	Unknown	601
T01	LA_01_01_007_00	Digital Library of Lao Manuscripts	1598	526
T02	TH_10_01_063_00	Wat Mahadhatu, Yasothon	1822	652
T03	TH_01_01_002_00	Wat Sung Men, Phrae	1836	573
T04	TH_01_01_003_00	Wat Sung Men, Phrae	1836	717
T05	TH_10_01_007_00	Wat Mahadhatu, Yasothon	Unknown	501
M01	TH_05_01_026_00	National Library, Bangkok	Unknown	571

References

Papangkorn Inkeaw, Jakramate Bootkrajang, Phasit Charoenkwan, Sanparith Marukatat, Shinn-Ying Ho, Jeerayut Chaijaruwanich: Rule-Based Page Segmentation for Palm Leaf Manuscript on Color Image *International Conference on Asian Digital Libraries (ICADL)*, pp.127-136, 2016

David Doermann, Karl Tombre: Handbook of Document Image Processing and Recognition *Springer*, Heidelberg, 2014

Suchada Srisetthaworakul: Developing Database of the Pāli Canon from the Selected Palm-leaf Manuscripts: Method of Reading and Transliterating the Dīghanikāya in Khom and Tham Scripts *Journal of Indian and Buddhist Studies*, Vol. 65, No. 3, 2017

Ronald Haentjens Dekker, Dirk van Hulle, Gregor Middell, Vincent Neyt and Joris van Zundert: Computer-supported collation of modern manuscripts: CollateX and the Beckett Digital Manuscript Project *Digital Scholarship in the Humanities*, pp.1-19, 2014

Elisa Nury: Visualizing Collation Results Elisa Nury *The Journal of the European Society for Textual Scholarship*, pp.75-94, 2019

Ciprian-Octavian Truica, Alexandru Boicea and Florin Radulescu: Asynchronous Replication in Microsoft SQL Server, PostgreSQL, and MySQL *International Conference on Cyber Science and Engineering*, 2013

http://lannakadee.cmu.ac.th/LannaOCR/

http://www.tipitaka.org/chattha

https://collatex.net/

Distinguishing Commentary from Canon: Experiments in Pāli Computational Linguistics

Dan Zigmond

Jikoji Zen Center
12100 Skyline Blvd
Los Gatos CA 95033
U.S.A.

Apple
1 Infinite Loop
Cupertino CA 95014
U.S.A.

djz@shmonk.com

Abstract

The *Tipiṭaka* or Pāli Canon is the canonical scripture of Theravāda Buddhists worldwide and is said to record the direct teachings of the historical Buddha. These texts were transmitted orally for several centuries before being recorded in written form in what is now Sri Lanka, likely around 100 BCE, in the Pāli language, a Middle Indo-Aryan dialect. A strong commentarial tradition evolved in the following centuries setting forth the orthodox interpretation of these texts, generally also written in Pāli. The oldest of these commentaries are now considered quasi-canonical themselves.

This paper explores the application of modern computational linguistics to these Pāli texts. We show that relatively simple analysis of word frequency allows us to distinguish canonical works from commentary. This builds on earlier analysis showing that the canonical texts themselves could be clustered using computational techniques to separate older and newer volumes. The success of these initial analyses suggests Pāli computational linguistics will be a fruitful area for future research.

1 Introduction

The *Tipiṭaka* or Pāli Canon records the oral teachings of the historical Buddha. They were codified in a series of "councils" in which the Buddha's followers gathered to recite his teachings orally and agree on their contents. The First Council is said to have been held almost immediately after his death around 400 BCE. The *Tipiṭaka* continued to be transmitted orally until the Fourth Council, held in what is now Sri Lanka around 100 BCE, when it was set in written form. The language used for this written edition was Pāli.

The word "Pāli" itself comes from the compound *pāli-bhāsa*, meaning "the language of the texts" (Geiger, 2005, xxiii). In other words, the language Pāli and the *Tipiṭaka* are inextricably linked. Although Pāli came to be used in other Buddhist literature, it is essentially unknown outside the Buddhist context.

Portions of the *Tipiṭaka* exist in other languages, but the Pāli form appears to be the oldest complete edition. Although the original manuscripts written on palm leaves are long-since lost, the volumes were painstakingly recopied over the centuries until the advent of automated printing. Even today, collections of hand-copied palm leaf manuscripts are preserved in many Asian countries. As Buddhism spread through Asia, the Buddhist community fragmented into a variety of sects and schools, many of which de-emphasized the *Tipiṭaka* in favor of newer scriptures.[1] However among the Therāvada communities still flourishing throughout Sri Lanka, Southeast Asia, and beyond, the Pāli Canon remains paramount.

Orthodox opinion among Theravāda Buddhists is that the *Tipiṭaka* records Buddha's literal teachings; in other words that Pāli is a representation of the spoken language of Magadha, the ancient kingdom in northern India where Buddha primarily lived and taught (Gombrich, 2018, 13). This assertion has long been viewed skeptically by scholars, particularly in the West.

[1] These schools would object to the description "newer," believing in many cases that the non-Pāli scriptures, generally recorded in Sanskrit, were rediscoveries of original teachings that had been lost.

Proceedings of the Computational Sanskrit and Digital Humanities, 18th World Sanskrit Conference 2023, pages 213–222

However, a growing academic movement holds that the earliest portions of the *Tipiṭaka* may indeed contain something very close to the actual words the Buddha spoke (see, for example, Sujato and Brahmali (2014) and Gombrich (2018)). Although the *Tipiṭaka* has certainly undergone significant change over the centuries—for example, to demean to role of women (Anālayo, 2016)—elements of these Pāli texts may well trace back to Buddha's time and capture Buddha's words. As Gombrich (2018, 1) puts it, Pāli itself may represent "the argot of the Buddha and his earliest followers, [...] the idiosyncratic language used by the Buddha as he toured northeast India." This possibility brings further urgency to the critical study of the *Tipiṭaka*, if only to determine the relative age of the various texts and to provide clues as to which may, in fact, have been "spoken by the Buddha" (Sujato and Brahmali, 2014, 7).

The name *Tipiṭaka* literally means "three baskets" and derives from the traditional division of the Canon into three distinct collections of texts:

- *Vinaya Piṭaka*, "Basket of Discipline," describing the rules for Buddhist monks and nuns, their origin, and their evolution.
- *Sutta Piṭaka*, "Basket of Teachings," compiling the oral teachings of the Buddha and a few of his most notable disciples.
- *Abhidhamma Piṭaka*, "Basket of Special Teachings" or "Basket About the Teachings," explaining and systematizing various Buddhist doctrines.

Over time Pāli became the preferred language for most Buddhist ecclesiastical writing in the Theravāda tradition.[2] A prodigious commentarial literature evolved, describing the orthodox interpretation of the *Tipiṭaka* for generations of Buddhists (von Hinüber, 1997, 100). Among the most revered of these commentaries are those believed to have been composed by the teacher Buddhaghosa, likely between 370 and 450 CE (von Hinüber, 1997, 103). Eventually, others composed commentaries on the commentaries (usually referred to as "sub-commentaries"), resulting in a vast, sprawling Pāli corpus.

Despite this extensive body of writing, Pāli has no fixed written form. It is traditionally transcribed using the native alphabets of the countries in which Therāvada Buddhism is practiced: Sinhala in Sri Lanka, Khom and Tham in Thailand, Burmese in Burma, Khmer in Cambodia, and Devanagari in India. In the West it is generally written in Roman script, using the International Alphabet of Sanskrit Transliteration long adopted for Sanskrit and other Indic languages. Thus, for example, *bhikkhu* and *bhikkhunī* (monk and nun) in Roman script are equivalent to भिक्खु and भिक्खुणी in Devanagari.

2 Pāli Computational Linguistics

Computational linguistics—the application of computational techniques to the study of language—is nearly as old as digital computing itself. The recent explosion in the availability of both computing power and electronic texts has caused a concomitant explosion of research in this field. Although much of this work was initially in military, governmental, and commercial contexts, recent decades have seen a flourishing of applications in the humanities (see, for example, Jockers (2013) and Jockers and Thalken (2020)). There has also been considerable success using computational techniques to solve the specific problem of determining the authorship of texts (see, for example, Rosen-Zvi et al. (2010)).

Historically much of this work was heavily biased towards English and a handful of other modern languages. By one estimate, as recently as 2007, "only a very small number (perhaps thirty) of the world's 6000+ languages currently enjoy[ed] the benefits of modern language technologies" (Scannell, 2007). Even among modern European languages, the Multilingual Europe

[2]As Buddhism spread to other countries within Asia, Pāli was also used as a means of communication between monks and nuns who did not share a native language. This practice seems to have died out, in part due to the spread of English as a second language. The last book on spoken Pāli appears to be have been published in 1951 (Buddhadatta, 1951) and is long out of print.

Technology Alliance found in 2013 that only English had consistently "good support" across technology categories, and only French and Spanish had consistently "moderate support" across all categories (Multilingual Europe Technology Alliance, 2013).

Fortunately this has started to change, with under-resourced languages receiving increasing attention in recent years. In particular, efforts to apply computational techniques to ancient languages is picking up speed. The Classical Language Toolkit provides resources for a wide variety of ancient languages (Johnson et al., 2014). Recurring international symposia have been held on Sanskrit computation linguistics since 2007 (Gerard, 2009).

Yet relatively little computational research has been applied to Pāli thus far. Elwert et al. (2015) began work on a structured electronic edition of the *Sutta Piṭaka* in Pāli, but this work was never completed and the corpus never published. Alfter (2015) developed several tools for analyzing Pāli texts in Java, but that work appears to be no longer maintained. More recently, Haribhakta and Nadageri (2017) have explored labeling parts of speech in Pāli sentences, and Basapur et al. (2019) describe a computational approach to the issue of Pāli word splitting, which (as in Sanskrit) is complicated by Pāli's sandhi rules for word combining and elision. (Basapur et al. (2019) use Devanagari rather than Roman script, which may make the work less accessible to some Pāli scholars.) Beyond this handful of papers, little else has been published.

Efforts are now in place to facilitate broader application of computational techniques to Pāli. Last year we published `tipitaka` (Zigmond, 2020), a package for Pāli computational linguistics using the R statistical software language (R Core Team, 2020). It is currently in a nascent stage, providing access to the *Tipiṭaka* in raw and lightly-processed form and a few basic tools for sorting and comparing Pāli words. Our first applications of this package to the analysis of the *Tipiṭaka* showed some promising results. For example, rudimentary word frequency analysis was able to separate older and newer volumes of the *Tipiṭaka* into the clusters that roughly matched the scholarly consensus on their relative age (Zigmond, 2021).

3 Distinguishing Commentary from Canon

The results described here extend that early work to include the Pāli commentary as well as the Canon. Here we focus exclusively on the *Sutta Piṭaka*, the most widely read and studied of the three baskets of the *Tipiṭaka*. As in our prior study, we divide our texts into two groups using k-means clustering (MacQueen, 1967; Lloyd, 1982), which can be thought of as a simple form of unsupervised machine learning. In this case, we use the algorithm to classify our texts into the two implicit categories of canon and commentary. As in Zigmond (2021), the frequencies of the global top 1,000 Pāli words (i.e., the 1,000 words most frequently found across the entire corpus) become our features, although past work suggests the results are typically robust across many frequency thresholds, both higher and lower than 1,000.[3]

The `tidy` (Wickham et al., 2019) and `tidytext` (Silge and Robinson, 2016) packages in R make the text processing tasks fairly simple. Like the `tipitaka` package, this work uses the Chattha Sangāyana Tipiṭaka version 4.0 (CST4) edition of the *Tipiṭaka* (Vipassana Research Institute, 1990). Illustrations of the resulting clusters were created with the `factoextra` package (Kassambara and Mundt, 2020).

Figure 1 shows the results of this clustering. Each file in the CST4 distribution is plotted separately, and the naming convention follows that of CST4 itself: `sttvvx`, where `s` denotes the *Sutta Piṭaka*, `tt` is a two-digit text number, `vv` is a two-digit volume number, and the final letter `x` is the character `m` for canonical or root texts (from the Pāli word *mūla*, root) or `a` for commentary (from *aṭṭhakathā*, explanation or commentary). Thus, for example, `s0502m` denotes the canonical fifth text (i.e., the *Khuddaka Nikāya*), second volume (the *Dhammapada*), while `s0502a` denotes the commentary on that same volume. Where an additional numeral

[3]It's important to note that that we use the term "word" loosely here to mean any string of letters delimited by white space, punctuation, or numerals. These strings can, in practice, represent multiple Pāli words due to sandhi. While this is not quite as large an issue in Pāli and Sanskrit, it nevertheless represents a limitation of this approach, as discussed both below in Section 4 and in our prior paper (Zigmond, 2021).

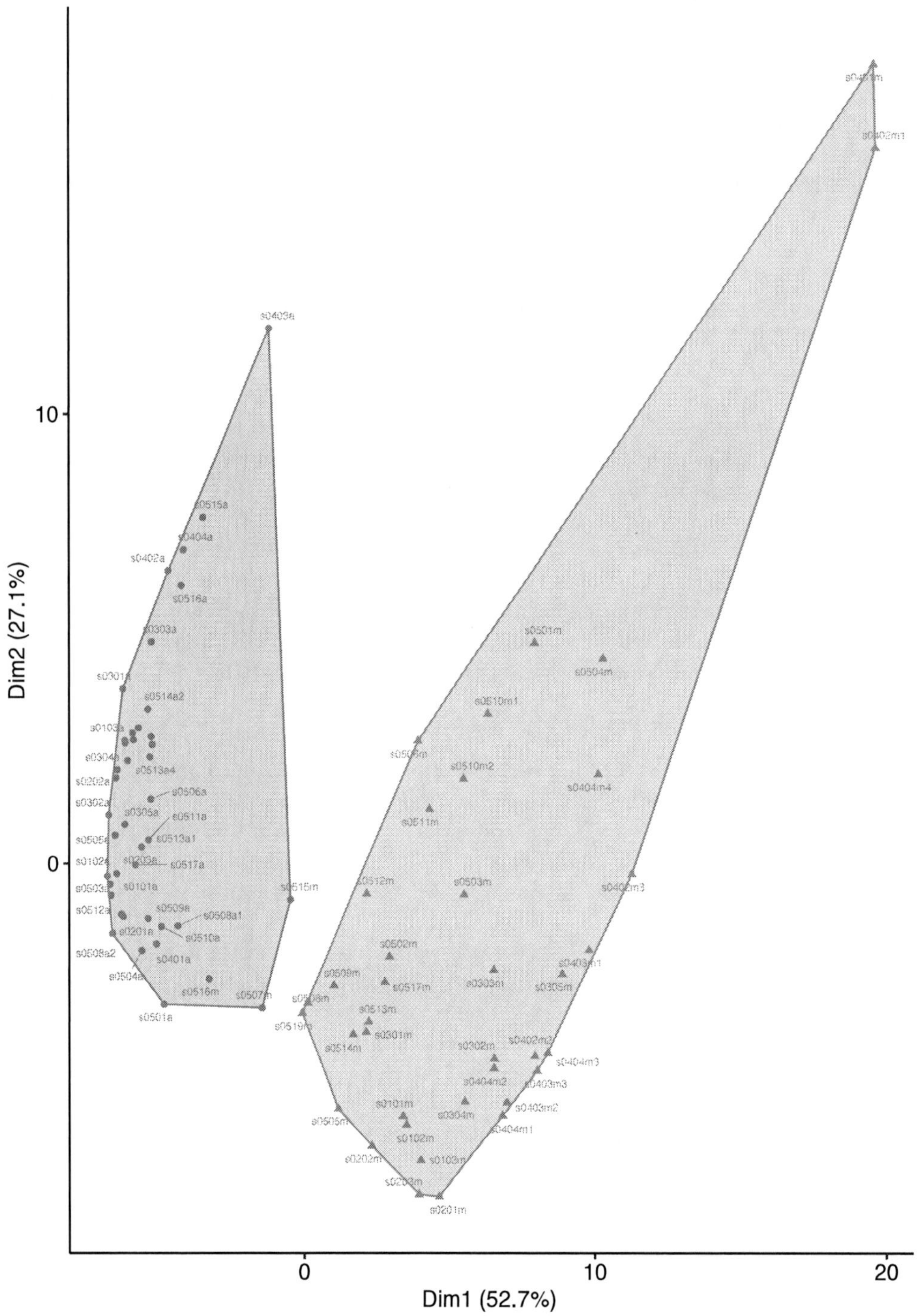

Figure 1: Clustering canon and commentary. On the right (blue) we see the canonical texts and on the left (red) we see *primarily* the commentarial texts, with three canonical texts (`s0507m`, `s0515m`, and `s0516m`, all near the bottom) miscategorized there. For naming conventions, see Table 1.

appears after this sequence, as in s0513a1, it simply means a single printed volume was split into multiple text files in the electronic edition of the CST4. A full list of CST4 file names and their corresponding *Tipiṭaka* text is given in Table 1.

We can see in Figure 1 that the two clusters separate the canonical texts from the commentary nearly perfectly, with the right cluster containing the root texts and the left cluster containing the commentary. There are three exceptions, where root texts appear to be incorrectly categorized: s0507m, s0515m, and s0516m. All of three come from the *Khuddaka Nikāya*, "the collection of short pieces" (Geiger, 1956, 19), a diverse set of texts generally considered the last part of the *Sutta Piṭaka* to be closed.

The latter two files, s0515m and s0516m, contain the *Mahāniddesa* and *Cūḷaniddesa*, respectively. These are an interesting case in that they are, in fact, commentaries on portions of the *Suttanipāta*. They are not attributed to Buddha but to Sāriputra, one of his chief disciples. They are believed to be much more recent than the original sutras, with estimates of their origin ranging from roughly 100 BCE to 200 CE (von Hinüber, 1997, 59). This is older than most of the other commentaries, but younger than most of the canon. It seems reasonable that such canonical texts could be "mistaken" for commentarial literature, since they are, in fact, both.

On the other hand, the characterization of s0507m file is more puzzling. This is another text of the *Khuddaka Nikāya*, the *Petavatthu*, a book containing "the stories of the departed ones (*petas*) who are suffering because of the bad actions they have committed during their previous existence" (Norman, 1983, 71). It is clearly also a late addition to the canon, likely added after the Second Council (von Hinüber, 1997, 51), perhaps "a short time before the third council" (Geiger, 1956, 20) or roughly 200 years after Buddha's passing (Norman, 1983, 71). Yet other texts in the *Khuddaka Nikāya* are of a similar age, including the *Vimānavatthu* (s0506m), which are not clustered with the commentaries by our algorithm. Age therefore cannot be the sole cause of the miscategorization.

It seems that this area of the clustering is somewhat unstable. The Burmese Theravāda lineages have traditionally included two additional volumes in the *Khuddaka Nikāya*: the *Milindapañha* and *Peṭakopadesa*, which are included in the CST4 as s0518m and s0520m, respectively, although the files are tagged as "miscellaneous" rather than canonical.[4] Because there is disagreement among Theravada traditions about the status of these texts, von Hinüber (1997, 76) calls them "paracanonical." If we add these to our corpus, our algorithm produces the clusters shown in Figure 2. Now only the *Cūḷaniddesa* (s0516m) is clustered "incorrectly," with the commentaries rather than root texts. Again, given that the *Cūḷaniddesa* and *Mahāniddesa* are both canonical and commentarial, it makes sense that their categorization is somewhat unstable between the two clusters, easily perturbed by other changes to the corpus of texts.

As mentioned above, eventually new commentaries were written to explain the older commentaries, referred to sub-commentaries or *ṭīkā*. Figure 3 shows the effect of adding the 16 *Sutta Piṭaka ṭīkā* included in the CST4 to the 40 *aṭṭhakathā*, 39 *mūla*, and 2 paracanonical files. (All sub-commentary file names end in t, as in sttvvt.) Here again, only the *Cūḷaniddesa* seems to be "miscategorized." All the volumes of sub-commentary are correctly clustered with the original commentaries.

4 Limitations and Conclusions

This work shows that simple k-means clustering based on unique word frequencies can reliably distinguish most Pāli canonical literature from the Pāli commentaries. The few errors we see are on the margins of the canon, with a few late additions to the *Tipiṭaka* clustered with the later commentaries. This bodes well for future applications of computational linguistics analyzing the age and authorship of Pāli texts.

That said, and as discussed in both Elwert et al. (2015) and Zigmond (2021), the Pāli Canon

[4]The *Nettippakaraṇa* (s0519m) is similarly paracanonical, but is not distinguished from other root texts in the CST4.

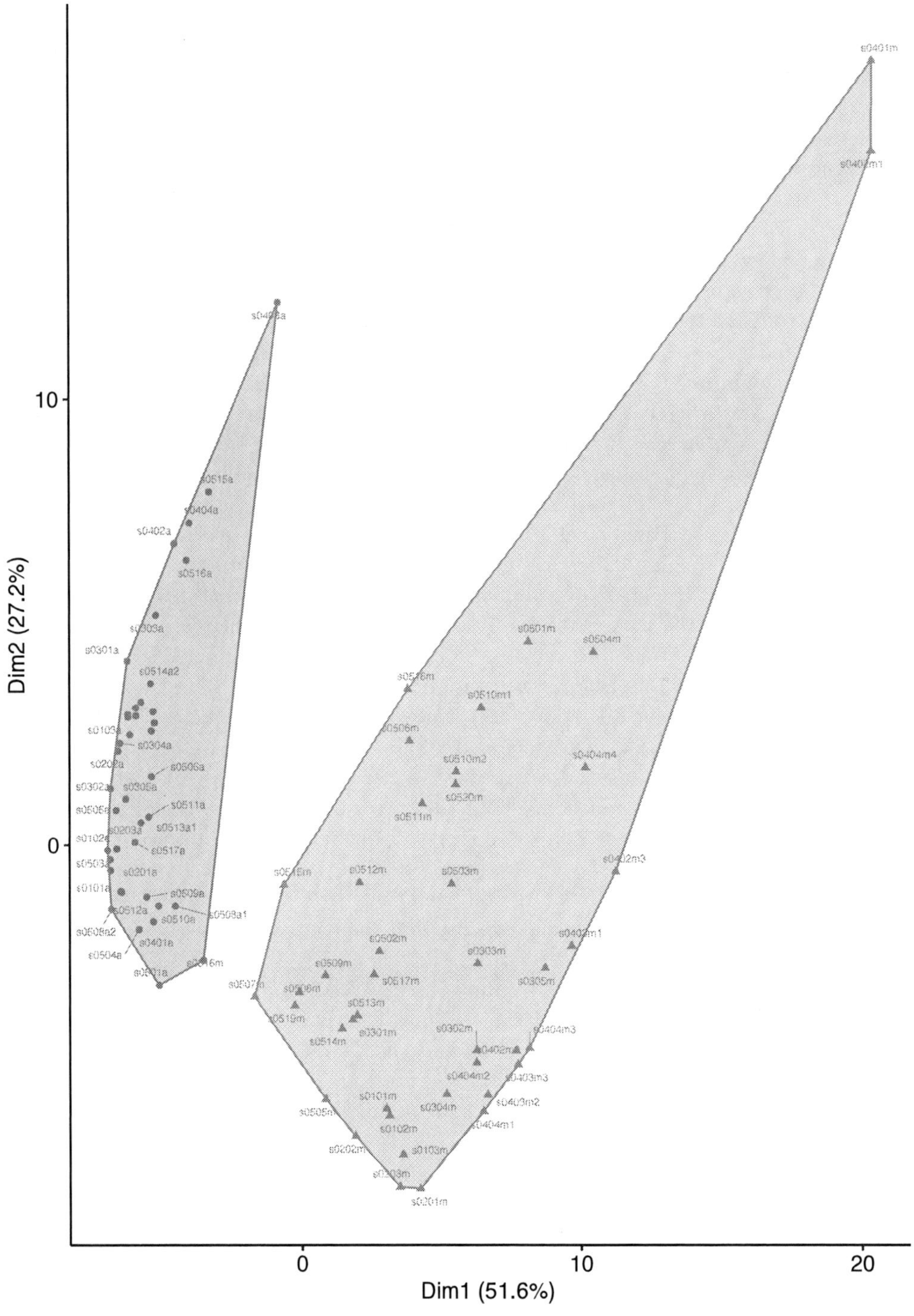

Figure 2: Adding two paracanonical texts (`s0518m` and `s0520m`) to our clustering. Again on the right (blue) we see the canonical texts and on the left (red) we see mostly commentarial texts, now with only one canonical text (`s0516m`) miscategorized.

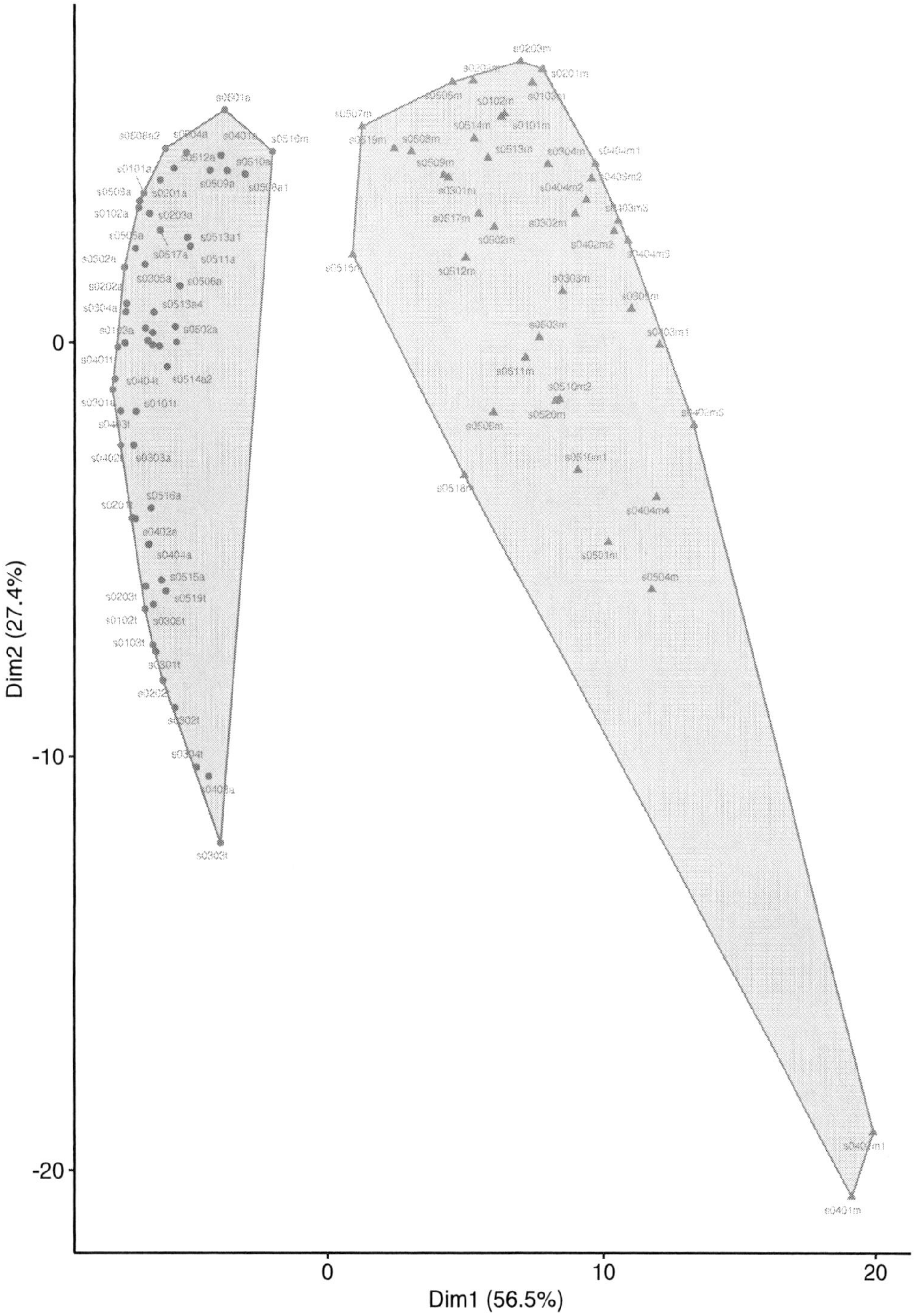

Figure 3: Adding the sub-commentaries (which follow the form to our clustering. Although the shape is different, the results are unchanged, with again only one canonical text (`s0516m`, now near the top) miscategorized.

File	*Tipiṭaka* text
`s01`*vvx*	*Dīgha Nikāya*
`s02`*vvx*	*Majjhima Nikāya*
`s03`*vvx*	*Saṃyutta Nikāya*
`s04`*vvx*	*Aṅguttara Nikāya*
`s05`*vvx*	*Khuddaka Nikāya*
`s0501`*x*	*Khuddakapāṭha*
`s0502`*x*	*Dhammapada*
`s0503`*x*	*Udāna*
`s0504`*x*	*Itivuttaka*
`s0505`*x*	*Suttanipāta*
`s0506`*x*	*Vimānavatthu*
`s0507`*x*	*Petavatthu*
`s0508`*x*	*Theragāthā*
`s0509`*x*	*Therīgāthā*
`s0510`*x*	*Apadāna*
`s0511`*x*	*Buddhavaṃsa*
`s0512`*x*	*Cariyāpiṭaka*
`s0513`*x*	*Jātaka* I
`s0514`*x*	*Jātaka* II
`s0515`*x*	*Mahāniddesa*
`s0516`*x*	*Cūḷaniddesa*
`s0517`*x*	*Paṭisambhidāmagga*
`s0518`*x*	*Milindapañha**
`s0519`*x*	*Nettippakaraṇa*†
`s0520`*x*	*Peṭakopadesa**

Table 1: File naming conventions in the CST4. Note that the individual volumes of the *Khuddaka Nikāya* are typically referenced by name, while the volumes of the first four *Nikāyas* are not. Also, * designates paracanonical volumes differentiated in the CST4, while † designates a paracanonical volume included as canonical in the CST4. The character `x` is always `m` for root (canonical) texts, `a` for commentaries, and `t` for sub-commentaries. Any number after the final letter (as in `s0403m1`) simply means the volume was split into multiple files due to length.

in raw form is a poor foundation for this sort of textual analysis. Similar words appear in a wide array of dissimilar forms, due to declensions, compounds, and sandhi. In addition, volumes are divided arbitrarily, extraneous words are sometimes added, and at times typographical errors have clearly crept in. Some of these artifacts may provide clues to the age of the texts—if, for example, different errors have appeared in different periods, or where word combining practices have evolved over time—but many of them simply add noise.

Although the present work shows that useful research can be carried out directly on the electronic edition of the CST4, Pāli computational linguistics is in dire need of a more refined corpus. At the very least, we would like to be able to run the same analysis on both raw and "corrected" or "normalized" versions of the texts. The very light pre-processing of the `tipitaka` package will not be sufficient in the long run.

Recently the Digital Pāli Tools (2021) project has embarked on an ambitious effort to create a more suitable corpus for Pāli computational linguistics and related applications. Once this work is complete, it should be possible to apply the tools and techniques used here against their new preprocessed texts. That will allow us to establish whether some of the anomalies in our results—such as the strange clustering of the *Petavatthu*—can be explained by artifacts in the raw text files. It should be relatively straightforward to adapt the `tipitaka` package to this corpus once it is available.

Many interesting analyses will be possible using these techniques against a more robust corpus. For example, we can begin looking below the level of full texts to compare verse passages to prose. We can use more advanced machine learning algorithms to attempt to classify individual chapters of heterogeneous works like the *Suttanipāta*, to explore when they may have been composed. We may be able to estimate more precisely when texts were added to the canon, taking us one step closer to determining which may be the actual words of the historical Buddha.

Acknowledgements

The files used in this analysis from the electronic edition of the CST4 were generously provided by Frank Snow of Tipitaka.org. This work was greatly facilitated by the software tools referenced earlier, including the `R` statistical programming language and the `tidy`, `tidytext`, and `factoextra` packages. I am also grateful to the four anonymous reviewers for the Computational Sanskrit and Digital Humanities section of the World Sanskrit Conference 2021–2023, who provided valuable feedback and several corrections.

References

David Alfter. 2015. Analyzer and generator for Pali.

Anālayo. 2016. *The foundation history of the nuns' order.* Projekt Verlag.

Swati Basapur, Shivani V, and Sivaja Nair. 2019. Pāli sandhi – a computational approach. In *Proceedings of the 6th International Sanskrit Computational Linguistics Symposium*, pages 181–192, IIT Kharagpur, India, October. Association for Computational Linguistics.

A. P. Buddhadatta. 1951. *Aids to Pali conversation and translation.* P.M.W. Piyaratna.

Digital Pāli Tools. 2021. A step-by-step process towards natural language processing of Pāli. https://bitly.com/dptvision.

Frederik Elwert, Sven Sellmer, Sven Wortmann, Manuel Pachurka, and David Alfter Jürgen Knauthand. 2015. Toiling with the Pāli Canon. In *Proceedings of the Workshop on Corpus-Based Research in the HumanitiesPage*, pages 39–48, Warsaw, Poland. Institute of Computer Science, Polish Academy of Sciences.

Wilhelm Geiger. 1956. *Pali literature and language.* University of Calcutta.

Wilhelm Geiger. 2005. *A Pāli Grammar.* Pali Text Society.

Huét Gerard. 2009. *Sanskrit computational linguistics first and second international symposia, Rocquencourt, France, October 29 - 31, 2007 ; Providence, RI, USA, May 15 - 17, 2008 ; revised selected and invited papers.* Springer.

Richard Gombrich. 2018. *Buddhism and Pali.* Mud Pie.

Yashodhara Haribhakta and Laxmi Nadageri. 2017. Parts of speech tagger for Pali language. *International Journal of Scientific Research in Computer Science, Engineering and Information Technology (IJSRCSEIT)*, 2(4):845–853, Jul–Aug.

Matthew L. Jockers and Rosamond Thalken. 2020. *Text Analysis with R.: For Students of Literature.* Springer International Publishing.

Matthew Lee Jockers. 2013. *Macroanalysis digital methods and literary history.* University of Illinois Press.

Kyle P. Johnson, Patrick Burns, John Stewart, and Todd Cook. 2014. Cltk: The classical language toolkit. https://github.com/cltk/cltk.

Alboukadel Kassambara and Fabian Mundt, 2020. *factoextra: Extract and Visualize the Results of Multivariate Data Analyses.* R package version 1.0.7.

S. Lloyd. 1982. Least squares quantization in pcm. *IEEE Transactions on Information Theory*, 28(2):129–137.

J. B. MacQueen. 1967. Some methods for classification and analysis of multivariate observations. In L. M. Le Cam and J. Neyman, editors, *Proc. of the fifth Berkeley Symposium on Mathematical Statistics and Probability*, volume 1, pages 281–297. University of California Press.

Multilingual Europe Technology Alliance. 2013. Meta-net white paper series: Key results and cross-language comparison.

Kenneth R. Norman. 1983. *Pāli literature incl. the canon. literature in Prakrit and Sanskrit of all the Hīnayāna schools of Buddhism.* Harrassowitz.

R Core Team, 2020. *R: A Language and Environment for Statistical Computing.* R Foundation for Statistical Computing, Vienna, Austria.

Michal Rosen-Zvi, Chaitanya Chemudugunta, Thomas Griffiths, Padhraic Smyth, and Mark Steyvers. 2010. Learning author-topic models from text corpora. *ACM Transactions on Information Systems*, 28(1):1–38.

Kevin Scannell. 2007. The Crúbadán project: Corpus building for under-resourced languages. *Building and Exploring Web Corpora: Proceedings of the 3rd Web as Corpus Workshop*, 01.

Julia Silge and David Robinson. 2016. tidytext: Text mining and analysis using tidy data principles in R. *JOSS*, 1(3).

Bhikkhu Sujato and Bhikkhu Brahmali. 2014. *The authenticity of the early Buddhist texts.* Buddhist Publication Society.

Vipassana Research Institute. 1990. Chaṭṭha saṅgāyana tipiṭaka version 4.0.

Oskar von Hinüber. 1997. *A handbook of Pāli literature.* Munshiram Manoharlal Publ.

Hadley Wickham, Mara Averick, Jennifer Bryan, Winston Chang, Lucy D'Agostino McGowan, Romain François, Garrett Grolemund, Alex Hayes, Lionel Henry, Jim Hester, Max Kuhn, Thomas Lin Pedersen, Evan Miller, Stephan Milton Bache, Kirill Müller, Jeroen Ooms, David Robinson, Dana Paige Seidel, Vitalie Spinu, Kohske Takahashi, Davis Vaughan, Claus Wilke, Kara Woo, and Hiroaki Yutani. 2019. Welcome to the tidyverse. *Journal of Open Source Software*, 4(43):1686.

Dan Zigmond, 2020. *tipitaka: Data and Tools for Analyzing the Pali Canon.* R package version 0.1.1.

Dan Zigmond. 2021. Toward a computational analysis of the Pali Canon. *Journal of the Oxford Centre for Buddhist Studies*, 20.